A MILLENNIUM PRIMER

THE OLD FARMER'S ALMANAC

A MILLENNIUM PRIMER

THE OLD FARMER'S ALMANAC

timeless truths and delightful diversions

by Tim Clark AND THE EDITORS OF *The Old Farmer's Almanac*

First printing. Printed in the U. S. A.

Editor: Sarah Elder Hale
Consulting Editors: Susan Peery, Mare-Ann Jarvela
Copy Editor: Barbara Jatkola
Art Director: Jill Shaffer
Layout Assistant: Sheryl Fletcher
Cover Illustration: Cindy Wrobel

ISBN 0-7370-0050-3 (hardcover)
ISBN 0-7370-0061-9 (softcover)
ISBN 0-7370-1133-5 (softcover mass market)

A milllennium primer: timeless truths and delightful diversions / by Tim Clark
  and the editors of Old Farmer's Almanac.
        p.   cm.
     ISBN: 0-7370-0050-3 (hardcover). – ISBN 0-7370-0061-9 (softcover)
      1. Twenty-first century – Forecasts Miscellanea. 2. Millennium Miscellanea. 3.
Life skills Handboooks, manuals, etc. 4. Almanacs, American.   I. Clark, Tim,
1950-   . II. (Old) Farmer's almanack.
CB161.M479 1999
303.49'09'05–dc21   99-23718
                                                     CIP

Distributed in the book trade by Time-Life Books

Time-Life Books is a division of Time Life Inc.

TIME LIFE INC.

PRESIDENT AND CEO: George Arlandi
EXECUTIVE VICE PRESIDENT: Lawrence J. Marmon

TIME-LIFE CUSTOM PUBLISHING

VICE PRESIDENT AND PUBLISHER	Neil Levin
Director of Acquisitions and Editorial Resources	Jennifer Pearce
Editor	Linda Bellamy
Director of Creative Services	Laura McNeill
Technical Specialist	Monika Lynde
Production Manager	Carolyn Bounds
Quality Assurance Manager	James D. King

TIME-LIFE is a trademark of Time Warner Inc. U.S.A.

Books produced by Time-Life Custom Publishing are available at a special bulk discount for promotional and premium use. Custom adaptations can also be created to meet your specific marketing goals. Call 1-800-323-5255.

Contents

How to Become a Prophet 331

Foreword

WHAT, WOULD YOU SAY, is the intent of this book?" I asked editor Sarah Hale after she informed me that, as the 12th editor of *The Old Farmer's Almanac,* I ought to write its introduction. (Oh, incidentally, Sarah and I are not related, at least not as far back as six generations. Before that, who knows?)

"Think of it as a suitcase you've packed for your journey into the next millennium," she said.

"A suitcase packed with *what?*" I asked. I guess I knew, sort of, but I wanted to be sure.

"Packed with all kinds of useful, entertaining, scientific, and enlightening articles and tidbits chosen from the past 207 years of *The Old Farmer's Almanac,*" she replied.

She paused for a moment and then tried to elaborate. "I mean, every year since 1792, the Almanac has been packed with exactly enough to carry all of us here in North America through the next 12 months..." Her voice trailed off.

"So now this one book is supposed to provide us with enough for the next one thousand years?" I asked incredulously.

"Well...," she began, with the sort of engaging smile that reminded me of my late mother's when *she* was in her thirties. Throughout her life, she'd used it to convince people of just about anything.

"Let's say this has enough for the next century," Sarah finally continued. "Then my grandchildren can compile a sequel. A hundred years and another couple of generations later, maybe book number three. Ten of these ought to carry us safely to the fourth millennium."

Well, I thought, *that's a tall order for even* ten *suitcases.* But I didn't say that to Sarah.

Instead, I immediately began to read the vast assortment of material she and other current editors of *The Old Farmer's Almanac* (Susan Peery and Mare Anne Jarvela, in particular) had chosen for this millennium suitcase of theirs.

Some of it, of course, I'd already read during my forty-one years (and counting) with the Almanac. I particularly enjoyed reading these familiar stories, anecdotes, and pieces of information again. It was like running into dear old friends from the past. Whenever I came across one of the late Guy Murchie's articles, for instance, I pictured the delicious lamb stew and fresh popovers his wife, Katie, prepared for our lunch each January, during which time we'd discuss his next Almanac assignment. Guy's morsels of wisdom were inevitably delicious, too.

Reading "Surefire Home Remedies for the Hiccups" brought back the fall day in 1984 when one of our editors got the hiccups and we tried some of those old-fashioned remedies on her — including having her wet a piece of red thread with her tongue, stick it to her forehead, and look at it. It worked, too. Trouble was, we laughed so hard that someone else began to hiccup. It was out of control.

There has always been laughter here at *The Old Farmer's Almanac.* It's a tradition. In fact, our founder, Robert B. Thomas, made sure that a certain amount of humor was an integral part of the 54 editions he created. In the 1829 edition, he even made it official. The mission of the Almanac, he wrote, was always "to be useful with a pleasant degree of humor." Every editor since, including yours truly, has managed to keep that mission statement very much in mind.

And, as I was pleased to note, so has Sarah Hale and all the other editors who compiled the material for this book. Even the time line that runs along the bottom of the pages made me smile. Certainly not your typical time line of oft-repeated dates in history, this one is full of the details of our everyday lives and common experiences, pieced together from myriad sources.

Finally, Tim Clark. Well, his introductions to the seven chapters made me laugh so hard that a couple of times I thought that I, too, was about to get the hiccups. Then again, Tim Clark, executive editor of the Almanac, has always had that effect on me. Like the Almanac itself, Tim is a complex combination of wisdom, practicality, know-how, and humor.

When at last I finished reading everything, I found I had only one small quarrel with Sarah. Contrary to her suggestion, there'll be no need for her grandchildren to compile a sequel a hundred years from now. The truths packed herein will remain useful and fun for at least the next thousand years. Probably longer. Heck, maybe forever.

Judson D. Hale, Sr.
Editor-in-Chief
The Old Farmer's Almanac

The Human Connection

AHOY! I'M USING the greeting that Alexander Graham Bell suggested for use on the telephone. Why not "hello"? In earlier days, saying "hello" to someone you didn't know was considered a sign of ill breeding.

It's an example of the eternal difficulties human beings have in communicating with each other. We yearn for connection, but we also hesitate to lower our guard to strangers.

And yet, as Guy Murchie points out in the first article in this chapter, we are all related. Each of us is, at worst, 50th cousin to each and every other human being on the planet, in spite of the great distances (and the prejudices and taboos) that separate us.

Permit me to illustrate the point through a familiar modern communication device — the personal ad. Sup-

Small forks for eating (derived from farmer's pitchforks) first appear in Europe. They are subject to widespread disdain and condemned by the clergy as inappropriate.

pose you were, say, a Foldi man of the Hyabites tribe of Arabia, an inbred clan distinguished by their extra digits. Here's how you might advertise for a mate:

> **ARABIAN KNIGHT** seeks eligible woman for marriage. I like long walks in the desert, moonlight at the oasis, and lattes with camel's milk. You must have six toes on each foot and five fingers plus thumb on each hand. Send letter, glove size to Box 93870.

Well, you say, I don't harbor such primitive superstitions. But read on. In Christine Schultz's story about the mysteries of hu-

man attraction, you will find that folk beliefs continue to influence us in seeking the perfect mate, so that a candid modern woman might write a personal ad like this one:

> **LONELY FEMALE SCHOOL-TEACHER** seeks male catalog model with forearms no longer than 18 inches to sniff my apocrine glands. I love canvasback duck, picnics under a waxing Moon, and men who look good in studded dog collars. No snorers. Send photo, underarm swab to Idle in Idaho, Box 99054.

Of course, our ideals of personal beauty change over time. According to Elenor Schoen, in 1770 Pennsylvania passed a law intended to protect men from being misled by women's cosmetics

1000s

Italian families begin handing down second names, or surnames, from father to son.

and figure-enhancing fashions. A skeptical Pennsylvanian of that time could have written:

I'M FEELING MY QUAKER OATS!
Law-abiding Pennsylvanian seeks virgin, maid, or widow. Purpose: betrothal. No scents, paints, cosmetic washes, artificial teeth, false hair, Spanish wool, iron stays, hoops, high-heeled shoes, or bolstered hips. Write Poor Richard, Box 01776.

Still, new scientific discoveries about the brain may be able to guide us in seeking a compatible partner. Jon Vara's "The Sinister Truth About Handedness" might produce a personal ad that reads something like this:

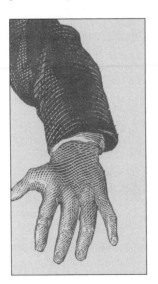

SLAVISHLY RATIONAL CAPTIVE OF THE LEFT HEMISPHERE
seeks wild, creative, insightful southpaw who stirs her sugar into her coffee counterclockwise. You write the poetry and choose the drapes; I'll do the taxes and handle the power tools. Let's overcome our veering biases together. Baden-Powell, Box 99431.

Different temperaments can also be a bar to communication, of course.

c. 1000

The first European colony is founded in the New World by Leif Eriksson. Called Vinland, the settlement is probably located in present-day Newfoundland but will be abandoned 15 years later.

Take crying, for example. Women are likely to cry four times more often than men, due perhaps to cultural conditioning but also perhaps to biological differences. Women's bodies, Jamie Kageleiry tells us in "For Crying Out Loud," contain 60 percent more prolactin, a hormone connected not only with the secretion of milk but also with emotional tears. It's not hard to imagine a woman using a personal ad to find a man who's not ashamed to show his emotions:

CRY, BABY! I'm looking for an Italian Ed Muskie. He-men and the prolactin-challenged need not apply. Write to Nadia, longhand (tearstains a plus!), Box 40822.

There's no avoiding the fact that attempting to reach out to another human being involves risk. We can't find true love without taking chances, but there is such a thing as going too far. I can just picture what Sam Patch would have written in his own personal ad:

PROFESSIONAL ENTERTAINER, single, risk taker, accustomed to high places. Enjoys sailboats, waterfalls, bears. Seeks daring woman willing to take the plunge. Write Yankee Leaper, Box 00675.

And where there is risk, there is inevitably loss. Powerful emotional attachments are not limited to other humans. I don't wish

1010

The Tale of Genji, considered the world's first novel, is published by Shikibu Murasaki, lady-in-waiting to the empress of Japan.

to give away the precise reason "Why My Great-Uncle Gave Up the Ministry," but after you have read it, you will see the real tragedy one might have found in a personal ad like this one:

WHERE'S TWINKIE? Grieving lady seeks information on disappearance of her beloved Chihuahua. Last seen shortly before pastoral visit by portly minister. Box 54398.

Tim Clark

1052

England's King Edward the Confessor orders the building of a new church, Westminster Abbey. It will be completed in 1065.

■ *Whether you work back through your ancestors or carry the theory forward to future generations, you will come, or so the theory goes, to the same conclusion: We are all members of a single family. Skeptical? Get out your calculator and figure it out for yourself.*

How Big Is the Family Tree?

BY GUY MURCHIE

ALTHOUGH FEW OF US SEEM TO realize it, man's relation to himself is fairly easy to measure and is surprisingly close. In fact, no human being (of any race) can be less closely related to any other human than approximately 50th cousin, and most of us (no matter what color our neighbors) are a lot closer. Indeed, this low magnitude for the lineal compass of mankind is accepted by the leading geneticists I have consulted (from J. B. S. Haldane to Theodosius Dobzhansky to Sir Julian Huxley), and it means simply that the family trees of all of us, of whatever origin or trait, must meet and merge into one genetic tree of all humanity by the time they have spread into our ancestries for about 50 generations.

This is not a particularly abstruse fact, for simple arithmetic demonstrates that, if we double the number of our ancestors for each generation as we reckon backward (consistently multiplying them by 2: 2 parents, 4 grandparents, 8 great-grandparents, 16 great-great-grandparents, and so on), our personal pedigree would cover mankind before the 30th generation. Mathematics is quite explosive in this regard, you see, for the 30th power of 2 (1,073,741,824) turns out to be much larger than the Earth's population 30 generations ago — that is, in the 13th century, if we assume 25 years to a generation.

But you cannot reasonably go on doubling your ancestors for more than a very few generations into the past because inevitably the same ancestor will appear on both your father's and your mother's sides of your family tree, reducing the total number (since you can't count the same person twice), and this must happen more and more as you go back in time. The basic reason it happens is that spouses are not just spouses, but they are also cousins (although the relationship is usually too distant to be noticed), which means they are related to each other not only by marriage but also by "blood," because somewhere in the past they share ancestors.

Another way of saying it is that your father's family tree and your

1054

Chinese and Japanese astronomers record the appearance of a remarkably bright star — what we know today as a supernova.

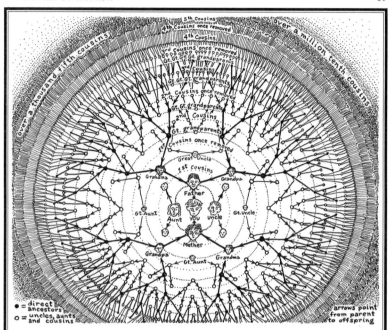

• = direct ancestors
○ = uncles, aunts and cousins

arrows point from parent to offspring

mother's inevitably overlap, intertwine, and become one tree as their generations branch out backward, a process forced by geometry until eventually all your ancestors are playing double, triple, quadruple, and higher-multiple roles as both sides — all quarters, eighths, and so on — of your tree finally merge with others into one common whole, and the broad tops of the family trees of all people alive and their families become identical

The family trees of all of us, of whatever origin or trait, must meet and merge into one genetic tree of all humanity by the time they have spread into our ancestries for about 50 generations.

with their ancestral world populations. These populations, of course, are the fertile portions of past societies and naturally cannot include "old maids" and "cautious bachelors" — or anyone who fails to beget at least one continuous line of fecund descendants to disseminate his genes into mankind's future.

If people all over the Earth always married at random, choosing their mates by lot regardless of what country, race,

1090

Killing one's enemies, especially for political gain, is given a name: assassination, from a Muslim sect called the *hashshashin,* "those who smoke hashish." This name eventually will evolve into its present form, assassins.

class, or religion they came from, it would take something like 35 to 40 generations for all their family trees to merge completely in common ancestors, the time beyond 30 generations needed because of the aforementioned slowdown in backward ancestral multiplication, a rate that progressively decreases from 2 to 1 and ultimately even below 1 when the family trees begin to encompass all mankind, whose numbers, of course, were smaller in earlier centuries.

But obviously people do not mate at random, for there have always been barriers to boys and girls getting together: oceans, high mountains, and vast distances between them; rigid marriage laws, religious sexual taboos, and innumerable racial and cultural prejudices. By contrast, there have been almost as many compensating influences tending to overcome these barriers and increase the scope of mating: long hunting trips for food, nomadic herding, expeditions for business or war with its spoils in slaves and women; also strict laws against incest and inbreeding, all naturally abetted by man's primordial appetite for novel amorous adventure.

Probably most significant of these factors, geneticists agree, are the nearly universal rules of endogamy (inbreeding) and exogamy (outbreeding) that respectively permit persons to pick marriage partners only from inside the membership of a specified larger, endogamous social group (such as a tribe or caste) yet also only from outside a specified smaller exogamous group (such as a clan). In many sophisticated countries today, of course, the endogamous group is nothing less than mankind and the exogamous group is one's own immediate family, which gives a man latitude to propose to practically any uncommitted female in the wide spectrum between his niece and a chim-

In many sophisticated countries today, of course, the endogamous group is nothing less than mankind and the exogamous group is one's own immediate family, which gives a man latitude to propose to practically any uncommitted female in the wide spectrum between his niece and a chimpanzee.

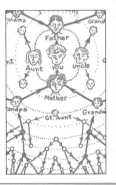

Priests in Europe start the first grammar schools.

panzee. But virtually all the more primitive of human societies have traditions that greatly restrict marriage. In rural tropical Africa, for example, the average tribesman is expected to marry inside his tribe of perhaps 10,000 people yet outside his family clan of 1,000 or 2,000, giving him a total population of some 8,000 to pick from.

In a few rare cases, tribal members have been even more restricted endogamically, as in the inbred clan called Foldi in the Hyabites tribe of Arabia, all of whose people have 6 toes on each foot and 5 fingers plus thumb on each hand and who have come to value their 24 digits so highly that they will kill any 20-digit baby born to them as the illegitimate issue of an adulterous mother. The same goes for the monkey-tailed clan of Kali, who traditionally refuse to keep any infant who doesn't have a tail.

Laws of exogamy can be at least as extreme in the opposite (outward)

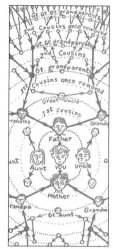

The inbred clan called Foldi in the Hyabites tribe of Arabia, all of whose people have 6 toes on each foot and 5 fingers plus thumb on each hand . . . have come to value their 24 digits so highly that they will kill any 20-digit baby.

direction, and the marriage law in much of western Europe during the time of the Crusades defined incest as extending out to fifth cousins. In some other parts of the world, the outbreeding groups were even larger, as in imperial China, where one was forbidden to wed anyone with the same family name, a rule that diverted the average Chinese bridegroom away from about a million of his closer relatives and undoubtedly contributed much to the homogeneity of that most populous nation.

It is practically impossible to set limits on where any man's family connection may reach upon the habitable Earth. And the very proliferation and complexity of his relations is incomprehensible to most of us, for, even if you assume only 2 children to a couple (a quote actually too low to permit humanity to survive), everyone on the average must have 4 first cousins (the children of his uncles and aunts), 16 second cousins (the grand-

Mount Etna in Sicily erupts, killing approximately 15,000 people.

children of his great-uncles and great-aunts), probably 64 third cousins, about 250 fourth cousins, roughly 1,000 fifth cousins, and some 1 million relatives as close as

Sleep with a mirror under your pillow for three nights, the third a Friday, and you will dream of your true love on the third night.

tenth cousin. Then, if you extrapolate on into the billions, which means extending your relatives to all humanity, it is evident that, even after allowing liberally for the shared ancestry of spouses and all

the barriers to intertribal and intercontinental marriages, the range of 50th cousins will still easily cover the planet.

Of course, a few snobbish people will protest, "But my family is an exception. We traced our ancestry back 1,100 years, and they all came from an isolated community on the Isle of Man, where they spoke Manx and never had any marriage contact with the outside world."

Statements of that sort cannot possibly stand up to close scrutiny. Genealogists, I admit, will often trace a prominent family name back hundreds of years — which involves only the relatively simple procedure of following one male line of descent. But the average person has approximately a million ancestors with some thousand names just in the past 500 years, and it is patently impossible to trace any large portion of them. Even such a well-publicized lineage as the *Mayflower* descendants from Plymouth, Massachusetts, can hardly begin to track down their relatives of 375 years, and a little knowledge of early Yankee seamanship and fecundity in the tea and slave ports of Asia and Africa, plus mathematics, will show that their ranks probably now include more than a million Chinese in China, a comparable number of Hindus in India and blacks in Africa — not to mention several million Americans and Europeans.

1182

In China and Europe, it is discovered that magnesium ore has properties that we now call magnetic. Its ability to point consistently in a north–south direction leads quickly to the development of the magnetic compass.

ANECDOTES & PLEASANTRIES

How Long Is a Thousand Years?

A MILLENNIUM may seem like a long time, but it takes surprisingly few human lifetimes to fill one. A baker's dozen lifetimes carry us from the year 1000 to the first decade of the 20th century — well into the lifetimes of several million octogenarian-plus Americans who will be here to celebrate in the year 2000.

1. Berenger of Tours, Christian scholar, 1000–1089
2. Suger, abbot of Saint-Denis, leading French churchman, ca. 1081–1151
3. Maimonides, Jewish philosopher and theologian, 1135–1204
4. Simon de Montfort, English baronial leader, ca. 1208–1265
5. Dante Alighieri, Italian poet, 1265–1321
6. Sir John Hawkwood, English mercenary, 1320–1394
7. Donatello, Italian sculptor, 1386–1466
8. Leonardo da Vinci, Italian artist and inventor, 1452–1519
9. Gerardus Mercator, Flemish cartographer, 1512–1594
10. Thomas Hobbes, English philosopher, 1588–1679
11. Jonathan Swift, English satirist, 1679–1754
12. Daniel Boone, American pioneer, 1734–1820
13. Florence Nightingale, English hospital administrator, 1820–1910

Courtesy of Jon Vara

1200

The University of Paris, regarded as the first modern university, receives its foundation charter. The university's beginnings date from c. 1170, when the "guild of masters" was recognized, attracting eminent scholars from across Europe.

FARMER'S CALENDAR

Ancestors

I HAVE SPENT the afternoon with my ancestors, although I have not the slightest idea who they were or what they did. They are here before me in daguerreotype. How boldly, how alone they stand! They could step from those cracked old frames and fill this attic, as real and alive as I am. For it is the wonder of this well-nigh forgotten art that the subject, though posed as stiff as a funeral lily, has the singular quality of arrested action — or, rather, enforced interruption from something he would much rather be about.

Look at them with me. Here the female coiffure flows, like glass; here ringlets stiffen into springs; this gentleman's hirsute adornments have been fluffed and brushed and greased to raffish distinction; each lively, clumsy, protesting body is molded to dreadful ease and elegance.

Scanning these ancient pictures, I am like the little boy before the wonderful cuckoo clock. The hour approaches, the hand moves, and presently the door will burst open and the cuckoo live his brief moment — ecstatically.

These are my ancestors unknown, forever posed. But is that so? Are they indeed but waiting for a door to open? Nonsense. I have looked too long. Obed and his little bride, the five black-bearded brothers — what can awake them now? Like the cuckoo, they have lived their time, proclaimed their hour.

1236

Theodoric of Lucca, a Dominican friar, is the first to suggest using opiates (opium or mandragora) to help patients through painful surgery.

A Handy Chart for Identifying Five Generations of Blood Relatives

ECHNICALLY, it's known as consanguinity — that is, the quality or state of being related by blood or descended from a common ancestor. These relationships are diagrammed herewith for the genealogy of five generations of one family. *Courtesy of Frederick H. Rohles Jr., Ph.D.*

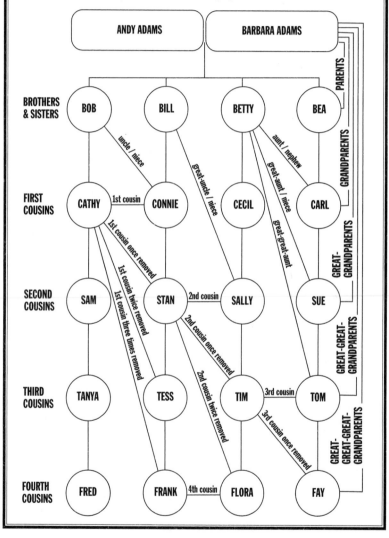

The Misericordia di Firenze,
the first known emergency
ambulance service, is founded
in Florence, Italy.

■ *Every ten years, since 1790, the federal government has compiled a census of our population. A few basic questions, a simple tally of family members — seems easy enough. Unless you happen to be one of the unfortunate folks hired to do the snooping, uh, data collecting. This article, from the 1990 edition of* The Old Farmer's Almanac, *celebrated the bicentennial of the U.S. census.*

200 Years of Counting Noses

BY TIM CLARK

EVER SINCE THE FIRST MONDAY in August 1790, when 600 assistant U.S. marshals from Vermont to South Carolina began 200 years of counting noses, Americans have had mixed feelings about the census. Jealous of our privacy but curious about our neighbors, we have regarded the decennial enumeration with a mixture of pride and suspicion.

The census was condemned as snooping as early as the 1840s, when a leading southern newspaper questioned whether it was "worthy of the dignity and high function of the Federal Government to pursue such petty investigations." A hundred years later, some citizens were outraged when the census asked whether they used a toilet or a privy.

By contrast, some people have attacked the census for failing to be snoopy enough. Required by Article I of the Constitution as a means of determining the size of the House of Representatives (and as a means of fairly apportioning the costs of the American Revolution), the census now determines where an estimated $100 billion in government aid is to be spent. That has made it a target of modern critics who say that the census consistently undercounts the number of blacks or Native Americans or members of other ethnic groups.

But even in 1790, the census was controversial. There was no permanent census office, so the job was given to the 16 federal district court marshals, under the direction of Secretary of State Thomas Jefferson. Jefferson apparently didn't trouble himself with the details, and the marshals and their hired assistants had only general guidelines to follow. As one historian put it, "The marshals were left practically on their own."

The first census asked only six questions: the name of the head of each family, the number in it of free

1250–1268

Glass lenses are being used to aid poor vision. Roger Bacon is instrumental in developing the magnifying glass. In China and Europe, magnifying lenses are fitted into frames to correct farsightedness. Lenses for shortsightedness won't come into use until the 16th century.

white males 16 years of age or older, the number in it of free white males under 16, the number in it of free white females (no ages asked!), the number of all other free persons, and the number of slaves.

The marshals were paid different amounts for each state, ranging from $100 each for Rhode Island and Delaware to $500 for Virginia, the most populous state at that time. The assistant marshals, who actually did the counting, received $1 for every 150 persons counted in rural districts, and $1 for every 300 persons in cities and towns containing more than 5,000 inhabitants. In some areas where the inhabitants were widely scattered, marshals were authorized to pay up to $1 for every 50 heads counted.

Jealous of our privacy but curious about our neighbors, we have regarded the decennial enumeration with a mixture of pride and suspicion.

Once assistants came up with a list of inhabitants for their areas, they were required to post that list for inspection in two public places so that the residents could check them for accuracy — a matter of no small importance, as both taxes and representation in Congress depended on the count. The marshals filed the completed lists with the clerks of their respective courts and sent copies to the secretary of state.

The lack of standardized forms and instructions gave the assistant marshals some room for creativity. Colonel Presley Nevill of Pennsylvania bound his report in fine wallpaper decorated with pink orchids. Another Pennsylvania enumerator went to the trouble of alphabetizing his 4,904 names.

The final count was 3,929,214 — a total that disap-

Marco Polo brings the recipes for water and milk ices, precursors to ice cream, to Italy from China.

pointed George Washington, among others. He suspected that many people had either lied about the number of persons in their families or avoided the census takers altogether, fearing high taxes. But subsequent counts showed that the 1790 census was remarkably accurate.

Still, the system was a creaky one. As succeeding censuses demanded more information about individuals and industry, the ramshackle arrangement of temporary assistants began to break down. Always prone to political favoritism — one census historian called it "an orgy of spoils" — the system spawned increasingly bizarre results. By 1843 the American Statistical Society was concerned enough to issue a report condemning the census as unreliable.

Among other aberrations, the society found that the number of colleges reported was probably twice the true number, that enumerators in some cases were counting every member of a doctor's family as doctors, and that in some counties apparently no one was employed at all. The statisticians reserved special scorn for the figures given for the incidence of idiocy and insanity, noting that "in

many towns, all the colored population are stated to be insane."

Popular comedians were also making hay at the expense of the census takers. Artemus Ward wrote of his own experience in the dialect style popular in 1860:

The Senses taker in our town being taken sick he deppertised me to go out for him one day, and as he was too ill to giv me informashun how to perceed, I was consekently compelled to go it blind. I drawd up the follerin list of questions which I proposed to ax the people I visited:

"Wat's your age? Whar was you born? Air you marrid, and if so, how do you like it? How many children have you? Did you ever have the measels, and if so how many? Wat's your fitin wate? Air you trubeld with biles? Do you use boughten tobaker? Is Beans a regler article of diet in your family? Was you ever at Niagry Falls? How many chickens have you, on foot and in the shell? Was you ever in the Penitentiary?"

But it didn't work. I got into a row at the fust house I stopt to, with some old maids. Disbelieven the ansers they giv in regard to their ages I endevered to look at their teeth, same as they do

Some citizens were outraged when the census asked whether they used a toilet or a privy.

An early form of fugue, considered by many to be the most complex and highly developed type of composition in Western music, is used by the French composer Jacques de Liège.

with hosses, but they floo into a violent rage and tackled me with brooms and sich. Takin the senses requires experiunse, like any other bizniss.

The sheer work of counting and preparing statistics was also getting out of hand. Fieldwork for the 1840 census took 18 months to complete, compared with the 9 months required for the 1790 count. Despite many reforms and efforts to modernize procedures, the situation grew worse as the 19th century drew to a close. The 1880 census employed 31,382 enumerators in the field and nearly 1,500 clerks in Washington, but the results were not made public until 1888. Wrote one historian, "If nothing was done, the census might have [had] to be abandoned altogether."

[An 1843 report showed that] enumerators in some cases were counting every member of a doctor's family as doctors and that in some counties apparently no one was employed at all.

One day two men walked through a room in which hundreds of clerks were painfully transcribing and tabulating the results of the 1880 census. One of them was Dr. John Shaw

Phillips, a physician in charge of compiling statistics on health. He said, "There ought to be some mechanical way of doing this job, something on the principle of the Jacquard loom, whereby holes in a card regulate the pattern to be woven."

His companion was Herman Hollerith, a young man from Buffalo who had recently joined the Census Bureau to collect data on power consumption in the iron and steel industry. An inventor, he taught briefly at the Massachusetts Institute of Technology (MIT), worked at the Patent Office, and experimented with air brakes. But his profound contribution, not only to the Census Bureau but also to the information age, was the first electric tabulating machine — the forerunner of the computer.

Mulling over Dr. Phillips's suggestion, Hollerith came up with a system employing punched cards — each card representing an indi-

1347

Bubonic plague, also known as the Black Death, begins its sweep through Europe, killing upwards of 25 million people, about one-quarter of Europe's population.

vidual person and each hole a bit of data. Clerks could press such cards in a "pin box," in which spring-activated pins would go through the holes and into tiny cups filled with mercury, completing an electric circuit and advancing a set of counters.

He tested his system while collecting vital statistics in Baltimore before the 1890 census. Using an ordinary railway conductor's punch, Hollerith punched 12,000 holes, and the system worked beautifully. But he found he'd lost all strength in his hand and wrist. So he invented a pantograph punch that allowed him to punch cards by tapping a key, like a telegraph key.

Hollerith's Electric Tabulating Machine saved the census and revolutionized information processing. By the end of the 1890 census, an average clerk could record 8,000 cards daily; one superman set a record of 19,071 cards in a day. The invention saved an estimated two years and $5 million.

Hollerith founded his own company, a direct ancestor of today's giant computer maker IBM. The permanent Census Bureau, founded in 1902, went on to pioneer in the use of statistical sampling in 1940 and the first computer, Univac, in 1950. For the 1990 census, virtually all forms were collected by mail, largely eliminating the armies of enumerators. And in years to come, new communication technologies may eliminate paper census forms altogether.

Ironically, it was the census of 1890, the first modern census, that provided the data on which historian Frederick Jackson Turner based his theory of the closing of the American frontier. No one recognized at the time that Herman Hollerith had opened a new frontier whose limits are yet to be discerned.

> *Hollerith's Electric Tabulating Machine saved the census and revolutionized information processing. . . . The invention saved an estimated two years and $5 million.*

The first mechanical clock, powered by the action of weights and gravity, is invented. It is very inaccurate.

ANECDOTES & PLEASANTRIES

Happy(?) Birthday

IN A STUDY published in *Psychosomatic Medicine* (and reported in the *New York Times*), it was discovered that elderly women are, statistically speaking, more likely to die from natural causes during the week just after their birthdays. Men, however, are more likely to die of natural causes during the week before their birthdays.

Why? According to Dr. David P. Phillips, a sociology professor at the University of California in San Diego who conducted the research, birthdays can be "a deadline or a lifeline." For men, birthdays may be a time of taking stock, of assessing one's lifetime achievements and failures. Maybe, if they're near death anyway, they'd just as soon let go before having to think again about things that may not have gone very well. For women, however, birthdays are often a time of increased attention from family and friends. So they may hang on to enjoy one more.

Those are theories. Dr. Phillips said that the actual biological causes of prolonging or shortening life around birthdays are not understood. Nonetheless, the statistics, based on 2,745,149 deaths from natural causes, cannot be refuted.

Courtesy of A. G. Frost

1381

John Wycliffe, a reformer and theologian, is responsible for the first popular translation of the Bible into English.

■ *What really happens when we flirt, kiss, and fall in love? It's more scientific than you might expect.*

Solving the Mysteries of Love (and Sex)

BY CHRISTINE SCHULTZ

A S SOON AS SHE SAW HIS PHOTO IN a catalog, she fell in love. All the other merchandise — the corsets, the garters, the studded dog collars — paled by comparison. "I am a lonely schoolteacher in the dismal hills of Idaho," she wrote to the catalog publisher. "Would you be kind enough to do your share in assisting a poor, forlorn teacher in her future happiness by sending this man advertised in your latest edition?"

Hers was a classic case of love at first sight, and though seemingly far-fetched, not one to be quickly discounted. As the philosopher Blaise Pascal once said, "The heart has its reasons which reason knows nothing of." Poets for centuries have agreed that the one certainty about love is its mystery. Today's scholars, however, armed with their studies and statistics, aren't so ready to concede. With clipboards in hand, they've taken notes on everything from the Flirting Sequence Gesture to the Copulatory Gaze to the effects of diet on the libido and the "love drug" on mice.

Although they have yet to crack the code, they've discovered some revealing clues about love. Our lonely Idaho schoolmistress would do well to take notes. Perhaps you would, too.

For starters, you should know that if you're a romantic, you're not alone. Scholars have mistakenly believed for too long that courtly love is a luxury invented by the 12th-century troubadours in Provence and handed down to us through Western culture. Recently they've learned (or admitted) that romantic love is, in fact, universal. Of 166 cultures surveyed by anthropologists William Jankowiak and Edward Fischer, 89 percent showed signs of romantic love. (It's true that many cultures still don't believe romantic love should be the basis of marriage, but the tide is shifting in the heart's favor.) That means you could stumble onto romance almost anywhere — in the Australian outback, in the Amazon jungle, even in the hills of Idaho.

You may wonder, nevertheless, what exactly to look for in a mate.

1386

Geoffrey Chaucer begins writing *The Canterbury Tales.*

Try measuring forearms. One study showed that men and women with the same size forearms were more likely to stay together. But if you forget your tape measure, the poets say not to worry — you'll know love when you see it. "Through the eyes love attains the heart: / For the eyes are the scouts of the heart" (Guiraut de Borneilh, c. 1138–1200). Surprisingly, some scientists agree that you should go with your instincts, since love at first sight most likely evolved to spur the mating process. "During the mating season a female squirrel needs to breed," explained anthropologist Helen Fisher. "It is not to her advantage to copulate with a porcupine. But if she sees a healthy squirrel, she should waste no time." For squirrels and humans alike, the key attraction lies in the health of the potential mate. Scholars tell us that despite all the worldwide variations, the one physical characteristic that attracts men and women

1415

The earliest extant Valentine's Day card is sent by Charles, duke of Orléans, to his wife while he is a prisoner in the Tower of London.

in every culture is a good complexion.

But it's not just how you look; it's how you smell. Foul odors do little to induce affection. Here's why: Located in our nasal cavities are 5 million olfactory neurons waiting like postal workers to sort through some 10,000 recognizable odors. They mail these perfumed messages directly to the brain's emotional headquarters (what scientists call the limbic system). Let's pretend, for instance, that the catalog model (we'll call him Marvin) meets our forlorn teacher (let's call her Myrna) in Idaho on a day when the liquid from her eccrine glands has mixed with bacteria on her skin. She hadn't really expected him to come all this way, and now that he has, it's too late to rid her

She hadn't really expected him to come all this way, and now ... it's too late to rid her body of that acrid smell. Marvin's smell sorters send nasty notes to his brain. He leaves. Poor Myrna, alone again in Idaho.

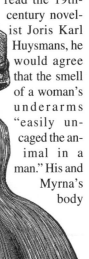

body of that acrid smell. Marvin's smell sorters send nasty notes to his brain. He leaves. Poor Myrna, alone again in Idaho.

Let's give her another chance. This time when Marvin arrives at her door, she's prepared; her body smells seductively sweet. Marvin doesn't know it, but his neuron messengers have keyed into the subtle scent released from Myrna's apocrine glands located around her armpits, nipples, and groin. Had he read the 19th-century novelist Joris Karl Huysmans, he would agree that the smell of a woman's underarms "easily uncaged the animal in a man." His and Myrna's body

Joan of Arc, the 19-year-old peasant girl who inspired the French army to fight against the English, is tried and convicted of heresy and witchcraft. She is burned at the stake.

odors hit it off after all. He understands at last what Napoleon meant when he wrote to his love, Josephine, "I will be arriving in Paris tomorrow. Don't wash."

Smells can do that to a man. If you're still not convinced, try this trick used by women in Shakespeare's day. Hold a peeled apple under your arm until the fruit becomes saturated with your scent, then present it to your lover to inhale. It'll do wonders for your relationship. Really.

Look how it works for the male black-tipped hang fly. He gets mates all the time by secreting his odor into a juicy aphid, daddy longlegs, or housefly and hanging the prize in the wind. Before long, a female catches the scent and stops by for food and procreative fun.

If scented houseflies just don't do it for you, you're best to stick to chocolates. Buried amid the calories are plenty of amphetamine-related substances sure to produce the erratic behavior common to infatuation. Food for the heart.

Who can resist a little courtship feeding, the old evolutionary way for a male to show his prowess as a hunter? To keep in shape for his forays, Marvin should fill up on roughage. Lots of it. That's the advice Dr. Frederick Hollick gave back in the 1840s. "To ward off impotence," he counseled, "fill up on potatoes, celery, parsnips, onions, mushrooms, truffles if you can get

them, olives, tomatoes, lima beans, and above all, asparagus. Canvasback duck also makes a potent pepper-upper." Those who need self-restraint should avoid those foods and eschew coffee — particularly, the good doctor said, if they are "disposed to involuntary emissions." In all cases, he advised that lovers would do well to avoid constipation

Dream of kisses, and you dream of treachery.

and to take care to let the stomach settle before proceeding to the bedroom. "Sexual indulgence just after eating is nearly certain to be followed by indigestion, even if it does not cause immediate vomiting."

Regrettably, not all in love is savory. If you're serious about finding love, you may wish to sample one of the many concoctions said to ignite the heart (if not the intestines). The Australian Aborigines brew a love potion from kangaroo testicles; others swallow the heart of a wild duck; those in Far Eastern

Johannes Gutenberg prints the first edition of the Holy Bible.

countries mix ginger in soft drinks, sweets, and tea; the Chinese look to ginseng and rhinoceros horn. If you have trouble finding kangaroo testicles in your local supermarket, you might just try a more accessible mixture: Stir rosemary, thyme, mint, rose petals, and lemon leaves into black tea. Drink it under a waxing Moon.

In fact, almost anything you do concerning love would be better done under the waxing or full Moon. Scientists and poets alike agree that the Moon plays a powerful role in our reproductive beings. Pliny believed that "lunar energy penetrates all things." Aristotle noticed that the ovaries of sea urchins swell during the full Moon. Darwin wrote that "man is subject, like other mammals, birds, and even insects, to that mysterious law, which causes certain normal processes, such as gestation, as well as the maturation and duration of various diseases to follow lunar periods." Not only is the average menstrual cycle the same length (29.53 days) as the synodic lunar month, but the average human gestation period is 10 lunar months. Furthermore, a statistically significant majority of births (7 percent) occur at the full Moon, and a study by Wesleyan University's psychology department found a 30 percent increase in sexual activity at the time of ovulation, which most frequently happens during the full Moon.

"Like other mammals that go into heat," wrote Paul Katzeff, "women apparently grow randier at ovulation." But they're not the only ones. Researchers also have documented that men, like women, have a greater sexual appetite once a month at the time of the full Moon.

For all we know, it could just be the added light that incites us to romance. When the Moon doesn't shine, we're left groping in the dark. The darkness signals our pineal glands to produce melatonin, and that puts a damper on sperm production, ovulation, and sexual interest. During a waning Moon, we'd be better off waiting for a picnic in the Sun. Sunlight raises the excitement level by revving up the pituitary gland and turning on the ovaries and testes.

With all these cosmic forces at play in our bodies, do our brains have any say at all in the matter of love?

"If only one could tell true love from false love," said Katherine Mansfield, "as one can tell mushrooms from toadstools." But even that's not such an easy thing. If you're no mycologist, take a quick lesson in body cues. The most obvious, of course, is the human "upper smile," combined with a one-sixtieth-of-a-second eyebrow lift; it's a worldwide indicator of interest. Don't, however, confuse the upper smile with the "nervous so-

1477

Future emperor Maximilian I presents Mary of Burgundy with a ring set with a diamond as a symbol of marital commitment. It is the first recorded diamond engagement ring.

cial smile." If Marvin, for instance, approaches with his lips pulled back to reveal his upper and lower teeth, Myrna should spot the response as one that evolved from the ancient mammalian practice of baring one's teeth when cornered. Myrna should back off.

She might try to relax Marvin with the Flirting Sequence Gesture, an age-old female courtship ploy diagrammed by ethologist Irenaus Eibl-Eibesfeldt like this: The woman smiles at her admirer, lifting her eyebrows in a swift jerky motion as she opens her eyes wide. Then she drops her eyelids, tilts her head down and to the side, and looks away. Often she will also cover her face with her hands and giggle nervously.

Then she drops her eyelids, tilts her head down and to the side, and looks away. Often she will also cover her face with her hands and giggle nervously.

Marvin may now be impressed. He may wonder, though, why he hadn't been the one to initiate such advances. Perhaps he hasn't heard of a study by Clellan Ford and Frank Beach in the 1950s that showed that in practice women around the world initiate sexual liaisons, or another study in which American women initiated two-thirds of the encounters. Their best pickup line went like this: "Hi." It worked 100 percent of the time. Men had only a 71 percent success rate with that same line. But at least it meant the ball was rolling. To keep it moving, watch for the next cue. If a woman turns her toes inward, that's the meekness stance, signaling openness for approach. If the man thrusts out his chest, he's trying to impress. Males throughout the animal kingdom puff themselves up to appear attractive. If these cues click, both male and female are interested; their eyes lock for two to three seconds with the pupils dilated. Scientists call this, the most striking human courtship ploy, the Copulatory Gaze. "The gaze triggers a primitive part of the human brain," said anthropologist Helen Fisher, "calling forth one of two basic emotions — approach or retreat."

If neither backs down, only one thing can happen next: The Kiss. Rhett Butler and Scarlett O'Hara did it best in *Gone with the Wind* — Americans rate that the most memorable kiss in movie history. (The

Late 1400s

Wallpaper is developed as an alternative to expensive tapestries in France and spreads to other parts of Europe.

runner-up is the beach kiss by Burt Lancaster and Deborah Kerr in *From Here to Eternity.*) Don't think for a minute that a kiss is just a kiss. On the contrary, it speaks volumes. The esteemed Dr. Bubba Nicholson wrote in the British *Journal of Dermatology* that kissing allows us to taste semiochemicals on a suitor's skin. Semiochemicals, according

---

Married in the merry month of June, Life will be one honeymoon.

---

to Bubba, transmit biological signals of attraction and compatibility. In the words of Carl Jung, "The meeting of two personalities is like the contact of two chemical substances; if there is any reaction, both are transformed."

So if Marvin and Myrna taste good to each other, they may well fall in love. They may find themselves dizzy with excitement, full of bumbling energy that keeps them up late into the night. They might tell you there's chemistry between them. And it would be true, literally. Michael Liebowitz of the New York State Psychiatric Institute said that during infatuation, the brain releases the chemical phenylethylamine, or PEA, a natural amphetamine. When scientists inject PEA into mice, they (the mice, that is) jump and squeal, exhibiting "popcorn behavior." A shot of PEA to rhesus monkeys makes them emit pleasure calls and smack their lips.

But extended romantic bliss may become too much for the brains of Marvin and Myrna. Liebowitz told us that 18 months is about all the brain can take in this revved-up state. Then the nerve endings become habituated to the stimulants, and the levels of PEA drop. A new set of brain chemicals called endorphins takes over. Endorphins calm the mind, kill pain, and reduce anxiety, leaving Myrna and Marvin comfortably settled in the attachment stage of love. Now they can talk and eat and sleep in peace. Myrna may discover for the first time that Marvin snores. Loud. She read somewhere that after sexual intercourse, male rats emit a contented high-frequency snore. Twenty-two kilohertz wouldn't be so bad. At least it wouldn't keep her awake like this jackhammer noise Marvin makes. Since she can't sleep, maybe she'll just go downstairs, do some reading, flip through a couple of catalogs to see what they have in stock.

1492

Columbus's shipmate Rodrigo de Jerez is the first European to smoke a cigar. The New World natives have been smoking the rolled tobacco leaves for at least 500 years.

■ *Cosmetics, perfumes, and personal adornments are nothing new. But it is astonishing, and sometimes horrifying, to learn the lengths to which women and men have gone in their pursuit of beauty. This article from the 1972 Almanac traces fashion and cosmetic trends over the past several centuries.*

Beauty Was in the Eyes (and Nose) of the Beholder

BY ELENOR L. SCHOEN

AMERICAN MALES SPENT MORE than $510 million on cosmetics in 1972. To historians, this is not a surprising development, just another swing of the fashion pendulum.

At the time of the early explorations in America, Indian males were much absorbed in painting their bodies for ornamentation. It was reported that one chieftain spent as much as eight hours decorating himself with lines and designs in multicolors. The Indians had found that various animal fats protected their skin from the cold and from insects. It was just a logical step for them to realize that such greasy substances were good under paint, since the paint could be more easily removed afterward. When an Indian was mourning some loved or revered person, he blackened his entire face with charcoal. If he was obliged only to be in "half-mourning," his face displayed some horizontal black lines. Although Indians learned how to make the dyes more lasting, they did not know how to preserve the fats they used. As a result, the average Indian was enveloped in a highly pungent scent.

In 1651 there was general dismay among the "upper classes" of American colonists because indentured servants and their like had the impudence to ape their betters and use cosmetics. The Gen-

The toothbrush is invented in China. It will not be widely used in Europe until the 17th century.

eral Court of Massachusetts expressed its indignation: "That men and women of meane conditions, education and calling should take upon the garb of gentlemen by wearing gold or silver lace, or buttons or points at the knees, or walk in great boots, or women of the same rank to wear silk, hoods or scarves." All "marks" of the gentleman or gentlewoman — such as hair powder, rouge, and perfume — were included in this exclusive listing.

Later, in 1770, a statute was adopted in Pennsylvania. This was designed to protect men from being misled by deceitful women. It read:

All women of whatever age, rank, profession or degree, whether virgins, maids, or widows, that shall from and after such Act, impose upon, seduce and betray into matrimony, any of His Majesty's subjects by the scents, paints, cosmetic washes, artificial teeth, false hair, Spanish wool, iron stays, hoops, high-heeled shoes, bolstered hips, shall incur the penalty of the law in force against witchcraft and like misdemeanors,

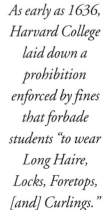

As early as 1636, Harvard College laid down a prohibition enforced by fines that forbade students "to wear Long Haire, Locks, Foretops, [and] Curlings."

and that the marriage upon conviction, shall stand null and void.

As early as 1636, Harvard College laid down a prohibition enforced by fines that forbade students "to wear Long Haire, Locks, Foretops, Curlings, Crispings and Partings, or Powdering of ye Haire."

Many of the early colonists brought fancy soaps and lotions with them from Europe. Sir Walter Raleigh had the forethought to bring "scents to perfume his leather jerkins."

The colonists resorted to many home concoctions as beauty aids. A covering of bacon on the face of a sleeper would soften her skin and ward off wrinkles. Eggshells were ground with toilet water to make an acceptable face powder. Lips were reddened by sucking lemons. Hair powder was made from sifted flour or powdered starch, combined with plaster of Paris and perfume. Scents were developed from musk, orrisroot, jasmine, violet, and iris.

When the wearing of wigs became common in England around

1504

German locksmith Peter Henlein creates a small timepiece that fits into a pocket. It will later be referred to as a watch, after the period of time that sailors and soldiers maintained guard.

1660, the colonists copied the custom. A wig for women was fashioned with at least a foot-high wire frame covered with material, and then hair was piled and curled over it. Scented powder was sprinkled on top. The hair was set with a lacquer of starch combined with pomatum (pomade). Men wore large wigs with much curly hair reaching their shoulders, which made them resemble shaggy lions.

Other cosmetics of Americans in the 17th century were bosom bottles (in which fresh flowers and water were placed), masks, patches, and skin lotions. The desire for pleasant and fresh fragrances in the home led the colonists to blend juices from bayberries and juniper berries in their candles. They also placed dried flowers and herbs in bowls and set these in every room.

An 18th-century American dandy usually owned a "dressing box" that held his razor cases, scissors, combs, curling irons, oil and

Men wore large wigs with much curly hair reaching their shoulders, which made them resemble shaggy lions.

scent bottles, powder puff, brush, and soap. In the morning after he shaved, rouge and powder were applied. Bits of gummed silk called patches were attached artistically here and there on the face. Originally, these were used to cover blemishes, but later they were just another decoration. Some patches were in various designs, such as stars, animals, and ships. During one period, a person indicated his political allegiance by which side he wore his patches on: On the right, he was a Tory;

1505

Law student Martin Luther is struck by a bolt of lightning during a thunderstorm. In his fear, he renounces the world, enters an Augustinian monastery, and eventually will become the leader of the Protestant Reformation.

on the left, he was a Whig.

Elaborate little boxes resembling modern powder compacts held these patches. Some were made of gold, silver, ivory, pewter, or tortoiseshell. A mirror was fastened to the inner side of the lid.

Most gentlemen had a special room in their homes called a powder closet. Here wigs could be powdered. A gown was first put on, and then, while a paper cone was held over the face, flour or starch might be sprinkled on through a perforated container. The powder might be light brown, blue, grayish pink, violet, or white. Gray was used only for mourning. A gentleman used perfume to overcome the tobacco smell that clung to his clothing.

Even soldiers wore wigs throughout the 18th century. One pound of flour was issued to each soldier for the purpose of powdering his wig.

At this time, ladies' wigs and coiffures were so elaborate that they were done up no more often than from three to nine weeks in the

At this time, ladies' wigs and coiffures were so elaborate that they were done up no more often than from three to nine weeks in the summer; a longer period elapsed in the winter.

summer; a longer period elapsed in the winter. The hair was never combed or touched in the intervals. Poison was applied to the head daily to control the vermin, sometimes unsuccessfully. Occasionally, after a month had passed, a lady's head was "opened" so that the various vermin might be removed. Many ladies resorted to probing their heads with long ivory scratchers, which they used even in public.

A description of a Saturday afternoon in Philadelphia during 1758 mentions barbers' boys busily delivering wig boxes after the wigs had been curled, powdered, and perfumed for Sunday.

Most 18th-century American gentlewomen had dressing cases that contained cold creams, bleaches made from citrus fruits, hair dyes, false hair, eye shadow made from lampblack or kohl, lotions, and oils. Bottles of water were also placed in the hair to keep flowers fresh.

To protect a lady's skin from the Sun, a mask made of velvet or satin was worn, or large fans made of lace, shell, ivory, or feathers were

Leonardo da Vinci completes his portrait *Mona Lisa* in Florence, Italy.

used. Some ladies retired at night wearing leather gloves dressed with almonds and spermaceti to soften and whiten their hands.

Doctors of the time frequently carried canes that, when tapped on the floor, released some perfumed disinfectant through a perforated lid on the cane's top. This was supposed to safeguard the doctor from disease.

Paste and powder were used on teeth only to make them white and sparkling, not to prevent decay. Brick dust was an occasional ingredient.

Some of the old cosmetics have intriguing names: Balm of Mecca (a liquid rouge), Damask Rose Water and Divine Cordial (both perfumes), Grecian Liquid (hair dye), Honey of Roses (wrinkle remover), and Imperial Royal Cream Marbled Wash Balls (soap).

One offering was Lady Molyneux's Italian Paste, which could enamel the hands, neck, and face a "lovely white. . . . Ladies who use it cannot be tanned by the most scorching heat, nor can the most severe frost crack the skin."

Royal Milk Water was promised to take pimples and spots off the face. Venetian Paste "entirely eradicates Carbuncles and other Heats of the Face, or Nose, and cracking of the lips." Spanish Papers were rubbed on the face to give color from their carmine dyes.

In America during the 19th century, the use of cosmetics declined. The elderly used them to conceal the marks of age. Frontier women used ground chalk for powder and freshly cut beet root

Lady Molyneux's Italian Paste . . . could enamel the hands, neck, and face a "lovely white. . . . Ladies who use it cannot be tanned by the most scorching heat."

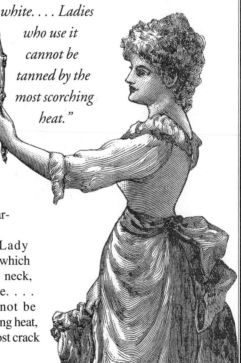

1520

The Aztecs introduce Spanish explorers to chocolate (extracted from the cacao bean), which they serve as a liquid. Hernán Cortés brings the cacao bean to Europe, but it will not be enjoyed there for nearly 100 years.

for rouge. More soap was used than creams. A combination of lard, rose water, and coconut milk made a popular hand lotion. To prevent crow's-feet at the eyes, strips of brown paper soaked in vinegar were applied to the face.

Men decided that cosmetics were effeminate and eliminated all cosmetics except hairdressing.

Men decided that cosmetics were effeminate and eliminated all cosmetics except hairdressing. For this, rich men used perfumed macassar oil, and pioneer men used bear's grease.

Ivan Golovin, exiled from Russia and a naturalized Englishman, wrote a book about the United States in 1855, *Stars and Stripes or American Impressions.* He commented, "The American ladies well deserve the name given to them by the Indians of *palefaces,* their paleness being excessive indeed. This is owing to rocking-chairs, to sexual excesses producing consumption, but particularly to absence of vegetation in the cities."

During the Civil War, northern profiteers started the expensive habit of powdering their hair with gold and silver dust. Empress Eugenie visited America and reportedly introduced mascara. Charles Meyers came to New York from Germany and brought with him a special recipe. From this, he formulated and sold the first greasepaint.

In 1866 it was discovered that zinc oxide could provide an excel-

1525

A system of secondary education, or high schools, is introduced in the Western world.

lent base for face powder. It was safe, held its color, and was low-priced. Talcum powder became generally used only in the United States. It was concocted of powdered magnesium silicate and perfume.

Between 1880 and 1900, only the least bit of cosmetics was fashionable. The mark of a true lady was her natural, untouched appearance.

The 20th century introduced the marcel wave. A Parisian hairdresser, Marcel Grateau, curled the hair in even waves with a special iron.

In 1906 Charles Nessler, a German living in London, announced his "permanent" wave. It took 8 to 12 hours and cost $1,000. During the first year, only 18 women dared to have one. This "permanent" process appeared in America in 1915; there it was improved and reduced in price.

More and more innovations came. There were lipsticks in oval tubes, powder boxes of gold and silver called compacts, eyebrow pencils, facial packs made of perfumed mud, "cold

Between 1880 and 1900, only the least bit of cosmetics was fashionable. The mark of a true lady was her natural, untouched appearance.

waves," and nail and hair lacquer.

Cosmetics became a major industry during World War I, and by mid-century retail sales were $1 billion annually. In the late 1960s, a drive was commenced to lure men to buy more and more lotions, perfumes, and the like. Male beauty preparations included an aftershave cream that claimed to have antiwrinkle properties, shampoos, bath foams, colognes, deodorants, moisturizers, a liquid bronze and face-color talc, hair creams, hair oils, hair tonics, hair color restorers, lip pomades, hair sprays, and weather lotions. Beauty kits for men contained as many as ten items.

To capture more dollars from men, various companies will no doubt continue to offer products for facial and skin treatments, hand care, and hair tinting. The 21st-century man will more and more resemble his 18th-century counterpart. We may comment, as did Zeno (a Greek who lived in the 4th century B.C.) upon meeting a man fragrant with perfume, "Who is this, who smells like a woman?"

1531

A comet is recorded this year and again in 1607 and 1682. Years later, English astronomer and mathematician Edmond Halley will determine that it is the same comet and predict its reappearance in 1758. Halley will be proved right in 1758, but he will die before the event. The comet is now known as Halley's comet.

FARMER'S CALENDAR

Nostalgia

I T'S THE STEAM WHISTLE on the old locomotive that sobbed and wailed and cried in the night.

It's the clop, clop of Ned and Dandy coming up the lane with the biggest load of hay.

It's the cough, cough and whine and buzz — and the dying drone — of the saw rig that made us our cordwood.

It's sawing ice on the ice pond and the icehouse and the smell of sawdust as we slid the great cakes in.

It's everything that isn't now, says the old-timer — and woe be it, says he, that these things are dead and gone.

Maybe that's so, old-timer, but let's whittle these memories down to size. You remember these things that have gone, mostly because they have gone and are surrounded now by the magic of nostalgia.

The truth is that we live in a very wonderful present, with a promise of a wonderful future. No sword hangs over our heads that has not always hung over the heads of the human race in some way or other from the beginning of time — time as we humans call it for ourselves. But, of course, time was here before we were. Time is so vast that for our own sakes, for our need of emotional being, we take the little span of it that we know and play the changes on it. And this we have then: a longing for things past, a joy and apprehension in the present, a hope and apprehension of the future. But here is a new year. That's tangible. Let's grab it and make the most of it.

1541

Spanish explorer Hernando de Soto is the first European to see the Mississippi River.

■ *There have always been a lot of theories having to do with "handedness." Only recently have we begun to learn the facts about people who are left-handed. And some are downright surprising.*

The Sinister Truth About Handedness

BY JON VARA

Why was I not born with two good hands? he thought. Perhaps it was my fault for not training that one properly. But God knows he has had enough chances to learn.

— Ernest Hemingway,
The Old Man and the Sea

WHEN HEMINGWAY'S OLD fisherman falls to scolding his cramped left hand, he is simply carrying on a tradition of left-hand disparagement shared by many languages and cultures. An En-glish speaker who pays someone a left-handed compliment, for example, is actually delivering a veiled insult. The French word for left, *gauche,* refers in English to clumsy or tactless behavior. Lefties also have been regarded as somehow, well, sinister. The English *sinister,* in fact, is identical to the Latin word for "left" or "on the left." (By contrast, the Latin word for "right," *dexter,* gives us the English *dexterous,* meaning "skilled" or "adept.") The left also figures prominently in any number of superstitions, including the belief that entering a house on the left foot will bring bad luck to its inhabitants. (Composer Frederic Chopin and author Samuel Johnson, among others, were strict observers of the left-foot-last rule.)

In reality, of course, lefties are no more diabolical than, say,

1542

Scotland's St. Andrews, the first major golf course (and the oldest still in use), is founded.

Rotarians. And although it is true that some very troubled characters have been left-handed — including Jack the Ripper, Billy the Kid, and John Dillinger — there have been many eminent left-handers as well.

Leonardo da Vinci and Pablo Picasso were lefties, as were Benjamin Franklin, Albert Einstein, Marilyn Monroe, Queen Victoria, Joan of Arc, and New York Yankees pitching star Lefty Gomez. Three of the last five presidents of the United States — Gerald Ford, George Bush, and Bill Clinton (maybe four if you count Ronald Reagan, who uses his left hand for some tasks) — have been southpaws. (*Southpaw*, incidentally, derives from baseball, where playing fields are often laid out so that the batter faces east, with the afternoon Sun at his back. The pitcher then faces west, with his left hand — or "paw" — to the south. For some reason, referring to right-handers as "northpaws" never caught on.)

> *Leonardo da Vinci and Pablo Picasso were lefties, as were Benjamin Franklin, Albert Einstein, Marilyn Monroe, Queen Victoria, Joan of Arc, and . . . three of the last five presidents of the United States — Gerald Ford, George Bush, and Bill Clinton.*

Quantitatively speaking, somewhere between 12 and 15 percent of the world's population is left-handed, or about one person in seven. Setting aside small-scale statistical anomalies — such as the three out of five presidents — that proportion seems to have remained fairly constant throughout recorded history.

Among the modern primates, humans seem to be unique in having any consistent, species-specific hand preference. Studies of gorillas, monkeys, and chimpanzees have found that only about half of all individuals tested show a preference for a particular hand, and they are evenly divided between left-handers and right-handers.

Researchers into handedness — or laterality, as the medical and scientific communities prefer to describe it — do not yet know why it should have evolved among humans in the first place, or even how

1543

Nicolaus Copernicus's book *De Revolutionibus Orbium Coelestium* (On the Revolutions of the Heavenly Spheres) is published. In it, he refutes the idea of an Earth-centered universe, claiming that Earth and all other celestial bodies revolve around the Sun. His theory will not be proved until the 17th century.

it is passed along from one generation to the next. Indeed, pairs of identical twins appear to be no more likely to share the same handedness than randomly chosen pairs of unrelated strangers.

But handedness does run in families, in a general way. The newborn child of two right-handed parents, for example, has something like a 10 percent chance of turning out left-handed. If Dad is left-handed and Mom is right-handed, the odds of the child being left-handed edge upward by a few percentage points. If Mom is left-handed and Dad is right-handed, the odds rise sharply to 20 percent, or almost double. And if both parents are left-handed, the incidence of left-handedness among the offspring nearly doubles again, to between 35 and 40 percent.

Is handedness somehow preordained, or is it simply learned? Psychologists are now convinced that nature, rather than nurture, is the deciding factor. Until just a few decades ago, it was widely believed that left-handedness was simply a bad habit, one that could be rooted out and eradicated if proper "corrective" action was taken early enough. Many adult left-handers retain vivid memories of the forceful, occasionally cruel, and generally fruitless methods used to convert them into right-handers.

The belief that training would carry the day reached its zenith in the turn-of-the-century Ambidextral Culture Society, which energetically promoted training both hands to perform skilled tasks. For a time, it enjoyed a large and influential following, including Robert Baden-Powell, Boer War hero and founder of the Boy Scouts. (Baden-

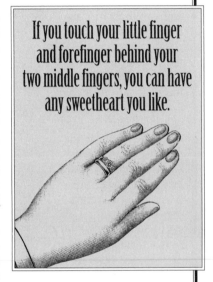

If you touch your little finger and forefinger behind your two middle fingers, you can have any sweetheart you like.

Powell even wrote an introduction to a popular book on ambidextrality, closing with two specimens of his signature, one written with each hand.)

The movement unraveled, however, as it became painfully obvious — as Hemingway's Santiago would later observe — that true ambidextrality is very difficult, if not impossible, for most people to achieve. Still more problematic, those who did turn the trick were

Mid-1500s

Cats (especially black ones) fall from grace as their population increases, and superstitions associating them with bad luck abound. This coincides with a period of witch hysteria in Europe.

hard-pressed to put their ambidextrality to practical use. The movement's most visible legacy seems to be the official Boy Scout handshake, created by Baden-Powell himself, which is still offered and accepted with the left hand.

The ambidextrality fad has run its course, but other half-baked ideas about handedness have appeared to take its place. The most popular notion now making the rounds is that left-handed people are more insightful and creative than right-handers, thanks to a supposed ability to draw directly on the right hemisphere of the brain. Right-handers, by contrast, are seen as the stolid, slavishly rational captives of the left hemisphere.

Unlike most pieces of folklore about handedness, that one at least portrays left-handers in a favorable light. And there is a grain of truth associated with it: The two hemispheres of the brain do control motor functions on opposite

Right-handed scissors and ice cream scoops can be annoying, but a southpaw who must struggle with a right-handed power saw or rotary meat slicer risks losing more than his or her composure.

sides of the body, which is why an injury to the left hemisphere — a stroke, for example — results in paralysis of the right side. But there is no evidence that the distribution of motor functions in the brain has anything to do with handedness or difference in thought processes.

Still, there probably are some minor differences in the neurological wiring of right- and left-hander brains. One difference shows up in what are sometimes called "veering biases." A right-handed person stirring sugar into a cup of coffee, for example, swirls the spoon in a clockwise direction, while a left-hander stirs counterclockwise. The same pattern carries over into larger-scale movements as well. Right-handers show a tendency to bear right upon entering a room, while left-handers typically bear left. The myth of left-handed awkwardness probably has less to do with a lack of grace on the part of left-

1556

Jean Nicot, the French ambassador to Lisbon, is credited with importing tobacco to Europe from America. The active ingredient, nicotine, is named after him.

handers themselves than with the right-handed majority's lack of practice in anticipating their movements.

In some cases, though, that can work to the southpaw's advantage. In sports such as boxing, fencing, and tennis, a left-handed competitor often finds it easier to keep a right-handed opponent off balance. (However, when two lefties compete against each other, both are at an equal disadvantage.)

Neurological differences are only part of the story. Several studies show left-handers to be disproportionately numerous in architecture and the arts, as well as among chess champions. They also tend to do better than right-handers on tests that measure the ability to visualize and manipulate three-dimensional images.

Do these findings mean that left-handers really are inherently more creative than right-handers? Probably not. It's more likely that left-handers — who, from childhood, must learn to adapt to right-handed scissors, ice cream scoops, writing desks, and other items — simply have more practice solving visual problems and gravitate naturally toward activities in which such

We live in an overwhelmingly right-handed world. Under the circumstances, the left-handed minority's refusal to knuckle under and be overwhelmed — despite centuries of distrust, scorn, and ridicule — has to be seen as inspiring.

skills are valued. The frustration lefties experience in using improperly designed tools and machines may also explain why left-handers tend to be both more cautious and more anxious than their right-handed counterparts.

Right-handed scissors and ice cream scoops can be annoying, but a southpaw who must struggle with a right-handed power saw or rotary meat slicer risks losing more than his or her composure. Not surprisingly, some studies suggest

1565

Graphite found in northern England is cut into rods, wrapped in a wooden casing, and used as the first modern pencil.

ANECDOTES & PLEASANTRIES

Does Anyone Care to Know the Origin of "Hello"?

To be even slightly interested in this question, you have to realize that the word "hello," as used today, didn't really exist back in the 19th century. They did call out "halloo" to incite hounds to chase or to hail someone from a long distance away. Like "Halloo! You up there on the roof." And the English did say "hullo," but not as a greeting. They used it as an expression of surprise as in "Hullo, what have we here?"

So how and when did "hello" begin as a simple greeting? Well, in a *New York Times* article by William Grimes, sent to us by no less than four readers, the "hello" mystery seems finally to have been, if not totally solved, somewhat clarified. It now seems likely that it originated with Thomas Edison and his telephone. Alexander Graham Bell is credited with inventing the telephone, of course, but Edison also developed one, which he envisioned as exclusively a business device with open lines at both ends.

"Are you there?" and "Are you ready to talk?" were suggested methods, initially, of starting a conversation on Edison's phones. His rival, Bell, however, was insisting on "Ahoy!" as the preferred initial greeting.

The reason we can now credit Edison with "hello" is due to a letter discovered by Allen Koenigsberg, a

---

that left-handers suffer more accidental injuries than right-handers, although that has not been conclusively proved.

Lefties can, of course, take some solace from the everyday items that actually favor them. Hand-cranked pencil sharpeners, for example, are cranked with the right hand, enabling a left-handed user to insert a pencil without first shifting it from the preferred writing hand, as a right-hander must. Most women's clothing is designed with the buttons on the left, so that it is most efficiently buttoned by a left-handed wearer (or a right-handed lady's maid facing her, which is how the convention got started). And the keyboards on most typewriters and computers are laid out in such a way that the operator's left hand is responsible for nearly three-quarters of the work.

But in the end, examples like these simply underscore the fact

---

1582

Pope Gregory XIII invents a calendar that follows the seasonal year more closely than the Julian calendar currently in use. To implement the new calendar, ten days are removed from the month of October this year.

classics professor at Brooklyn College, New York. It had been stored away for more than a hundred years in the American Telephone and Telegraph Company archives in lower Manhattan. Dated August 15, 1877, it is addressed to one T. B. A. David, who was preparing to introduce Edison's version of the telephone to the city of Pittsburgh. "Dear David," Edison began, "I don't think we shall need a call bell as 'hello' can be heard 10 to 20 feet away. What do you think?" Signed, "Edison."

From then on, according to Professor Koenigsberg, "hello" became the recommended greeting in telephone operating manuals. It also became something of a social liberator and leveler, in that it cut through 19th-century etiquette that said you don't speak directly to someone unless you've been introduced.

For us this solves yet another mystery. We've always wondered why, when he first spotted Livingston in the jungle, Stanley said, "Dr. Livingston, I presume." Why not a simple "hello"? As we now know, the word did not yet exist.

that we live in an overwhelmingly right-handed world. Under the circumstances, the left-handed minority's refusal to knuckle under and be overwhelmed — despite centuries of distrust, scorn, and ridicule — has to be seen as inspiring.

And even though the righties have the upper hand at the moment, it's possible that the shoe may someday be on the other foot. Some researchers speculate that the small but consistent pool of left-handers in the population may represent a sort of evolutionary ace in the hole — a hedge against the possibility that an unforeseeable turn of events may someday work against the survival of the right-handed variety of *Homo sapiens.*

That may sound unlikely, and it probably is. But maybe, just maybe, the southpaws will one day inherit the Earth. They certainly will have earned it.

1587

Virginia Dare is born on Roanoke Island, off the coast of North Carolina. She is the first child born of English parents in North America.

■ *Crying is an elemental human function, but relatively little is known about it. One thing is for sure: There's a story in every teardrop.*

For Crying Out Loud (or Otherwise)

BY JAMIE KAGELEIRY

A WOMAN STANDS AT A SINK. WE can't see what she's doing, but she's slumped over a bit. Her hair hides her face. She sniffles. Then her hand comes up and brushes her cheek. A tear? She's crying. Has her husband been cross to her? Or is she peeling an onion?

Humans cry. There are unproven anecdotes of crying elephants and tearful golden retrievers, but humans are virtually the only creatures to shed emotional tears. Although *Bartlett's Familiar Quotations* has far fewer entries for *cry* and *crying* than it does for *love,* popular music relies heavily on the word (either using it in lyrics or evoking an emotion that moves you to tears). Until recently, scientific resources were scarce on this most elemental of human functions. There has been research on infant cries but not much about the rest of us. As Dr. William Frey (director of the Ramsey Dry Eye and Tear Research Center in St. Paul, Minnesota) and Jeffrey Kottler (author of *The Language of Tears*) have

discovered, crying is no simple thing.

The woman at the sink, for instance. If we could scoop up that brushed tear and analyze it, we might know why she is crying. If her tears are due to a tiff with her husband, they will contain more proteins — complex elemental substances that include essential compounds such as enzymes or hormones — than if her eyes are merely irritated by peeling an onion. Although other scientists aren't sure yet, Frey thinks this difference means that "something unique happens when people cry emotional tears." Frey was able to isolate in emotional tears the hormone prolactin, which is released by the pituitary gland at times of intense emotion or stress and makes its way to the lachrymal (tear) glands. Too much prolactin in your system can become toxic, so crying is a way of cleansing the body of this during stress, just as irritant tears help cleanse the eye of smoke, onion fumes, or a stray eyelash.

Late 1500s

Fashions in Europe include the first pockets in trousers.

The fact that crying flushes away excess prolactin during stress probably accounts for the fact that 85 percent of women and 73 percent of men say they feel better after crying, and why some studies even indicate that men who do not cry, or who consider crying a sign of weakness, are more apt to suffer stress-related illnesses such as colitis.

Imagine the woman, let's name her Nadia, at the sink again. We've discovered that she's sad. Chances are, she cries emotional tears four times more often than her ogre of a husband. No surprise — women average 5.3 cries a month. When men cry, it's often hard to tell — usually their eyes brim, but not many tears escape down the face.

Before puberty, boys and girls cry about the same amount. Then, by some combination of a "big boys don't cry" culture (at least in this country) and biological differences, women pull way ahead. Men's and women's tear glands are structurally different, but there's something else that

may cause women to cry more — that sneaky prolactin again. Not only is the hormone present during emotional times, but it's crucial in promoting the secretion of milk. Women need prolactin to nurse

Her hair hides her face. She sniffles. Then her hand comes up and brushes her cheek. A tear?

their babies, and their bodies contain 60 percent more of it than do men's.

Time Is a River of Tears

So a woman stands crying. Only this time, it's not at a sink. It's be-

1590

William Shakespeare writes his first play, *The Comedy of Errors*. The first performance of the play will be in 1594; the first printing of the play in 1623.

side a fire, and she is early *Homo sapiens*. A neurophysiologist named Paul MacLean thinks that humans first began to cry 1.4 million years ago when they started using fire. He pictures the smoke from the first fire making those standing around it cry irritant tears. Then, as tribespeople habitually gathered around the fires for social activities — cooking, tending the sick, even disposing of loved ones in cremation ceremonies — tearing became a conditioned reflex associated with separation. MacLean suggests that it is the ability to cry tears in response to separation from loved ones that sets us apart from other animals. (Although there is the story of the lost golden retriever. His owners finally tracked him down hundreds of miles away from home. As they walked up to the shelter to get him, out he came with tears running down his face.

Nadia can tell by the sharpness of her baby's cry that he is hungry, and she picks him up and soothes him. His cries have stimulated milk production in Nadia, and she feeds him.

But we didn't run into many of these stories.)

Jeffrey Kottler notes that Charles Darwin — who believed that no human behavior is useless but is naturally selected based on its adaptive value in helping an organism survive — could think of no use for tears. But think about babies. And, once more, picture Nadia at the sink. This time, she stops what she is doing and turns her head quickly. Her three-month-old baby is crying. She listens for a second: Is he just trying to get to sleep? Is he hungry? Or sick? Or wet? Studies have found that although fathers can correctly identify their own child's cry out of a group 84 percent of the time, mothers are nearly infallible, and mothers are better than fathers at being able to discern what their baby's cries mean. Nadia can tell by the sharpness of her baby's cry that he is hungry, and she picks him up and soothes him. His

The first opera — Jacopo Peri's *Dafne,* with text by the poet Ottavio Rinuccini — is staged in Florence, Italy.

cries have stimulated milk production in Nadia, and she feeds him. He won't be able to speak words for another year, but he has gotten his message across and his needs met.

Take a different look at Nadia. She stands in her office at a major law firm where she works as the chief litigator. Her boss has just spoken crossly to her — probably even more sharply than her husband did that morning. But she stands with her hands on her hips, dry-eyed. As women move into traditional male worlds, the tears aren't as automatic. Nadia cries at home. She would never cry at work. In our culture, where more people of both sexes tend to cry more often than those of other cultures, one's occupation is as good a predictor as any for this tendency: Nurses cry, doctors don't (as often); therapists cry, engineers

In our culture, where more people of both sexes tend to cry more often than those of other cultures, one's occupation is as good a predictor as any for this tendency: Nurses cry, doctors don't (as often); therapists cry, engineers don't.

don't. And, as with Nadia, it all depends on where you are when you feel like crying.

"Laugh, and the world laughs with you; Weep, and you weep alone."

Well, that all depends on your culture. If you're English, you might cry only in private. If a tear slips out in public, chances are those with you will look away in embarrassment or discomfort. An Italian, though, is more likely to cry in public, whether happy or sad.

If you are one of the Bosavi people of New Guinea, it gets more complicated. If visitors from another village come, for instance, they are expected to perform a night of singing and dancing for their hosts. Suddenly, a local villager will grab a torch and burn one of the visiting Bosavins on the shoulder. The victim will not cry or even show he is in pain. The villagers,

1602

English navigator Bartholomew Gosnold discovers Cape Cod, in what is now southeastern Massachusetts.

though, will scream, cry, and carry on all night. The longer and harder the crying, the more successful the ritual is deemed to be. This ceremony, writes Kottler, is one "of grief, of violence, of tribute and reciprocity. . . . The object of this exercise is to elicit strong emotional reactions in the participants, to

> **A judicious silence is better than truth spoken without charity.**

make them cry." Anthropologists observing the Bosavi people think the songs are presented not as taunts but in the same spirit of sympathy with which the guests themselves weep at the end of the ceremony for their hosts who have suffered. The entire ritual is a way of contriving tragedy so that everyone may cry in the end.

This may sound bizarre, but when you think about it, it's not much different from what we do when we purposely play a song that makes us cry, or go to an opera or film that we know will make us weep. "Both within the culture of the Bosavi," says Kottler, "and in our own community, we have institutionalized 'tear ceremonies' that help us to reflect on our feelings about our own existence through the lives of others" — allowing us to experience our emotions safely, without rocking the boat too much.

The ability to turn on tears, or even to withhold them as Nadia did at work, functions as communication. Think about the late Senator Edmund Muskie. In 1972 Muskie, then seeking his party's presidential nomination, purportedly wept at a rally in Manchester, New Hampshire, while denouncing a newspaper publisher for printing a derogatory letter about his wife. His "weakness" did in his campaign. Yet the 1996 campaign season was, according to the *Wall Street Journal,* "the weepiest on record." Bill Clinton and Bob Dole were both comfortable blubbering in public. It had become, in the words of one reporter, "increasingly cool to cry."

So perhaps the next time we see someone sobbing at the sink, it may be Nadia's husband or her son crying over *Field of Dreams.* Or maybe it's just onions.

1603

Thomas Ravenscroft of London writes the verse and melody of "Three Blind Mice," the earliest printed secular song still sung today.

The Golden Rule
(It's true in all faiths.)

Brahmanism

This is the sum of duty: Do naught unto others which would cause you pain if done to you.

— *Mahabharata 5:1517*

Buddhism

Hurt not others in ways that you yourself would find hurtful.

— *Udana-Vargas 5:18*

Confucianism

Surely it is the maxim of loving-kindness: Do not unto others what you would not have them do unto you. — *Analects 15:23*

Christianity

All things whatsoever ye would that men should do to you, do ye even so to them; for this is the law and the prophets.

— *Matthew 7:12*

Taoism

Regard your neighbor's gain as your own gain and your neighbor's loss as your own loss.

— *T'ai Shang Kan Ying P'ien*

Zoroastrianism

That nature alone is good which refrains from doing unto another whatsoever is not good for itself.

— *Dadistan-i-dinik 94:5*

Judaism

What is hateful to you, do not to your fellowman. That is the entire Law; all the rest is commentary.

— *Talmud, Shabbat 31a*

Islam

No one of you is a believer until he desires for his brother that which he desires for himself.

— *Sunnah*

Courtesy of Elizabeth Pool

1603

Italian alchemist Vincenzo Cascariolo combines barium sulfate and powdered coal to create not gold, but a substance that glows in the dark, which he calls *lapis solaris*.

■ *There are humans among us who push harder, run longer, and reach higher, often at enormous personal peril. Was it fame that drove Sam Patch, the "Yankee Leaper," to take such terrible risks, or purely the thrill of taking the human spirit to the very edge?*

Alas, Brave, Foolish Sam Patch

BY TIM CLARK

ON MARCH 17, 1830, AN UP-state New York farmer chopped a hole in the ice of the Genesee River to water his horses. There in the frigid water, near where the river empties into Lake Ontario, he found the lifeless body of Sam Patch, who four months earlier had leaped into the river from a platform erected atop Genesee Falls — a distance of 125 feet — before a crowd of thousands.

When Sam Patch made his fatal leap — on Friday the 13th, November 1829 — he jumped out of the realm of history and into legend. He had been a popular sensation for just two years, dating from his first spectacular plunge of 70 feet from the top of Passaic Falls in September 1827. Sam repeated the stunt 10

Sam had been jumping to entertain himself and his friends, just as he had as a boy in Pawtucket, Rhode Island, where he and other daredevils jumped from the bridge above Pawtucket Falls.

months later, then raised the ante by leaping 90 feet from the masthead of a sloop anchored off Hoboken, New Jersey. This feat was seen by hundreds of onlookers in boats and on the shore, and it propelled Sam Patch to new fame.

Up to that point, Sam had been jumping to entertain himself and his friends, just as he had as a boy in Pawtucket, Rhode Island, where he and other daredevils jumped from the bridge above Pawtucket Falls or from the roofs of the cotton mills where they worked. But when the news of Sam Patch, the "Yankee Leaper," began to spread throughout the eastern part of the nation, Sam lost control of his destiny. He would be pulled onward by money and popular acclaim to greater and greater heights and more terri-

1605

The first part of *Don Quixote,* a novel by Miguel de Cervantes, is published in Madrid, Spain. The second part will be published in 1615.

ble risks, until fate caught up with him at Genesee.

A year after the Hoboken jump, the citizens of Buffalo were planning a gala to celebrate the dynamiting of Table Rock, which overhung Niagara Falls on the Canadian side. An earlier stunt — sending an unseaworthy brig over the falls with a crew of bears, foxes, geese, a buffalo, and an effigy of Andrew Jackson — had been a big hit in 1827. Looking for a way to top that, the folks decided to invite Sam Patch to leap down the falls while another empty boat was deliberately wrecked.

The date was set for October 6, 1829, and a large crowd was on hand to see Sam, who for some reason failed to arrive on time. But Sam was not deterred. He distributed posters in the city advertising a 120-foot plunge over the falls on October 17. On the appointed day, Sam made his way to Goat Island, which overlooks the falls, and climbed a swaying platform made of four trees that had been lashed together. Reaching the top, he capered about for 10 minutes to demonstrate his balance, then, after kissing an American flag,

1608

Dutch spectacle maker Hans Lippershey invents the telescope.

stepped into space. One observer says the crowd shouted, "He's dead, he's lost!" Another maintains there was a shocked silence. But then Sam's head broke water in the river below the falls, and the shoreline rocked with cheers as he swam in.

Less than two weeks later, Sam was advertising a new jump, from the falls at Genesee. There, on November 6, before a crowd estimated at 5,000, he once again successfully defied fate by plunging 100 feet into the river, this time accompanied by a pet bear, who also survived.

By this time, Sam was the darling of the nation's newspapers and a bona fide tourist attraction. He won the backing of a group of sponsors for his next jump, which would be from a 25-foot platform set up on the heights above Genesee Falls, in order to achieve a new record. Taverns and hotels did a record business as the curious came from all around in special excursion coaches and schooners. The attraction was heightened by the fact that it was advertised as "Sam's Last Jump." Was it an advertising ploy? Or was the "Jumping Hero"

beginning to have second thoughts? On the day of the jump, some observers thought Sam staggered as he walked to the platform, as if he had been drinking. Others claimed he asked, before beginning his climb to the top, that his prize money — about $400 — be sent to his mother should he fail.

Drunk or not, there was no doubt that this leap lacked the style and precision of all his others. Usually he fell in a rigid upright position, feet down, entering the water in such a way as to curve back to the surface feet first. But on his last jump, Sam's form faltered — his body struck the water at an angle, with arms and legs extended in a desperate effort to regain a vertical position. He never came to the surface.

At that point, the machinery of legend took over. Although the river was dragged, Sam's body was not found immediately, leading to rumors that he was still alive. Sam had found an underwater cave before the jump, some said, where he had cached food and clothing that al-

> *Drunk or not, there was no doubt that this leap lacked the style and precision of all his others. . . . He never came to the surface.*

Galileo builds his own version of the telescope and increases its magnifying power. With it, he sees mountains and craters on the Moon and four satellites of Jupiter. He also discovers that the Milky Way is actually a dense collection of stars.

lowed him to escape quietly. He was reportedly seen in Albany, in Pittsford, in Canandaigua, and points south on the way to New Jersey.

On November 30, the *New York Post* printed a letter claiming that Sam had never jumped into the river at all, but had tossed down a dummy filled with sand and stones. The weight in the dummy was not properly distributed, the letter said, resulting in "a rascally jump." He said it was all "a capital joke" and promised that "when I come to Boston you will see me jump for nothing." It was signed, "The Real, no mistake, SAM PATCH of New Jersey."

Even after the body was found — both shoulders dislocated — Sam's legend gained momentum. Preachers used his death as a text on the sin of pride. Editors mourned the passing of one who had sold so many newspapers. A spurious autobiography was rushed into print. Even Nathaniel Hawthorne used Sam's death as a moral in an essay called "Rochester": "Was the leaper of cataracts more mad or foolish than other men who throw away life, or misspend it in pursuit of empty fame, and seldom so triumphantly as he?"

Sam's posthumous glory shone brighter still when, in 1836, a comic actor named Dan Marble starred in a play called *Sam Patch; or, The Daring Yankee.* It played to packed houses in Buffalo, Boston, and New York, and led to sequels such as *Sam Patch in France; or, The Pesky Snake.*

The climax of every show came when Marble would leap from the top of the stage onto a spring bed

If you don't want anyone to know, don't do it.

piled high with bags of wood shavings, hidden behind a painted "river." Marble can hardly be accused of exploiting Sam's fame without risk; these leaps ranged from 40 to 70 feet. On at least one occasion, Marble was injured seriously enough to miss a performance, forcing an understudy to take his place. That young man so fortified himself with drink before taking the plunge that he missed his target completely and fractured

1614

American Indian princess Pocahontas, daughter of an Algonquian chief of the Tidewater region of Virginia, marries John Rolfe, a Jamestown colonist.

a leg. In show business, this is known as getting your first big break.

There are even reports that a sort of "jumping mania" took hold:

> **Never descend to flatter or withhold a deserved compliment.**

farmers leaping over fences, clerks bouncing over counters. Sam's name became a catchphrase, as in "He was off before you could say Sam Patch!"

Sam's currency lasted far longer than his short life (he was in his twenties when he died). Forty years after the fatal jump, a children's picture book, *The Wonderful Leaps of Sam Patch*, was published, celebrating jumps that by then included transatlantic jaunts from Washington to London and back. He was mentioned in congressional debate as late as 1891.

There was a torrent of bad verse written about Sam's life and death, much of it dredged up by folklorist Richard Dorson, who published several articles on the "Yankee Leaper." The tone of the poems ranges from highfalutin oratory:

> *Napoleon's last battle proved his dreadful overthrow,*
> *And Sam's last jump was a fearful one, and in death it laid him low.*

To earnest moral instruction:

> *He jumps! He sinks! The waters roar*
> *Above him and he's seen no more;*
> *And as their breath the people catch,*
> *They sigh, "Alas! Brave, foolish, Patch!"*

To a popular piece of doggerel that went:

> *Poor Samuel Patch — a man once world renownded.*
> *Much loved the water, and by it was drownded.*
> *He sought for fame, and as he reached to pluck it,*
> *He lost his ballast, and then kicked the bucket.*

But perhaps the best comment on the life and times of Sam Patch was the laconic epitaph some unknown admirer wrote on the wooden headboard of Sam's grave in Rochester, New York: "Here lies Sam Patch; such is Fame."

1636

The first written version of the fairy tale "Sleeping Beauty" is published by Giambattista Basile in Italy. In 1697 Charles Perrault will include this story in his collection of fairy tales.

Why My Great-Uncle Gave Up the Ministry

(A true reminiscence by Marcia Barnard Chandler.)

THE FOLLOWING sad but true little tale concerns my great-uncle, a wonderful, jolly, beloved man who was over 6 feet 4 and probably weighed close to 300 pounds. He was also very well educated (Colgate University, doctor of divinity), and in the early 1900s he became a full-time Baptist minister. A kindly, gentle man despite his enormous size, Uncle Alden Bentley's only real fault seemed to be that he was terribly clumsy.

One day when he was a young minister, he was paying a pastoral call to a lady's home in Dillon, South Carolina, when he inadvertently sat on the lady's Chihuahua, Twinkie, and killed it. As the lady searched and called for her dog throughout the house, Uncle Alden felt underneath his hip and, realizing what he had done, suddenly pan-

icked and slipped the dead dog into his coat pocket. Although he was devastated, he could not bring himself to admit to the woman what had happened.

Five years later, he returned to the same home for an overnight visit and resolved to unburden himself by finally telling the woman the next morning exactly what had happened to Twinkie. The lady had just had the guest room repapered and had hung brand-new curtains. To make Uncle feel welcome, she placed a large pitcher of ice water and a glass on the bedside table, as well as a pen and a bottle of ink so that he could work on his sermon before retiring.

Uncle liked to sleep with the window open and got up in the night to open it. As he did, however, he knocked over what he assumed to be his full glass of water. Then, groping along the walls in an unsuccessful search for the light switch, he retraced his steps several times before raising the window and settling back on the bed for the night. When he opened his eyes the next

1636

Harvard College, the first college in the English-speaking American colonies, is founded. It is named after its benefactor, John Harvard.

morning, he was horrified. The fresh wallpaper on two walls was covered with great black blobs. The crisp white curtains were thoroughly smudged with the prints of Uncle's huge paws. It had not been the water glass he'd overturned during the night — it had been the ink bottle.

In a shaken state of mind and knowing that he must face his hostess, Uncle dressed hurriedly and started down the stairs outside the guest room. As he approached the landing, his foot slipped. He grabbed wildly for the nearest object for support, which happened to be a beautiful electric brass candelabra mounted in the stairwell wall. The fixture was hissing and smoking as he ripped it from the wall and toppled down to the landing below, still clutching it in his hand.

"Are you hurt?" his hostess cried as she rushed to Uncle's side.

"No," said Uncle as he rose to his feet, "but I have demolished your home." With that, he walked out the front door and at the end of the walk turned and said to his hostess with deep reverence, "Twinkie had a Christian burial."

He then retired from the ministry and was a teacher of philosophy for many years at a private preparatory school in Massachusetts.

Old English Prayer

GIVE ME a good digestion, Lord,
And something to digest.
Give me a healthy body, Lord,
And sense enough to keep it at its best.
Give me a thoughtful mind, dear Lord,
To keep the pure and good in sight,
And when seeing Sin is not appalled,
But finds a way to make it right.
Give me a mind that is not bored —
That does not whimper, whine, nor cry.
Do not let me worry overmuch, dear Lord,
About that fussy thing called I.
Give me a sense of humor, Lord,
Give me the grace to see a Joke;
To get some happiness from Life
And pass it on to other folk.

Courtesy of Mrs. C. B. Terrell

1638

William Penn builds America's first brewery in Pennsylvania.

Good Health,
Good Food

MEMO

To: Sarah Hale

From: Tim Clark

Re: Health and Food Chapter

SARAH, I THINK you should look for somebody else to write this introduction. I'm glad to help out, but I think I'm temperamentally unsuited for the job.

Let me try to explain. This chapter starts with Guy Murchie's essay "The Breath We Share," which explains that each breath any one of us takes contains at least a million atoms breathed personally sometime this year by each and every person on Earth.

Well, in some people, that would be an awesome, inspiring thought. It makes me want to tape the windows and doors shut. How do you think things like the Great Lowell Measles Epidemic got started?

It's the old half-full, half-empty glass problem. To me, the glass is not only half-empty, it's half-empty because somebody drank out of it while I wasn't looking, and that somebody is likely to harbor some dread disease.

1640s

The Society of Friends, or Quakers, is founded in England. The Quakers are persecuted for their beliefs and will later flee to America.

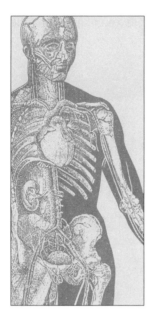

You remember "Do You Really Know Yourself?" — that little list of facts about the human body? The first one says, "If all 600 muscles in your body pulled in one direction, you could lift 25 tons." I only got as far as the first eight words, then I had to go lie down for a while.

It's an old problem with me. Take bleeding. *Please*. I don't even like to *think* about bleeding, much less read a whole chapter called "The Blood-stoppers." It may be wonderful, but I'll never . . .

• • •

Sorry, I had to put my head between my knees for a while.

Please understand, I'm not criticizing the articles. I freely admit it's my attitude that's the problem. It affects the way I read articles like "The Top Ten Feel-Good Herbs." My eye goes right to the final sentence of each descriptive paragraph — you know, the part that warns you about side effects, like, oh, I don't know, death. (How can death be a *side* effect? Isn't it the *main* effect?)

I'm much happier with folk remedies. These, I am convinced, are remedies that were invented by folks like me. They never involve puncturing the skin with sharp objects. They're *easy*. Cure the hiccups? Eat a spoonful of peanut butter. Cure the common cold? Chicken soup will do the trick. Hay fever? The Roman scholar Pliny suggested kissing the nostrils of a mule. OK, it sounds disgusting, but it's noninvasive (except to the mule).

1642

The first real kitchen utensil made in America (Lynn, Massachusetts) is a three-legged cast-iron pot known as the Saugus pot.

Which brings me to the cooking stuff. It's not that I don't like to eat. I love to eat. But I was blessed with a mother who is a good cook and a wife who is a good cook, and except for a few years of college food, all I've ever eaten has been made by one of those two fine women.

Here's another argument against my writing this introduction: I *liked* college food. I gained about 20 pounds in college, and this was before the days of salad bars and "Thai Nights" in college dining halls.

Now that I think about it, there was one summer while I was in college that I cooked for myself. I had a job on campus and lived in a dingy little apartment without a kitchen. I had a hot plate in the closet, as I recall, and I pretty much stuck to one basic menu:

1 canned peach half on 1 leaf iceberg lettuce, garnished with cottage cheese

1 can Del Monte green beans (add package of slivered almonds for company)

1 can Franco-American SpaghettiO's, with a splash of sherry

Do you really want this introduction written by a man whose idea of a cookbook is the *Boy Scout Handbook*?

I've also never done very well in restaurants. My interest in the exotic (noticeably absent when cooking for myself) has often gotten the best of me when I'm paying someone else to cook. I remember once, when I was in France, ordering something I roughly translated as "hunter's stew," and I ate it with gusto. Afterward, a malicious friend informed me that its main ingredients were the internal organs of wild animals, and I spent the rest of that night fertilizing a French cornfield.

1644

England's Parliament, under Oliver Cromwell, bans Christmas observances. Across the Atlantic, Massachusetts will follow suit in 1659. England will repeal its law in 1660, Massachusetts in 1681.

Once — it was a long, long time ago — I tried to impress a date by ordering whale steak. It came to the table looking a lot like beefsteak, and the illusion sustained me through the first bite. "Tastes just like beefsteak," I said suavely. The second bite tasted just like Number 2 fuel oil. (Historical note: This was at a restaurant in Cambridge, Massachusetts. Can you imagine what would happen if you ordered whale steak in Cambridge, Massachusetts, today? You'd be publicly executed by harpoon.)

One result of these misadventures has been an extremely conservative attitude about trying anything unusual in the way of food. I'm willing to accept Georgia Orcutt's assertion that the sweet potato is "The Healthiest Vegetable of All," but that's no argument in favor of eating a "fleshy root." If the per capita consumption of sweet potatoes is indeed six pounds, I'm not pulling my oar. And I must say it annoys me when food snobs like the North Carolina

SweetPotato Commission ask me not to call a sweet potato a yam. I say it's a yam, and I say the hell with it.

The story about presidential cooking reports that George Washington once advertised for a cook: "No one need apply who is not perfect in the business," he wrote. *Perfect* in the business! That's exactly what I'm talking about! The only presidential recipe I could manage is Mrs. Wilson's clam dip, which calls for a can of clams, a package of cream cheese, a little onion, some salt and pepper, and an electric mixer. (I might add a splash of sherry . . .)

1669

Mount Etna in Sicily erupts again
(it last erupted in 1169), this time causing
approximately 20,000 deaths.

See what I mean? I have a basic lack of appreciation for the process of cooking. I'm absolutely with Al Sicherman, who wrote the article on meat loaf, when he calls pâté "meat loaf taken to several logical extremes and left there." In fact, my recipe box at home contains nothing but the phone numbers of every take-out emporium within a 50-mile radius, indexed according to ethnic varieties (Italian pizza, Greek pizza, American pizza . . .).

I'm a busy guy. I don't have time for all this finicky stuff. "In the Event You Have a Cow . . ." gives detailed instructions on making your own butter, cottage cheese, and ice cream. Well, I don't *have* a cow, I don't *want* a cow, and the strongest argument against ever *getting* a cow to make my own ice cream is summarized in the last sentence of the article: "In an hour or two, eat!"

Or look at Leslie Land's story on making a perfect cup of coffee (there's that *p*-word again!). "For *absolutely* the best coffee, you would have to start by roasting your own beans," she says. Why stop there? Why not grow your own beans, harvest them, and bring them down the mountain on your own mule? Come to think of it, that might be handy if you suffer from hay fever.

So think it over, Sarah, and drop off a memo when you get the chance. I'll tear off some tape so you can slide it under my door.

Tim Clark

1681

The dodo, an unusual bird found on the island of Mauritius in the Indian Ocean, is proclaimed extinct.

■ *Whether you live in Ohio, Arizona, or Wisconsin, your very next breath will probably include a million-odd atoms of oxygen and nitrogen once breathed by Buddha, Christ, Plato, Newton, and Einstein.*

The Breath We Share

BY GUY MURCHIE

IT IS ESTIMATED THAT THE AVERage human breath contains as many as 10 sextillion atoms, a truly unimaginable number that can be written as 10,000,000,000,000, 000,000,000 or, in modern notation, 10^{22}. And since the entire atmosphere of our planet is calculated to contain the equivalent of some 10 sextillion breaths, each breath rather mystically turns out to be midway in size between an atom and the world. Thus, every time you inhale, you are inhaling an average of about one atom from each of the breaths contained in the whole sky. And every time you exhale, you are breathing back the same average of one atom for each of these breaths. This exchange, being repeated 20,000 times a day by more than 4 billion breathing people (not to mention other creatures), has the surprising consequence that each breath anyone takes anywhere must contain at least a quadrillion (10^{13}) of the same atoms breathed in and out by the rest of mankind within the past few weeks and more than a million atoms breathed per-

sonally sometime this year by each and every person on Earth.

The rapidity with which these unseeable, almost unimaginable, atoms and molecules mix and diffuse in the sky is obviously a factor in such a calculation. So is the speed of the wind, which moves air all the way around the world within two to three weeks. Knowing this, it should be relatively easy to understand how an American taking a breath in, say, Ohio or Arizona today cannot help but breathe in a million-odd atoms of oxygen and nitrogen once breathed by Buddha, Christ, Muhammad, Plato, Newton, Einstein, or anyone you can think of, including many trillions from the Chinese in China within a fortnight, from Pygmies in the Congo or Eskimos in Greenland within a few days. And, returning to other life, you could add a few hundred million molecules from the wallowing dinosaurs in pre–Ice Age swamps, from Hannibal's elephants puffing up the Alps, even from the gentle transpirations of the vegetable kingdom, the rain

1683

Viennese bakers create croissants, pastries shaped like the crescent on the Turkish flag, to commemorate the city's stand against the invading Turks. Austrians gobble up the pastries as a patriotic gesture.

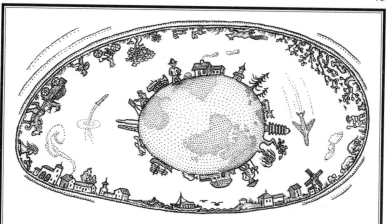

forests of Brazil and Malaysia or the soggy emanations of the Sargasso Sea in the North Atlantic.

Human breath, along with that of all creatures and not excluding the Earth's own breath, the wind, was once called *anima,* or "spirits." This was before the 17th century, when Evangelista Torricelli, Galileo's pupil, invented the barometer and proved the existence of air, thereby preparing the way for such epic future inventions as the balloon, the parachute, and the airplane. Before that time, strange as it now seems, people regarded the wind as

An American taking a breath in, say, Ohio or Arizona today cannot help but breathe in a million-odd atoms of oxygen and nitrogen once breathed by Buddha, Christ, Muhammad, Plato, Newton, Einstein, or anyone you can think of.

more or less supernatural, not really part of the material world. There were words for fire and air, of course, but no one knew what these were made of, and many looked upon their functions with superstition, as did Job, who said (7:7), "O remember that my life is wind." Air in particular was often regarded almost as a religious manifestation.

Then Torricelli, after long labor, demonstrated in 1643 that air actually has measurable weight and substance. He brought it into science and thus overcame much of the popular terror of the sky, at the same time emancipating the whole idea of flying. Admit-

1690

French physicist Denis Papin proposes a road vehicle powered by a piston engine. (Papin also invented the pressure cooker.)

tedly, we still use the expression "light as air," but it is something of a deceptive phrase in view of the now known fact that the atmosphere of the Earth, about 500 miles deep, weighs more than 5,000,000,000,000,000 tons. Such a mass naturally exerts a ponderable gravitational pull, hugging the airy sky to the Earth with such force that very few of its molecules can hope to escape. To do so, in fact, any air molecule would have to attain an upward speed of 7 miles per second (mps), rather a lot more than any recorded hurricane or tornado has achieved. On the Moon, by contrast, a mere 1¼ mps is escape velocity, which largely explains why the Moon has less

Torricelli, after long labor, demonstrated in 1643 that air actually has measurable weight and substance. He brought it into science and thus overcame much of the popular terror of the sky, at the same time emancipating the whole idea of flying.

atmosphere than the Earth.

A few decades after Torricelli, a Dutchman named Antony van Leeuwenhoek made himself a series of tiny but powerful magnifying glasses that enabled him to discover and establish the microcosm, including the never-before-known life of microbes in dust and raindrops. This eventually revealed that not only is the atmosphere the habitat of birds and bats, but it is also home to a wide range of invisible life forms, of which those hidden in the air are known as aeroplankton. Indeed, scientists have recently found that every cubic centimeter of air within ten miles of the solid or wet Earth holds at least several

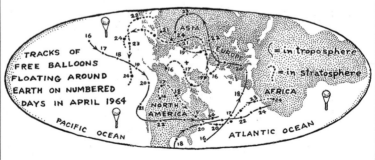

TRACKS OF FREE BALLOONS FLOATING AROUND EARTH ON NUMBERED DAYS IN APRIL 1964

= in troposphere
? = in stratosphere

ASIA
EUROPE
AFRICA
NORTH AMERICA
PACIFIC OCEAN
ATLANTIC OCEAN

1692

Nineteen men and women are hanged as witches in Salem, Massachusetts.

dozen invisible particles of dust, and if the air happens to be over a smoggy city, the number can reach into the millions.

The nuclei of this dust may be anything from salt crystals evaporated from ocean spray to smoke spicules to the spores of algae, fungi, bacteria, or larger plants, grains of pollen, or the powder-size seeds of orchids. And living on them almost always are animal microbes that are dormant when dry or cold but that awaken and start swimming when a cloud droplet happens to condense around them, perhaps eventually conveying them to Earth inside a raindrop. In fact, the clouds are the most fertile parts of the sky, and every puff of cumulus is unquestionably alive with tiny animals and plants that live there for generations (a microbe's generation often lasting less than an

The clouds are the most fertile parts of the sky, and every puff of cumulus is unquestionably alive with tiny animals and plants that live there for generations — eating, breathing, excreting, floating, swimming, competing, reproducing.

hour) — eating, breathing, excreting, floating, swimming, competing, reproducing. These aeroplankton, don't forget, are alive in your lungs, too, as you breathe them in and out, further evidence (if any be needed) that the sky permeates us all.

The year 1983 was the 200th anniversary of the invention of the balloon, which freed man to ascend into the sky for the first time in 1783. It also was the 100th anniversary of the famous volcanic explosion of Krakatoa, an island near Java, which sent air waves seven times around the Earth and proved the sky's dominance over the sea. My point in saying this is that scientists, who at first supposed that the Krakatoa-generated sea waves (slower and repeatedly blocked by land) could not keep up with the Krakatoa-generated air waves, were surprised when both kinds of

1695

In England, a new tax is levied on bachelors.

waves were reported to have arrived simultaneously at Panama, San Francisco, and the English Channel. Careful study of the evi-

tific fact that invisible events in the sky really do change the face of the deep below.

To wind up this essay on breath and the sky, let us add only that, like you and all warm-blooded creatures, Earth maintains herself in temperature and humidity and breathes in her own way. Indeed, our planet's atmosphere, composed largely of oxygen and nitrogen, gets its oxygen primarily from the exhalations of forests and other plant life and almost all its nitrogen from the exudations of living soil microorganisms, both of which are alive and able to regulate themselves for survival. Likewise has Earth as a whole maintained her temperature and humidity (as proved in fossil evidence) over the 4.3 billion years of her existence, despite the fact that the Sun is now putting out more than twice as much heat, light, and energy as it did when Earth was born. That means that Earth is alive. And if a planet can breathe gases, no doubt a galaxy can breathe stars. In similar ways, your own breath can be seen as an integral part of all life everywhere, significantly including that of Earth herself, which, it is becoming increasingly evident, is but a cell in the life of our solar system. In turn, our solar system is a mere corpuscle in the billionfold vaster Milky Way, which is hardly a speck in the life of the living, breathing universe.

TO CURE A HEADACHE:
Lean your head against a tree and have someone else drive a nail into the opposite side of the tree.

dence, however, eventually convinced them that only the air waves were a direct effect of the volcano's explosion and that the sea waves recorded on tidal gauges in America and England must have been induced by the air disturbance. Thus it became an accepted scien-

1697

Charles Perrault writes the first known version of "Little Red Riding Hood," in which both the grandmother and the little girl are eaten. Versions of the tale in which Red Riding Hood's life is spared will appear later.

ANECDOTES & PLEASANTRIES

The Great Lowell Measles Epidemic

(or how the telephone number was invented.)

IN THE BEGINNING, which was in 1879, a mere three years after Alexander Graham Bell made the first phone call, the Lowell (Massachusetts) District Telephone Company hired teenage boys to run the switchboard.

"Give me John Smith," a subscriber would ask, and the lad on duty would plug the call into John Smith's line.

However, as time went by, changes had to be made.

"First off, young women were hired to handle the switchboard," said Peter Cronin, spokesman for New England Telephone Company several years back. "It was discovered that the women's voices were better adapted for the work than the boy's voices.

"Once the women took over the switchboard, and the public began to accept the idea of the telephone, business improved for the

Lowell District Telephone Company. By late 1880, 4 operators were on duty at the switchboard. The phone company had over 200 customers by then."

Alas, in December, a few days be-

1702

In Russia, men with beards must now pay a tax.

fore Christmas, the trouble started. One of the operators phoned in sick.

Back then a sick operator, even if she was missing for only a day, rocked the foundation of the brand-new telephone company. She knew the name of each and every subscriber in the Lowell area.

Still, the three switchboard girls managed to keep things going — until the very next day, when a second operator phoned in sick. At this point, company president W. A. Ingham put through an emergency call to Dr. Moses Greeley Parker, who, in addition to being the best doctor in town, also happened to be a big stockholder in the new company.

"If you can't get these two women back on the job in a hurry, we'll be out of business," Ingham told him. "Those other two operators will collapse from exhaustion."

So Dr. Parker visited the two ill telephone operators and then went directly to the phone company office.

"You'll have to train substitute operators," the good doctor informed Ingham. "They both have the measles."

"It will take weeks to train substitutes," stated Ingham. "The new girls will have to memorize more than 200 names."

"But," Dr. Parker interrupted, "instead of names, why don't you use numbers?"

"Numbers, doctor?" responded Ingham. "I don't know what you mean."

"It's rather simple, Ingham," said the doctor smoothly. "Instead of identifying your subscribers by name, identify them by numbers, and put a corresponding number

over their holes on the switchboard. For example, since I had the first phone in town and I am in the first-hole position on your board, I can be number one!"

Ingham began to get the message, but he scoffed at the idea. "Our subscribers," he said, "will never accept your idea, Dr. Parker. People have names. They are not numbers."

"Be that as it may," countered Parker, "it's either numbers or we go out of business if those other operators get the measles."

And so numbers it was.

Courtesy of Barbara Craig

1709

Jean Baptiste Farina, an Italian barber in Cologne, Germany, concocts the first eau de cologne.

■ *There is no shortage of helpful suggestions on how to cure a cold — many of them quite creative, to say the least — but none seems to be the ultimate answer for which the eventual discoverer will likely receive the Nobel Prize. The Almanac published this anecdotal overview in 1982.*

Cures for the Common Cold

BY TIM CLARK

CASE HISTORY. THE PATIENT, A VIGorous man in his late sixties, went out riding on December 12, 1799, a day of cold rain, sleet, and strong winds. Arriving at home late for dinner, he sat down to eat before changing his clothes. The next day, he complained of a sore throat and stayed indoors for the morning. In the afternoon, he went out to mark some trees to be cut down. That same evening, he was hoarse but refused suggestions to take medicine. "You know I never take anything for a cold," he said. "Let it go as it came."

At about 3:00 A.M., the patient awakened his wife to complain of chills. He was having trouble speaking and breathing. Near dawn, he was offered a mixture of molasses, vinegar, and butter but was unable to swallow it.

A doctor was summoned, and he took one pint of blood from the pa-

1709

Daniel Gabriel Fahrenheit (also called Gabriel Daniel Fahrenheit) makes the first practical thermometer, using alcohol instead of mercury. Mercury will come into use in 1714.

tient. The patient then soaked his feet in hot water and had a piece of flannel soaked in salve wrapped around his neck. Hot compresses and mustard packs also were applied, along with various gargles and inhalations. More blood was taken. On December 14, the patient died.

What killed George Washington? Was it pneumonia or a strep infection, as some historians believe? Or was it, as others have suggested, the most ordinary of diseases, the common cold, aided by "remedies" such as bleeding?

Washington himself believed that he had a cold, and the remedies he and his doctor applied were considered the normal treatment for a cold in those days. They may sound quaint, but after nearly 200 years modern science is not much closer to a cure for the common cold, also known as coryza, or nasal catarrh.

The cold has bedeviled mankind throughout history, and the effects of the illness are recorded in ancient literature. A 15th-century writer, for example, described the plight of one Swanus, a pilgrim

Washington himself believed that he had a cold, and the remedies he and his doctor applied were considered the normal treatment for a cold in those days.

who, on the road to Jerusalem, "dyed by the waye of colde that he had taked of goynge barefote."

The very word *cold* refers to the commonly believed cause of the illness — becoming chilled by exposure to cold, overexertion followed by rapid cooling off, or even "goynge barefote." But one of the few things that scientists can say with any certainty about the common cold is that it is *not* a result of such chilling. Volunteers have spent many hours attesting to this fact by standing in drafty hallways wearing wet clothing. They were chilly and uncomfortable, but they caught no more colds than other volunteers kept warm and dry. During World War I, military doctors noticed that men who had to sleep in wet trenches during the winter had fewer colds than those who lived in comfortable barracks behind the lines. Eskimo communities were free of colds until they were visited by ships from warmer climates.

One reason for the common connection between the illness and feelings of chill may be that sufferers often feel a greater sensitivity to

1716

The first recorded rowing race is held on the Thames River (England).

temperature changes during the early stages of a cold. So when you start shivering and think, "I'd better put on a sweater, or I'll catch cold," you may already have it.

Most colds seem to occur between September and May, with an abrupt increase between September and mid-October. Researchers think that has more to do with the fact that people are indoors a lot during the winter months — where they are more likely to be exposed to people with colds, and where warmer, drier air tends to dry out the protective mucus that lines the nasal passages, allowing the viruses that actually cause colds to take hold — than with the temperature outside.

There are more than 100 different viruses that can cause a cold, the most important of which are called rhinoviruses, which cause 25 to 30 percent of all adult infections. The rhinoviruses are different from and much smaller than the viruses that cause influenza. Antibiotics do not affect viruses, and although vaccines can be developed to combat them, the large number of cold viruses makes that approach impractical.

Statistics on the common cold are hard to gather because the cold resembles many other illnesses and often is not considered important enough to report. Some authorities think that Americans suffer as many as a billion colds a year. The National Center for Health Statistics announced in 1978 that

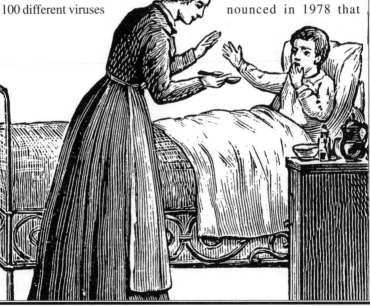

1718

Edward Teach, aka Blackbeard the pirate, is killed by Virginia naval officer Robert Maynard on the James River.

Americans annually reported almost 100 million colds, resulting in the loss of 30 million workdays and 30 million school days and in 276 million days of "restricted activity." The common cold accounts for one out of five acute illnesses in the United States.

Other studies provide a wealth of information about who gets colds

TO CURE A HEADACHE:
Rub cow dung and molasses on your temples.

and how often. One said that 75 percent of all people have at least one cold a year, while 25 percent have four or more. At Cornell University, 25 percent of all the students have 75 percent of all the reported colds. Children under four average eight colds a year, but the number declines with increasing age, so that adults average only two colds a year. Women have more colds than men and tend to spend more time in bed or in restricted activity.

The economic costs of colds, in terms of work time lost, have been estimated in the billions of dollars. Americans spend more than half a billion dollars a year on drugs aimed at fighting colds, but so far there is no pharmaceutical cure.

Folk remedies for colds are legion. They may be based on conceptions about colds that are outdated by scientific research, but people still believe in them, and some research indicates that belief may be the most important element. In one five-year experiment, a variety of cold vaccines were tested, while a control group, which had been told it was receiving a vaccine, was actually injected with distilled water. More than a third of the control group reported that their "medication" had cured or improved their colds. "Such results explain why it is so easy to become enthusiastic about any preparation for the treatment of colds," one expert said.

A look through history provides a representative sampling of popular folk remedies for colds, which seem to fall into several distinct categories.

Diet. A wide variety of herbal teas are recommended for colds, including teas made from coltsfoot, peppermint, yarrow, boneset, mint, catnip, verbena, horehound, and sage. Garlic is frequently recommended, as are licorice and lemon in many forms. A Vermont doctor

1732

Benjamin Franklin publishes the first edition of *Poor Richard's Almanack.*

prescribed chewing on a honeycomb to clear sinus passages. Another Vermonter, Dr. B. J. Kendall, suggested the following treatment in a pamphlet called *The Doctor at Home Illustrated: Treating the Diseases of Man and the Horse* (1888): "Take of molasses one-half cupful, Jamaica ginger one heaping teaspoonful, soda or saleratus one-fourth teaspoonful. Mix and beat thoroughly. Dose, one teaspoonful, repeated every hour."

Onions figure in many cold cures from the early days in this country. A mixture of onions and butter was placed on the throat and chest. Cooked onions were put in a muslin bag and worn around the neck. To protect children, it was agreed that a large red onion should be tied around the bedpost.

As recently as 1978, Dr. Marvin Sackner, chief of medicine at Mount Sinai Medical Center in Miami Beach, reported that chicken soup cleared mucus from sinus passages

Garlic is frequently recommended, as are licorice and lemon in many forms. A Vermont doctor prescribed chewing on a honeycomb to clear sinus passages.

faster than other hot beverages. Dr. Sackner's findings were published in the medical journal *Chest*.

According to *Grannie's Remedies* by Mai Thomas (1965), "In some country districts (in England) there are still many folk who believe that swallowing a spider will cure them."

The nose. People have suggested washing out the nose with hot water, soap, sodium bicarbonate, ammonium bicarbonate, cod-liver oil, cream, salt water, vapors of ammonia, eucalyptus oil, iodine, and formalin. Sniffing aspirin, pepper, snuff, and cinnamon have been tried. Several authorities have recommended that cold sufferers can reduce the length of their illness and avoid more serious sinus and ear infections by refraining from blowing the nose. Some colonial Americans pared orange peels, rolled them up inside out, and stuffed them into the nostrils.

Inventor Norman Lake of Lancaster,

1736

British doctor Claudius Aymand performs the first successful appendectomy.

Pennsylvania, discovered in 1953 that he could make a cold go away by wearing a clothespin on his nose. In 1977, after much research, he patented a device he called the Cold Clip, which closed the nose to viruses or pollen. Despite tests by a local physician showing that half of the volunteers who used the Cold Clip were able to halt or shorten the duration of colds, the U.S. Food and Drug Administration (FDA) told Lake that he could not advertise his device as a cold cure but only as a way of "keeping foreign material out of the nose."

Alcohol and drugs. A traditional cure known to some as the Hungarian Hat Trick is performed as follows: Place a hat on a bedpost. Get into bed and start drinking. When you see two hats, stop drinking.

Actually, alcohol has been found to dilate small blood vessels in the skin and help reestablish circulation in the mucous membranes of the nose, along with raising the temperature of those membranes to

Inventor Norman Lake . . . discovered in 1953 that he could make a cold go away by wearing a clothespin on his nose. . . . [The] FDA told Lake that he could not advertise his device as a cold cure but only as a way of "keeping foreign material out of the nose."

help neutralize viruses. It also produces a feeling of comfort and drowsiness.

The National Academy of Sciences has reported that the claims of most nonprescription cold remedies to prevent or relieve cold symptoms cannot be supported by science. The FDA also believes that many of the claims made in labeling and advertising these substances are misleading or exaggerated.

Although many people believe that taking vitamin C will prevent or reduce the severity of a cold, long-range studies have so far not found conclusive evidence that this is so. The use of vitamin C in very large amounts may lead to undesirable side effects.

Another drug that appears to be effective against colds, but with unacceptable side effects, is opium. Thomas DeQuincy, who wrote *Confessions of an English Opium-Eater,* testified that he had never suffered from a cold while addicted.

Other. Another of *Grannie's Remedies* suggested for the pre-

Ann Lee founds the Shakers, a millenarian sect, in England. The first American Shaker community will be established in the 1770s in upstate New York.

vention of colds goes like this: "Walk with the toes turned outward. Walk with the chin slightly above the horizontal line, as if looking at the top of a man's hat in front of you, or at the eaves or roof of a house. Walk a good deal with your hands behind you. Sit with the lower part of your spine pressed against the chair back."

Sir Christopher Andrewes, in his book *The Common Cold* (1965), cataloged the 100 remedies for colds that had been sent to him by helpful laymen. Most of them could be included under such general categories as drugs, diet, and treatment for the nose, but a number of them defied pigeonholing:

Under miscellaneous remedies these occurred: smoking tobacco, inducing daily shivering, rubbing methylated spirit into a bald head, rubbing the body with Vaseline, "naturopathy," transient exposure to tear gas or other war gas (two letters), wearing a gas mask for an hour, inhaling powdered dry licorice leaves, working with lime, taking up fencing, avoiding people with poisonous auras, mental concentration (especially on mathematics), growing a mustache right up to the nostrils, sweeping chimneys, standing on one's head under water, or wearing on the back between the kidneys a bag containing onions. Cure of colds was reported to have followed an electric shock, a car smash, and destruction of one's home by a V-1

bomb. *Finally, several letters pointed out the value of attention to psychology, a subject that probably had considerable relevance to the prescriptions of the other ninety-odd of our correspondents.*

Curing the common cold has become a sort of Holy Grail to some researchers, an ideal at once infinitely desirable and seemingly unattainable. The person who achieves it should be able to accept the Nobel Prize as his just deserts.

The Sun in your dream bestows favor and health to the sick.

Indeed, one famous Nobel laureate, Dr. James D. Watson, accepted his prize with these words: "It is an important thing we have accomplished, but we have not done away with the common cold — which I now have."

1757

Benjamin Franklin writes, "Early to bed and early to rise, / Makes a man healthy, wealthy, and wise" (and many other maxims) in the last edition of his *Poor Richard's Almanack.*

FARMER'S CALENDAR

Folk Remedies

PLINY THE ELDER, the Roman scholar whose *Natural History,* in 37 volumes, forms an encyclopedia of the ancient world's knowledge of the natural sciences, education, art, and society, had some quaint ideas about medicine. He believed, for example, that kissing the nostrils of a mule cured hay fever. He believed that an owlet's brains, eaten, were good for a sore throat. Pliny didn't invent these cures; he was a reporter only. Therefore, presumably, thousands of afflicted Romans must have been seen every day making unwelcome advances toward mules and chasing after owlets who ran for their lives. And so the question arises, If Pliny didn't think this stuff up, who did? How did anybody first get the idea, for a third instance, that epilepsy could be treated by feeding the sufferer the afterbirth of a donkey?

Some of Pliny's cures make even other folk remedies look perfectly plausible by comparison. In fact, much of the antique medical lore has a kind of magical logic, rigorous enough in its own way. If you believe the common wildflower Solomon's seal to have some mystic connection with the ancient king of Israel, it makes a kind a sense to suppose that by grinding up the plant and eating it, you will gain fame, wisdom, and the queen of Sheba for a girlfriend. Beside Pliny's regimens, that sounds no more extreme than "Take two aspirin and call me in the morning." Where, in contrast, is the logic behind Pliny's idea that a colicky baby can usefully be served roast lark? We'll never know. One thing is clear, though. Pliny was killed in the eruption of Mount Vesuvius in A.D. 79, when he apparently got a little too close to the action — proving to the most skeptical that a nearby volcano is a sovereign cure for natural history.

1759

Joseph Merlin of Belgium, a musical instrument maker, designs and makes the first practical pair of roller skates.

■ *Consult some old-time lumberjacks around the country and in Canada, and many would have a story or two concerning blood-stoppers, people with the gift of stopping the flow of blood by mental power. Superstition? Hogwash? Well, the power of the human mind is often underestimated.*

The Bloodstoppers

BY MARGO HOLDEN

O NE MUST PLACE IT UNDER "folklore," we believe, this ability that some people have of stopping blood by merely knowing that someone is bleeding badly

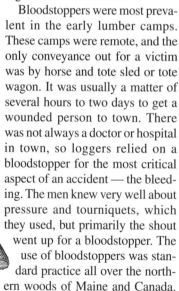

and needs their help. The blood-stoppers tried to get to their patients, or patients were brought to them, but usually they did their bloodstopping after merely receiving word of an accident.

Bloodstoppers were most prevalent in the early lumber camps. These camps were remote, and the only conveyance out for a victim was by horse and tote sled or tote wagon. It was usually a matter of several hours to two days to get a wounded person to town. There was not always a doctor or hospital in town, so loggers relied on a bloodstopper for the most critical aspect of an accident — the bleeding. The men knew very well about pressure and tourniquets, which they used, but primarily the shout went up for a bloodstopper. The use of bloodstoppers was standard practice all over the northern woods of Maine and Canada.

I saw a bloodstopper work back in 1924 at a lumber camp. A fellow with a deep ax cut in his leg was car-

1760s

Englishman John Spilsbury makes "dissected maps," later called jigsaw puzzles, to teach children geography.

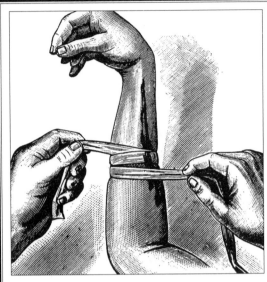

ried in by the two fellows with whom he had been working. He was very white and weak, and blood kept running down and dripping from the stocking that was over his boot. The cook, who was the bloodstopper, was stooped over taking cookies out of the oven. When the men entered, they shouted for him. He paused in taking the cookies out, looked at the wounded fellow a long half minute, and then proclaimed, "The bleeding is stopped." The men carried their chum to his bunk in the

Loggers relied on a bloodstopper for the most critical aspect of an accident — the bleeding. The men knew very well about pressure and tourniquets, which they used, but primarily the shout went up for a bloodstopper.

bunkhouse, cut his pant leg off, removed his clothing, and announced the bleeding was indeed stopped. In about a week's time, the fellow could stand the trip out, and he was taken to his home. We heard he was back on the drive that spring.

I saw the same bloodstopper stop a violent nosebleed that the cookee had. However, the cookee was a nonbeliever, and after the nosebleed had been stopped, he began decrying the fact that the bloodstopper had anything to do with it. He worked himself up to such a pitch that his nose started bleeding again. The cook would have nothing to do with him the second time. After a day and a night of bleeding, the cookee left the camp and never came back.

We know of another close friend, Amos, who sank an ax into his foot, nearly severing it in two. A bloodstopper was called by camp phone, and about that time the

1760

John Montagu, the fourth earl of Sandwich (England), is credited with making the first sandwich.

bleeding stopped. When I asked Amos later what it had felt like, he said it was as if someone had pressed twice very firmly on the cut. This led me to ask a blood-stopper once how he did his work. He said that it was nearly impossible to explain, but that he forgot everything and concentrated on the person hurt. He imagined himself right there holding the blood back and saying, "It's stopping, it's stopping, it's stopped."

Another time a small child had a severe nosebleed. None of the usual remedies seemed to help. I knew the mother well, and she and I had often talked about the veracity of all these stories of the bloodstoppers and of how handy people like them had been in the lumber camps. Of course we knew that a certain amount of superstition was involved, and although we had seen them stop blood, we ourselves did not wholly believe in their ability. However, after her little boy had had this nosebleed for three days and nights, had been cauterized twice by a doctor to no avail, and was weakening, she began to talk about going to see the bloodstopper. The whole family encouraged her; they were tired of staying up nights with the young fellow, afraid he would choke. I said, "Go ahead; I won't tell anyone."

She drove to the bloodstopper's house. He saw the car drive into the driveway, and he hobbled out to the porch. He took in the scene at once — the wan little boy at the window holding a bloody rag to this nose, the distraught mother. He raised his hand as if in salute and said, "The bleeding is stopped." So it had. The little fellow did not have another nosebleed for two years.

Because the topic has interested me, I've asked around the state of Maine for more information. I've found that all old people who have worked in the woods can tell of times when a bloodstopper has helped

TO MAKE A WART GO AWAY:

Rub it with seven kernels of corn, then feed the corn to your neighbor's chickens.

someone. I have also found that many young people have heard of it from their old folks, and some claim to have bloodstoppers in their own

1762

The first instrument specifically designed as a safety razor is invented by professional barber Jean Jacques Perret in France.

families. One far-fetched story concerns a grandmother on whom the family, and in fact the neighborhood, depended. She had only recently died when one of the young children cut himself. All efforts to stanch the blood seemed in vain. One of the family lamented, "If only Grandma were here now. How I wish she were here to help us." The bleeding stopped suddenly.

Stories and stories. There is still a lively belief in the art of blood-stoppers. Today maybe there isn't such a desperate need for them as in the old days in the lumber camps. Today we have radios in about all the camps, and we also have mobile units. We have planes that can get into even the smaller lakes. Better woods roads allow ambulances to come into most of the camps. We have put our faith in these newer things. But the drastic urgency of events in the old days, when people mostly took care of each other, led to another kind of solution, the efficacy of which they never doubted.

ANECDOTES & PLEASANTRIES

Fingernails

CUT YOUR fingernails on Monday,
　cut them for wealth.
Cut your fingernails on Tuesday,
　cut them for health.
Cut your fingernails on Wednesday,
　cut them for news.
Cut your fingernails on Thursday,
　cut them for a new pair of shoes.

Cut your fingernails on Friday,
　cut them for woe.
Cut your fingernails on Saturday,
　a journey to go.
Cut your fingernails on Sunday,
　cut them for evil,
And be all the week as cross
　as the Devil.

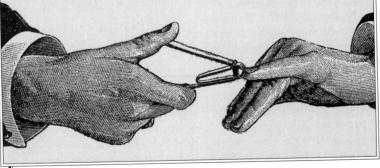

1764

Wolfgang Amadeus Mozart composes his first symphony. He is eight years old.

■ *"Newly improved!" "Scientifically advanced!" "A revolutionary new herbal breakthrough!" Would you guess that these phrases advertise medicines that, in some cases, have been used for thousands of years?*

The Top Ten Feel-Good Herbs

BY MARTHA WHITE

NATURAL REMEDIES HAVE ENjoyed a resurgence of interest, and rightly so. The "feel-good" herbs are the latest rage, from the controversial yohimbe (touted as an aphrodisiac for men but potentially fatal in excess) to the popular ginkgo biloba (a circulation enhancer believed to aid memory and the libido). With all the hype and glory, it can be difficult to know what to believe. Luckily, in most cases, there are centuries of tradition and experience to guide us about the usefulness of these ancient herbs.

Calendula. Creams and balms of this "pot marigold" *(Calendula officinalis)* are often effective as an antiseptic and anti-inflammatory agent for diaper rash, chapped hands and lips, and other minor skin irritations. Various commercial varieties are available. Your grandmother probably made her own salve, and you can do the same (see the recipe on page 92). The purest forms use just the petals, but many include the entire flower head. Do not confuse this plant with the French marigold *(Tagetes patula),* often used as an insecticide.

Echinacea. Commonly known as purple coneflower, echinacea *(Echinacea purpurea* or *E. angus-*

ECHINACEA

1767

The first iron rails are used in the mines of Coalbrookdale, England.

Calendula Salve

dried fresh calendula flowers
olive oil
beeswax
benzoin tincture

CHOP THE DRIED flowers and cover them with olive oil. Cover and soak for about 2 weeks. Strain through muslin, composting the plant parts, and add up to 4 parts beeswax to every 10 parts calendula oil. A few drops of benzoin tincture will help the salve keep well over time. Store in a covered container. Apply externally to sunburn, minor scrapes and bruises, and chapped lips.

tifolium) is an herb used in teas, capsules, and tinctures to enhance immunity to colds and flu and to fight kidney and mucous infections. Perhaps more than any other herbal remedy, echinacea has enjoyed a widespread new popularity, and its role is being studied in many immunity-related diseases. The root is the part generally used, although the flower can be used as well. Echinacea is sometimes adulterated, so buy it from a reputable source or grow your own. Short-term use (up to two tablespoons of dried herb steeped in water and taken as often as three times a day) is generally advised; at higher doses, you risk nausea or dizziness. Some commercial teas combine goldenseal (see page 94) with echinacea, which may create uncertain dosage.

Feverfew. For brainpower and enhanced memory, feverfew (*Chrysanthemum parthenium* or *Tanacetum parthenium*) is a vasodilator that is considered to enhance blood circulation to the brain and, sometimes, to relieve or prevent migraines. Midsummer daisy and featherfew are other, old names for this herb, but do not confuse it with feverwort. Traditional uses for feverfew are for menstrual cramps and indigestion, but not — as you might think — for fever. One leaf, up to three times a day, can be chewed (stop if mouth sores form) or used as a tea. Capsules are also

1770

British mechanic Edward Nairne finds that the substance caoutchouc, tapped from trees in Mexico, is good for rubbing out pencil marks. Noted chemist Joseph Priestley agrees and gives the substance its new name — rubber.

FEVERFEW

available, but only good-quality sources contain the active ingredient. Avoid feverfew if you are pregnant or on blood thinners.

Ginkgo biloba. The Chinese have been using ginkgo, from the *Ginkgo biloba* tree, also called the maidenhair tree, for thousands of years for conditions related to aging, such as headaches, hearing loss, and dizziness. More recent German and French studies suggest that ginkgo leaves in a tea may help concentration, memory, and Alzheimer's symptoms. (Avoid the seeds, which can cause headaches or skin trouble.) For impotence, ginkgo leaves taken in a tea once or twice a day is suggested because of its circulation-enhancing effect. "Vitality" and "libido" remedies often contain ginkgo.

Ginseng. First, know your ginsengs. The root of the American ginseng *(Panax quinquefolius)* is considered to be a digestive aid. The Asiatic ginseng root *(Panax ginseng)* is supposed to provide short-term aid for exhaustion, concentration, and resistance to stress; it also may help regulate hormones, thus enhancing fertility. A third, the closely related Siberian ginseng *(Eleutherococcus senticosus),* is considered even more invigorating to the nerves. Pure sources of any of these are rare, however, and some reputed ginseng remedies and teas contain none of the true herb, which

GINKGO BILOBA

1775

The modern flush toilet is designed by Alexander Cumming of England.

Risky Herbs

Seek expert advice before using any of the following herbal remedies.

Borage oil. Restricted in some countries; can damage liver.

Calamus. Carcinogenic.

Celandine. Restricted in some countries; poisonous in large doses.

Chaparral. Can damage liver.

Coltsfoot. Can damage liver.

Comfrey. Can damage liver.

Eucalyptus. Best used externally rather than ingested; oil is highly toxic.

Germander (occasionally sold as skullcap). Sometimes sold in weight-control remedies; can damage liver.

Jin Bu Huan. Can damage liver.

Lemon balm. Linked with inhibiting thyroid hormones; avoid if you have Graves' disease or other thyroid difficulties.

Licorice (the medicinal variety, not the candy, which rarely contains real licorice).

Prolonged use can destroy electrolyte balance.

Life root. Can damage liver.

Lobelia (also called puke-weed). A controlled substance in some countries; can affect breathing.

Ma huang (also called ephedra). Restricted in some countries; excess can damage nerves or cause stroke.

Pokeweed. Toxic.

Sassafras. Carcinogenic.

Skullcap. See germander.

Wintergreen oil. Toxic.

Yohimbe. Can be fatal in excess.

---

is relatively expensive. Pure ginseng can be highly stimulating, so short-term use (less than three weeks) is advised, except perhaps for the elderly with degenerative conditions such as Alzheimer's. Avoid taking true ginsengs with other stimulants, including caffeine, and be alert for signs of hyperactivity or increased anxiety or tension.

Goldenseal. When applied externally to cleansed wounds such as canker sores and cold sores, a compress made by steeping the leaves of goldenseal (*Hydrastis canadensis*) in hot water for up to 20 minutes may be modestly effective. A wash of goldenseal also might remedy athlete's foot. Goldenseal tea (about one-quarter teaspoon of dried leaves in a cup of hot water)

1780

Machine-made steel-point pens, manufactured by John Mitchell in Birmingham, England, replace quill pens.

ST. JOHN'S-WORT

St. John's-wort. You know it's an ancient remedy when it's named for one of the beheaded saints. The true herb *(Hypericum perforatum)* "bleeds" red when crushed, which can help you identify fresh sources. The flowers in a tea are reputed to ease depression and calm the nerves. Some call it "nature's Prozac." Up to 400 milligrams of dried herb can be taken three times a day, but beware of photosensitization (increased Sun sensitivity). St. John's-wort is an expectorant, analgesic, antibacterial, and antiviral and is often considered a remedy for sore throats and cold symptoms. It is especially popular in Germany,

has astringent, antibacterial, and antiviral effects and may be taken as a short-term cold remedy or immunity booster. Avoid it if you are pregnant or have high blood pressure. Beware of adulterated sources, which may contain bloodroot (a powerful laxative).

Gotu kola. Also called Indian pennywort, the leaves, stems, and flowers are considered a relaxant, digestive, diuretic, and nervine. Short-term use is recommended. Two versions are commonly sold: The weaker, though more available, is *Hydrocotle asiatica,* sometimes taken in capsules of up to 400 milligrams a day; the stronger is *Centella asiatica.* Relatively little is known about either, so caution is advised.

VALERIAN

1781

In England, William Herschel, an organist, music teacher, and composer, discovers the planet Uranus.

A Cautionary Note

GOVERNMENT regulations prevent herbal suppliers from making medical claims about herbs unless costly scientific tests substantiate the results. Consequently, labels may not offer much practical information and will often carry disclaimers, such as "These products are not intended to diagnose, treat, cure, or prevent any disease." To protect yourself, buy only from a reputable source and begin slowly. For utmost safety, consult a qualified health practitioner before proceeding on any course of internal remedies, especially if you are pregnant or nursing, have other conditions such as high blood pressure or diabetes, or are taking any prescription drugs.

where it is taken for anxiety and used as a skin ointment (in balm form). It's also being studied for possible use in treating AIDS.

Saw palmetto. This is a popular remedy for benign prostate enlargement. To promote healthy prostate function and urinary flow, consider saw palmetto *(Serenoa serrulata* or *Sabal serrulata),* but continue your routine checkups as well. Seek a reputable source for an oil-based extract of the berries; 320 milligrams per day in capsule form is suggested by some practitioners. It's a diuretic and urinary antiseptic. Be aware that saw palmetto use can influence blood tests in misleading ways and sometimes interferes with prescription drugs, so keep your doctor informed.

Valerian. "Generally recognized as safe" by the U.S. Food and Drug Administration (FDA), valerian *(Valeriana officinalis)* can be taken in a tea (made by steeping one to four grams of the fresh or dried root in hot water) or in the popular capsule form to ease insomnia and aid relaxation. Valerian is sometimes recommended for muscle cramps and spasms as well. After smelling and tasting the tea (reminiscent of sweaty sneakers), many people find they prefer the capsules. Start slowly; too much can cause vomiting, headaches, dizziness, and depression. Traditional remedies also recommend the smelly herb for rat-trap bait and for attracting cats!

1782

German educator Friedrich Froebel, founder of the first kindergarten, is born.

> ■ *The medical community is hard at work finding a cure for hiccups. In the meantime, most people continue to rely on their own home remedies. In 1985 the Almanac came to the rescue of hiccup sufferers with a long list of folk remedies from which to choose.*

Surefire Home Remedies for the Hiccups

BY TIM CLARK

ICCUP, HICKE UP, HIKUP, hickop, hickhop, hecup, hiccop, hickup, hicket, hickok — it sounds like a bad attack of a condition that has plagued or amused (depending on your point of view) humanity since the dawn of time. In reality, it is a list of the different ways people have spelled the word in English, dating back as far as 1544, when the accepted medical practice was "to cast colde water in the face of him that hath the hicket."

The British, by the way, persist in spelling it "hiccough" (while still pronouncing it "hiccup"), which even their own *Oxford English Dictionary* suggests "ought to be abandoned as a mere error." Put that in your next cough of tea and drink it. But not too fast, for it might trigger an attack, along with eating too fast or too much, smoking, pregnancy, certain illnesses, exercising too strenuously, nervousness, laughing hard, or recent surgery.

Hiccups have nothing to do with coughing, nor are they, as some people have supposed, unsuccessful efforts to inhale or to vomit. In fact, according to the world's leading authority on the biology of hiccups, the muscle spasm in the diaphragm that causes a sudden intake of air, ending with a "hic" as the glottis snaps shut, may be one

HIC!

HAMMOND

1783

The Montgolfier brothers demonstrate the first untethered flight of a hot-air balloon in France.

of the most ancient behaviors in the animal kingdom, with links to breathing, digestion, and even reproduction.

Dr. Terence Anthoney, a specialist in animal behavior at Southern Illinois University, believes the hiccup originated millions of years ago as a gasp, a primitive form of breathing. Even now, he points out, some dying patients with respiratory problems begin to hiccup in the last moments of their lives, as if reverting to the most basic form of breathing. Eventually, more efficient forms of respiration evolved, but when such improvements occur, Anthoney says, "nature doesn't throw the old behavior away." It persists, held in reserve, perhaps adapting to some new function. In the case of hiccups, Anthoney believes that the new function was regurgitation of food to feed the young, a behavior still found in many mammals. Along with the new behavior evolved the ability to close the glottis, to prevent food from being sucked into the lungs, and thus was heard the primal "hic!"

Dr. Terence Anthoney, a specialist in animal behavior at Southern Illinois University, believes the hiccup originated millions of years ago as a gasp, a primitive form of breathing.

Although human beings today don't regurgitate digested food for their young to eat (at least not in polite circles), Anthoney cautions against assuming that hiccups have no function. In years of study, he has found clues linking hiccups in infants to improved digestion, and his discovery that women, as a rule, have much more frequent bouts with hiccups than men has led him to investigate the possibility that hiccups may be connected with the human reproductive cycle. "The belief that hiccups have no purpose is a lot of hooey," Anthoney says. "It's just so common we don't look closely at it."

Although much of Anthoney's research has involved animals, one of his most fascinating cases was that of Charles Osborne of Anthon, Iowa, who started hiccuping one day in 1922 and hasn't stopped since. Osborne, a retired farmer and livestock trader, has been hiccuping anywhere from 10 to 40 times a minute for nearly 63 years — a total of somewhere around half a billion hiccups. Anthoney believes the cause of this phenomenon was a minor

1784

Benjamin Franklin
invents bifocal
eyeglasses.

stroke Osborne suffered that day in 1922, while trying to lift a 350-pound hog. That stroke probably destroyed a part of the brain that inhibits the hiccup response. Unlike many victims of prolonged hiccuping, who have lost great amounts of weight or even died of exhaustion (Pope Pius XII suffered prolonged hiccuping before dying of a stroke in 1958), Osborne seems to have thrived. He is 90 years old, has fathered eight children, and, since his first appearance on a radio program in 1936, has achieved a measure of worldwide celebrity. He is listed in *The Guinness Book of World Records* along with an unnamed young man, admitted to an English hospital in 1769, whose hiccups could be heard at a distance of half a mile.

Prolonged hiccups can be stopped by surgery, but it can inhibit breathing, and so Charles Osborne prefers to live with his condition. He has, of course, tried thousands of folk remedies. One well-meaning friend fired both barrels of a shotgun behind him in an effort to startle the hiccups away, but nothing has worked.

Recent experiments with valproic acid have shown promise, but most people continue to depend on their own surefire home remedies. Most of these remedies rely on forcing a deep breath, either by startling the victim or by increasing the carbon dioxide content in the blood by breath holding, hyperventilation, or breathing into a bag. Others appear to work by irritating nerve endings in the back of the throat when various substances are swallowed. Some depend on pure magic, such as the mystical numbers three, seven, and nine. And some have no rational explanation at all.

VARIOUS CURES FOR HICCUPS

- "The hickot is cured with sudden feare or strange newes" (1584).
- "Sneezing doth cease the Hiccough" (Francis Bacon, 1626).
- "You must in the very instant that the Hickup seizes the Party pull his Ring-Finger, and it will go off" (1727).
- Cover your head with a pillow.
- Spit on a rock, then turn it over.
- Hold your breath and stick out your tongue.
- Pant like a dog.
- Bite your thumbs and blow hard against them for a minute.
- Drink a glass of water with a pencil in your mouth.
- Eat a spoonful of peanut butter.
- Eat a spoonful of sugar.

1790

The first U.S. census is taken. According to the census, there are 3,929,214 people living in the country.

- Eat a spoonful of salt.
- Eat a spoonful of vinegar.
- Eat a spoonful of Worcestershire sauce.
- Eat a spoonful of crushed ice.
- Drink nine swallows of water from your grandfather's cup without taking a breath.
- Drink water through a folded handkerchief.
- Drink from the wrong side of a cup.
- Drink water while holding your ears and nostrils closed.
- Take a mouthful of water and swallow it in three gulps. Repeat three times while standing perfectly still and breathing through your nose.
- Breath into a paper bag.
- Stand on your head for 5 minutes.
- Stand on your head and drink a glass of water.
- Lay over a chair on your stomach and drink a glass of water.

- Put the head of a burnt match in your ear.
- Place a matchstick on top of your head and count to nine.
- In a baby, place two broom straws in the baby's hair.
- Lay a broom on the floor, bristles to the right, and jump over it seven times.
- Lay a broom on the floor and jump over it three times. Walk around it once, then leave it where it lies.
- Hold your left elbow for 7 minutes.
- Hold a dime against the roof of your mouth for 30 minutes.
- Wet a piece of red thread with your tongue, stick it to your forehead, and look at it.

- Accuse the victim of something he has not done.
- Turn your pockets inside out.
- Stand nose to nose with the victim and stare at him.
- Tighten a belt around your chest.
- Stick your head under water and count to 25.
- Place a wastebasket on your head and have somebody beat on it.
- Say, "Nine sups from a cup cures the hiccups" three times without taking a breath.
- Say, "Hiccups, hiccups, stand straight up; three sups in a cup are good for the hiccups" three times without breathing.
- Stand in the middle of the road and say, "Hiccup, stickup, not for me, hiccup, stickup." (*Editor's note:* Keep an eye on the traffic while doing so, or the cure is likely to be permanent.)

The U.S. Supreme Court is organized. Until 1935, when it will move into its own building, the Court will meet in a small chamber in the Capitol Building.

Do You Really Know Yourself?

(As a matter of fact, you're pretty wonderful.)

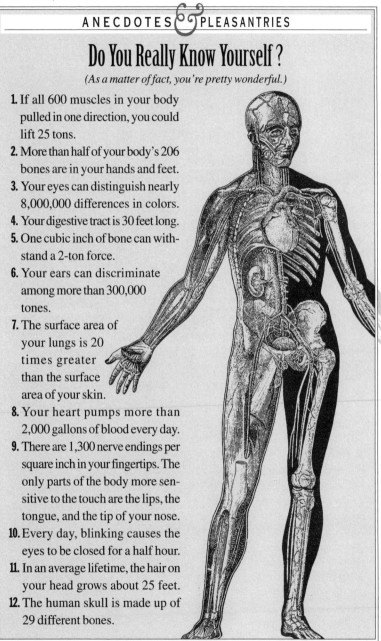

1. If all 600 muscles in your body pulled in one direction, you could lift 25 tons.
2. More than half of your body's 206 bones are in your hands and feet.
3. Your eyes can distinguish nearly 8,000,000 differences in colors.
4. Your digestive tract is 30 feet long.
5. One cubic inch of bone can withstand a 2-ton force.
6. Your ears can discriminate among more than 300,000 tones.
7. The surface area of your lungs is 20 times greater than the surface area of your skin.
8. Your heart pumps more than 2,000 gallons of blood every day.
9. There are 1,300 nerve endings per square inch in your fingertips. The only parts of the body more sensitive to the touch are the lips, the tongue, and the tip of your nose.
10. Every day, blinking causes the eyes to be closed for a half hour.
11. In an average lifetime, the hair on your head grows about 25 feet.
12. The human skull is made up of 29 different bones.

1792

Mount Unzen in Japan erupts, killing approximately 14,500 people.

> ■ *Sweet potatoes have amazing virtues that not everyone knows about. So perhaps it's time to learn how best to grow them and how best to cook them.*

The Healthiest Vegetable of All

BY GEORGIA ORCUTT

SWEET POTATOES ARE MANY things to many people. One woman we know used their fiery orange flesh as a color swatch for her kitchen wall. While making supper one night, she cut into a baked sweet potato and saw at last the color she'd been searching for. She popped a slice into a plastic container and headed for the paint store. "The man mixing the paint looked at me strangely," she reported, "but I got the accent color I wanted for one wall."

To nutritionists, sweet potatoes are food for thought. By some measures, they rank as the healthiest vegetable we can eat. An excellent source of vitamin A and a good source of vitamin C, high in iron and dietary fiber, sweet potatoes also provide their eaters

with potassium and vitamin B_6. Of special note is their high percentage of beta-carotene — four times the recommended daily allowance per cup. (Beta-carotene, which the body converts to vitamin A, is especially valued for its ability to re-

1792

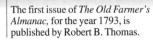

The first issue of *The Old Farmer's Almanac,* for the year 1793, is published by Robert B. Thomas.

duce the risk of certain cancers.)

To George Washington Carver, the sweet potato was the key to unending possibilities. Before World War I, he urged rural southern farmers to think beyond cotton and grow this easy, cheaply raised crop with its high nutritional rewards. To cut back on the use of precious wartime wheat, Carver recommended using two cups of cooked, mashed sweet potato for every six cups of flour in preparing bread. He went to Washington in 1918 to extol the virtues of sweet potato flour, but the end of the war curtailed the commercial application of his ideas.

To gardeners, especially those in the South, sweet potatoes have earned their place as an easy, economical, and tasty crop. Most at home in U.S. Department of Agriculture (USDA) Zones 8, 9, and 10, sweet potatoes prefer rather poor, dry, sandy soil and need it to be nice and loose, so they have room to develop. They like moisture but don't enjoy being constantly wet. In fact, they like resisting drought. When planted in rich, acid soil, they tend to make all leaves and very poor fruits.

Sweet potatoes are planted from slips or sprouts, which you can buy from mail-order seed and plant purveyors or start yourself. A month before warm weather (60° F nights) sets in, suspend a sweet potato on

SWEET POTATO FACTS

- Never put sweet potatoes in your refrigerator unless they have been cooked first. They will develop a hard core and sunken spots and will spoil much faster than if you keep them at room temperature.

- Leading varieties are 'Beauregard', 'Jewel', 'Centennial', 'Georgia Red', 'Nugget', and 'New Jersey Orange'.

- One cup of cooked sweet potato provides 30 milligrams (50,000 IU) of beta-carotene. (It would take 23 cups of broccoli to provide the same amount.)

- One medium sweet potato contains 135 to 155 calories.

- The ranking states for production of sweet potatoes for 1992 were California, North Carolina, Louisiana, Texas, Alabama, Georgia, Mississippi, New Jersey, South Carolina, and Virginia, according to the USDA.

- The per capita consumption of sweet potatoes is approximately 6 pounds.

- The National Cancer Society cites sweet potatoes as an excellent food to aid in the prevention of several common types of cancer.

1792

The Philadelphia Mint is established to make silver half-dimes and dimes.

toothpicks in a glass with its lower half in water. As shoots develop, cut them off, root them in water, and plant them. (A sweet potato suspended in water also makes a remarkable houseplant, sending out rampant vines and delighting kids of all ages.)

Depending on the variety, sweet potatoes need 120 to 150 frost-free growing days. Some gardeners prefer planting them in mounds about 16 inches apart, leaving room for their trailing vines. Keep at least two leaves from each slip above ground and water them well after planting. When the plant tops turn black after the first frost, they are ready to harvest. (In areas where there is no frost, they are ready to harvest four months after planting.) Dig them carefully and handle them as you would eggs. Their tender skins bruise easily.

For northern gardeners, sweet potatoes offer a true challenge that has been successfully met as far north as Canada. One gardener in the Yukon plants sweet potatoes in a lean-to cold frame against his house and reaps a small but rewarding yield. Another Canadian grower reports harvesting one sweet potato that weighed ten pounds.

Ken Allan of the Garden Research Exchange in Kingston, Ontario, advocates growing sweet potatoes in USDA Zones 6b, 5a, and 5b under clear plastic mulch, which warms the soil and retains heat. "Make a slit to plant them, and use sand or sawdust to keep the plastic close to the ground around the slit," he advises. "You don't want to have a flap for the air to come in and out. That's just like leaving a door open in your garden." If May brings some warm days, Allan recommends planting sweet potatoes by the 15th. As for variety, he's sold on 'Georgia Jet'.

The late James Crockett advocated planting sweet potatoes in bushel baskets, one slip per basket. He noted that sweet potatoes grown in such confinement often outproduce those allowed to roam in garden soil. And if early frost threatens, you can simply move the baskets to a warmer spot.

Although it may be tricky to grow sweet potatoes in the North, they are, ironically, well suited to storage in colder climates. "The sweet potato is an ideal root crop

> *One gardener in the Yukon plants sweet potatoes in a lean-to cold frame against his house and reaps a small but rewarding yield. Another Canadian grower reports harvesting one sweet potato that weighed ten pounds.*

1794

America's first cracker bakery opens in Newburyport, Massachusetts.

for those northern gardeners with central heating in their homes," Allan says. "Temperatures of 55° to 60° F are ideal for long keeping. If you see a sweet potato with sunken circular spots, that's a sign that it has been stored at too cold a temperature. Below 50° F, they suffer chilling injury and develop a hard core and spotting."

Proper curing enhances sweet potato flavor by converting starch to sugar and hardening their skins for storage. Unlike new potatoes,

The Great Yam Scam

ARE SWEET POTATOES the same as yams? No . . . , and yes. Literally and botanically speaking, the two are not related. Yams are large, starchy, edible tuberous roots that belong to the genus *Dioscorea*. They grow in tropical and subtropical countries and require eight to ten months of warm weather to mature. Yams can grow 2 to 3 feet long, and some can weigh as much as 80 pounds. According to horticulturist U. P. Hedrick, the word *yam* means "to eat" in the dialect of Guinea. In the United States today, it is possible to find true yams in some urban Hispanic markets.

Both the yam and the sweet potato grow underground and have yellowish orange flesh, but there the similarity ends. The two became entwined in this country by household vernacular in part through the work of a pub-

THE YAM

licity campaign. Sweet potato promoters attached the word *yam* to the deep orange, moist-fleshed varieties of sweet potatoes and left the words *sweet potato* to the smaller, yellowish, and drier-fleshed varieties. The two types of sweet potato are interchangeable in cooking but bring different tastes, textures, and colors to your plate. 'Centennial' and 'Puerto Rico' are two popular moist-fleshed (formerly called yam) varieties; 'Nemagold', 'New Jersey Orange', and 'Nugget' have the lighter and drier (sweet potato) flesh.

Today it is common to find either or both words used in supermarkets, although sweet potato promoters wish we would all stop saying yam. The North Carolina SweetPotato Commission currently urges the world to spell "sweetpotato" as one word, but it's an uphill battle. If your mama called them yams, for certain you will, too.

1795

Ludwig van Beethoven performs publicly for the first time in Vienna, Austria.

which are a delicacy, newly harvested sweet potatoes are watery and bland. To cure homegrown sweet potatoes, keep them at 90° F for five to ten days at high humidity. Some people use heaters in closets; others get good results from an incubator or a carefully moni-

TO CURE A HEADACHE:

Soak your feet in hot water to draw blood from your head.

tored light bulb in a box. Allan puts his crop in brown paper bags, folds over the tops, and puts them in his back bedroom with a 1,500-watt heater. "I suppose a sauna would work well, too," he says.

To the cook, sweet potatoes are easier than pie. They can simply be scrubbed, poked with a fork in a few places, and baked at 400° F for 35 minutes to 1 hour, until they give a bit when you squeeze them. In the microwave, a whole sweet potato baked on high will be ready in 4 to 6 minutes. (Let it stand for 5 minutes to soften.)

Sweet potatoes can also be steamed or boiled whole and unpeeled for about 40 minutes, or until tender, but they are tastier baked.

Immerse cut raw sweet potatoes in water until you're ready to cook them; otherwise they will darken. As a general rule, don't substitute sweet potatoes for regular potatoes in recipes (the two aren't related). Sweet potatoes don't hold together the way white potatoes do, and their strong flavor can overwhelm a dish meant for a milder potato taste. But they make a fine substitute for pumpkin, especially in desserts.

There is one thing a sweet potato is not, and that is a potato. Unrelated to its white namesake, the sweet potato is a member of the morning glory family (Convolvulaceae), *Ipomoea batatus*. It also is not a tuber, but a fleshy root originating in South and Central America. Many varieties were being grown by the time Columbus came to America in 1492. Ships' logs from the early 16th century note sweet potatoes traveling from Honduras to Spain, where their popularity spread to Europe and beyond.

Pork and Sweet Potato Stir-Fry

1 pork tenderloin (about 12 ounces)
2 tablespoons oil
2 medium sweet potatoes, finely diced
**   or julienned**

1796

The first American passport is issued to Francis Maria Barrere.

1 medium yellow pepper, chopped
1 medium sweet red pepper, chopped
8 ounces fresh or frozen snow peas
2 cloves garlic, minced
1 tablespoon grated fresh gingerroot
2 tablespoons soy sauce
3 tablespoons water
1 tablespoon cornstarch
2 tablespoons hoisin sauce (available in the Asian foods section of supermarkets)

2 teaspoons baking soda
1½ teaspoons cinnamon
¾ teaspoon ground ginger
¼ teaspoon ground cloves
¼ teaspoon freshly grated nutmeg
½ teaspoon salt
2 cups mashed cooked sweet potatoes
1½ cups vegetable oil
4 eggs
1 cup chopped nuts

Cut the pork diagonally into ¼-inch slices. Have the remaining ingredients ready. Stir-fry the pork in the hot oil over high heat until no longer pink. Add the sweet potatoes and toss until they begin to soften. Add the peppers, snow peas, garlic, and gingerroot, and continue stir-frying until the peppers are crisp-tender. Combine the soy sauce, water, and cornstarch in a small jar, shake well, and add to the pan, stirring well. Cover the pan, lower the heat, and cook briefly, then uncover and stir in the hoisin sauce. Serve with rice or noodles. Makes 6 servings.

Sweet Potato–Chocolate Nut Cake

The colors and flavor of this moist cake are a knockout.

4 ounces semisweet chocolate
1 teaspoon vanilla extract
3 cups flour
1½ cups sugar
2 teaspoons baking powder

Butter and lightly flour a 10-inch tube pan. Place the chocolate and vanilla in a small saucepan and set, covered, in a larger pan that you've just filled with boiling water.

Sift together all the dry ingredients and set aside. In a large bowl, beat the sweet potatoes and oil together, then beat in the eggs one by one until well blended. Slowly add the dry ingredients and mix well; stir in the nuts. Put one-third of the mixture in another bowl and stir in the chocolate, which should be melted smooth by now. Alternate the batters in the tube pan as you would for a marble cake. With a knife, cut through the two batters to swirl together slightly.

Bake in a preheated 350° F oven for 1 to 1¼ hours, or until the sides have shrunk away from the pan, the top is springy, and the tester comes out dry. Let cool for 10 minutes and then remove from the pan and cool on a rack. If desired, drizzle with a thin confectioners' sugar glaze (beat 2 to 3 tablespoons boiling water into 1½ cups confectioners' sugar).

1797

London haberdasher John Etherington designs the top hat.

ANECDOTES & PLEASANTRIES

The Birthplaces of Our Vegetables

POTATOES came from far Virginia;
Parsley was sent us from
　　Sardinia;
French beans, low grown on the
　　Earth,
To distant India trace their birth;
But scarlet runners, gay and tall,
That climb upon your garden
　　wall —
A cheerful sight to all around —
In South America were found.
The onion traveled here from
　　Spain;
The leek from Switzerland we
　　gain;
Garlic from Sicily obtain;
Spinach in far Syria grown;
Two hundred years ago or more,
Brazil the artichoke sent o'er;

And southern Europe's seacoast
　　shore
Beet root on us bestows.
When 'Lizabeth was reigning here
Peas came from Holland and were
　　dear.
The south of Europe lays its claim
To beans, but some from Egypt
　　came.
The radishes both thin and stout,
Natives of China are, no doubt;
But turnips, carrots, and sea kale,
With celery so crisp and pale,
Are products of our own fair land;
And cabbages — a goodly tribe
Which abler pens might well
　　describe —
Are also ours, I understand.

Amicus, from Goldthwaite's
Geographical Magazine

c. 1800

John Chapman, aka Johnny Appleseed,
sets out on foot to plant apple seeds along
the roadways and rivers and in the
forest clearings of the Midwest.

■ *Surely all of us, at one time or another, have "eaten like kings." Now we can eat like presidents.*

From the Highest Table in the Land

A SELECTION OF PRESIDENTIAL FAVORITES

For a quarter of a century, Louis Szathmary, author of seven cookbooks and owner of Chicago's highly acclaimed The Bakery Restaurant, collected all manner of cookbooks and food-related memorabilia. Upon his retirement, he donated more than 200,000 items to Johnson and Wales University in Providence, creating the world's largest archives and museum related to the culinary arts and hotel and restaurant management.

A unique collection within the collection is the U.S. presidential material, which museum curator Barbara Kuck refers to as the "First Stomach" collection. It includes more than 100 original handwritten or typewritten documents by our presidents and first ladies.

Here is a sampling of recipes from the archives, along with notes

1801

Italian astronomer Giuseppi Piazzi is the first person to discover an asteroid, or tiny planet.

and comments from Barbara. These dishes can easily be incorporated into your own family traditions, to become all the more special because a president savored them, too.

THE MARQUIS DE LAFAYETTE RE-turned to America after the Revolutionary War in the fall of 1784. After Lafayette's stay at Mount Vernon with his beloved friend George Washington, one of Major Andrew Lewis's boys accompanied him to Fredericksburg to pay his respects to the general's mother. They found her in her garden in a short gown, petticoat, and cap, raking leaves. Unaffectedly, she greeted Lafayette, and together they went into the house. She made him a mint julep, which she served with spiced gingerbread. Listening with pleased attention to the Frenchman's praises of her son, she replied only that "George was always a good boy."

Here's the recipe for the cake Washington's mother served on that visit.

Lafayette Gingerbread

½ cup butter
⅔ cup excellent brown sugar
½ cup warm milk
2 teaspoons powdered ginger
¼ heaping teaspoon cinnamon
¼ heaping teaspoon mace
¼ heaping teaspoon nutmeg
1 cup molasses
4 tablespoons brandy or coffee
3 eggs
3 cups flour
1 teaspoon cream of tartar
juice and grated rind of 1 large orange
1 teaspoon baking soda dissolved in a little warm water
1 cup seeded raisins or Zante currants, soaked overnight in brandy or water and drained

Cream the butter and brown sugar with a paddle. Add the warm milk. Mix all the spices together and add to the butter and sugar mixture. Mix in all the other ingredients. Pour into a prepared 9x13-inch pan. Bake at 350° F for about 30 to 40 minutes, or until a toothpick inserted in the center comes out clean.

Courtesy of Mrs. Vivian Minor Fleming, Military Regent, Washington-Lewis Chapter, Daughters of the American Revolution, Fredericksburg, Virginia

1804

Parisian Nicolas Appert successfully tests his method of preserving food by hermetically sealing glass bottles and then boiling them. He will open the first commercial cannery in 1810.

ONE OF THE FIRST ADVERTISE-
ments to appear in an American newspaper after George Washington assumed office was this one,
written personally by the first president.

A COOK

Is wanted for the family of the President
of the United States. No one need apply who is not perfect in the business,
and can bring indubitable testimonials
of sobriety, honesty, and attention to
the duties of the station.

Significantly, the ad ran for a
long time before a suitable appli-
cant was found.

Martha Washington had her
hands full running the households
at Mount Vernon and in Philadelphia, which was then the nation's
capital. Her handwritten books include some simple recipes, such as
Olives of Beef. This type of meat-
ball was one of the favorites of our
first president, who, as we know,
had difficulty with his dentures and
appreciated the fine taste of pure
beef without the effort and discomfort that chewing it involved.

Olives of Beef

⅔ cup short-grain Carolina or Louisiana
    rice
3 cups water
1½ teaspoons salt, divided
2 pounds beef (combine a lean ground
    beef, such as ground round or ground
sirloin, wth a somewhat fattier
    ground beef)
1 egg
½ teaspoon freshly ground black
    pepper
¼ teaspoon paprika
1 to 2 tablespoons oil or shortening

In a 2- to 3-quart pan under cover,
boil the rice in the water with 1 teaspoon of the salt until very tender,
about 1½ hours. The rice must cook
to a mush, and never mind the extra
water. It's also very important that
the beef, the rice, and the water it is
cooked in are really cold at preparation time. Transfer the rice with
its liquid to a chilled dish and refrigerate until cold (or place in the
freezer after cooling slightly). Keep
the beef in the refrigerator also.

Measure the cooked rice and liquid, and if necessary add enough ice
water to make 3 cups. Pour over the
ground beef in a large bowl. Add the
egg, remaining ½ teaspoon salt, pepper, and paprika, and work ingredients together until completely
mixed. Cover with plastic wrap or
aluminum foil and refrigerate for 2
hours or longer. (This much of the

1810

English merchant Peter Durand creates the tin
can for food storage. During the War of 1812,
the Royal Navy will find the cans indispensable
for storing rations.

recipe you can do in the morning or even the night before.)

Transfer the chilled mixture to a flat surface and form it into an oblong piece about 1 inch thick. With a wet knife, divide it into 1-inch pieces. With wet hands, roll the pieces into the shape of olives or little sausages. Chill again.

About 30 minutes before serving, fry the pieces for 2 to 3 minutes in a heavy skillet in a very small amount of hot oil or shortening, just enough so that the meat won't stick to the pan. Or bake at 450° F for 12 to 15 minutes. Don't overcook.

Serve with fluffy mashed potatoes and a big salad. Any kind of sauce will help the "olives" if you use them as a main course, which serves 8, but if you want to be authentic, try the sweet-and-sour sauce also adapted from a Martha Washington recipe.

Martha Washington's Sweet-and-Sour Sauce

4 tablespoons butter
4 scant tablespoons flour
2 cups beef broth or consommé,
  or 2 beef bouillon cubes dissolved
  in 2 cups boiling water
1 tablespoon white vinegar
1 teaspoon sugar
2 tablespoons chopped fresh parsley
2 tablespoons rinsed, chopped capers
  or chopped green olives (optional)

Melt the butter in a heavy saucepan over medium heat. Add the flour in small sprinklings, stirring constantly with a wooden spoon. Let the mixture bubble, then remove from the heat and gradually stir in the broth. Add the vinegar, sugar, and parsley, return to medium heat, and bring to a boil. Immediately reduce the heat and simmer, stirring, for 3 to 4 minutes. Add the capers or olives, if you like, before serving.

If you like a thinner sauce, add 2 to 3 tablespoons more broth or water. If you like a thicker sauce, cook for a couple of minutes longer.

This simple, basic, very old-fashioned sauce is also good with a few tablespoons of white wine instead of vinegar. If the white wine is sweet, use less sugar or omit altogether.

THE FIRST LADIES OF HISTORY busied themselves to varying degrees with the important task of feeding the president. Most were good housewives and fine homemakers. Even if they personally didn't get involved with the cooking, they certainly kept an eye on what would be served and what table linen, china, silver, and crystal would be used.

1811

An earthquake shakes the sparsely settled Midwest, causing the Mississippi River to come to a standstill, roll backward, and then surge ahead in huge tidal waves.

Mrs. Lincoln owned a copy of *Directions for Cookery in Its Various Branches* by Miss Leslie, one of the most popular sources of recipes at the time. She consulted it often. One of Mrs. Lincoln's most enduring recipes is a delicious cake invented by Monsieur Giron, a Lexington, Kentucky, caterer, who created it in honor of the 1825 visit to that city of his famous fellow Frenchman Lafayette. The Todd family acquired the recipe and cherished it ever after, and it later became known as Lincoln Almond Cake. The baking powder was added at a later date.

the sugar and butter. Sift together the flour and baking powder three times; slowly add to the butter and sugar mixture alternately with the milk, in small amounts at a time. Mix thoroughly.

Add the chopped blanched almonds and vanilla to the mixture. Continue beating until thoroughly mixed. In a separate mixing bowl, stiffly beat the egg whites with the salt. Gently fold them into the first mixture.

Pour the mixture into a greased and floured angel food cake pan or Bundt pan. Bake for approximately 1 hour, or until a toothpick inserted in the center comes out clean. Turn the cake out on a wire rack and allow to cool upside down for a few minutes until you are able to gently remove the cake from the pan. Before serving, gently cut the cake with a serrated bread or cake knife to avoid tearing it.

Lincoln Almond Cake

- 2¼ cups sugar
- 1 cup butter
- 3 cups flour
- 1 tablespoon baking powder
- 1 cup milk
- 1 cup chopped blanched almonds
- 1½ teaspoons vanilla (or almond) extract
- 6 egg whites
- ½ teaspoon salt

Preheat oven to 350° F. With an electric mixer, first cream together

PRESIDENT WARREN G. HARDING was a great lover of good food and good drink, mainly good Bordeaux wines. One of his handwrit-

1812

Jacob and Wilhelm Grimm publish the first volume of *Nursery and Household Tales* (later known as *Grimm's Fairy Tales*), a collection of folktales gathered from the people they met on their travels through the countryside. A second volume will be published in 1815 and a third in 1822.

ten letters mentions a dinner at which "the pheasants and venison were very fine. The pity is that we never get any Limburger and onion, but I guess the town smells bad enough without them." Lovers of good cheese and good wine may enjoy this pungent presidential cheese spread.

President Harding's Limburger Cheese Spread

4 ounces ripe Limburger cheese
4 ounces (½ cup) soft unsalted butter
1 tablespoon finely chopped scallions, green part
1 tablespoon finely chopped scallions, white part

In a blender or with a fork, mix the cheese and butter well. Fold in the chopped scallions. Serve at room temperature with toast points, dark bread, or crackers. Generously serves 6 to 8 as a cocktail spread or cheese course.

PERHAPS THE SIMPLEST RECIPE IN the presidential legacy is one written down in pencil on the back of a 3x5-inch index card by Mrs. Woodrow Wilson, a first lady who was not among the greatest cooks. Still, her clam dip was often served to the president.

Clam Cream Cheese Dip

1 small can clams, drained
1 8-ounce package cream cheese
2 to 4 tablespoons grated onion
salt and pepper to taste

Mix all the ingredients slowly in an electric mixture until thoroughly incorporated. Chill and serve with crackers.

> **Potatoes, tomatoes, and hot spices are foods for fidelity.**

1814

Francis Scott Key writes the poem "Defense of Fort M'Henry," which will be set to music and renamed "The Star-Spangled Banner." It will become the national anthem of the United States in 1931.

■ *Who says you have to go to a fancy restaurant to get great food? Remember that thick slice of Mom's meat loaf?*

Meat Loaf Can Be Quite Personal

BY AL SICHERMAN

WHEN I WAS A KID IN MILWAUkee, we didn't make a big deal out of eating — at least not the way some people do now. We ate. Sometimes, at holiday dinners, for example, we ate a lot; that was a great meal by definition. If you came away from the table groaning, you had been in the presence of great food.

But much of the food that I remember from my growing-up years, while it was great in that sense, was not great in the contemporary sense — it wasn't fancy. No miniature cream puff appetizers, no amazing dessert that belonged in an art museum.

We did have a lot of very nice meat loaf.

Oh, it's true enough that big-time restaurants on the East and West Coasts have lately been treating some traditional home-style recipes as though they were newly unearthed ancient treasures: macaroni and cheese, bread pudding, mashed potatoes and gravy. But even if the cognoscenti in Los Angeles are suddenly dining on meat loaf,

1816

Scottish engineer John Loudon McAdam is recognized for his new approach to road building — a three-layer design that will be called macadam and then, when a layer of tar is added to the top, tarmacadam, shortened to tarmac.

chances are very strong that they aren't dining on your *mom's* meat loaf.

Meat loaf can be quite personal, after all. Although all meat loaves may well trace their origins to a single prehistoric loaf that was formed while the Earth was still cooling, many different recipes evolved over time from that one. And your mom's meat loaf probably continued to change even after she started making it. That's because there's lots more room for variations in the ingredients and their amounts in a batch of meat loaf than there is, say, in roast beef or grilled cheese sandwiches.

Maybe, for example, once — long ago, while dinosaurs roamed the Earth — your mom's hand slipped while she was adding the ketchup, and a whole lot extra went in. If everybody liked it that way, she kept on making it with extra ketchup. Then, maybe, one day years later she added some green onions when she was out of garlic, and that became part of her recipe. (Or, if your fam-

ily wasn't as lucky, maybe she added some peanut butter when she was out of garlic.) In any case, chances are your mom's meat loaf is unique.

Sometime after my widowed father moved into an apartment, he passed along to me a small loose-leaf recipe book that my mother had been adding to for years. That recipe book was a real piece of time travel for me. Not only was it full of those tried-and-true pretty-good recipes, but lots of them were attributed — many to people whose names I had almost forgotten: long-gone relatives, my grandmother's canasta-playing friends, neighbors from several houses and many years before. My mother's kitchen was in those pages.

Over the course of my checkered career in comestible journalism, I've acquired an awful lot of cookbooks, some of them very good indeed. But many of my favorite recipes are in that homemade volume.

Such as meat loaf.

Just in case you somehow don't have any meat loaf recipes to

> *Then, maybe, one day years later [your mom] added some green onions when she was out of garlic, and that became part of her recipe. (Or, if your family wasn't as lucky, maybe she added some peanut butter when she was out of garlic.)*

Mary Wollstonecraft Shelley publishes her novel *Frankenstein*.

pass along, or in case you're in the generation that is now waiting for its parents to start typing out their meat loaf recipes but you're kind of impatient, here are three very nice, very simple versions. Two of them are in my mother's loose-leaf recipe book. The third (the teriyaki one) is a slight modification of a recipe from my newspaper colleague Mary Hart. (She likes meat loaf, too.) I'm also tossing in a rather complicated recipe, just so you don't get the wrong impression about life (not *everything* is easy). It's for pâté, which is meat loaf taken to several logical extremes and left there. Believe it or not, this recipe is simpler than many pâtés. I like it, but if you're not into liver, you might want to pass.

May I make one final none-of-my-business suggestion before we do recipes? If your mom is still around, go cook a meal with her. It'll be a favor for both of you.

Crunch-Top Meat Loaf

2 tablespoons butter
2 cups soft bread cubes, divided
1 egg
1½ pounds lean ground beef
½ cup ketchup
2 tablespoons chopped onion
1 teaspoon salt
½ cup water

Melt the butter in a large saucepan. Toss 1½ cups of the bread cubes in the melted butter. Beat the egg lightly. In a large bowl, combine the remaining ½ cup bread cubes with the beaten egg, ground beef, ketchup, chopped onion, salt, and water. (If you can find a way of doing this that doesn't ultimately involve plunging your hands into it, good for you.) Pack the mixture into a loaf pan or a round cake pan. Press the buttered bread cubes on top. Bake at 350° F for 1 hour. Serves 6.

Barbecue Meat Loaf

1 medium onion
1 egg
1½ pounds lean ground beef
1 cup bread crumbs, fresh or dried
2 (8-ounce) cans tomato sauce, divided
1 teaspoon salt
¼ teaspoon pepper
½ cup water
2 tablespoons prepared mustard
3 tablespoons brown sugar
3 tablespoons vinegar
2 teaspoons Worcestershire sauce

Peel and chop the onion. Lightly beat the egg. In a large bowl, combine the onion, egg, ground beef, crumbs, ½ can of the tomato sauce, salt, and pepper. (We're speaking of the same kind of messy operation you ran into in the previous recipe. Some folks recommend putting your hands into plastic bags for an exercise like this. I dunno. Wash them anyway.)

1820

John James Audubon sets off from Philadelphia to pursue his dream of drawing life-size pictures of the birds of America.

Pack the mixture into a loaf pan or round cake pan. Combine the remaining 1½ cans tomato sauce, water, mustard, brown sugar, vinegar, and Worcestershire sauce. Pour on enough sauce to cover the loaf. Bake at 350° F for 1½ hours, basting occasionally with the remaining sauce. Serves 6.

Teriyaki Meat Loaf

3 (8¼-ounce) cans crushed pineapple in syrup
1½ pounds lean ground beef
¾ cup soft bread crumbs
½ cup chopped onion
6 tablespoons soy sauce
1 tablespoon Worcestershire sauce
2 cloves garlic, minced
1 teaspoon salt
½ teaspoon pepper

GLAZE
1 tablespoon cornstarch
1 teaspoon ground ginger
3 tablespoons soy sauce
3 tablespoons dry sherry

Drain the pineapple. Reserve the syrup and ⅜ cup of the pineapple for the glaze. Combine the remaining pineapple, ground beef, crumbs, onion, soy sauce, Worcestershire sauce, garlic, salt, and pepper. Pack the mixture into a loaf pan and bake at 350° F for 1¼ hours.

When it is almost serving time, prepare the glaze. In a saucepan, combine the cornstarch and ginger. Stir in the reserved pineapple syrup, soy sauce, and sherry. Bring to a boil and continue to boil for 1 minute. Stir in the reserved pineapple. Spoon some of the glaze over the meat loaf; pass the rest. Serves 6.

Liver Pâté

2 shallots
1 apple
1 clove garlic
1 small onion
1 orange
½ cup shelled pistachios (from 4 or 5 ounces of pistachios in their shells)
3 tablespoons butter or margarine
1 pound chicken livers
1 pound lean ground pork
¼ cup brandy
¼ cup heavy cream
juice of 1 lemon
2 eggs, lightly beaten
2 tablespoons flour
1 tablespoon salt
1½ teaspoons pepper
½ teaspoon ground allspice
¾ pound lean bacon

NOTE *for those who don't read recipes through first but just go sailing right in:* The pâté must be chilled after baking, so allow an extra 6 hours or so, preferably overnight.

Peel and mince the shallots. Peel and core the apple and slice it thin. Peel and mince the garlic. Peel and chop the onion. Peel and section

1822

Clement Clarke Moore writes his poem "A Visit from St. Nicholas," which will later be commonly referred to by its first line, " 'Twas the Night Before Christmas."

the orange, removing any seeds. Shell the pistachios. Set the orange sections and pistachios aside. Sauté the shallots, apple, garlic, and onion in the butter until the onion is translucent and the apple is soft.

Chop the chicken livers finely by hand or in a food processor. In a large bowl, combine the livers, pork, and sautéed mixture. Add the brandy, cream, lemon juice, and eggs. Mix well. (If you thought the mixtures in the other recipes were hard to take in this condition, this one is appalling. Seriously consider plastic bags or kitchen gloves for your hands.) Add the pistachios, flour, salt, pepper, and allspice.

Completely line a loaf pan with strips of bacon — across the bottom, up the sides, and up the ends. Allow any extra lengths to hang over the sides and ends. Pack half the meat mixture into the pan. Arrange the orange sections in a row or two, making sure that there are no lengthwise spaces without any orange on them (so that every slice of pâté will have some orange showing), then cover with the remaining meat mixture.

Cover the top of the mixture with additional lengthwise strips of bacon, tucking them in on the ends. Set the loaf pan in a larger pan of hot water and bake at 350° F for 1¼ to 1½ hours. Test for doneness by inserting a knife. Juices should run clear yellow, with no trace of pink.

While the pâté is still hot, pour the fat out of the pan (being careful not to pour out the pâté at the same time). Cover the pâté with a sheet of aluminum foil, put another loaf pan on top of that so that the bottom of the second pan is atop the pâté, and put several pounds of weights into the second pan (4 or 5 cans of soup or whatever will do). Let stand at room temperature for several hours, until fully cool, then refrigerate for at least 4 hours. Unmold before slicing and serving.

Serves 12 or more, depending on how much they like pâté. Could serve an army of people who prefer meat loaf.

IF YOU SUFFER BACKACHES, *empty your pockets, wear looser clothing, and don't cross your legs.*

1823

John Howard Payne writes the song "Home, Sweet Home," which ends with this line: "Be it ever so humble, there's no place like home."

■ *Who knows? The days when every family had a milk cow might return, so let's not forget the basics.*

In the Event You Have a Cow...

HERE'S HOW TO MAKE YOUR own butter and cottage cheese — and ice cream!

Butter

1 quart heavy cream (35 percent butterfat)

Heat the cream in a double boiler to 160° to 165° F, stirring frequently. Chill quickly to 50° F. Pour into a large mixer bowl. Make a cover for the bowl from heavy aluminum foil and insert the beaters through a hole made in the center. (This is to prevent spattering.) Beat at high speed until flecks of butter show. Then turn to low speed and beat until the butter comes and the buttermilk separates. Pour off the buttermilk. (Save for baking.)

Add cold water equal in quantity to the buttermilk poured off. Beat at the lowest speed for a short time. Pour off the water and repeat, using slightly colder water each time, until the water drained off is clear. This is "washing" the butter. Work out the rest of the water by pressing with a wooden spoon. Salt the butter, ½ teaspoon to 1 pound of butter. Mold and cover with a moisture-proof wrap. This butter can be frozen.

Old-Fashioned Cottage Cheese

Heat very slowly 1 quart unpasteurized naturally sour skim milk in a double boiler. Put in a strainer lined with cheesecloth and drain. Rinse with about a quart of warm water and repeat rinsing two more times. Let drain until the curd is free of the whey. Moisten with cream and salt to taste.

Cottage Cheese (Without a Cow)

Use pasteurized skim milk or reconstituted instant nonfat and pasteurized dry milk. It takes 1 gallon of milk to make about 1 pound of cottage cheese.

A starter culture is needed to make the cheese. Two days before you intend to make the cheese, prepare this culture. Have 2 pints of pasteurized milk and refrigerate 1 pint. To the other pint add 1 tablespoon of fresh buttermilk and keep it at 70° to 75° F for 16 to 24 hours, until it curdles. Then, with a scalded and cooled teaspoon, add 1 teaspoon of the curdled milk to the reserved pint of milk and culture this fresh pint until it curdles (12 to 18 hours). This is the starter for the cheese.

1826

James Sharp of Northampton, England, builds the prototype for the first practical gas stove for use in his home. He will start to manufacture these stoves in 1836.

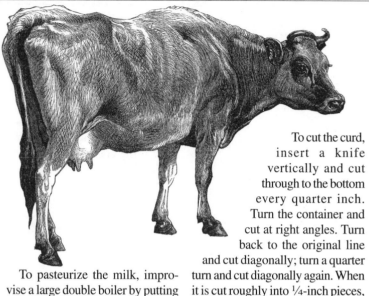

To cut the curd, insert a knife vertically and cut through to the bottom every quarter inch. Turn the container and cut at right angles. Turn back to the original line and cut diagonally; turn a quarter turn and cut diagonally again. When it is cut roughly into ¼-inch pieces, let stand for 10 minutes.

To pasteurize the milk, improvise a large double boiler by putting a smaller pan inside a larger kettle. Heat water in the outer container until the milk in the inner container reaches 145° F and keep the milk at this temperature for 30 minutes. Cool the milk to 72° F by emptying the outer kettle and filling it with cold water.

The milk to be made into cheese should be kept at about 72° F until the curd is formed and cut (best done by keeping it in another container of water). Add ½ cup or more of starter. Cover with a clean cloth and let stand for 16 to 24 hours. Test to see if the curd is ready for cutting by inserting a spatula into the curd at the side of the container and gently pulling the curd. When it breaks quickly and smoothly, it is ready to be cut.

Add water at 72° F to the outer container and heat the water slowly to raise the temperature of the curd and whey to 100° F (should take 30 to 40 minutes), stirring gently with a large spoon every 4 or 5 minutes. Heat the curd to 115° F during the next 15 minutes; stir more frequently and keep at this temperature for 30 minutes. Stir constantly and test for firmness. When firm enough, stop heating, dip off most off the whey, and put the remaining curd and whey into a colander lined with cheesecloth. Drain for 2 to 3 minutes.

Gather the corners of the cheesecloth and dunk the bag of curd in a pan of cool, clean water for 2 to 3 minutes to rinse. Then rinse thor-

1827

The friction match is (accidentally) invented by John Walker in Stockton-on-Tees, England.

oughly again in ice water to chill. Put the bag of curd in a colander to drain. Transfer the curd to a mixing bowl and add 1 teaspoon of salt for each pound of curd and ¼ cup of either sweet or sour cream or half-and-half. Mix thoroughly.

Vanilla Ice Cream

4 cups cream, divided
1 cup sugar
⅛ teaspoon salt
1½ teaspoons vanilla extract (or a vanilla pod heated in the cream)

Heat 1 cup of the cream very slowly, but do not boil. Stir in the sugar and salt until dissolved. Chill. Add the remaining 3 cups cream and vanilla. Freeze (see below). Makes 1½ quarts.

Strawberry or Peach Ice Cream

1 cup sugar
⅛ teaspoon salt
2 cups mashed fruit
1 teaspoon vanilla extract
4 cups cream

Add the sugar and salt to the fruit and let stand until dissolved. Chill. Add the other ingredients and freeze (see below).

To Freeze

Scald the freezer can and chill. The mixture to be frozen should be cold. Fill the can two-thirds full, cover, and try the crank to see that it's turning the can properly.

Fill the tub around the can with 3 parts crushed ice to 1 part coarse rock salt. (Measure out by scoopfuls.) Pack the crushed ice (or snow) about one-third of the way up, then put in the remaining ice and salt in layers to the top of the can. Pack down the salt and ice tightly. Wait for 5 minutes, then turn the crank slowly and steadily. First one child turns, and the other sits on the freezer (covered with a thick pad of newspaper); then the other child has a turn at cranking. It will take 5 to 10 minutes to get the ice cream mushy; crank as hard as possible until you feel it is frozen solid. More ice and salt should be added, in the same proportions, when the level goes below the top of the can.

Drain the freezing salt water, take the dasher from the can (the kids get to lick it), pack down the ice cream firmly with a spoon, and put on a solid cover. Repack the freezer with 4 parts crushed ice to 1 part salt. Cover tightly with newspaper or old carpeting. In an hour or two, eat!

The color green helps soothe nerves and promotes general healing.

> ■ *Just because people have been brewing coffee for hundreds of years doesn't mean they have been doing it right. Not that it's difficult: All it takes is perfect water at the perfect temperature, poured over the perfect beans, freshly roasted and ground just to perfection.*

Anyone Can Make
a Perfect Cup of Coffee

BY LESLIE LAND

THE MELANCHOLY TRUTH IS THAT the two most commonly used American ways to make coffee result in the worst coffee in existence. You'd think the main villain was instant coffee, for which 1,175,000 bags of green coffee (enough to make 4,272,727,200 cups) were imported in 1984. But the real offender is perked coffee, made in a percolator, glub-a-glub-a-glub, the inescapable sound of morning for several wholly misguided generations. Mostly it's awful because it is boiled, the one thing that coffee should never be. Boiling disperses the fragile, rich aromas that are so important to flavor, while it concentrates acids, extracts extra tannin, and intensifies bitterness.

For *absolutely* the best coffee, you would have to start by roasting your own beans. Fragrance and flavor deteriorate quickly after green coffee is roasted, and from its ancient Middle Eastern beginnings to the turn of the 20th century, almost everyone everywhere who made coffee roasted the beans as needed. This is, however, a modest proposal, so we will simply insist that the coffee be as freshly roasted as possible, ground at the last minute.

Although the beans are obviously crucial, water is the main ingredient in coffee. If the water doesn't taste good, the coffee won't taste good. Avoid using very hard water or water that has been artificially softened, heavily chlorinated,

Followers of Reverend Sylvester Graham, an outspoken pioneer of health and hygiene, are inspired to make the graham cracker, a whole-grain cracker that aids digestion.

or otherwise made to taste bad. In some places, this means using bottled water.

Draw fresh cold water (hot might pick up impurities from the pipes) and put it on to boil. Use hot water to rinse the china, earthenware, stainless steel, glass, enamel, silver, or gold (but *not* tin or aluminum) coffeepot, so that it will be warmed up. Do the same with the cups. If you intend to use milk, put it in a double boiler to heat up gradually. Cream should be allowed to come to room temperature.

Decide which kind of coffee you want to make. Filtered coffee is light in body and aftertaste, but very clear, refreshing, and sediment-free. Steeped coffee is a heavier, richer product because none of the superfine flavoring compounds have been trapped and filtered out.

For filtered coffee: Put the pot where it will keep warm — in a larger pan of simmering water, on a heat spreader, or at the side of the woodstove. When you hear the water about to boil, grind the coffee quite fine, not quite to a powder. Put the filter holder over the pot, line it

Be sure to use a wide-bottomed, high-spouted pot, so the grounds have plenty of chance to sink out of the liquid and stay sunk at pouring time.

with filter paper, and for each cup of coffee add 1½ to 2 tablespoons of ground beans. Tamp down lightly, so that the water will take more time to filter through. When the water boils, turn off the heat and let its temperature fall back a few degrees, then pour on only enough to dampen the coffee. Allow the grounds to swell for about 2 minutes, then add the rest of the water, in batches if necessary. Serve as soon as filtering is completed. (*Note:* Filter papers are pretty close to tasteless when they leave the factory but will pick up strong odors — garlic, cheese, tobacco smoke — if stored near them.)

For steeped coffee: Follow the instructions above, except:

1. Be sure to use a wide-bottomed, high-spouted pot, so the grounds have plenty of chance to sink out of the liquid and stay sunk at pouring time.

2. Grind the coffee (2 tablespoons per cup) only to the texture of rough cornmeal. Put it in the pot, pour on the not-quite-boiling water, and stir well.

1830

Edward Budding applies for a patent on the world's first lawn mower.

3. Let the coffee infuse for 4 minutes, stir again briefly, and let steep for 2 to 5 minutes more, depending on how strong (and clear) you want the product to be. Dash in a few drops of cold water, which will sink through the hot coffee, carrying stray particles to the bottom of the pot. Serve at once, not letting the liquid sit around on the grounds for very long.

About that egg. Many recipes call for eggshell, egg white and shell, or an entire egg at the end of the process. The idea is to have the albumen in the egg bond with the floating coffee particles, carrying them out of the liquid. It isn't really necessary, and it certainly isn't too tasty.

Choosing the Right Beans

A well-stocked coffee store can be uncomfortably reminiscent of a well-stocked wine store, a place where it's easy to feel daunted by an exotic and unknown array. You can just taste until you figure out what you enjoy — unlike wine, almost all specialty coffee is pretty good, and even the most expensive is a

Arabicas are labeled (and valued) according to place of origin. Generally speaking, the higher the elevation at which the coffee grew, the better the flavor will be.

bargain if you look at the cost per cup.

Although about a dozen species of coffee shrub (*Coffea* genus) are cultivated, only two have major commercial importance. *Coffea robusta* is easier to grow than *Coffea arabica*, and more prolific, hence a great deal cheaper. Though rich in caffeine, it is bitter and poor-flavored. Robustas are mainly used as cheap fillers and for the manufacture of instant coffee. Arabicas are labeled (and valued) according to place of origin. Generally speaking, the higher the elevation at which the coffee grew, the better the flavor will be.

The roast: Green coffee beans improve with age, but their flavor must be developed and made soluble by roasting. Heat breaks down fats and carbohydrates as it develops the coffeol, an oily, volatile, aromatic (and still somewhat poorly understood) substance that is the soul of the coffee. The longer the roasting, the darker the roast, which leads to a sort of false impression. Roasting reduces both acid and caffeine and brings coffee oils to

1832

Private bathtubs are installed for the first time in homes, in a row of model houses in Philadelphia.

the surface, so those sinister-looking, shiny black beans are actually much milder in effect than the ones that look like milk chocolate. The reputation of dark-roast coffee for bitter strength is more a function of the intense ways it is brewed than anything else.

And there you have it, all the ingredients for a flavorful, aromatic, bracing, soothing *perfect* cup of coffee.

ANECDOTES & PLEASANTRIES

Let's Have Another Cup of Coffee
(Two points of view.)

1657, England
From the *Public Advisor:*

IN BARTHOLOMEW LANE ON THE back side of the Old Exchange, the drink called 'Coffee' is for sale. It is a very wholesome and physical drink, having many excellent virtues, closes the orifice of the stomach, fortifies the heat within, helpeth digestion, quickens the spirits, maketh the heart lightsome, is good against eyesores, coughs or colds, rhumes, consumption, headache, dropsy, gout, scurvy, Kings evil, and many others. Is to be sold both in the morning and at three o'clock in the afternoon."

1977, United States
From *Commentary:*

JUST ONE CUP OF COFFEE DOES amazing things to the body. The temperature of the stomach jumps 10 to 15 percent; salivary glands double their flow; the heart beats 15 percent faster; the lungs work 13 percent harder; blood vessels dilate in the brain and near the heart; the metabolism rate goes up 25 percent and the workload of the kidneys doubles." (And, at $4 a pound or thereabouts, it also flattens the purse!)

Courtesy of H. L. Miller

1837

Parole, with stringent supervision and restrictions, is offered to prisoners in Australia as part of their rehabilitation process.

The Art of
Self-Reliance

(Note to readers of this book: In this chapter, you will learn how to catch fish, grow vegetables, shovel snow, fix shoes that pinch, tell time by the stars, and find north without a compass. Oh, you already know all that? Then proceed to the next chapter.)

Notes for a Commencement Speech

CONGRATULATIONS, SENIORS. You have had four more years of education and lived to tell the tale. Before this ceremony is over, you will hear a lot of people praise you for all that you have learned and remind you of the priceless value of knowledge.

But not from me. I am here to say three cheers for ignorance.

Somebody has to — ignorance has few defenders. We hear it decried everywhere. Americans, we are told, are ignorant of geography, of mathematics, of science, of grammar, of their own history. We have to fight ignorance. Let's declare war on ignorance.

Let's not. Instead, let's try to understand, accept, and perhaps even celebrate our ignorance.

First cheer: *Ignorance rules!*

The last thousand years have seen a continuing and astounding increase in our awareness and understanding, from the intri-

1837

Charles Lewis Tiffany opens a fancy goods and stationery store in New York City. He will gradually concentrate on jewelry.

cacies of atomic and subatomic structure to the awesome grandeur of the universe and its beginnings.

But ironically, every increase in knowledge — every step up this mountain — has given us wider, grander views of what we don't know. We have moved from a time in which one intelligent person might reasonably expect to learn, in one lifetime, almost everything known, to a time in which all of us, collectively, have no chance whatsoever to learn even the tiniest percentage of what is knowable. As physician and writer Lewis Thomas put it, "The greatest of all the accomplishments of 20th century science has been the discovery of human ignorance."

The more we know, the more we know what we don't know. "Our knowledge can only be finite," said philosopher Karl Popper, "while our ignorance must necessarily be infinite."

So what do we do about this apparently hopeless situation? That brings me to my second cheer: *Ignorance is bliss!*

Not long ago, an international team of physicists announced their discovery that neutrinos have mass. Don't ask me to explain it — my ignorance of physics is nearly perfect. It was big news, got headlines all over the world, threw physicists everywhere into a tizzy. "It's very exciting," said Nobel Prize winner Leon Lederman of the Fermi National Accelerator Laboratory. "It also exacerbates and emphasizes our total confusion."

About the only thing that makes a scientist happier than proof of success is proof of failure. Failure of a theory means we don't

1838

Charles Dickens finishes his novel *Oliver Twist.*

know what we thought we knew, and that's good — there's more to be learned. Another physicist, Heinz Pagels, wrote, "The capacity to tolerate complexity and welcome contradiction, not the need for simplicity and certainty, is the attribute of an explorer."

Ignorance will not only make you happy — it will cure your melancholy. My favorite book is *The Once and Future King* by T. H. White. It is the story of King Arthur. One day, when the boy Arthur is feeling depressed, he goes to his tutor, Merlin the magician, who gives him this advice:

> *The best thing for being sad is to learn something. That is the only thing that never fails. You may grow old and trembling in your anatomies, you may lie awake at night listening to the disorder of your veins, you may miss your only love, you may see the world about you devastated by evil lunatics, or know your honor trampled in the sewers of baser minds. There is only one thing for it then — to learn. Learn why the world wags, and what wags it. That is the only thing which the mind can never exhaust, never alienate, never be tortured by, never fear or distrust, and never dream of regretting. Learning is the thing for you. Look at what a lot of things there are to learn — pure science, the only purity there is. You can learn astronomy in a lifetime, natural history in three, literature in six. And then, after you have exhausted a milliard lifetimes in biology and medicine and theocriticism and geography and history and economics — why, you can start to make a cartwheel out of the appropriate wood, or spend 50 years learning to begin to learn to beat your adversary at fencing. After that you can start again on mathematics, until it is time to learn to plow.*

1839

Kirkpatrick Macmillan of Dumfries, Scotland, completes the first workable bicycle, complete with brakes and pedals, a vast improvement over the earlier (1818) velocipede, used for coasting.

Isn't that beautiful? Ignorance represents the potential for learning. Ignorance is the *prerequisite* for learning. Ignorance is the vacuum that nature won't tolerate, the well that never goes dry, the itch that can't be scratched away. Chet Raymo, a science writer for the *Boston Globe*, put it this way: "Ignorance is a vessel waiting to be filled, permission for growth, a foundation for the electrifying encounter with mystery."

And finally, my third cheer: *Ignorance will keep you humble!*

There's a story told about the great Danish physicist Niels Bohr. He was walking along a beach one day with a student, and the student was telling Bohr what a great man he was, how much he knew about the workings of the universe. Bohr picked up a stone and showed it to the student. "This," he said, "is what I know." Then he

turned away and threw the stone into the ocean. "And that," he said, pointing to the endless sea, "is what I don't know."

Bravo for Bohr, who knew how to respond to sycophants! More human misery has been caused by people certain of their own wisdom than by people who aren't absolutely sure they're right. Joshua Slocum, the man who first sailed around the world alone, once remarked that he was never so frightened at sea as when he was aboard a ship whose captain always knew exactly where he was. And the people who framed our Constitution understood the same thing: They weren't interested in an efficient form of government. They wanted an inefficient government, a clumsy, hog-tied, slow-moving Rube Goldberg form of government, which

1839

William F. Harnden takes out an ad in the *Boston Transcript* offering his services as an express messenger to New York City once a week. With this ad, the express business is born.

couldn't decide anything of importance very quickly. They wanted an ignorant government, because they knew that an infallible government — better known as the "divine right of kings" — was a constant threat to the liberty of its people.

I've quoted philosophers, doctors, writers, and scientists in this speech — let me close with a jokester. Josh Billings was the pen name of Henry Wheeler Shaw, a 19th-century humorist who specialized in puncturing windbags. He gave ignorance its due in fewer and better words than anyone: "It is better to know nothing than to know what ain't so."

Good luck, seniors. Here's wishing you a future full of uncertainty, doubt, and confusion. May you remain ignorant all your days and look at the world with stupid, wondering eyes.

Tim Clark

1840

Postage stamps are used for the first time in England.

■ *Despite the fact that man has been building fires for tens of thousands of years, there seem to be many differing opinions as to the right way to do it. You surely have your own advice to give on this subject, but do try to keep an open mind.*

The Forgotten Art of Building a Long-Lasting Fire

BY RAYMOND W. DYER

THE FIRE ON THE HEARTH IS ONE of the very few things that has been passed down all the way from primitive cave dwellers to modern man. The fireplace warms all — the room, the conversation, and the people about. However, we often have many fireplaces and all too few fires burning in them — probably because we have lost the art of building a long-lasting fire without constant and bothersome attention.

Most people begin with no ashes in the fireplace and proceed to build the fire with paper and dry kindling wood laid directly on top of the andirons. This explodes into a large, scary blaze. As soon as it dies down, so that one can get close to it, larger logs are thrown on top, and another large, uncontrollable blaze quickly burns and dies out.

All of this results in a fire constantly needing attention and always either too hot or too cold, too large or too small. It also can result in a scorched mantel or a second good fire up in the chimney.

All of this amateur nonsense is the result of too much draft — which in turn results from the improper use of the andirons. You should not think

1842

For the first time, a surgical operation is performed on an anesthetized patient. Dr. Crawford Long of Georgia gives James Venable ether before removing a tumor from his neck. Venable feels no pain during the surgery.

of the andirons as a grate but simply as uprights to prevent the logs from rolling out of the fireplace.

To build a fire of good steady heat with a small blaze and minimum use of wood, the fireplace should be covered with a bed of ashes about one or two inches above the andirons' legs. If ashes are not available, sand may be used.

Now choose a log eight to ten inches in diameter. Place this, called the back log, against the brick back of the fireplace, with a slightly smaller log balanced on top of it. Then place a log four to six inches in diameter in the front of the fireplace, just in back of the andirons. This is called the fore log. It is essential that these logs be well bedded down in the ashes, as the point is to keep the flames and draft out from under the logs so only their tops and faces burn.

It is essential that [the back and fore] logs be well bedded down in the ashes, as the point is to keep the flames and draft out from under the logs so only their tops and faces burn.

Build the fire between the back and fore logs, starting with paper and kindling and gradually building up to four- to six-inch logs. Once the fire is lit, the fore and back logs will eventually burn through. As this happens, move them into the center of the fire and replace them with new logs, once more well bedded in ashes.

This results in a fire that burns with a hot blue flame and red-hot coals. The face of the back log burns red-hot and reflects the heat of the fire. The fore log holds the fire in and prevents air from passing under it.

If you want less fire, you can dampen this arrangement by putting a shovel of ashes on it. If you prefer more blaze, a few small sticks of kindling can be added to the top of the fire.

If a good fire remains when you retire for the night, cover it with ashes from the side of the fireplace. This will hold all night, and when you uncover it the next day, or even the next evening, you will find a bed of red-hot coals upon which to build a new fire.

This is how heat and fire were maintained from day to day in colonial homes, when such fires were a hard necessity.

It goes almost without saying that a hardwood such as oak, maple, cherry, or birch is the best to burn. This must be cut in late winter or early spring so that it can dry and cure in the hot summer sun. A drying and curing period of at least six months is necessary.

1843

The first commercially printed Christmas cards are available in London.

FARMER'S CALENDAR

Wood Sniffing

SPLITTING FIREWOOD is widely appreciated as exercise for the upper body and as an aid to reflection, but the work deserves to be better known as an adventure in connoisseurship in the most rarefied realm, that of the nose. We have been given our five senses to enable us to discriminate, to mark differences and similarities between things. Smell is the finest discriminator of all. Learn to use your nose while you're splitting hardwood, and it will open for you a rich volume of distinctions.

Compare the heavy smell of olives that comes from a fresh-split block of red oak with the similar but far more delicate smell of white oak or with the smoky, almost musky olive smell of butternut. Beech is faintly sweet; paper birch has a stronger, sweeter scent; and black birch smells like bubble gum. Maple, to me, has little character besides a kind of vague vegetative smell, and ash is odorless. No doubt a finer nose than mine could make something of the last two woods as well.

Let no one imagine that wood sniffing is a mere frippery. The potential is there for hard financial advantage. Why couldn't a really educated woodpile nose attain the kind of refinement we hear the whiskey tasters of Scotland possess? They can sniff a glass of Scotch and tell you not only which district it came from but also which glen, which brook, which distiller. Since there's a good deal of money in Scotch, a lot can hang on the findings of an expert nose. Why couldn't the same apply to wood sniffing? Firewood dealers are a tough lot, almost the last of the old-time freebooting capitalists. The buyer needs all the help he can get. A sniffer who could knock ten bucks off the price of a load for an off scent would be a valuable man.

1844

Alexandre Dumas writes
The Three Musketeers.

■ *For those rare occasions when you leave home without your compass, we suggest you learn how to keep from getting lost. One method involves your wristwatch; another two stakes in the ground; and many utilize stars, certain plants, and even animals.*

Some Good Ways to Find North Without a Compass

BY DOUGALD MacDONALD

M Y SCOUTMASTER INSISTED I would never get lost if I looked for the moss that grows only on the north side of trees. Well, maybe, but it never worked for me; given enough shade and moisture, moss will grow just about anywhere. Such imprecision is typical of most of the so-called natural compasses heralded in survival manuals; nevertheless, there are some that can be quite accurate, as well as fun to test.

For instance, you may notice that deciduous trees grow predominantly on the south side of hills, but conifers are usually found on the north. In the high Rockies, limber pines grow on the south and east sides of mountains, Engelmann spruce on the north. Plants often adapt to the existing conditions: Trees grow fuller on the south side, and evergreens are usually bent away from the prevailing wind direction (if the wind is usually from the northwest, the treetops will grow to the southeast). In the desert, the giant barrel cactus always leans to the south. Such tendencies can indicate directions to a knowledgeable observer. The pilot weed, whose leaves grow in a north–south line, helped guide the first settlers across the Great Plains and became known as the "compass plant of the prairies."

Other natural signs are supported less by empirical proof than by long tradition. Spruce gum drawn from the south side of trees is said to have a clear, amber color, but that from the north side will be soiled and grayish. Leonardo da Vinci was the first to report that the north side

The pilot weed, whose leaves grow in a north–south line, helped guide the first settlers across the Great Plains and became known as the "compass plant of the prairies."

1845

Elastic bands are patented by Stephen Perry of London.

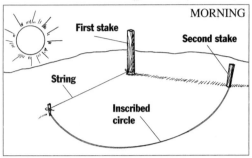

MORNING

First stake
Second stake
String
Inscribed circle

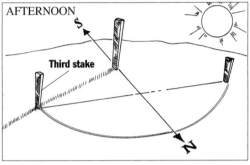

AFTERNOON

Third stake

S

N

is a mistake, however, to assume that the Sun rises in the east and sets in the west. It does approximately, of course, but depending on your latitude, the shape of the horizon, and the time of year, sunrise and sunset may be as much as 40 degrees off the cardinal points. The Moon, too, reaches its highest point above the horizon at due south, but this can be predicted conveniently only once a month — exactly at midnight at full Moon.

of most trees has thicker bark and wider growth rings to protect against chill north winds. Spiderwebs can show direction, too: Given a choice, spiders will orient the web facing southeast to catch the morning sun. In practice, however, they can only lay the first thread with the wind, so most webs face parallel to the prevailing wind. Animals like a warm, sunny home as much as people do, and most birds' nests, squirrels' nests, and even anthills are found to the lee of the prevailing wind, often facing toward the Sun.

The Sun was probably man's first natural guide. At noon, it lies due south every day of the year. It

It is easy to find north within just a few degrees by tracing the movement of shadows. At midmorning, anytime from 8:30 to 11:00 A.M., drive a stake into the ground and mark the end of its shadow with

N

S

1846

Artist John Banvard unveils the world's largest painting, *Panorama of the Mississippi.* The painting is 12 feet high and 3 miles long.

another stake. Tie a string to the first stake, and using the distance between the two stakes as the radius, inscribe a circle in the dirt around the original stake. As the Sun gets higher, the shadow will fall within the circle. After noon, the shadow will grow longer; with a third stake, mark the point where it hits the circle again. Now measure the distance between the two points on the circle and locate the middle (try taking the distance with the string and halving it); the midpoint and the original stake will be the end points of a north–south line.

Another method that sacrifices some accuracy but takes only a few minutes uses a wristwatch. Place the watch on a level surface and hold a match or small stick upright against its edge — a thin enough object will cast a faint shadow even on overcast days. Now turn the watch slowly until the stick's shadow is aligned with the hour hand. A line drawn from the center to a point halfway between the hour hand and 12 on the dial will point toward south.

On a clear night, you can use the stars to find directions by tracing their relative movements. Drive a stake at eye level in an open clearing. Drive another, taller stake behind it, so the two tips line up on a bright star. After a few minutes, the star will seem to have moved across the sky (actually, the stars only *seem* to move as the Earth rotates beneath them). The apparent movement indicates the direction you are facing: If your star moves up, you are facing east; if it moves down, you're facing west; right means south, and left means north.

Of all the natural direction finders, however, only one is truly reliable. The North Star, Polaris, lies directly over the North Pole. It can be found by connecting the two stars marking the end of the familiar Big Dipper and tracing a line across the sky to the next bright star — about the distance from your outstretched thumb to your middle finger held at arm's length. Long before the compass was invented, before magnetism had been discovered, mariners were navigating by the North Star. It moves only slightly during the year and is by far the most accurate of nature's beacons.

> *The North Star, Polaris, lies directly over the North Pole. . . . Long before the compass was invented, before magnetism had been discovered, mariners were navigating by the North Star.*

1846

The eighth planet, Neptune, is discovered.

FARMER'S CALENDAR

Snow to Water

ROM A SAFE DISTANCE, anything that's possible looks easy. It's the theoretical point of view: If you *can* do a thing, you will. Then experience intervenes, and you learn that the street of reality has high curbs.

Nowhere is the gap between the possible and the practical wider than in the beliefs of those who move to the country from places having more complete amenities. Your house is without a modern stove? No problem: There's a wood-burning range with an oven. We'll cook the turkey in that. How hard can it be? Need six cords of wood to heat the house in the winter? No problem: We'll cut it on the weekend; after all, there are trees all around. It'll be fun.

You learn fast. I remember the first time a winter storm knocked out our electricity and left us without running water. I took it well at first because we had a couple of feet of fresh snow on the ground. What is snow, I reflected, but water? We don't really need running water; we'll just melt snow. I wasn't wrong, of course, but reality is in the ratios, and the water-to-snow ratio is not favorable to the comfort I felt in the fact that snow is nothing but water. I found that the five-gallon pot we use for lobsters (our largest) yielded about a quart of water when filled with snow and heated. That's good news if all you need is a cup of tea, but it's not much help if you want to bathe, do a wash, and clean up the dirty dishes. Yes, you *could* melt, say, 1,000 gallons of snow, but you won't. You'll do what I did: Wait disconsolately for the power to come back on and reflect on the difference between the way you know things to be and the way they are.

1848

The California gold rush starts when gold is discovered along the American River at Sutter's sawmill. San Francisco's population of 800 will more than triple in the next two years.

ANECDOTES & PLEASANTRIES

How to Estimate Distances Easily
(A bona fide "rule of thumb.")

YOUR ARM is about ten times longer than the distance between your eyes. That fact, together with a bit of applied trigonometry, can be used to estimate the distance between you and any object of approximately known size.

Imagine, for example, that you're standing on the side of a hill, trying to decide how far it is to the top of a low hill on the other side of the valley. Just below the hilltop is a barn, which you feel reasonably sure is about 100 feet wide on the side facing you.

Hold one arm straight out in front of you — elbow straight, thumb pointing up. Close one eye and align one edge of your thumb with one edge of the barn. Without moving your head or arm, switch eyes, now sighting with the eye that was closed and closing the other one. Your thumb will appear to jump sideways as a result of the change in perspective.

How far did it move? (Be sure to sight the same edge of your thumb when you switch eyes). Let's say it jumped about five times the width of the barn, or about 500 feet. Now multiply that figure by the handy constant 10 (the ratio of the length of your arm to the distance between your eyes), and you get the distance between you and the barn — 5000 feet, or about 1 mile. The accompanying diagram should make the whole process clear.

With a little practice, you'll find that you can perform a quick thumb-jump estimate in just a few seconds, and the result will usually be more accurate than an out-and-out guess. At a minimum, it will provide some assurance that the figure is in the ballpark — which, in many cases, is as close as you need to get.

Courtesy of Jon Vara

├─ 500' ─┤

Barn (approx. 100')

5000'

(Diagram not to scale)

20"

2" (distance between eyes)

1851

A new daily newspaper, the *New York Times*, hits the streets. Its slogan, "All the news that's fit to print," will come later, in 1896.

■ *Here's the best advice you're likely to get on fishing, boiled down to four basic steps. Good luck!*

The Four Fundamentals of Successful Fishing

BY HAROLD F. BLAISDELL

1 BE IN THE RIGHT PLACE AT THE RIGHT TIME.

Assess the potential of your immediate vicinity by prospecting. For more distant waters, you can write to the appropriate state or provincial fish and game department. General rules regarding the right time are as follows:

Trout: When water temperatures are between 50° and 55° F. Fish metabolism and feeding reach their highest rates when water temperatures are rising from the 40s and entering the optimum range. For the fly fisherman, it's when mayflies are hatching and trout are feeding at the surface. The earliest hatches of the season usually occur in the middle of

the day, but in summer they are mainly dusk-to-dark affairs. For the bait fisherman, the right time is early spring, and later on, when stream levels rise from summer showers. In lakes, fish with bait at the mouths of brooks whenever they are roiled by sudden storms and are sweeping dislodged food items into the lake.

Smallmouth bass: During the spawning season (late May and early June) wherever the law allows. (Cast to the shoreline with fly-rod lures: popping bugs or streamer flies.)

Largemouth bass: All-season feeders, with depth of more importance than time. However, large-

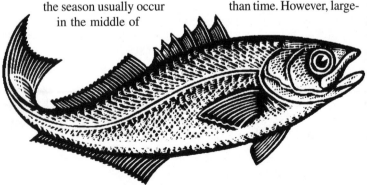

1852

Butchers in Frankfurt, Germany, create the frankfurter. It is nicknamed the "dachshund sausage" and then rechristened the "hot dog" in America.

mouths often cruise the shoreline after dark and will smash at surface lures that kick up a commotion. (Use flashlight or lantern only sparingly.)

Northern pike and pickerel: All-season biters also.

Walleyes: During spawning runs (late April and early May) where legal. After spawning (late May and well into June) along the shoreline, where they tend to cruise in schools.

Landlocked salmon: From ice-out until surface temperatures approach 60° F.

Panfish: More all-season biters.

Bullheads, larger catfish, and eels: All feed most actively at night.

2 FISH AT THE PROPER DEPTH.

Determining the right depth is of critical importance, especially in lake fishing. Northern pike, pickerel, largemouth bass, and panfish tolerate warm water containing relatively little oxygen. Consequently, they can be caught throughout the season in the shallow water that borders weed beds, around sunken brush, and in the shade of overhanging trees. (Cast to the edge of the cover in which they lurk, or anchor so that bait can be lowered close to this edge.)

During warm weather, trout, walleyes, and smallmouth bass seek the cooler water and higher oxygen content of the thermocline. This is a relatively thin layer of water that, in lakes of substantial depth, separates the warm surface layer from the cold and somewhat stagnant layer at the bottom. The depth at which the thermocline forms varies from lake to lake, but it usually lies between 20 and 35 feet beneath the surface. However, fish are not evenly distributed throughout the thermocline. Instead, they are attracted to those places where the bottom lies within this comfort zone. Such hot spots exist where sunken reefs rise into the thermocline and where the bottom drops away sharply to enter it. Electronic depth finders are of great help in finding such reefs and drop-offs, but they can also be located by trial-and-error sounding. Once you've found them, fish natural baits within inches of the bottom. Should you elect to troll, use sufficient weight to hold the lure equally close to the bottom.

3 USE THE CORRECT BAIT OR LURE.

All natural baits and artificial lures will take a wide variety of species of fish, but most species have particular preferences. The following list matches species with the baits and lures to which they respond most readily.

Trout: Best baits include night crawlers, small earthworms, virtually all insect larvae that can be hung on a hook, very small crayfish, and small minnows. Appropriate lures include dry flies, wet flies, streamers, and small to tiny spoons, wobblers, and spinners.

Largemouth bass: Big minnows and large crayfish are top baits. Effective lures consist of surface and underwater plugs, popping bugs, large streamers, bucktail jigs, so-called spinner baits, metal spoons, and specially rigged plastic worms.

Smallmouth bass: Medium minnows, crayfish, night crawlers, small frogs, hellgrammites, grasshoppers, and crickets. Among strike-winning lures are medium popping bugs, streamers, surface and underwater plugs, plastic worm rigs, and virtually all metal lures designed for use with spinning gear.

Walleyes: Small to medium minnows and night crawlers. One or two night crawlers hung on a worm gang and trolled behind a No. 4 spinner is an old standby. Trolled plugs and wobblers are also effective. Walleye baits should be fished within inches of the bottom, and trolled baits and lures should be weighted to hold them just above the bottom. Troll very slowly.

Northern pike and pickerel: Both feed almost exclusively on small fish, so minnows are the logical bait. Large, flashy spoons will produce savage strikes. In this category, the time-tested red-and-white Dardevle is without peer. For hair-raising strikes, tempt northerns with king-size popping bugs. Use a short wire leader or trace ahead of baits and lures, for both pike and pickerel will chop off fabric or monofilament lines with their sharp teeth.

Large, flashy spoons will produce savage strikes. . . . For hair-raising strikes, tempt northerns with king-size popping bugs.

Landlocked salmon: Smelt, drifted alive or laced on a hook and trolled. Trolled streamers or small metal wobblers are standards. Trolling speed should be faster than when trolling for other species. Landlocks will rise to dry flies during a hatch, furnishing one of the top thrills of fly-fishing.

Panfish: Worms and grubs for all except crappies. These are best tempted with very small minnows. Bluegills will rise readily to large dry flies and small popping bugs, affording a source of fly-fishing fun that is often overlooked.

Bullheads, big catfish, and eels: Night crawlers or cut bait, fished on the bottom. These species do not respond to artificial lures, although channel catfish are an exception sometimes.

1856

The first commercial creamery opens in the United States, offering an alternative to hand-churning butter at home.

Best Fishing Days
(And other fishing lore.)

Probably the best fishing time is when the ocean tides are restless before their turn and in the first hour of ebbing. All fish in all waters — salt or fresh — feed most heavily then.

Best temperatures for fish species vary widely, of course, and are chiefly important if you are going to have your own fishpond. Best temperatures for brook trout are 45° to 65° F. Brown trout and rainbows are more tolerant of higher temperatures. Smallmouth black bass do best in cool water. Horned pout take what they find.

Most of us go fishing when we can get off, not because it is the best time. But there are best times:

■ One hour before and one hour after high tide, and one hour before and one hour after low tide. "The morning rise" — after sunup for a spell; "the evening rise" — just before sundown and the hour or so after. Still water or a ripple is better than a wind at both times.

■ When there is a hatch of flies — caddis or mayflies, commonly. (The fisherman will have to match the hatching flies with his fly — or go fishless.)

■ When the breeze is from a westerly quarter rather than north or east.

■ When the barometer is steady or on the rise. (But, of course, even in a three-day driving northeaster, the fish isn't going to just give up feeding. His hunger clock keeps right on working, and the smart fisherman will find something he wants.)

■ When the Moon is between new and full.

4 USE THE PROPER PRESENTATION.

You can be in the right place at the right time, fish at the correct depth, use appropriate baits and lures — and still return empty-handed because of faulty presentation. First, it is important to understand that the technique of winning bites or strikes splits into two completely different categories. Natural baits and their imitations appeal directly to fish hunger. Flashy, non-imitative lures draw strikes by exciting

1857

James Merritt Ives joins Nathaniel Currier in his printmaking firm. Their firm, Currier & Ives, will produce thousands of scenes of 19th-century American life over the next 50 years.

fish to the point that they attack the lure.

Accordingly, natural baits and their imitations must be presented in a manner carefully calculated to eliminate or disguise, to the greatest possible extent, all reasons for

It's of no use to carry an umbrella if your shoes are leaking.

alarm or suspicion. To fool a critical trout, for example, a dry fly must respond freely to the whims of the current that bears it. For the same reason, a live minnow will tempt a cautious smallmouth only if it seems to swim naturally, ostensibly unimpaired by the circumstances of its attachment to hook and line.

The problem, then, is that of minimizing the restraining influences of hook, sinker, and line. This is best accomplished by using the smallest hooks, the lightest sinkers, and the lines and leaders of the finest diameter that can be employed practically in a given situation. The inhibitive effect and anomalous appearance of big hooks, heavy sinkers, and coarse lines and leaders are grounds for immediate alarm and suspicion, and their use is perhaps the greatest single reason for lack of fishing success. Therefore, use every delicacy of presentation that circumstances will allow. Obey this "commandment," and increased catches are guaranteed!

Effective use of provocative, non-imitative lures is an altogether different matter. Here the "secret" of success is not finesse but instead erratic retrieves. Try a fast and steady retrieve, for example. Then, on the next cast, bring the lure back in short spurts. Let floating lures lie motionless for substantial periods, then apply the lightest possible twitches. Recast, and bring the same lure back to the boat so fast that it churns the water. Experiment constantly with the infinite variations that lie between these suggested ploys.

And if all fails, welcome to the club. Be not bitter, but seek consolation in respect for your quarry. They meet fishermen on even terms, and only a poor loser begrudges a worthy opponent his share of victories.

1858

Mailboxes first appear on the streets and roads of America.

FARMER'S CALENDAR

Shovel with Style

I F YOU SHOVEL SNOW, remember two rules: (1) The snow is bigger than you are — don't try to move it all at once, and don't try to move it too far. (2) The solace of work that is essentially vain, futile, or meaningless is style — and if you're shoveling snow, your work is futile, if any work is.

Watch your neighbors; see how they shovel snow. The man you see struggling to pitch an enormous shovel, on which is poised a block of snow the size of a hay bale, is an amateur. If you're his friend, advise him to take it easy — or get a snowblower. If you're his life insurance agent, insist. In your own snow shoveling,  use a big shovel by all means but take small bites. Don't heave the snow out of your path if you can help it; rather just twist your wrist and let the snow slide off the shovel beside the path. And try to get to your shoveling soon after the snow has stopped falling. The longer you wait, the more time the snow has to settle, increasing its weight and your work.

Try to shovel with style. Reflect that the goal of snow shoveling is an unsatisfactory one: You will never see the end of it; there will be more tomorrow. Still, today's snow must be shoveled. Therefore, make the *act* of shoveling, not the result, the object of your care. Take pains to shovel your paths straight, to make them of uniform breadth, and to cut your corners neatly. Take your time. Make unneeded paths, detours, shortcuts, oxbows, and dead ends. If you have animals or small children, they will thank you. And you will have the satisfaction of knowing that you have overcome winter in the only way you ever can — by submitting to it, but gracefully and with style.

1860

Frederick Walton of England obtains a patent for linoleum, a floor covering made from flax *(linum)* and oil *(oleum).*

> ■ *With careful observation and a little practice, you'll have an accurate celestial clock — one that never needs winding or batteries.*

How to Tell Time by the Stars
AND
How to Check Your Watch by the Stars

BY EDWARD BARNATOWICS

BEFORE THE ADVENT OF THE modern clock, the time of day was determined by the position of the Sun. But did you ever wonder how our ancestors stayed on schedule after the Sun went down?

They told time simply by looking at the stars.

To be able to use our "star clock," you first have to be able to identify the Big Dipper (Ursa Major), whose two pointer stars (Merak and Dubhe) are used to locate the North Star (Polaris).

The Big Dipper is a circumpolar constellation, which means that for anyone north of 40 degrees latitude, it never rises or sets. It just keeps revolving around Polaris, making a little more than one revolution a day.

An imaginary line that connects the two pointers and Polaris makes up the single hand of our star clock. If our single hand swings completely around Polaris in 24 hours, it follows that if the hand rotated through 90 degrees (one-quarter of

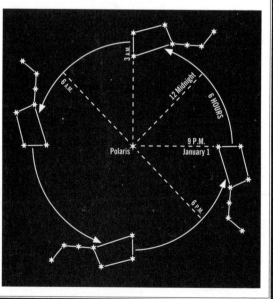

San Francisco bartender
Jerry Thomas mixes
the first martini.

a revolution), 6 hours would have passed (one-quarter of 24 hours is 6 hours).

As an example, the diagram illustrates the position of the Big Dipper on January 1 at about 9:00 P.M. Using this 6-hour quarter circle as a convenient increment, we can further increase our accuracy. For example, if our hand rotated through 45 degrees from its 9:00 P.M. position, it would be 3 hours later, or 12:00 midnight.

With some practice, you'll surprise yourself at being able to tell time to within 15 minutes!

And if you're a stickler for accuracy, you might be interested to know that man has yet to develop a timepiece as accurate as the apparent movement of the stars. In fact, the world's most accurate clocks are checked by star time.

Here is how you can check how much your favorite timepiece is gaining or losing each day. This method is accurate to within one second.

As mentioned before, the stars complete one revolution in slightly less than one day, actually in 23 hours, 56 minutes, and 4 seconds. This means that a star will reach the same position in the sky 3 minutes and 56 seconds earlier each night.

Looking out a window on the west side of your house, find a bright star that is just about to disappear behind some prominent object. With a felt-tip pen, place a dot on the window to mark the star's position just as it disappears, then look at your watch. Write the time on your window. Now with two pieces of masking tape, make a V on the window, with your "posi-

Plow deep while sluggards sleep, And you will have corn to sell or keep.

tion" mark at the vertex. This forms your rear sight. The next night, simply note the exact time the star disappears again. For example, if on the first night your star went down at 9:00, in order to be right on time your watch would have to read 9:00 minus 3 minutes and 56 seconds, or 8:56 and 4 seconds, on the next night. If it reads any less, it's gaining by that amount. If it reads any more, it's losing by that amount.

Now you have the information you need to check that expensive watch — or maybe you'll decide to throw it away and use the stars!

1861

Portraits first appear on U.S. paper currency.

■ *You don't need a big backyard to produce a bounty of fresh vegetables. Heck, even if you do have the space for a grand-size garden, you might opt for the small intensive type.*

Growing Vegetables in Small Spaces

BY HELEN TOWER BRUNET

FOR ANYONE WHO WANTS TO grow vegetables but is short on space, intensive vegetable gardening may be the answer. Started in France in the 19th century, this system enabled French produce farmers to increase their production at astonishing rates. If you have a plot of ground, no matter how small, that receives at least six hours of sunlight a day, you might want to try intensive gardening. Here is a nine-point plan for starting one.

1. Planning the beds. Intensive gardening is best done in individual beds of any length, but not more than four feet wide, which enables the gardener to care for the plants without stepping on the bed itself and compacting the soil. If an arrangement of several beds is used, paths should be set permanently between them. The beds may be the same level as the paths (or slightly higher due to the addition of organic material), or, in areas where drainage is a problem, the beds may be raised above ground level using walls of wooden

slats, railroad ties, or cinder blocks. In planning the size of the bed the first year, it is best to start small and add on later. A good beginning would be one bed four feet wide and perhaps ten feet long. The next year another bed could be placed next to it, with a path made between. Because the plants are placed closer together than in the traditional vegetable garden, yields are much higher per square foot of space.

2. Double digging. This is the essential step in setting up an intensive garden, and one that scares a good many gardeners away, because it is very heavy work. The good news is that it has to be done only once. What the double digging does is provide deep (at least two feet), rich, well-drained soil for the vegetables to grow in. The roots go a long way toward producing superior harvests. Here's how you go about double digging.

As soon as the ground can be worked in spring, dig a trench about three spades wide and as long as you want the garden to be. As you

1862

To raise funds for the Civil War, the first income tax is levied in the United States. In 1881 the tax will be deemed unconstitutional.

remove the first foot of soil, place it to one side. This will be mostly topsoil. Then dig into the next layer at the bottom of the trench, down another foot into the subsoil, and place this soil on the other side of the trench. Now fill up the trench, alternating layers of topsoil, subsoil, and at least three inches of organic material such as compost or rotted cow manure. When the first trench is complete, make another one adjoining it on one side and repeat the whole procedure. It usually takes two trenches side by side to make a fourfoot-wide bed. In a very sandy soil, more organic matter may be needed. In a heavy clay soil, builder's sand may be added in addition to the organic material to improve drainage.

Started in France in the 19th century, this system enabled French produce farmers to increase their production at astonishing rates. If you have a plot of ground, no matter how small, that receives at least six hours of sunlight a day, you might want to try intensive gardening.

When the trenches are finished and the soil is back in place, if you are still interested in intensive gardening, sprinkle 3 pounds of superphosphate and 1 pound of muriate of potash per 100 square feet over the entire bed and scratch it into the surface. Then water with a sprinkler until the water penetrates 10 inches below the surface (check it with a stick or ruler) and wait at least a day to plant.

Double digging may be done in the fall, too, when leaves, grass clippings, green cow manure, and rough organic material may be used in place of the compost or well-rotted cow manure required in the spring. If used in the fall, these materials have a chance to break down over the winter.

1863

The world's first subway system opens in London.

If hand-digging is impossible, a thorough power tilling may be used instead, but it is not as effective in layering the different soils as the double-digging method.

3. What to plant. When you are making the most of a very small vegetable garden, you have to be selective about what you grow. Plant what you like most and only as much as your family will use. Consider also the length of time a particular crop remains in good eating condition. For instance, it's easy to have too much lettuce all ready at the same time. But crops such as carrots and beets can stay in the ground (or in cold storage) almost indefinitely until you are ready to use them. Of course, size is very important — how much space the different crops take compared to what they yield. Corn requires a fairly large stand for

When you are making the most of a very small vegetable garden, you have to be selective about what you grow. Plant what you like most and only as much as your family will use.

good wind pollination and so may crowd the small garden. Cabbage takes up a lot of space and yields a single harvest, whereas summer squash, which requires even more space, produces over and over. Tomatoes, either staked or grown in wire cylinders, are the champion producers for the space they require. Any crop that can be trained to grow up — such as pole beans, peas, and cucumbers — is a good bet. The main thing is to grow exactly what you like.

4. Plant spacing. In the intensive garden, plants are spaced much closer together than in the vegetable garden, which is planted in rows with walkways between. The elimination of single rows is a real breakthrough. It allows space for more plants, and the plants themselves serve to help each other

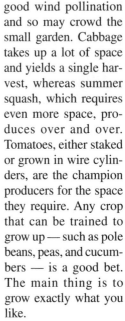

fight off insects as well. The elimination of the walkways between the rows cuts down on the harmful soil compaction under the walkways, which sometimes spreads into the rows on either side.

When spacing plants within the beds, stagger them, using the distance recommended on the seed packet for spacing *within a row,* and ignore the suggested spacing between rows, because you aren't planting in rows. For instance, beets would be planted 2 inches apart all the way around and summer squash 16 to 18 inches apart all the way around. The suggested between-row spacing for these plants is 12 to 18 inches for beets and 36 to 60 inches for squash. This is where the greatest space saving takes place — the elimination of rows.

Many plants may be planted in broad bands 12 to 18 inches wide. When using this type of planting, follow the general rule of planting small seeds ½ inch apart and large seeds 2 to 3 inches apart. Cover the seeds thinly and tamp with a board or the flat edge of a hoe. Crops that respond to broad-band planting are beans, peas, carrots, onions, Swiss chard, spinach, beets, parsnips, and radishes.

5. Interplanting. Another method used in intensive gardening to increase yield is interplanting, or double cropping. This simply means planting fast-growing vegetables between slower-growing ones to utilize the space temporarily available. For example, you may scatter carrot seeds and radish seeds together in a broad band. The radishes will mature before they crowd the carrots. Or, if you have a garden large enough for corn, pumpkins or melons may be planted between the stalks.

Procrastination is the thief of time.

6. Succession planting. Similar to interplanting is succession planting, which enables the intensive gardener to extend the growing season in a small area. By the time the early cool-weather crops such as lettuce and spinach are dying out in the heat of early summer, prestarted plants of tomatoes, melons, eggplant, and peppers may be placed in their space.

Ideally, there is never a speck of bare ground in the intensive garden, but this takes quite a bit of planning. It's a good idea to have some extra plants growing in small

1863

The National Bank Act of 1863 standardizes U.S. currency. Before the act, individual banks could issue their own money.

containers in a protected area of the garden so that they may be slipped into spaces that become available, usually in midsummer. Depending on the climate, cool crops for fall also may be started as seeds in the empty spaces, such as more lettuce, kale, leeks, and spinach. Or the gardener may elect to pop an annual in the empty space, especially the helpful marigold or nasturtium, both of which repel certain insects.

7. Feeding. When succession plantings are made, the area to be planted may be presoaked with a liquid fertilizer, preferably the organic type, which makes a longer-lasting contribution to the soil. This could be fish emulsion, liquid seaweed, or dried cow manure. One of the cheapest and easiest to use is manure tea, made from the dried cow manure sold in most gar-

One of the cheapest and easiest [fertilizers] to use is manure tea, made from the dried cow manure sold in most garden centers. Soak the manure overnight — one part manure to ten parts water. This liquid fertilizer may . . . be poured over the entire bed.

den centers. Soak the manure overnight—one part manure to ten parts water. This liquid fertilizer may also be poured over the entire bed at intervals during the summer. In well-prepared soil, little feeding is necessary. Since the best-tasting vegetables are usually the young, small, and therefore more tender ones, heavy feeding to produce huge specimens is pointless.

8. Watering. Watering is extremely important in growing good vegetables, which themselves are mostly water. Young plants must have a constant supply available. But when the plants are established and the leaves begin to shade the soil, much less water is required than with the traditional row garden.

9. Pests. A gardener's first line of defense against garden pests is a watchful eye. The area around the garden should be kept clear of any debris or rubbish.

Some insects may be picked off by hand or washed off with a forceful stream of water. The next strongest step would be the use of one of the botanical sprays on the market, such as pyrethrum, rotenone, and ryania. Being made from plants themselves, they are the safest to use. The last resort would be the safer of the chemical sprays — Diazinon, malathion, and sevin — used strictly according to package directions.

IN THE FALL, WHEN ALL THE PLANTS have been harvested, clear off the garden bed completely. This is a good time to add coarser organic material that can break down over the winter, such as shredded leaves, grass clippings, shredded cornstalks, hay, or cow manure, which at this time of year does not need to be rotted. These ingredients may be forked under the soil, then the whole bed should be covered with a mulch of whatever is available in the area — leaves, hay, wood chips, seaweed, and the like. The following spring, any covering that has not decomposed may be pulled off several weeks before planting to allow the ground to warm up. The intensive gardener will find waiting under the mulch dark, rich humus ready to be planted again and again.

ANECDOTES & PLEASANTRIES

A Tricky Method for Fixing Shoes That Pinch

THE AUTHOR Roald Dahl wrote a letter to the venerable *Times* of London that the *Times* printed in full. Dahl wrote that he had recently purchased a pair of gym shoes and found they pinched his toes. He said that fortunately he remembered his school physics course, which taught that "10 volumes of water at zero degrees centigrade expand to 11 volumes at freezing point. So I pushed a plastic bag deep into each shoe and filled it with water. I placed the shoes in the deep freezer compartment of the refrigerator and closed the door. The next morning the water inside the shoes had frozen solid and expanded in all directions by 10 percent." The shoes fit perfectly. Dahl said the system also works with Wellington boots.

Courtesy of the Boston Globe

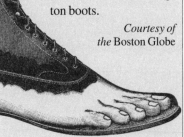

1865

Count Leo Tolstoy begins his epic novel *War and Peace,* which he will finish in 1869.

FARMER'S CALENDAR

Blackflies

I N EARLY SUMMER, the blackfly is the cruel overseer of gardeners and other stooped workers. Imagine a scene inspired by *Uncle Tom's Cabin:* a cotton field; slaves bent over the endless rows; striding among them the fiendish overseer, cracking his long whip just above the harvesters' heads, so that anyone who stands for a moment's relief from his work feels the sting.

In blackfly season, that little humpbacked bug no bigger than a gnat becomes a slave driver of a sadism exquisite and relentless. As long as you remain down close to the ground — weeding the garden, thinning, fixing the lawn mower, changing a tire — he will leave you alone. The moment you can finally no longer bear your bent-over position and stand, the flies will descend on you. You find your head and shoulders in a cloud of them. Quickly you kneel again.

No doubt the blackfly's persecution of gardeners who slack off their work is accounted for by some arcane force, operating automatically on the lives of insects, that makes them fly at a certain height above the ground at certain times. The effect on us is the same as if the fly's merciless hounding was bought with a planter's gold.

In the woods, the mosquito and the deerfly work a subtle variation on the blackfly's cruel attentions. Suppose you are cutting wood, using a chain saw. You will find that the bugs spare you as long as the saw is running — that is, as long as you are actively at work, on your task. Turn off the saw (to rest, say), and the mosquitoes and deerflies will immediately close in. No doubt they are kept away by the racket of the saw's engine, by the smoke of its exhaust, and not by a deliberate neglect that lasts just as long as you are at your job. The effect is the same as it is with the blackflies outside the woods. Loggers know: The bugs work for the boss.

1866

Chewing gum comes to the United States when exiled Mexican leader Antonio López de Santa Anna shares his chewy *chictli,* a tasteless resin from the sapodilla tree, with New Yorker Thomas Adams. Adams will begin marketing it as a jaw exerciser in penny pieces in February 1871.

■ *It's one thing to listen to the weather forecast or compare notes with fellow gardeners. But to truly beat the frost, you have to know the exact situation for your garden.*

How to Predict a Frost Accurately

BY CALVIN SIMONDS

MY GARDEN IS IN A VALLEY that is 600 feet above sea level, and on still nights the cool air puddles at the bottom of the valley. I wish I had a dollar for every time I've stood at the foot of my garden watching the Sun descend, trying to figure out how low the temperature would go. The big-city forecaster is never much help. He or she sits in the midst of an urban "heat island" and plays the averages for the city and its suburbs. But my garden is not in an average location, and when I listen to the weather forecast at night, I have to subtract about 15° F from the lowest temperature estimates.

In matters of frost prediction, there's no substitute for knowing your own situation. Here are some factors.

Temperature. When the temperature of the air around your plants falls to 32°F, you have a frost. But there is a tremen-dous variation between the daytime temperature and the low point for the night. Where I live in the Northeast, the following rule of thumb works pretty well: If the high temperature for the day is above 75° F, I don't have to think about the possibility of frost. In drier climates, cautious gardeners might have to use 80° F, or even 85° F, as their guideline.

Wind. On a still, cool night, the air tends to sort itself into layers, with the colder air at the bottom. The longer and stiller the night is, the more time the air has to do this. Unfortunately, the wind at sunset isn't a very good indication of what the wind will be like at dawn. Thus, when I'm deciding whether or not to cover my plants, I take the evening wind into account only if it's very still or if it's blowing vigorously and I have good reason to believe it will continue to blow

1866

American outlaw Jesse James and his band commit their first bank robbery. They will soon branch out to rob trains and stagecoaches, too.

all night and keep the air layers mixed.

Clouds. Clouds, even very high clouds, can keep temperatures from falling farther than they otherwise might. Remember, though, that the clouds at sunset may not be the same as the clouds at dawn. Notice the trend of the clouds. If the sky has been covered by low, gray clouds that begin to break and thin as the Sun sets, I worry. If the Sun sets through an increasingly dense network of vapor trails and mare's tails, however, I don't worry.

Ground conditions. If the soil is cold and dry, the atmosphere near the ground can cool more rapidly. If the ground is moist and warm, it lends its heat and moisture to the atmosphere. But the soil temperature isn't much of a factor unless it is up in the 70s. Generally, you can count on the soil temperature to help you a little in the fall and not much in the spring.

Length of night. The longer the night, the more time there is for the Earth to lose heat to the sky. During the fall frost season, nights can be

If the sky has been covered by low, gray clouds that begin to break and thin as the Sun sets, I worry. If the Sun sets through an increasingly dense network of vapor trails and mare's tails, however, I don't worry.

as much as two hours longer than during the spring frost season.

Regional weather situation. Unseasonable frosts commonly occur in only one meteorological situation: under the crest of a continental polar or arctic air mass that follows the passage of a low-pressure area. Then the skies clear, winds diminish, the air is dry, and nighttime temperatures plummet.

Phase of the Moon. I believe that frost is more likely under a full or new Moon. The Moon makes tides in the atmosphere just as it makes tides in the ocean. The highest tides in the atmosphere come during the new and full Moons. If the high Moon tides are added to the effect of a high-pressure area as described above, doesn't it seem reasonable that frost is more likely?

Dew point. The dew point is the temperature at which the water vapor in the air condenses into water droplets or ice crystals. When the air reaches the dew point, water in the air starts to condense in the form of dew or fog. This condensation

1868

Christopher L. Sholes invents the first typewriter that makes it possible to type faster than a person can write. Sholes will continue to make improvements, and in 1873 he will contract with Remington Arms to manufacture and sell his machine.

releases heat, thus warming the air along the ground, and also serves as a little extra insulation for plants. The best source for determining the dew point is a television weather broadcast, often given as part of a printed display. My rule of thumb is not to worry about frost if the dew point is above 45° F on the evening weather report. You can also guess at the dew point: If the air is murky, the horizon is hazy and ill-defined, and stars are indistinct, you know the dew point is high. If you can see every detail of distant structures, the Moon comes up the color of platinum, and the stars come out in the thousands, the dew point is low. On such a night, the wise tomato cringes.

Frost protection. Any device that holds an insulating layer of warm air around a plant will offer considerable frost protection. Cover your plants with old milk cartons, sheets of plastic, moth-eaten blankets, bedspreads, or anything else that will contain warm air. Just remember to remove the covers in the morning when the temperature gets above the freezing point. You can save yourself a lot of grief by carefully choosing the site of your garden. Slopes help because they keep the cold air from puddling in your garden (remember, cold air is heavier than warm air). Water sources also help by raising dew points and by enveloping your plants in a protective mist.

Relative Hardiness of Common Garden Plants

IF YOU'RE in a frost-prone area, you can concentrate your gardening efforts on those crops that can withstand the threat of cold. Consider these categories when choosing garden plants.

Hardy (able to withstand freezing temperatures): broccoli, brussels sprouts, cabbage, chives, collards, garlic, horseradish, kale, kohlrabi, leeks, onions, peas, rhubarb, rutabagas, sage, salsify, scallions, spinach, thyme, turnips.

Half-hardy (can withstand short-term exposure to subfreezing temperatures): artichokes (Jerusalem), beets, carrots, cauliflower, celeriac, celery, chard, dill, endives, escarole, fennel, lettuce, mustard, parsnips, potatoes, radishes, rosemary.

Tender (fruit and leaves injured by light frosts): artichokes (globe), basil, beans, corn, marjoram, soybeans, squash (summer), tomatoes.

Very tender (need temperatures above 70° F for growth): beans (lima), coriander, cucumbers, cumin, eggplant, loofah, melons, okra, peppers, potatoes (sweet), pumpkins, squash (winter).

1868

The British Post Office begins hiring cats to control the mail-eating mouse population. The cats receive a weekly allowance of 4 pence each.

■ *Sounds crazy, but a test in Germany has shown that gardens cultivated on cloudy, Moon-less nights produce 78 percent fewer weeds. Hey, it's worth a try!*

A Case for Weeding in the Dark

BY JON VARA

WHERE DO ALL THOSE GARden weeds come from? They come from seeds — seeds that, in most cases, are an integral part of the garden itself.

Microscopic scrutiny of a sample of fertile garden soil inevitably turns up a disheartening number of unwanted seeds — the product of generations of weeds that have grown, matured, died, and been incorporated into the soil. A single pigweed plant, for example, may produce several million seeds.

Moreover, buried weed seeds may remain viable for the better part of a century. During that time, they lie dormant and await conditions that will allow them to germinate, grow to maturity, and produce seeds of their own. Those conditions include relatively warm temperatures, adequate soil moisture, and — according to recent research by German botanists — exposure to light.

According to the German study, reported in the journal *Naturwissenschaften*, the seeds of most common field weeds contain chemical triggers called phytochromes, which induce germination only when stimulated by light. Very brief flashes of light lasting only a few thousandths of a second will cause germination, even if the briefly exposed seeds are immediately reburied (as is likely to be the case during plowing, harrowing, sowing, and other soil-disturbing activities).

That is not particularly startling news in itself. As every experienced gardener knows, tilling the soil before planting also promotes weed growth, and attacking the initial weed crop with a hoe a few weeks later lays the groundwork for a successive crop of weeds.

What is intriguing about the German study is its suggestion of a novel approach to breaking the cycle of soil disturbance, light exposure, and weed growth. Rather than seeking to avoid disturbing the soil — as modern agribusiness does by replacing mechanical cultivation with chemical herbicides or in some cases by no-till planting — the researchers tried eliminating the germination-inducing light. The results, they found, were "quite astonishing."

1869

The United States celebrates the completion of its first transcontinental railroad.

By performing all soil-disturbing operations after dark, they discovered that weed germination could be reduced by as much as 78 percent. Weeds typically covered only 2 percent of night-cultivated test strips, while adjacent strips cultivated during daylight hours were 80 percent covered with weeds.

Apparently, even the odd twinkle of starlight can be enough to activate some seeds; the researchers found that weed suppression was most pronounced when cultivation took place on cloudy, Moon-less nights. Light from artificial sources, such as headlight beams, also was enough to stimulate weed seed germination. To prevent such unwanted exposure, tractor drivers participating in the study used sophisticated infrared night-vision equipment to maneuver across the fields in near-total darkness.

Few home gardeners will want to go to such extremes. Still, significant reductions in weed growth may be obtained by performing soil-disturbing operations on moonlit nights or at dawn or dusk.

For best results, the German researchers say, the soil preparation before crops are planted — plowing, harrowing, or other tillage — should be performed near noon on a bright sunny day. That will help to draw down the so-called seed bank by stimulating a large initial flush of weeds. Four weeks later, the immature weeds may be destroyed by nighttime cultivation, followed by nighttime seeding of crops.

A WORD OF CAUTION

The authors of the study suggest that it may be prudent to practice night cultivation only in alternate years. Although the vast majority of the millions of weed seeds slumbering in the soil will require the stimulus of light to germinate, a few light-independent renegades are inevitably present. If these dark germinators are allowed to mature and produce seeds of their own, the resulting progeny are likely to inherit the trait as well. After a few generations of such unintentional — and unwanted — selective pressure, the seed bank could become permeated with light-independent weed seeds, robbing nighttime cultivation of its effectiveness.

1871

The first correspondence courses are offered by the Chautauqua (New York) Methodist School for students living far away.

ANECDOTES & PLEASANTRIES

The Ultimate Example of Yankee Ingenuity

YOU'RE FLYING a Cessna with your nine-year-old daughter when the hydraulic fluid to activate the landing gear leaks out. What do you do?

It happened on a flight from Orlando, Florida, to Athens, Georgia. Piloting the Cessna was Alan Frankel of West Virginia. His passenger was his nine-year-old daughter, Alexis. About 15 minutes out of Orlando, Frankel discovered that there was no hydraulic fluid in the landing system. That meant the wheels couldn't go down.

First thing Frankel did was show his daughter how to keep the plane level while he crawled to the rear and poured some milk from a carton they happened to have with them into the plane's drained hydraulic line. But it wasn't enough to lower the wheels. Alexis, meanwhile, said later she had just one thing on her mind: "Help!"

Frankel was about resigned to a crash landing when he suddenly thought of something else. He decided to pee into the hydraulic line. Well, actually, he filled the milk carton with urine, poured it in, and then had Alexis do the same. They took turns — and finally, miracle of miracles, it was enough to lower the front wheels!

But, alas, the rear wheels didn't budge. So they eventually made a successful emergency belly landing at the Gainesville, Florida, Regional Airport. Neither was hurt.

Alexis said afterward that she wasn't sure she'd ever fly again. We don't know what her father said — but we'd guess that from now on he'll probably always be inclined to have that extra cup of coffee before climbing into the cockpit. You just never know.

1872

The United States establishes its first national park, Yellowstone, covering 2,219,791 acres in Idaho, Montana, and Wyoming.

Fellow Creatures

SOME OF THE STORIES in the following chapter are frankly unbelievable. I don't believe them.

Take "The Cat Who Came to Dinner," for example. We are asked to believe that (1) some jokers fired a cat out of a cannon; (2) the cat passed entirely through the body of a "highly accomplished and interesting lady, and the mother of seven children, the eldest being six years old"; (3) the cat's head was driven through a one-inch-thick board; and (4) the cat survived!

Seven children in six years? Come on!

Or how about "Jim, the Wonder Dog"? Supposedly this black and white setter understood and carried out orders in foreign languages, identified different species of trees, and, just before the 1936 World Series, correctly predicted that the Yankees would beat the Giants.

1875

The first Kentucky Derby is held at Churchill Downs, in Louisville. The winner: Aristides.

Well, duh. The Yanks won the pennant by *nineteen and a half* games that year, and with rookie Joe DiMaggio joining Crosetti, Lazzeri, Rolfe, Chapman, and Dickey in the lineup, they were prohibitive favorites.

You see what I mean? You have to take these outlandish stories about animals with a grain of salt — or a full shaker. (For anyone interested in a more in-depth discussion of this subject, I rec-

ommend "Animal Apocrypha: A Deconstructionist View of Meta-Language in Non-Human Discourse Modes" by Jacques le Chien Merveilleux, Distinguished Professor of Folklore at the Sorbonne.)

As Sy Montgomery points out (in "Who's Smarter: Cats or Dogs or Human Beings?"), it's impossible to determine the intelligence of an animal with a test designed for human beings.

Such tests, she says, are "about as useful as giving an American a multiple-choice exam in a foreign language." (Actually, Americans don't do so well on multiple-choice tests in their own language, but that's another story.)

What we need to separate fact from fiction is an IQ test that any species can take. Always eager to help, I have worked up a few sample questions.

AN IQ TEST FOR ALL SPECIES

1. You have been thrown into prison and are seeking to escape. After sneaking out of your cell, you are preparing to climb the high stone outer wall when suddenly the beam of a bright spot-

1875

George F. Green of Kalamazoo, Michigan, patents the first electric dental drill.

light falls directly on you. You should:

a. Secrete mucus from your epidermis and burrow into the soil.

b. Lose your balance and flop about so that you will be put outside.

c. Lighten the color of your carapace to match the color of the wall and scuttle off sideways out of the light.

d. Make "shadow bunnies" with your hands.

2. You go into a singles bar, order a drink, and notice an attractive female sitting by herself at a table for two. You should:

a. Lift your wing casings at a 45-degree angle and rub them together.

b. Knead her chest with your tiny paws.

c. Check to see if she's roughly the same length as you, then embrace her with your seta.

d. Circle her head, whining, buzzing, and biting.

3. You come across a murder scene in the woods. The body is still warm, and there are four bullet holes in the victim's back. The ground around the body is undisturbed, except for a slip of paper with a message written in a strange language. You should:

a. Send the body to the coroner and the slip of paper to Jim, the Wonder Dog.

b. Run home and bark frantically until Timmy calls his mom.

1876

Alexander Graham Bell makes the first successful telephone transmission.

c. Eat the body, converting it into a fine colloidal humus.

d. Lay your eggs in it.

4. You are in a room with four doors. Only one of them is unlocked and has food behind it. You should:

a. Call the super.

b. Sit in front of one door and whimper.

c. Pick a door and scratch the hell out of it.

d. Emit a high-pitched whine resembling a power saw going through a piece of cracked wood until the experimenter opens the damn door to shut you up.

5. It is 1928. While demolishing a building erected 31 years earlier, you discover a live horned toad in the cornerstone. You should:

a. Bat it around until you get bored, then break its neck and drop it on your owner's pillow as a present.

b. Gobble it down, go home, and throw it up on the new carpet.

c. Ignore it, make a home in the rubble, breed at an incredible rate, and spread disease.

d. Take it to the White House to meet President Calvin Coolidge. See which one looks more lifelike.

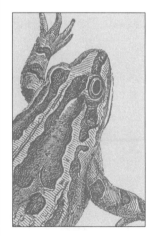

• • •

Actually, as any pet owner knows, the best measure of animal intelligence is how much the animal can get you to do for it. (This applies to human parents and children as well: Interestingly, the child's IQ, at Einstein level immediately after birth, declines as he ages and, upon having children of

1876

Mark Twain publishes
The Adventures of Tom Sawyer.

his own, plunges to that of a member of the House of Representatives. This is called the circle of life.)

By that definition, the smartest animal you will read about in the next few pages is the humble cricket. Kathleen Kilgore relates how she kept her pet cricket in a glass jar, gave him everything he wanted to eat and drink, cleaned up after him, and blew gently on him to arouse him from his normal torpor to sing.

Elvis really was a genius, wasn't he?

Tim Clark

1880s

The Old Judge Tobacco Company packs the first baseball cards with its cigarettes to stiffen the packages. Other tobacco companies will follow suit, and in 1933 the cards will begin appearing in packages of bubble gum.

■ *The age-old debate: Was the world and everything in it created in six days as described in the Bible, or did life on Earth evolve gradually over millions of years? Well, read this and argue no more.*

Solving the Evolution Riddle Once and for All

BY GUY MURCHIE

IN THE BEGINNING WAS THE Word." That is how the apostle John explained the genesis of Earth in abstract biblical terms. "And the Word was made flesh, and dwelt among us," an abstraction that turned into matter while matter turned into life.

In this subtly profound statement at the outset of the fourth book of the New Testament, one finds a key to divine terrestrial creation that does not violate any law of nature established by modern science. For today's biologists, geologists, and paleontologists, even though they have dug up massive evidence that life has existed on Earth for hundreds of millions of years, have not specifically attempted to explain the origin of life or seriously tackled the question of whether life as we know it somehow managed to spark itself into being on our previously sterile planet or whether it may instead have been wafted here through space in meteorites or dust spores from some other more viable world. This failure, moreover,

has to do with the fact that science, by its nature, concerns itself only with things that are measurable and therefore feels decidedly uneasy at any suggestion that it take on the issue of the origin of life, which so far has eluded measurement.

At the same time, of course, it is more than conceivable that astrobiologists will one day prove that the carbon compounds they find in meteorites do include viable spores that originated beyond Earth, but such proof obviously would not resolve the basic riddle of genesis. Rather, it would merely project the question outward from one world (ours) to another.

It appears, therefore, that science, for all its extraordinary discoveries of life forms evolving over unimaginably long periods on Earth, even of species spawning species, has never denied that life ultimately began with the Word or that "the Word was God." And the real question at issue in our schools thus turns out to be not *whether* God created life on Earth, but only *how* he created it.

1880

James Albert Bonsack of Virginia invents a cigarette-making machine.

Did he create it all at once, as the Book of Genesis symbolically suggests — all in one divine six-day week? Or did he take his time, of which he seems to have an inexhaustible supply, and unfold life inchmeal over billions of years, as science is demonstrating?

If you accept that God breathed the breath of life into Adam's nostrils all in one sublime puff, you are taking the Bible's symbolism literally, as is your right, although it might be worthwhile to consider how long a sublime puff might last. And what might constitute a "day" or an eon in the career of God?

It appears . . . that science, for all its extraordinary discoveries of life forms evolving over unimaginably long periods on Earth, even of species spawning species, has never denied that life ultimately began with the Word or that "the Word was God."

If, however, you think that the findings of thousands of scientists over the centuries — Charles Lyell's discoveries of fossils, Louis Agassiz's realization of the ice ages, Charles Darwin's and Alfred Russel Wallace's concepts of natural selection — reveal a different kind of creation by gradual evolution, you are applying what is generally called reason to the issue. You are questioning Bishop James Ussher's famous 17th-century calculation of the date of creation as 4004 B.C. and accepting that Earth-wide selection among quadrillions of organisms over billions of years is

1882

Thomas Edison opens the first electric power station on Pearl Street in New York City. The six generators in the station can cover approximately six square miles.

a more likely elucidation of just how the Creator carried out his creation, of how he "let there be a firmament" of stars and galaxies that slowly arranged themselves on a majestic scale out of elements evolving from simple hydrogen into more and more complex atoms and molecules and dust, of how he eventually "let the land bring forth grass . . . and cattle . . . and every thing that creepeth upon the Earth after his kind."

As it hardly seems feasible as yet to achieve worldwide agreement on the date of life's genesis as between the extremes of 4004 B.C. and 4,000,000,000 B.C., it may be of interest here to point out another and basically different concept of life that has long been mentioned in philosophical circles,

Thales, the Greek philosopher, in the sixth century B.C. . . . taught that all matter — including minerals, gases, and stars — is alive. . . . Anaxagoras propounded his panspermic theory that invisible "ethereal germs" are dispersed everywhere in the world, giving rise to all its creatures, including man.

and which may well eventually settle the issue. I refer to the principle of Omnipresence (explained in detail as the third mystery in my book *The Seven Mysteries of Life*), which seems to have been articulated first by Thales, the Greek philosopher, in the sixth century B.C., when he taught that all matter — including minerals, gases, and stars — is alive. Shortly afterward, Anaxagoras propounded his panspermic theory that invisible "ethereal germs" are dispersed everywhere in the world, giving rise to all its creatures, including man. Later, in Rome, Lucretius wrote in his famous *De Rerum Natura* that "multitudes of animals are formed out of the earth. . . . First the various breeds of birds . . . then the mam-

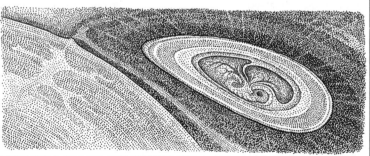

1883

The Indonesian volcano Krakatoa erupts. It is one of the most catastrophic eruptions in recorded history.

mals ... as the earth passes through successive phases." Inevitably, the question of "spontaneous generation" emerged, and the range of thinking on this crucial issue, even into the 17th century, is suggested by the recipe for creating mice propounded by none other than the great Flemish chemist Jan van Helmont: "Put a pile of soiled clothes in a dark, quiet corner, sprinkle them with kernels of wheat and within 21 days mice will appear." This had never been known to fail.

Usually it is so easy to tell a rock from a potato that most people don't regard them as comparable at all, or are apt to think that all rocks are dead. Yet ponderable evidence is accumulating that the whole mineral kingdom has a very real life of its own that takes only time, patience, and a little sensitive contemplation to reach our understanding. For many rocks actually do grow, if very slowly. And they get around, eat in a manner of speaking, become ill (yet not without some capacity to heal their wounds), and even bear offspring through their own simple system of reproduction. Rocks are crystals, you see, and it is the nature of a crystal to maintain its molecular lattice structure, to restore any distortion, to gradually fill up any crack (in effect healing the wound), and to grow by the natural tendency of passing molecules made of similar material to attach themselves to

the crystal's microscopic crevices, into which they exactly fit. The receptivity of these "friendly" molecules indeed amounts to an elementary attraction that, chemically speaking, approaches what could be termed "love." And this mysterious force, incidentally, seems to be the key to crystal reproduction, which is probably the simple but vi-

When sheep collect and huddle, Tomorrow will become a puddle.

tal technique of procreation that must have enabled Earth's very earliest "life" forms to maintain themselves, spread, and eventually evolve into all the millions of species of vegetables and animals we see around us today. From the naturalist's point of view, it would actually demean God if one were to cling to the primitive or literal interpretation of the Bible that he performed his creation in a series of instantaneous miracles, like waving a wand, instead of using the infinitely more impressive method of intricate and endless unfolding of form

1885

Vaudeville sharpshooters Annie Oakley and her husband, Frank Butler, join Buffalo Bill's Wild West Show. Oakley will perform her act for 17 years.

after form, out of which developed motion after motion, behavior after behavior, sense after sense, thought after thought, and ultimately spirit upon spirit.

Surprisingly, there does not appear to be any limit anywhere to this extraordinary process. Nor is Mother Earth herself exempt from the phenomenon, or from taking on her own global attributes of life. In fact, science is well on its way toward establishing our planet as a truly viable superorganism. For the power to maintain a fairly constant level of body temperature and humidity despite a changing environment is certainly a mark of life, as sweating and shivering humanity well know. And there is growing fossil evidence that Earth has literally kept a steady temperature through all her 4 billion years of existence, despite the fact that the Sun has increased its radiation of energy, light, and heat by some 200 to 300 percent (by current astrophysical estimates) during the same period. And if Earth may, therefore, be considered alive, so, in logic, must other planets and, by not unreasonable extrapolation, the solar system, the Milky Way, and — who can gainsay it? — the universe.

The whole concept of life, thus presented, is admittedly mysterious. Inevitably so, for Mystery (with a capital *M*) is an apt synonym for divinity, and, to the degree that instinct leads us to accept Mystery as the essence of a world in which our bodies function through the "wisdom of the inward parts" and the Milky Way churns perpetually upon nothing, we will humbly accept the divinity inherent in life's creation, be it engendered by swift wand or slow evolution.

Where the world is taking us is a question few philosophers have had the temerity to guess at. But some have noted that there seem to be many aspects to evolution, all interweaving their paths as the centuries and millennia unfurl. The human form and face, for example, have slowly taken shape as the worm and the fish crawled on dry land and the reptile became a mammal. Diseases evolve unseen in their own secret microcosm. Machines now boldly emerge in an accelerating sequence from the lo-

Science is well on its way toward establishing our planet as a truly viable superorganism. For the power to maintain a fairly constant level of body temperature and humidity despite a changing environment is certainly a mark of life.

1886

The first Tournament of Roses
New Year's Day parade is held
in Pasadena, California.

comotive to the atomic generator, from the abacus to the chip computer. The miracles of yesteryear become the necessities of today. Even virtues evolve across time as the spear-wielding heroes of millennia past are replaced by the spiritual statesmen who must forge the world federations of tomorrow.

As the germination of Earth thus becomes more established, we realize that the first victory of a machine over an animal in 1839 (when a steam engine outdistanced a horse) led a century later to a thousandfold increase in travel speed in the Apollo program — and comparable explosions have been occurring in population, communication, exploration, liberation, education, computation, standardization, and, we trust, political organization. Yet evolution is not the least explosive of these, as man, having won the tournament of animal competition, now, for the first time, must face eugenics: the task of breeding not just dogs or horses but — much more difficult — himself. It is a challenge also of the spirit, quite appropriate to this soul school called mortal life on Earth. And it more than hints that man has mounted, figuratively speaking, a bigger, wilder steed than he yet knows how to ride. He is still young enough to learn, however, and his eagerness to risk his neck, if not his soul, may be exactly what it takes to tame not only the mount but also, in time, even the unruly rider.

ANECDOTES & PLEASANTRIES

How Happy IS a Clam?

WE WILL PROBABLY never know exactly what makes a clam happy, but people usually list a long life and true love among their hopes. Thus, by human standards, a clam has good reason to be happy. According to Dr. Ida Thompson of Princeton University, the clam is the foxy grandpa of the invertebrate kingdom. Dr. Thompson determined that the bands one finds on a clamshell correspond to the rings found in a tree trunk and can be used to determine the clam's age. By this method, she discovered that clams live as long as 150 years (assuming they are not made into chowder), show no signs of aging (other than adding bands), and remain sexually active throughout their lives. In fact, Dr. Thompson questioned whether clams ever die of old age.

Courtesy of Tim Clark

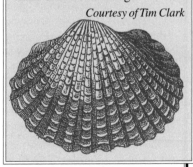

1886

Josephine Cochrane of Shelbyville, Illinois, patents her invention, the dishwasher.

■ *As a species, we humans might be a mere blip on the evolutionary time line. To survive the long haul, a species must be free from disease, superbly adapted to its environment, and able to assimilate its diet and eliminate wastes perfectly. If you think such a creature doesn't exist, it's time to go outside and turn over a spadeful of soil.*

The Only Potentially Immortal Creature on Earth

BY PEG BOYLES

I*T IS A MARVELLOUS REFLECTION that the whole . . . expanse has passed, and will again pass, every few years through the bodies of worms. The plough is one of the most ancient and most valuable of man's inventions; but long before he existed the land was in fact regularly ploughed, and still continues to be thus ploughed, by earthworms. It may be doubted whether there are many other animals which have played so important a part in the history of the world, as have these lowly organised creatures.*

These are the words of the great Charles Darwin, who in 1881 after more than 40 years of painstaking research, published what he considered his magnum opus, "The Formation of Vegetable Mould Through the Action of Worms with Observations on Their Habits."

It is both a tribute to Darwin's genius and a sad commentary on the scientific priorities of our time that his classic treatise stands unchallenged and unsurpassed even today as the definitive work on earthworms. Few modern investigators are directing their attention toward these "lowly organised creatures" that Darwin rightly placed at the pinnacle of importance within the animal kingdom.

For earthworms have always played a central role in the biodegradation of the Earth's wastes and in the creation and maintenance of productive agricultural soils. Some investigators even offer compelling evidence suggesting that without the stable agricultural base created by the soil-tilling, humus-creating efforts of certain active earthworm species, complex human civilizations might never have developed.

Earthworms belong to the phylum Annelida, the soft-bodied segmented worms. Close relatives of leeches and other marine worms,

1886

The Statue of Liberty in New York Harbor is dedicated.

earthworms have gradually over the millennia adapted to soil environments. Even today, many earthworm species inhabit swamps and wetlands, and all must remain continuously moist to survive.

Earthworms are further classified as Chaetopoda and the order Oligochaeta, both categories of bristle-footed worms. The bristles, called seta, are recessed into the worms' body walls and assist in locomotion, in anchoring the worms in their burrows, and in embracing a partner during mating. Of the 14 earthworm families, the most important commercially and agriculturally in North America is the family Lumbricidae.

Although some 1,800 species of earthworms have already been identified, it is postulated that there may be more than 5,000 species in all, with 70 or more species inhabiting the soils of North America. Each has its unique habits, food preferences, range of preferred condi-

Earthworms have always played a central role in the biodegradation of the Earth's wastes and in the creation and maintenance of productive agricultural soils.

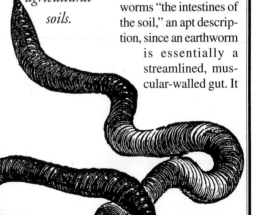

tions, and contributions to waste breakdown and soil creation.

One of the most fascinating among hundreds of mysteries surrounding these lowly creatures is just how long an individual earthworm can live. Free from disease, superbly adapted to its environment, assimilating its diet and eliminating wastes perfectly, the earthworm is potentially immortal. A worm usually succumbs to sudden changes in soil temperature or chemistry (many agricultural chemicals are lethal to earthworms) or falls prey to birds or rodents.

Aristotle called earthworms "the intestines of the soil," an apt description, since an earthworm is essentially a streamlined, muscular-walled gut. It

1886

Coca-Cola is invented by pharmacist John Styth Pemberton of Atlanta, Georgia.

literally eats its way through its environment, ingesting leaf litter, animal manure and remains, twigs, dead roots, and garden debris, as well as soil and mineral particles.

Each species has definite taste preferences. Worms use a muscular lip to push aside unpalatable objects or particles too large to ingest. The food mass taken in through the mouth opening is ground in a gizzard by sand and mineral particles, then moved by powerful muscular contractions into the main feature of a worm's internal anatomy, a long intestine. Here microbes and enzymes digest and assimilate the food. The remains that pass out through a posterior opening are known as castings, a fine colloidal humus rich in available plant nutrients. Most worms eat their weight in food each day and evacuate nearly an equal amount of castings.

An earthworm's circulatory and nervous systems are rudimentary, with no true heart or brain. Worms have no eyes but are extremely light sensitive, due to the presence of photoreceptor cells in the dorsal epidermis. Light activates a worm's burrowing instinct — a necessary survival mechanism, since worms are quickly killed by exposure to ultraviolet rays.

Although earthworms do mate to reproduce, they are hermaphrodites.

The many sensory cells in the epidermis give earthworms the exquisite tactile sense that alerts them to the slightest movement on the soil surface or in the earth around them, providing them with their chief means of surviving the approach of predators.

Gland cells, also located in the epidermis, secrete mucus, which helps keep worms constantly moist, allows the respiration of gases through their body walls, and lubricates the worms so that they can burrow through the most compacted of soils without injury. Deep-diving species such as *Lumbricus terrestris* use this mucus to cement the walls of their burrows.

A special mucus is exuded around the worms' genital openings during mating, protecting the spermatozoa being exchanged. Although earthworms do mate to reproduce, they are hermaphrodites — an important factor in their mind-boggling reproductive rate, since each individual worm produces offspring.

For their reproductive segments to coincide, worms mate with partners of roughly the same length. Using their seta, they hold each other in long embrace, while the sperm are exchanged and stored in

---

1887

A. E. Fick, a Swiss physician, invents the contact lens. Made of glass, it is very uncomfortable. A plastic lens will be made in 1938, but the first truly comfortable lens will not be introduced until 1950.

the partner's internal sperm receptacles until the eggs have matured.

The clitellum, a swollen, saddle-shaped band near the middle of a mature worm, then exudes a thick substance, containing both eggs and sperm, that hardens and is eventually sloughed off. The resulting egg-shaped capsule is where actual fertilization takes place. In most species, one or two worms will eventually hatch from each capsule, and a mature worm may produce a capsule each week.

Under favorable conditions, the eggs will hatch within 14 to 21 days, although earthworm capsules possess the extraordinary ability to hold the fertile eggs until conditions are right for survival of the newly hatched progeny. The little earthworms grow rapidly, reaching sexual maturity in 85 to 100 days.

The well-known regenerative powers of earthworms are amazing indeed, although considerably more modest than popular opinion holds. In any case of injury or severing, no more than one earthworm can result, and a worm will survive only if its neurological and reproductive systems are intact. Regeneration may take weeks or months depending on the species and the extent of the injury. A worm will never regenerate more segments than it possessed originally.

Earthworm populations can constitute a third of the soil's biomass and up to 95 percent of the weight of soil fauna. Productive agricultural soils may contain from half a million to more than 3 million worms per acre and contribute up to 50 tons or more of rich compost annually per acre of soil.

Yet, incredibly, no full-scale research has ever attempted to assess the full potential contribution earthworms might make to this nation's agriculture. At the same time, many

Bats flying late in the evening foretell a fine next day.

present agricultural techniques severely deplete earthworm populations.

Here are but a few of the well-documented contributions made by earthworms to agriculture.

1. Earthworm castings are a compost rich in available plant nutrients. Compared to the soil in which they are found, castings may contain 5 times the available nitrogen, 7 times the phosphorus, 3 times the magnesium, 11 times the potassium, and 1.5 times the calcium. Castings are always of near-

1888

The first issue of *National Geographic* is published in Washington, D.C.

neutral pH, making them an ideal pelletized fertilizer for most crops.

2. Some species, notably *L. terrestris* (night crawlers), construct permanent burrows up to 15 feet deep. Their burrowing helps break up hardpans and compacted soils, leaving channels that are filled eventually by biologically active topsoil. These channels can become

Dream of birds, and you dream of friends and fortune.

fertile tunnels for easy penetration by crop roots. Deep-burrowing worms ingest particles of mineral-rich subsoil, which then become available for plant use when they are excreted in castings left on or near the soil surface.

3. Earthworm castings contribute greatly to the improvement of soil structure, assisting in the development of a stable humus, the most desirable form for soil organic matter. The colloidal castings form soil aggregates, helping to keep the soil open and porous whether wet or dry. Soils rich in earthworms will drain four to ten times faster than those without worms, while still retaining water and dispensing it slowly for use by crops.

4. There is evidence that nitrogen fixation by anaerobic bacteria may take place in an earthworm's gut. This would mean that encouraging a sizable earthworm population could lessen a farmer's need for nitrogen fertilizers. Unfortunately, many commercial nitrogen fertilizers prove lethal to earthworms, thus interfering with a free natural means of maintaining soil fertility.

5. Earthworm castings are invariably higher in pH than the surrounding soil, yet the potential of this contribution to agriculture has never been gauged. (Most crops require a soil pH just shy of neutral.)

For all its vaunted efficiency, our modern Western agriculture withdraws 12 calories of nonrenewable fuel energy for each calorie it returns as food. Certainly in a time when the need to develop energy alternatives is so pressing, our agricultural and scientific institutions need to overcome the largely psychological barriers to an all-out study of what these "lowly organised creatures" might contribute to a solar-based agriculture.

The earthworms' medium is their message. The soil — it sustains us all. And as the worm turns, so may the future of our soils and their ability to feed the people of Earth.

1888

The first formal rodeo is held in Prescott, Arizona.

FARMER'S CALENDAR

Analyzing Ants

EXCEPT ON PICNICS and in their kitchens, most people evidently like ants. We feel a friendship for them that is unlike our response to any other insect. No insect has had better press from poets and authors, including our very best and biggest. Why? What is it about ants?

Not their looks. Many of the animals we most enjoy are animals that somehow look like people: frogs, geese, bears. Ants don't look like anything but ants. Others of our favorite animals don't look like us so much but seem to have the same kind of minds we have: dogs, cats, horses, dolphins. But nobody ever made friends with an ant. They hardly exist as individuals. That, perhaps, is our clue: We mostly experience ants in numbers, operating collectively. It is as a community that ants, severally almost invisible, make their appeal to us.

But only so far. "The ants are a people not strong, yet they prepare their meat in the summer," says the proverb. Laborious, thorough, and  completely willing to submerge the individual in and for the mass, ants succeed, and we like them just because we understand their individual insignificance and recognize their collective power. But we are seldom willing to work as hard or — especially — to sink our own pride as low. And so our affection for the ant is complex and includes a measure of superiority, the kind of negative admiration we may feel for those who possess virtues we acknowledge but are in no hurry to imitate.

1889

A dam breaks above Johnstown, Pennsylvania, and the ensuing flood claims about 2,200 lives.

■ *Ever consider a cricket for your next pet? They're easy to manage, won't last very long, and don't eat much. And you'll love (or hate) their singing.*

The Case for a Pet Cricket

BY KATHLEEN KILGORE

I'VE NEVER MET ANother American family that keeps pet crickets, although they are prized in Japan and probably China. My mother got the idea from a 1925 kindergarten teacher's textbook.

A field cricket is shiny black with brown wings. There are no green crickets — Hollywood's Jiminy Cricket to the contrary. A fully grown male is a bit less than an inch long, and a female about 50 percent longer. They are easy to tell apart, and telling them apart is vital if you want one for a pet, because the female does not sing. At his rear, the male has two thin, pronglike sensory organs. The female has three prongs, the middle and longest one being her ovipositor, with which she injects eggs into the soil. A cricket is shorter and stubbier than a grasshopper and stays close to the ground. The cricket won't jump except in desperation.

The female lays her eggs in the ground in the fall. They hatch in May or early June, producing thousands of tiny black crickets swarming in the tall grass. They molt rapidly, and by the time they are large enough to start singing in late July or early August, they have become not only bigger but also more cautious. The male selects a den to which he can retreat at a moment's notice — a tiny hole in the ground, a crack in a cement wall, a crevice under a piece of bark — and begins to sing.

Unlike the grasshopper, the cricket doesn't sing by rubbing his legs together. He lifts his wing casings at a 45-degree angle and rubs them together. The insides are lined with tiny sawtooth projections.

The cricket sings to attract a mate. But in captivity, he also will sing when you give him food (crickets can eat and sing at the same time). Some crickets become so tame that they will sing when you blow gently on them — they seem to like the warmth. Like all insects, crickets are cold-blooded, and they sing faster or slower depending on the temperature.

From my own experiments, it seems that the cricket's song is territorial. One fall I recorded the

1891

Dr. James Naismith, the physical education instructor at the YMCA Training School in Springfield, Massachusetts, invents the game of basketball. The first game is played with two peach baskets nailed to the balcony of the gymnasium.

cricket's song on tape. When the recording was played across the room, he showed no interest. But when I played it near his cage, he went wild, clawing at the sides to get at his rival. After a few more tries, I determined his territory to be about two feet in diameter. In China, male crickets were made to fight like roosters by putting two at a time in a pottery jar. They will fight whether a female is present or not. And they fight fiercely, losing legs and antennae, often continuing until one dies.

It's best not to keep two males in a cage. And don't take pity on

The cricket sings to attract a mate. But in captivity, he also will sing when you give him food. . . . Some crickets become so tame that they will sing when you blow gently on them — they seem to like the warmth.

your frustrated male and give him a female unless you have kinky voyeuristic tastes. The female is much bigger, and in a cage the male has no chance to escape. After their amour, you'll probably find Madam polishing off the remains of her lover.

I've experimented with several kinds of cages, jars, and fishbowls and found that the best cricket house is a medium-size pickle jar with holes punched in the lid. By far the worst home for a pet cricket is a cute sandalwood and bamboo cricket cage imported from Japan. The cricket can squeeze

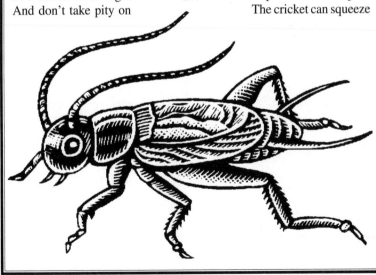

1892

The first U.S. horseshoe-pitching club is established in Meadville, Pennsylvania.

between the bars or, failing that, simply chew through the bamboo.

After you get your cricket, you can add sand or clean soil and leaves to the bottom of his container. A piece of bark makes him feel more at home. If a pickle jar is out of place in your decorating scheme, you could put him in a fishbowl or terrarium bottle. But the top must be covered tightly with wire mesh, and even with that crickets can sometimes squeeze underneath the edge, or hurt themselves trying. You're safer with a ventilated screw top.

Now comes the hard part — the hunt. Crickets abound in fields and front lawns, but the minute you get within a few feet of a cricket, he shuts up and retreats into his hole. The best place to catch him is on your own turf. In the fall, crickets often come inside, attracted by the

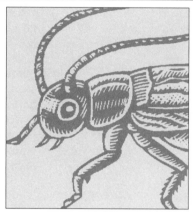

Now we come to the sad part. A cricket's life span is very short. . . . Outdoors, the first frost kills the crickets, but even in a warm house with good care, they won't winter over. If you catch one in good condition in August or September, he should last until Thanksgiving.

warmth. Anytime you hear one singing in a bathroom or cellar, you have a potentially easy catch.

Once you have what you are pretty sure is a cricket in your hand, be careful. Their legs and antennae can break off, and they can bite like crazy. Your pickle jar is sitting on the shelf miles away, so the next best thing is a cotton handkerchief. Wrap this loosely so that he won't suffocate, and try to get him home as soon as possible.

The best place to transfer the cricket to his jar is the bathtub. After he settles down and becomes tame, you can put him safely in another jar while you clean the old one by tipping it up. He will slide down the glass, but a newly caught cricket will make desperate attempts to escape. Close the drain and shower curtains — a glass-enclosed shower stall is ideal.

1892

The Pledge of Allegiance, written by Francis Bellamy, appears in the September 8 issue of *The Youth's Companion* for children to recite on Columbus Day (October 12).

Once he is safely in the jar, you will have to be careful about using insect sprays. They can kill him as well as harmful insects. He needs both food and water every day. For water, the most convenient dish is the lid of a plastic medicine jar. It can be put in with tweezers or a bacon turner, then filled by drawing water through a straw and releasing it in the lid. The water dish should be cleaned and refilled every day. I had one cricket who used to sit in his water dish all day, but generally they just drink from it.

Crickets will eat almost anything, including your woolens, if they escape. They like cereals of all kinds: cornflakes, oats, granola. They are crazy about birdseed, especially sunflower seeds, and will also eat apple peelings, lettuce, raw carrots, and other raw vegetables. It's best to go easy on the food; they eat very little. Any food should be removed every day so that the jar will not grow mold. I usually clean the jar and put in fresh dirt every two or three days.

Now we come to the sad part. A cricket's life span is very short. In fact, this is one pet children will not get tired of before it dies. Outdoors, the first frost kills the crickets, but even in a warm house with good care, they won't winter over. If you catch one in good condition in August or September, he should last until Thanksgiving. But I have never had one make it to Christmas.

Sometimes you will just find the cricket lifeless in the morning. Sometimes he will seem to lose his balance and flop about. When that happens, I put the cricket outdoors where I won't have to watch him die. Occasionally, one night the cricket's song will just get fainter and fainter, like Tinker Bell in *Peter Pan,* until it fades away by dawn. Then dump the jar out on the lawn, give it a good washing, and put it away for next fall.

Cows give more milk and the sea more fish when the wind's from the west.

1892

Peter Tchaikovsky's ballet *The Nutcracker* is performed in St. Petersburg, Russia, for the first time. It receives very poor reviews.

We are taught to take the good with the bad, but there are some nasty creatures out there that have sorely tested our best efforts at fairness. Animals that arrive in our country by accident, or simply through bad judgment, give new meaning to the term "immigration and naturalization." The stories behind several unfortunate intrusions appeared in the 1988 Almanac.

Unforgettable Gifts from Pandora's Box

BY ART SORDILLO

SEVERAL YEARS AGO, A FAMILY from Massachusetts moved to the San Fernando Valley in California and unknowingly brought along what could have been a devastating plague: the gypsy moth. Nine of the insects and three egg masses were found in a dollhouse tucked away with the family's belongings. The California Department of Food and Agriculture moved quickly to destroy this unfussy eater. California, still reeling from the $100-million problem caused by the Mediterranean fruit fly, didn't need any more exotic pests.

Well established in the Northeast, the gypsy moth arrived because of one man's desire to become rich in the silk industry. Leopold Trouvelot hoped to make his fortune in Medford, Massachusetts, in 1869 when he sent to Europe for some gypsy moth speci-mens. Hoping to crossbreed the gypsy moth with the mulberry silkworm, Trouvelot committed an unforgivable sin: Some gypsy moth larvae somehow got away from him and found the New England environment perfect for lack of predators or parasites.

The gypsy moth is a classic example of an invited pest that is here to stay. "Feeding" this pest has burdened us with more than an unmanageable grocery bill. In a "lean" year, the gypsy moth defoliates more than 2.5 million acres of forest in the Northeast.

Gypsy moths have an infamous track record, but a new problem surfaced in Rochester, New York, in 1987. Health officials there blamed gypsy moth caterpillars for polluting the city's water supply. Residents had to boil their water because tons of caterpillar droppings were getting into the reservoir. (The

1893

Mildred and Patty Smith Hill of Louisville, Kentucky, compose the melody that will later (1924) be used for the song "Happy Birthday to You."

bacteria count was so high that some theorized there were human bodies lodged somewhere in the system.)

And so we create our own predicament. The ancient Greeks in their myths blamed the first woman, Pandora, for the miseries we suffer. Pandora was give a box by Zeus. Her curiosity getting the better of her, she opened it, thereby letting out all the evils and distempers of the human race.

INVITED PESTS

■ Eugene Schieffelin was a man with two loves: Shakespeare and birds. This combination gave Eugene a cause: He decided to import every bird mentioned in the plays of Shakespeare. Some birds did not survive in their new home, but one line from *Henry IV* gave Eugene some hope: "I'll have a starling shall be taught to speake nothing but 'Mortimer.'" That one line has caused Americans to speak nothing but unspeakables about the starling, introduced in 1890. Released in New York, starlings are now found in all 50 states. Wintering flocks of starlings mingle with blackbirds and create enormous problems. In Tupelo, Mississippi, swarms of 3 million are common. Not only are the birds a nuisance, but they also are a health threat. If many birds are allowed to roost in the same location, a fungus that causes histoplasmosis, a respiratory illness, develops in the soil contaminated by the birds' droppings.

■ Sparrows were first brought to New York around 1850. They didn't take long to roost in the New World. In 1884 the sexton of St. John's Church in Providence destroyed 970 eggs. Quite a pest, the sparrow destroys buds and blossoms of fruit trees as well as grain crops.

In Stillwater, Oklahoma, 2,000 nesting sparrows in the downtown area caused a health problem in the

1893

Whitcomb Judson patents his "clasp locker," later improved by Gideon Sundback (1913) and named the zipper by B. F. Goodrich (1923).

late 1980s. The birds refused to eat poisoned bait, turned a deaf ear to the cannons that were set off, and ignored the rubber snakes. Exasperated, the city manager proposed that model airplane owners organize a mobile air force to dive-bomb the stubborn birds. We don't know whether there were any takers.

■ In 1936 a young woman brought some snails back to Oahu from her visit to Formosa. Thinking her "pets" — giant African snails — would look nice in the garden, she let them loose. Voracious eaters, they are now well established in the Hawaiian Islands. Attempts to kill them with the rat poison warfarin failed; the snails thrive on it.

■ Snyder, Texas, considers itself the clam center of West Texas. Darrell Callahan, supervisor of the water system, said, "It's something we're not proud of." The Asiatic clam is a nickel-size pest that has been nickel-and-diming 35 states to the tune of a billion dollars per year. It clogs water pipes, so much so that a nuclear power plant in Arkansas had to shut down because of damage to the internal cooling pipes. The clams are virtually indestructible — they have been found still moving inside poured concrete. Although it's somewhat of a mystery as to how these clams got here, the prevalent theory is that they were imported as an Asian gourmet food around the turn of the 20th century. University of Texas biologist Dr. Robert McMahon said that they are "the most damaging pest species introduced into fresh water." Control is always difficult with any hermaphroditic species; one clam can produce 400,000 larvae.

■ A fish culturist for the U.S. government, Rudolph Hessel, introduced the carp to this country in 1877. By 1883, 260,000 carp were divided among 298 congressional districts, and soon this wonder fish

1894

Newspaper magnate Joseph Pulitzer runs the world's first full-color comic strip in the *New York World*.

was released into public streams. Carp eat everything green and take food out of the mouths of many game birds as well as game fish. Control is difficult: One female is capable of laying 500,000 eggs.

■ Domestic swine were introduced to California by the Spaniards in 1769. Some pigs escaped and began to breed in the wild. In 1923 European wild boars were introduced into the Carmel Valley and began crossbreeding with the feral hogs.

By the late 1980s, the feral pig population was somewhere in the range of 100,000. The pigs lived up to their name and were consuming just about anything that grew. The problem was so bad that the Golden Gate National Recreation Area hired a "contract" hunter. He kept pretty busy: A pig population, under ideal conditions, can double every four months.

HITCHHIKERS

■ Malacologists, people devoted to the study of mollusks, believe that most of the slugs that are

The pigs lived up to their name and were consuming just about anything that grew. . . . A pig population, under ideal conditions, can double every four months.

chomping their way through gardens across the continent are descendants of stowaways, imported Europeans that entered this country in the folds of travelers' clothing or perhaps hidden in some suitcase recess. Slugs, never a favorite of the barefooted, can be quite large: The great yellow slug of Colorado can grow to be ten inches long and weigh a quarter of a pound.

■ British general William Howe enlisted the aid of Hessians in an effort to deal with the rebellious colonists in 1776. The Hessians brought over many supplies, including their own mattresses. Hidden in the bedstraw was a small fly that has be-

---

1894

The first kinetoscope parlor opens in New York City. Banks of kinetoscopes are available for individual viewing of motion pictures.

come quite a pest. Wheat farmers across the country are familiar with the Hessian fly. In the 1980s, it was responsible for more than $25 million annually in damage and control costs.

■ Bad luck comes in threes — as in rats, death, and disease. Brown rats are said to have been introduced to North America sometime around the Revolutionary War, arriving as stowaways in ships' holds.

Rats must constantly chew to wear down their front teeth. If a top tooth is knocked out, the bottom tooth will grow unimpeded by the natural grinding of chewing and actually pierce the brain cavity, causing death. But don't count on it. Rats are here to stay, contaminating food supplies and transmitting diseases such as the plague (outbreaks of this "medieval" disease occurred in San Francisco, 1907; New Orleans, 1914; and Galveston, Texas, 1920). Attempting to control this pest is futile. A single female may produce 10 litters of 10 a year, which means that 1 pair of rats has the potential of adding 350 million offspring to their family

A single female may produce 10 litters of 10 a year, which means that 1 pair of rats has the potential of adding 350 million offspring to their family tree in 3 years.

tree in 3 years. Experts estimate that rat-damage costs average $1 per rat each year.

■ In 1912 a law was passed making it illegal to import plants rooted in soil. Unfortunately, the failure to implement the law immediately allowed the most infamous hitchhiker of the century to arrive in this country — the Japanese beetle. Most entomologists agree that the beetles entered the country as grubs in soil on Japanese iris roots. These copperwinged pests were first spotted in a nursery near Riverton, New Jersey, in 1916. By 1920 eradication programs were dropped; the beetle proved to be too prolific a breeder. Not a choosy eater, it dines on more than 200 species of plants.

■ Lampreys usually start life in a swamp, later migrating to the ocean. Yet there are two notable ex-

1895

The game of volleyball is invented in Holyoke, Massachusetts, by William G. Morgan.

amples of landlocked lampreys in Lake Champlain and Lake Ontario. But are they really landlocked? Or are they most likely the by-products of canals that were in operation as early as 1825? Most of the Great Lakes are infested to some degree with these horrible creatures. Lake sturgeon, trout, pike, and lake herring all have succumbed. Lampreys attach themselves to the side of a fish and suck out a fatal meal of blood. On the U.S. side of Lake Huron, the average annual catch of lake trout before World War II was 860 tons; after the lamprey came, it fell to 2.5 tons in 1948. The average "kill" for a lamprey during a 25-month period is 20 pounds of fish.

■ An aggressive, dangerous Asian mosquito, *Aedes albopictus,* commonly known as the Asian tiger mosquito, has established itself in the United States. Entomologists have theorized that this insect arrived in this country via shiploads of used tires, which are imported for recapping. "These mosquitoes are very aggressive," said Daniel Sprenger, a mosquito control expert from Harris County, Texas. The Asian tigers are well established around Houston, New Orleans, and Memphis. The most serious problem is that the mosquito transmits dengue, or breakbone fever, which causes seven to ten days of fever, rash, and joint pain, and in severe cases has resulted in death.

■ All the cockroach species in this country were inadvertently introduced from somewhere else. The latest cockroach introduction will surely spoil your appetite: the Asian cockroach. Scientists have not yet agreed on an official name, but it's likely they will come up with something soon, especially when you consider the bug was first found in Tampa, Florida, and has worked its way to Maryland in less than a year. This new species has a disturbing behavior pattern unlike any other cockroach found in the country — it's *attracted* to light, such as TV sets. And it just loves to pounce on white shirts.

Wish on a spring frog for good luck.

1896

Fannie Merritt Farmer's *Boston Cooking School Cook Book* is published.

ANECDOTES & PLEASANTRIES

Animal Hero: Horace the Frog

IN THE LATE SPRING of 1972, a fire broke out in the science laboratory of a private grammar school in western New York (to remain nameless at the request of school officials). The students were quickly evacuated and grouped on the lawn, when suddenly two sixth-grade boys broke from the crowd and dashed into the building by the rear door. Moments later both boys emerged, one of them clutching Horace, a large frog. As the two boys were being lectured for their recklessness by their biology teacher, Horace wriggled free and started hopping across the lawn, right into the path of a fireman who was rushing toward the side door of the building, now spewing a cloud of thick black smoke. Horace, only recently having left the damp confines of his laboratory home, was wet, so when the poor fireman stepped on Horace, he went flying. The fall stunned the man for a minute or two, during which time the roof of the laboratory collapsed in a flaming roar. Had the fireman made it into the side door, he surely would have perished in the holocaust. For saving the fireman's life, Horace was awarded a medal by the entire sixth-grade class —
posthumously,
of course.

Courtesy of
Yolanda Jarvis

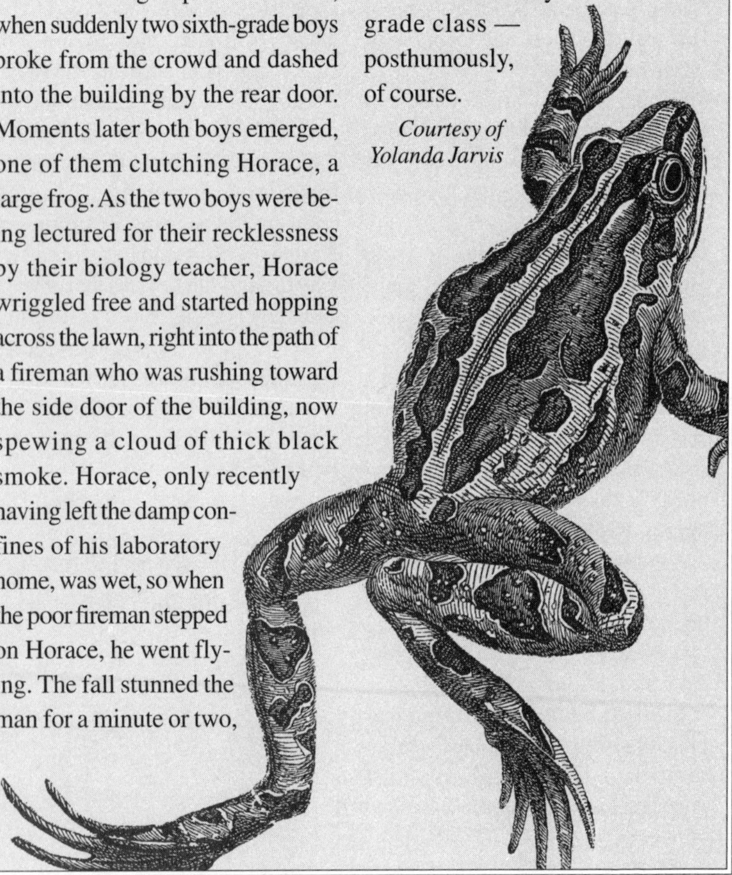

1896

The first modern Olympic Games are held in Athens, Greece. The ancient Olympic Games were abolished in A.D. 394.

FARMER'S CALENDAR

Cold-Blood Envy

WARM-BLOODED CREATURES like ourselves are supposed to have the best of this Earth, but you have to wonder. We go to a lot of trouble. On a May morning, for example, I wake up freezing. I crawl into my two-ton pants and a couple of sweaters. I may even pull on a wool hat — indoors, like a fool. I make my way downstairs and put on the water to heat. I wait, blowing on my fingers. Presently I'll be able to start pouring down the hot coffee. All this because I have to make my heat inside myself.

Then, by eleven o'clock, the Sun will be high and a day will have arrived that is in reality an early-summer day. I'll be tearing off clothing like an Eskimo trapped in a Turkish bath. The fire that I kindled with shivering fingers in the kitchen stove four hours ago will have heated the house intolerably. I'll throw open the windows and sit outdoors on the step. By suppertime, I'll be back in my sweaters and the stove will be cold, the fire out. I'll have to start it all over again. Because I carry my thermostat deep within, I must spend the whole day setting it up or down.

I have never heard snakes, turtles, and lizards praised for their brains. Their magnificent ancestors, the dinosaurs, were long believed to have died out pretty much through sheer stupidity, as I recall the story. On the grand ladder of evolution, the reptiles are assigned a fairly humble rung. But who thought up that ladder? We did. Maybe we were jealous. The reptiles, cold-blooded, can get by at whatever

temperature's on the market. They don't have to scurry around adjusting themselves. No grass snake has ever been made a fool of by a spring day.

1896

"March King" John Philip Sousa writes "The Stars and Stripes Forever."

■ *Finally, we're learning to appreciate some of the common, every-day mysteries of our natural world.*

Nature's Amazing Laws of Speed and Locomotion

BY GUY MURCHIE

HAVE YOU EVER WONDERED HOW a cheetah can run so fast? How he can stalk and then charge an antelope 100 yards away and run it down within 300 yards? Yet a hungry lion only 40 yards from the same antelope will decide that it is hopelessly out of range.

Have you ever wondered why an ostrich cannot fly? How a school of a thousand herring can sort itself into a crystalline formation in which every fish is perfectly matched in size and speed with all his fellow swimmers?

What are nature's speed laws for predators and prey, and how do the individuals conform so that not only does the predator get the food he cannot live without, but his prey at the same time will survive in reasonable contentment? How does running speed relate to size? How many failures can a predator tolerate between successful charges?

More and more convincing answers to such questions are being discovered every year as zoologists research details of animal behavior in the wild, often by attaching radio transmitters so they can track the creatures at will. That is how scientists learned the true nocturnal habits of hyenas, which are not really the despicable scavengers they were always thought to be. And that is how the "big bad wolf" finally proved himself to be a loving parent with no record of having attacked any human being anywhere.

Speed and Size: Why the Ostrich Can't Fly

Animal speed in running depends not only on the animal's size and weight but also on whether it must make an all-out dash to seize the prey or can wear it down in a patient all-day pursuit. It is true that a large animal tends to move faster than a similar small one in proportion to the square root of its linear dimensions. That is known as Froude's law of the correspondence of speeds. It seems to have grown out of Galileo's famous principle of similitude, in which he showed how the geometrizing of God applies without exception to everything in nature. Galileo was probably the first man to observe that trees on Earth cannot grow more than about

1897

Eighteen runners race in the first Boston Marathon on April 19 (Patriots Day).

100 feet high, while terrestrial buildings and conveyances are similarly limited by the fact that their supporting surfaces, having only two dimensions, cannot increase as fast as their weights, which, having volume, must expand in three dimensions.

Froude's law, covering all kinds of locomotion, explains why the ostrich does not fly:

Being about 25 times as tall and long as a sparrow, he would have to move at the square root of 25, or 5 times as fast. That is about the speed of a small airplane, which necessarily has many times an ostrich's "horsepower."

As for efficiency in running, fast animals like ... the horse, ostrich, and kangaroo have long thighs and keep their heavy leg muscles close to the body.

As for efficiency in running, fast animals like the hare and hound, as well as the horse, ostrich, and kangaroo, have long thighs and keep their heavy leg muscles close to the body, where they need not swing so far or so fast as shorter-legged runners. Supreme in this respect are the sprinting cheetah (credited with 70 mph for a short distance), the remarkable loping camel (115 miles in 12 hours), and the horse, whose light hoof-shank system includes marvelously elastic ligaments that save energy by automatically restraightening the fetlock joint and snapping the foot backward like a released spring every time it leaves the ground.

Another speed factor derives from the flexibility of the spine, notable in the cheetah, which greatly increases an animal's length of stride and can actually enable its foot to move in a smooth elliptical

1898

Caleb Bradham of New Bern, North Carolina, introduces Pepsi-Cola.

orbit in respect to the rest of its body — not very different from the cyclic path described by any point on the rim of a wheel or by the revolution of a planet circling the Sun.

Why Fish Swim in Schools

The mass maneuvering of animals in large numbers follows different rules that are crucial to their survival. Herds of reindeer may run in a V formation, but when cornered by wolves, they invariably curve into tight defensive circles like wagon trains attacked by Indians. And huge schools of fish and flocks of birds maneuver by subtle influences that still puzzle scientists. Vast bird flocks, like the formation of an estimated 150 million slender-billed shearwaters reported in Bass Strait between Australia and Tasmania several years ago, sometimes show a complex three-dimensional motion that includes convexity over a thousand square miles, as if it were part of the living skin of the planet, and that seems to be affected by the local winds and pressure patterns as much as by factors having to do with migration.

Schools of fish, being more amenable to laboratory study, are better understood than birds. Their formations in the sea vary in shape from square to diamond to elliptical to amoeboid, and, like sand grains on windswept dunes, the individual fish automatically sort themselves out by size and speed. The newly hatched fry begin to swim very slowly at first but steadily gain in both speed and size, their speed increasing (by Froude's law) in direct proportion to the square root of their increasing length. They keep a few inches apart, swimming irregularly, until

1899

L. Frank Baum tells a story to his children that he writes down and has published the following year as *The Wonderful Wizard of Oz.*

they are nearly half an inch long.

At this stage, they suddenly and instinctively begin to feel regimentation, swimming side by side or parallel to one another for short distances, responding to each other visually, conforming more and more exactly to the regimen of their fellows as they grow bigger. They also come relatively closer together as they grow, reducing the distance to half a body length by the time they are four inches long. They use a special pressure sense that fish have to help maintain the distance. Because smaller fish cannot keep pace with larger ones of the same species, they inevitably lag behind in ratio to their size, and that is what winnows them into their discrete grades or classes. It is a process crucial in the schooling of minnows. A mark of its widespread success among fish is that an estimated 16,000 species (80 percent of all fish) have adopted it, perhaps because predators tend to become confused by mass-regimented fish and therefore leave more of them to survive. Fish in schools are also known to have greater endurance in swimming and greater toleration of stresses; this probably relates to their mutually beneficial body radiation in close formation and lower consumption

Predators tend to become confused by mass-regimented fish and therefore leave more of them to survive.

of oxygen per fish (proven in diverse experiments).

Another advantage in schooling is improved efficiency through specialization. Fish swimming at the edges of a school, for instance, serve as the "eyes" of fish in the center, so the latter neither have to hunt for food nor be wary of danger as long as they can respond within about a sixth of a second to any change in direction or speed initiated by the "eye" fish (one-sixth of a second having been clocked in a California laboratory as the average fish school's response time). School specialization sharpens the awareness and effective intelligence of the school as a whole so that it can avoid a net or migrate to a safe spawning ground more successfully than any member fish alone. And in its transcendent superiority, it knows both how to move slowly and compactly to decrease its chances of meeting a predator and, when hunting, how to accelerate in looser formation to increase its chances of meeting prey.

There exist some small school fish that have evolved an amazing ploy to avoid being eaten. They do something called podding, which means breaking ranks when alarmed and huddling into a compact mass called a pod, in which they literally touch each other in tight layers. This curious performance, comparable to the Greek phalanx, has been known to save lake fish from an attacking loon. And mullet, spent and spawning in cold water, have been seen to pod perhaps for warmth or reassurance.

The Eater Meets the Eatee

You may think predation is such a deadly competition that the two sides are trying to eliminate each other to whatever extent is possible. But the eater and the eatee actually have no such goals, for they really need one another. In fact, they are playing a continuous game that, like all games, has rules. And a prime rule for the predator is this: He kills only what he needs to sustain him. To exterminate the prey or even make it scarce would be to eliminate his own food supply. No, the predator is basically a conservationist.

Being a conservationist, however, does not mean that the wolf or lion ever consciously moderates his hunting or holds back from killing with a thought for tomorrow or next month. He doesn't need to exercise such restraint — because killing is just not that easy. In fact, on Isle Royale in Lake Superior, where wolves and moose have been confronting each other for many years, only 1 in 13 wolf attacks on moose results in a kill. In other parts of the world, the "batting average" for li-

ons, hyenas, leopards, and other predators, including hawks, is about the same.

There is a delicate balance to predation and countless complexities, such as the compulsion to defend one's territory or the need to find one's place in the pecking order of one's social unit. Another complexity is the factor of extravagance: The most vulnerable of creatures, such as newly hatched fish, exist in such extravagant numbers that they defeat their most voracious and powerful predators simply by proliferating into such vast hordes that even if tens of thousands of them are gobbled up, there inevitably remain enough survivors to live to grow up and procreate their species. And it has long been a philosophical challenge to weigh the survival of the individual against the survival of the species, to balance mortality against immortality or even finitude against infinitude.

1901

The first license plates appear on New York cars.

FARMER'S CALENDAR

Allies and Adversaries

THE EARLIEST SCIENTIFIC OBSERVERS of nature found that wild birds and animals had lives that resembled those of people, not individually but politically, so to speak. Aristotle in his *History of Animals* (ca. 330 B.C.) describes a complicated system of enmities and alliances subsisting between creatures of various kinds. Most often, according to Aristotle, adversaries in the world of animals and birds are pitted against each other because they compete for food or because one is food for the other: "The eagle and the snake are enemies, for the eagle lives on snakes." Here the accuracy of the report seems plain enough, but it's remarkable that the author invariably expresses predator-prey relationships not as matters of simple survival but as warfare.

The alliances Aristotle discovered in nature are more interesting and curious than the oppositions: "The crow and the heron are friends, as also are the sedge-bird and the lark." While conflicts among animals are practical and based on survival, their alliances seem to involve subtler affinities. Friendships in the animal world are traditional, *historic,* we might almost say, like the friendship between England and the United States.

It's all pretty quaint. These observations are the product of a time when science had our eyes but not our minds. Today we are constantly on guard against the "pathetic fallacy," in which we attribute to animals human thoughts and feelings. Aristotle's natural history took the fallacy a large step further, giving to the birds and animals not only ideas and emotions but also foreign relations.

1902

Nabisco introduces Barnum's Animal Crackers in the circus-design box complete with string handle.

> ■ *Throughout history, many animals have performed remarkable deeds. Following are short tales of three pets who really left their mark.*

Three Incredible Pets Who Will Never Be Forgotten

Jim, the Wonder Dog

JIM WAS JUST A PLAIN BLACK AND white setter, but among all dogs there has never been anything his equal. Psychology professors from Washington University in St. Louis and the University of Missouri were puzzled by the uncanny things he could do. Even his master, Sam Van Arsdale, could offer no clue to his remarkable gift. Jim earned his reputation during the 1930s, when he gave demonstrations that hinted of a power beyond the comprehension of mortal man. So unique were this dog's

talents that he became a national celebrity: Jim, the Wonder Dog.

I first met Jim one warm summer day in the little town of Warsaw, Missouri, down on what is now the Lake of the Ozarks. Noticing a crowd gathering around some sort of commotion on Main Street, I drifted over.

Sam was talking. "What would I do," he asked, "if I had the stomachache?" Jim gave him a sympathetic look, wagged his tail, and trotted over to where Dr. Savage, the town physician, was standing. He nudged the doctor gently.

Sam stroked Jim's ears for a moment. "What made Henry Ford rich?" he asked next. The dog walked over to the curb and stood looking at a Model T Ford.

"See if you can find me a car," requested Sam, "with this license," and he gave a number. Jim crossed the street, looked up and down, and placed his paws on the running board of the county tax collec-

1902

The teddy bear gets its name from Rose and Morris Michtom, who are inspired by a cartoon of President Theodore ("Teddy") Roosevelt sparing the life of a mother bear with cubs while on a hunting trip.

tor's car. The license number was the correct one.

Then someone in the crowd spoke a few words in French. Van Arsdale looked apprehensive, since he didn't understand the language. But Jim slipped through the crowd and began nudging an interested spectator. It was our Methodist minister.

Van Arsdale turned to the questioner. "What did you say to Jim?" he asked.

"I asked if there was a Bible in the crowd," replied the French-speaking spectator.

The pastor had a quizzical look on his face as he reached into an inside pocket and produced a Bible.

I learned later that Jim could understand and would carry out orders given to him in Greek, German, French, and Spanish, or any other tongue for that matter, even though his master could not speak a foreign language and did not know the content of the question.

Jim was born in Louisiana in March 1925, one of a litter of seven pups. When he was a couple of months old, his owner sold him to Van Arsdale, who was living in West Plains, Missouri, at the time.

In quick succession then, at his master's suggestions, [Jim] found a walnut tree, a cedar, an ordinary stump, and even a hazel bush. It was the first real inkling that Jim was something special.

Sam placed the young dog in a kennel, where he was to be trained as a hunting dog. Jim required little training. He seemed to know instinctively where the quail were and how to make a perfect point.

When Jim was three, Van Arsdale moved to Sedalia, where he had bought a hotel. One warm fall day when the two were out in the fields hunting, Van Arsdale said, "Let's sit in the shade of that hickory tree and rest." Jim walked over to a hickory tree and sat down.

Bemused, Van Arsdale told Jim to show him an oak tree. Jim did. In quick succession then, at his master's suggestions, he found a walnut tree, a cedar, an ordinary stump, and even a hazel bush. It was the first real inkling that Jim was something special.

Jim rapidly acquired a national reputation. Although everyone was amazed, Van Arsdale himself was intensely interested in finding out how Jim could perform as he did. Searching for an answer, he arranged for a demonstration at the University of Missouri, with skeptical Dr. A. J. Durant, head of the School of Veterinary Medicine, conducting the proceedings. Durant was assisted

1903

The first narrative motion picture, Edwin S. Porter's *The Great Train Robbery,* is a hit.

by Dr. Sherman Dickinson of the College of Agriculture. The Paramount motion picture company was there to film the event.

As a starter, Dr. Durant gave Jim a thorough examination. He could find nothing abnormal or different from any other dog. Jim then demonstrated his skills by responding promptly and accurately to a variety of commands in several languages.

At the conclusion of the tests, a thoroughly convinced Dr. Durant told the crowd he was certain that Jim possessed an occult power that may never come again to a dog—at least for many, many generations.

Such were Jim's powers that he could even look into the future and foretell coming events. For seven years in a row, he was shown a list of entries in the Kentucky Derby and picked the winner each time in advance of the race. With equal ease, he could correctly predict the sex of babies yet unborn.

In 1936, just before the World Series, Van Arsdale, in the presence of friends, placed before Jim two pieces of paper upon which the names of the teams had been written. He explained, "Jim, I have here the names of the two teams that will be playing in the World Series. Will you show us the one that will win?" Jim placed a paw on the slip bearing the word *Yankees*. The end of the series proved him correct.

Again in 1936, Jim was asked to predict the winner of the presidential race. The names of Roosevelt and Landon were each written on separate pieces of paper and placed in a hat. The slips were drawn out by two ladies. Then Van Arsdale said, "Now, Jim, one of these ladies holds the name of the next president of the United States; will you show us who it will be?" Jim went immediately to one of the women. She unfolded her slip and read the name *Roosevelt.*

Although Jim could apparently predict the outcome of any future event with certainty, Van Arsdale refused to take advantage of the knowledge by wagering on Jim's foretelling; neither would he permit anyone else to reap a profit from Jim's uncanny ability. He

For seven years in a row, he was shown a list of entries in the Kentucky Derby and picked the winner each time in advance of the race. With equal ease, he could correctly predict the sex of babies yet unborn.

1903

Windshield wipers are invented by Mary Anderson.

rejected all offers with this explanation: "I feel that Jim's powers are beyond my comprehension, and I do not care to commercialize on them in any way."

On the morning of March 18, 1937, Van Arsdale and Jim headed for a fishing trip. Shortly after they arrived at the Lake of the Ozarks, the dog suddenly collapsed. Sam rushed his faithful companion to a veterinary hospital in Sedalia. The dog breathed only twice after being put on the table.

Because Van Arsdale considered Jim one of the family, he wanted to have the dog buried in the family plot in Ridge Park Cemetery in Marshall. The authorities would not permit this, so Jim was buried in a specially built casket just outside the cemetery gate. The cemetery has since been enlarged, and Jim's grave is now within its boundaries. Officials report that more people visit his grave than any other in the cemetery.

— Henry N. Ferguson

The Toad Who Took a Nap

EASTLAND, TEXAS, ON U.S. HIGH-way 20, 100 miles west of Fort Worth, is the hometown of the late "Old Rip," the horned toad who in his day gained more publicity than many famous and accomplished people.

In the fall of 1897, the town of Eastland was celebrating the laying of the cornerstone for a new courthouse. At the proper moment in the ceremony, county officials began placing inside the cornerstone the usual assortment of items that custom dictates must be deposited inside such a vault. Present that day was young Will Wood, whose father was playing in the town band for

1903

Crayola crayons, made by Binney & Smith, appear in stores. They cost a nickel a box.

the occasion. Will happened to have a horned toad in his pocket. Watching the proceedings, he felt compelled to contribute to the collection of memorabilia. He did, by dropping in his pet. The cornerstone was capped and tapped into place. It would be 31 years before anyone would see its contents again.

In 1928 Eastland was preparing to tear down the old courthouse and build a new one. On February 28, a crowd of some 2,000 onlookers was on hand to see the old cornerstone opened. Historian Edwin T. Cox, who was present, gave this account of what happened on that day:

One end of a chain was fastened to the cornerstone, the other end to a tractor. Moments later the cornerstone was pulled free of the wall. County Judge Ed S. Pritchard reached into the small vault, removing a Bible and other items from their three-decade hiding place. Again the hand was thrust into the opening. This time the judge gingerly lifted out a flat, dust-covered toad, which he dangled aloft by a hind leg so all might see.

Once-quiet Eastland became a seething mass of people wanting to see the frog. Reporters and photographers converged, and the wire services picked up every detail about the famous creature.

Suddenly the inert toad gave a convulsive shudder and began to swell up as it took a deep breath. Without benefit of food, water, or fresh air, the spiny little fellow had endured for 31 years. Now, through some strange circumstance, it had come alive again.

The toad was immediately christened "Old Rip" in deference to the legend of Rip van Winkle, and as word spread, the publicity gate opened. Once-quiet Eastland became a seething mass of people wanting to see the frog. Reporters and photographers converged, and the wire services picked up every detail about the famous creature. Old Rip had surpassed the achievement of the original Rip van Winkle, who had slept a mere 20 years.

Will Woods, who had placed the toad in the cornerstone, exhibited Old Rip on a tour of the United States. In May of that year, Old Rip was invited to visit President Calvin Coolidge in the White House. Legend has it that "Calvin broke several engagements in order to see the toad."

1904

The first ice cream cones are eaten at the St. Louis World's Fair.

Unfortunately, the little reptile's traveling days were of short duration. Eleven months after his emancipation from the cornerstone, the January 20, 1929, issue of the local *Daily Telegram* carried the banner headline DEATH ENDS RIP'S CAREER. Official cause of death was listed as pneumonia.

Preparations were immediately made for the body of Old Rip to lie in state at the Barrow undertaking parlors for several days so that people might pay their respects. People came from all parts of the country to walk past the bier for a glimpse of Eastland's famous toad.

Town officials had the body embalmed. Today Old Rip and his legend remain very much a part of Eastland. He may still be seen, resting in his plush-lined casket inside a glass and marble case in the lobby of Eastland's courthouse.

— *Henry N. Ferguson*

The Cat Who Came to Dinner

Seldom are we called upon to record a more horrible or shocking occurrence than that described in this extract from a letter dated Boieville, Mississippi, August 13, 1835:

A MOST SINGULAR AND TRAGICAL incident took place in this village, that has cast a gloom over the spirits of all the citizens, and clothed one of our most respectable families in mourning. Preparations had been in the making for some time to erect a large, four-story mill and manufactory in the east part of the village, and Tuesday last was appointed for the raising. As it was a matter in which the public had taken

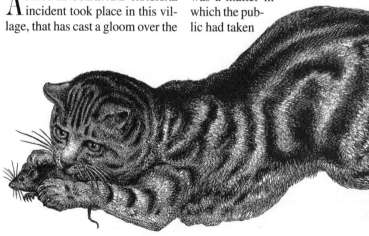

A new organization for young farmers and homemakers begins in Minnesota. In 1920 it will be named the 4-H (head, heart, hands, and health) Club.

a great interest, the whole population of the surrounding country assembled, arrangements were made for a large dinner party, and a bough-house was erected for the females. With a view of surprising the young women, some young men had the night previously secreted in a thick grove of bushes, about 200 yards from the bough-house, a nine-pound fieldpiece, heavily loaded, intending to discharge it while the party were seated at table. Unfortunately it was pointed directly at the opening of the bough-house. Some wretch in the meantime had taken a cat, confined its legs, and placed it in the gun. When the party were seated at the table the cannon was fired. Mrs. Blakeson, the wife of the chief magistrate of the village, who was at the head of the table, had at that instant risen for some purpose, when the cat struck her just below the shoulders and passed through her body; she uttered a single scream, and fell lifeless into the arms of a lady who was next to her; she was a highly accomplished and interesting lady, and the mother of seven children, the eldest being six years old. The cat passed over the whole length of the table, upsetting several decanters and pitchers, and its head was driven through an inch board at the east end of the bough-house, where it lodged; and what is most extraordinary, although stunned and apparently dead, it has recovered, and is now alive and well! The authorities have offered a reward of $100 for the conviction of the miscreant who was the author of this diabolical piece of mischief.

With a view of surprising the young women, some young men had the night previously secreted in a thick grove of bushes . . . a nine-pound fieldpiece, heavily loaded, intending to discharge it while the party were seated at table.

Reprinted from the Times *(London), October 26, 1835. Courtesy of Kenneth W. Mirvis*

Dream of a cow, and you will receive favorable news.

1905

Alfred Binet and Théodore Simon of France devise a test to measure intelligence, later known as the IQ test.

■ *Some scientists are beginning to believe that standard tests used to measure animal intelligence are often about as meaningful as giving an American a multiple-choice exam in a foreign language.*

Who's Smarter: Cats or Dogs or Human Beings?

BY SY MONTGOMERY

QUESTION: *OUR DOG OFTEN TAKES the posture of Rodin's famous statue,* The Thinker. *He sits there, chin on paw, thinking… what?*

ANSWER: *Owing to the artificially complex life led by city dogs of the present day, they frequently lapse into what comes very close to mental perplexity. I myself have known some very profoundly thoughtful dogs.*

The question and answer were made up by humorist James Thurber, but they illustrate a thought common to all dog and cat owners: What strange beast is this that comes slouching forth at dinnertime? In other words, just how smart are they? And which — dog or cat — is smarter?

Psychologists stepped in to solve the mystery. If human intelligence can be measured, why not animal IQ? Modeling their experiments after those used to test the intelligence of prespeaking children, they set about their task.

The psychologists were in for a shock. One early test was designed to measure how fast one dog could learn from watching another. One dog was taught to jump onto a box at a given signal to receive a food reward. A second dog watched all the while. Dog 1 repeated the trick 110 times. Dog 2 never got even a glimmer of the idea.

Then there was the animal version of *It's Academic.* An oft-cited 1967 experiment pitted cats against mink, ferrets, and skunks in a test of how long it would take them to figure out that they would be rewarded for choosing one of two different-looking objects in a set. After 200 problems, mink got the idea, and after 350 trials, their scores were almost perfect. Ferrets performed similarly. But after attempting 600 problems, the cats had barely begun to score higher than chance. At this task, they stank even worse than the skunks. At least the skunks eventually got about 70 percent of the problems right.

In another classic test, an animal faced four doors arrayed in an arc. One door was unlocked so the ani-

1906

San Francisco is rocked by a devastating earthquake. Fires destroy 514 city blocks, and more than 450 people die.

mal could go through it and get food. The door unlocked in the previous trial was never unlocked in the succeeding one. The animal was supposed to learn to avoid the last door that worked.

People and our kin, the monkeys, do well on this test. After 100 trials, we all get the idea and avoid the previous door.

But only 14 percent of the dogs tested got it, and a mere 9 percent of the cats. Of all the creatures tested, only horses and gophers fared worse. None of them figured it out at all.

The psychologists' verdict was in: "Certain animals are numskulls," animal psychologist Vance Packard summed up in his 1950 book *Animal IQ,* "grade-A morons." Lassie was dismissed as a lamebrain and Kitty labeled a knucklehead. Cats and dogs, it seemed, were about equally stupid.

Pet owners were horrified. An angry executive wrote Packard in defense of dogs: "I have an old setter dog that can tell a Buick from a Cadillac by its sound. I know because when I come home in a Buick he appears, but Cadillacs can go by all day, and he pays no attention to them. Are your

chimpanzees and orangutans that mechanical?"

Even in the face of data giving the dog a slight numerical edge over the cat in IQ tests, the great dog lover Albert Payson Terhune was finally convinced that the cat was smarter from watching a thirsty cat and a thirsty dog at a water faucet. The dog sat beneath the faucet waiting for a person to turn it on for him. The cat leaped up and pushed the tap open with her paws.

The psychologists responded that these animals only seemed to be thinking and learning, remembering and reasoning. What they were really doing was behaving by instinct. In other words, when they did something smart outside the laboratory, it didn't count.

But as the psychologists continued testing other species, they began to note some confusing results.

A startling experiment carried out at a well-known university pitted 27 white rats against 38 college students. Both species set about learning their way through a large, enclosed maze. The results were a disgrace to the human race: The rats learned the way three times faster than the college students.

Similarly disturbing results were obtained on other tests as

1906

Alfred Carl Fuller begins selling his Fuller Brushes door-to-door in Hartford, Connecticut.

well. On some visual tasks, chickens outperformed dolphins. On a test of short-term memory, wasps outscored all the mammals.

Results like these suggested that there might be something going on that the psychologists didn't understand. Perhaps, in these battles of wits, the losing contestants weren't stupid. Perhaps the tests were.

Ethologists, scientists who study animals' natural behavior (usually outside the laboratory), offered some obvious facts the psychologists had ignored. How could rats outscore college students? Because rats have lived in labyrinthine underground burrows for millennia. Why did Flipper flub? Because out of water, dolphins don't see as well as chickens do.

Terhune was finally convinced that the cat was smarter from watching a thirsty cat and a thirsty dog at a water faucet. . . . The cat leaped up and pushed the tap open with her paws.

grade school. But as for testing the intelligence of cats and dogs, the tests were about as useful as giving an American a multiple-choice exam in a foreign language.

The situation is like one once pictured in a "Far Side" cartoon: Notebook-toting animal psychologists stand perplexed before a dolphin tank. "Matthews," says one scientist to his colleague, "we're getting another of those strange 'aw blah es span yol' sounds."

The problem with these IQ tests is that cats and dogs interpret and understand the world differently than we do. We live in a world dominated by images. To see something is to believe it. So most of the tests we make up measure ability to solve visual problems — like figuring out whether a teacup or a saucer will elicit a food reward.

Why do dogs and cats fare so poorly on IQ tests? "These are artificial, human-centered tasks," said Randall Lockwood, a vice president of the Humane Society of the United States. Such tests may be perfectly fine for predicting how high a typical human toddler might later score on exams in a typical American

1907

The Hurley Machine Company of Chicago introduces the first self-contained electric clothes washer.

Further, cats and dogs are as different from one another socially as we are from them sensually. Cats are stealthy, solitary ambush hunters; dogs live in well-organized packs and hunt cooperatively. And this explains, at least partly, why a dog will work — well, doggedly — for hours solving laboratory experiments, and cats will walk away in the middle. (In her university studies, Vicki Hearne learned what the message in all this was for animal psychologists: "Don't use cats. They'll screw up your data.") Cats and dogs can't be simply compared or equated.

Cats and dogs do have good vision. Although their eyes lack a fovea, the area of the retina that lets people quickly distinguish objects at a distance, they have better peripheral vision and see better at night than we do. But vision pales beside their ability to smell. In the membrane lining the nose, cats have 19 million nerve endings devoted to smelling; dogs, with 220 million such nerve endings, can identify the scent of a human fingerprint that's six weeks old.

Dogs live in well-organized packs and hunt cooperatively. And this explains, at least partly, why a dog will work — well, doggedly — for hours solving laboratory experiments.

Not only do our simpleminded tests underestimate the intelligence of dogs and cats, but new evidence from the leading-edge theorists of artificial intelligence suggests that we may also be underestimating the nature of intelligence itself.

Humans, with a paltry 5 million such nerve endings, could well be considered "nasally challenged," to use the modern euphemism. As author, philosopher, and animal trainer Vicki Hearne put it, "A dog who did comparative psychology might easily worry about our consciousness or lack thereof, the way we worry about the consciousness of a squid."

Efforts to build an "intelligent" machine have long focused on duplicating those human abilities we hone in classrooms. Systems have already been developed that solve geometrical analogy problems and

1908

West Virginia is the first state to celebrate Mother's Day. It will become a national holiday in 1914.

play games like checkers and chess.

Vision, on the other hand, was thought to be so simple a process to duplicate by machine that about 25 years ago the director of MIT's Artificial Intelligence Laboratory is said to have assigned "solving the vision problem" to an undergraduate student as a summer project. Mental skills such as the processes by which creatures sort, interpret, and analyze information gathered with eye, ear, and nose were dismissed as "only" senses.

Today we have computers that can beat champions at chess. Meanwhile, no one has yet invented a computer that knows how to see.

Researchers are exploring each sense as a kind of intelligence in itself. In the realm of the senses, dogs and cats excel. Cats can hear two octaves higher than people (and one octave higher than dogs) and can hear a fly buzzing in another room. A dog can smell human sweat in concentrations as low as one part per million and hear the ticking of a watch 40 feet away. Some new research shows that dogs even have infrared detectors in their noses — which may be why Saint Bernards are able to tell whether a climber buried in an avalanche is alive or not.

Both species may possess senses of which we are not yet aware, allowing them to solve problems that would baffle a person. Animals' high-level survival skills are just as impressive as humans' abilities to play complicated board games — and just as worthy of exploration. A German zoologist once borrowed some cats from their owners, placed them in covered boxes, and drove around and around the city of Kiel. Finally he drove to a field where he had constructed a large, enclosed maze with 24 passages. Here, in turn, he let each cat go. The majority of the cats instantly chose the exit passage pointing them directly toward home.

Rather than creating more championship chess programs, suggested Beth Preston, a philosopher at the University of Georgia's artificial intelligence program, "artificial intelligence might find itself profitably devoting its energies to the construction of a better mousetrap in the form of an artificial feline intelligence."

As scientists are wising up to dogs' and cats' minds, we once again find ourselves impressed and humbled by our canine and feline companions. After all, as one researcher put it, "dogs and cats have got many thousands of years on us on the biggest IQ test going — survival."

1908

The Federal Bureau of Investigation (FBI) is established as part of the U.S. Department of Justice.

ANECDOTES & PLEASANTRIES

Animal Hero:
Rags, the Farm Dog

ON A STORMY MORNING in July 1964, Harold Peterson, a farmer from Shell Lake, Wisconsin, awoke and dressed with difficulty before stumbling to the barn to milk his cows. In shock, not feeling any pain, Harold didn't realize that he'd been struck by lightning as he'd slept. A lightning bolt had pierced his open bedroom window, leaving third-degree burns over 50 percent of his body. His iron bed was blackened, yet the bedcovers were unscorched.

Rags, Harold's beloved herd dog — a small, scruffy black mutt — knew something was wrong as he followed his master to the barn. In a dreamlike state, Peterson struggled through the motions of hooking up the milkers while Rags whined nearby.

Then Peterson collapsed in a gutter, unconscious.

Rags immediately raced out of the barn and across half a mile of cornfields to the farm of Peterson's brother, Alf. Although Rags had never been to Alf's farm, he seemed to know instinctively that it was the place to go for help. When Alf saw the little dog scurrying back and forth and barking, he quickly drove to Harold's farm.

Harold Peterson was in intensive care for three months recovering from his burns. After several skin grafts and extensive therapy, he returned home to resume farming. Rags, his faithful dog, remained his constant companion for many years to come.

Courtesy of Donna M. Steen (Harold Peterson's stepdaughter)

1908

Sir Robert Baden-Powell organizes the Boy Scouts in England.

■ *The cat's purr is a lot more mysterious than the cat's meow (or hiss, yowl, or roar).*

Why (and How) Do Cats Purr?

BY JEAN BURDEN

EVERYONE KNOWS THAT PUSS speaks with a voice box, just the way people do, if not in the same language. Some cats are more "verbal" than others. Besides meowing, they also yowl (in pain or in love), caterwaul, produce a trill spelled "pr-r-r-t," and hiss. All originate in the larynx or throat and are perfectly translatable to keepers of cats. But purring? Not so simple.

Experts have long disagreed on how a cat purrs. In the not-so-distant past, the purr was explained as a vibration of the soft palate at the back of the cat's throat that was "tuned up" by the breath.

Another explanation — much more complicated — was put forth by veterinarian W. R. McCuistion of Fort Worth, Texas, who wrote an article for *Veterinary Medicine/Small Animal Clinician* in June 1966 in which he attempted to explain the dynamics of purring in a way heretofore unheard-of. He asserted that a purr did not originate in the voice box at all, but in the *chest.*

The doctor's interest in the cat's purr was sparked when he was treating a Manx cat that had been torn up by a dog. The cat's diaphragm was ruptured and its trachea severed in the lower neck region. The vet inserted a tracheal tube, and lo and behold, although there was no voice, the cat still purred quite audibly from the thorax near the point where the tracheal tube had been inserted. From this study and cases involving diaphragmatic hernia in cats, Dr. McCuistion decided that purring

---

1908

Out of concern for public health, Hugh Moore develops disposable paper cups.

originates in the thorax, where the vena cava (a large blood vessel) is constricted into a funnel shape as it passes through the liver and diaphragm. Vibration is heard, Dr. McCuistion asserted, when the blood increases in velocity and rushes through the funnel.

Mildred Moelk has a much simpler explanation. In an article for the *American Journal of Psychology* (57:184) titled "Vocalizing in the House Cat," she opined that purring originates not in the larynx as we understand the word, but in two membranes nearby called *false* vocal cords.

Zoologists know that all cats — big or little, wild or domestic — have two sets of vocal cords: true or lower, and false or upper. Basic Cat is spoken by the true vocal cords, purring and roaring by the false. A nerve impulse from the brain (purring is voluntary) relaxes the true cords and lets the cat's breath vibrate the false cords. (I like this explanation better if only because I can understand it, but I sometimes wonder about that Manx cat with its severed trachea.) Take your pick of theories; no one ever dissected a purr.

Like Gaul, all cats are divided into three parts, or genera: *Felis* (36 species), *Acinonyx,* and *Panthera.* Of the *Felidae,* most of the family

is thought to be capable of purring, including the cougar, ocelot, lynx, jaguarundi, and, of course, *Felis catus,* our friend by the hearth.

Cheetahs (the only example of the genus *Acinonyx*) have a range of vocalization similar to that of our favorite tabby, and they do a lot of purring. I can testify to that because I patted a cheetah once and he did indeed purr — with a rasping sound delightful to hear.

The *Panthera* (lions, tigers, leopards, jaguars) do not bother with purring but instead open their mouths and let their false vocal cords out full force in a roar. Perhaps they don't purr because of the difference in size of their sounding boards, or perhaps they don't have much to purr about.

Which brings us to the next point: *Why* do cats purr? Or *when?*

In the beginning was the purr — that is, Mama Cat, after giving birth to a litter of babies, begins to purr with a rumble loud enough to be felt *by vibration alone* by her blind and deaf kittens. As soon as a kitten begins to suckle, it begins to purr, alerting the others that nourishment is *here,* not there. This initial purring on the part of a very young kitten is accompanied by the kneading motion of its tiny paws as it pushes

> *I patted a cheetah once and he did indeed purr — with a rasping sound delightful to hear.*

against its mother's breast to make the milk flow faster. In an adult cat, kneading still frequently goes along with purring, especially if the cat has just jumped up on your lap or has discovered the soft blanket under which you are having a nap — softness reminiscent of maternal fur.

Drawing on my experience with my own cats, I notice that they always purr when I touch them. They purr when sprawled on my stomach or sitting on my lap, or when I pick them up. It seems to go along with physical intimacy as well as pleasure. They purr with their mouths closed; the sound on inhaling seems louder than the sound on exhaling. I can put my fingers on their throats and feel the vibration. Sometimes I can feel it even when I can't hear it. My male cat, Linus, purrs much more emphatically than his sister, Lucy. That goes with everything else about him — he is clearly head honcho around here, and in all ways big and little lets us know about it.

Most people believe that a cat purrs only when it is contented. But like many feline myths, this is only partly true. Cats also purr under conditions of anxiety, as in a veterinarian's office. An examination by stethoscope is often, therefore, an exercise in futility. Old cats sometimes purr as they wait for death in the last stages of terminal illness. Why, I have no idea.

There are many reasons I sometimes envy a cat, but among the biggest is its ability to purr. Oh, to be able "to resound / with an enclosed and private sound"* every time I felt like it! I just don't have the palate for it — or the vena cava — or the right kind of vocal cords. Whatever. It is a motor solely and wholly owned by cats. Music in a troubled world.

*From "Catalog" by Rosalie Moore, *The New Yorker* © 1940, 1968.

ANECDOTES & PLEASANTRIES

Animal Hero: Dumb-Dumb the Cat

DUMB-DUMB was a half-Siamese cat who attacked a burglar trying to break into her family's home in Wichita, Kansas, in 1978. The cat struck the would-be robber so suddenly and so fiercely that the intruder was actually felled, leading to his quick arrest.

Courtesy of Yolanda Jarvis

1909

American explorers Robert E. Peary and Matthew Henson, along with four Inuit, reach the North Pole and mark the spot with the American flag.

FARMER'S CALENDAR

Uncouth Jays

THIRTY OR 40 YARDS from my house, at the edge of a meadow, I keep a kitchen garbage dump that I call a compost pile. Four blue jays who live on the property call it a free lunch and avail themselves of its provender liberally in all seasons, but especially so in winter. They rise from the pile with a great flap and squawk as I approach with a new pail of table scraps. When I return to the house, they descend immediately and commence flinging the stuff all over the snow, keeping up a loud palaver the whole time, like a hall full of drunken undergraduates.

Blue jays are the most human of birds. We recognize them easily as creatures that are more like us than most other birds are. What is it we recognize? It's sin. The qualities we think birds have that make them resemble us are never good qualities. The cock is proud, the crow thieving, the goose a bully. Whoever felt kinship with any bird for its charity, devotion, or high-mindedness? The principle extends to animals, but not perfectly. Domestic animals, we say, may have human traits that are admirable: Dogs are loyal and loving, cats dignified, horses stalwart. Wild animals, however, when we find them to have human qualities, have traits we hesitate to praise: the fox's low cunning, the weasel's blood lust, the bear's clownishness.

Still, we admire them; we admire them all. Blue jays are rapacious, greedy, disorderly, noisy, evidently irresponsible. They are also beautiful, but that bright outfit and that rakish crest could not belong to a good citizen. The qualities we admire in creatures, like those we admire in some people in novels, are ones we are not so apt to admire in our friends and neighbors.

1910

Spokane, Washington, holds the first Father's Day celebration. It won't become a national holiday until 1972.

■ *The next time you are asked the most roundabout of questions, be ready with this most straightforward answer.*

Which *Really* Came First — the Chicken or the Egg?

BY GUY MURCHIE

CHICKEN OR EGG? WHICH ONE started it all?

First let me say that although the chicken, like all other living creatures, is mysterious enough, the egg is more so. For an egg not only contains the equivalent of a clock, a compass, nest-building instructions, menus, sheet music, and sometimes a map of stars, but it also can talk and hold a conversation, and it is immortal.

Would a talking egg surprise you? Consider the fact that most eggs, particularly birds' eggs, are laid one at a time, and a clutch of them may appear during a span of a week or more. Yet it is vital that they hatch within a few hours of each other so that the last baby bird to emerge will not be trampled to death by his much older and bigger brothers and sisters. For this reason, the eggs of many different ages must somehow coordinate their hatching, which is done by direct communication, egg to egg, and often egg to mother and mother to egg. For a day or two before the egg hatches, some air accumulates in it, and in this air the developing chick starts to utter peeping sounds and eventually to peck against the shell. Since eggs in a nest generally touch each other, the sounds in them are easily transmitted from one to the other as a sort of telegraphic code.

The immortality of an egg derives from the abstract nature of its genes, for these can produce a bird who, even if kept indoors and pre-

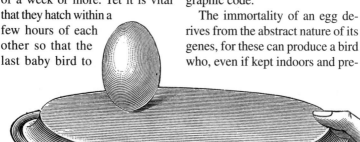

1910

The Boy Scouts of America is founded.

vented from seeing or hearing any other bird, can nevertheless sing the songs of his species and navigate by stars he never knew existed. Furthermore, the egg does not have to die, for it normally just grows into an adult bird, specifically into a bird who in turn may lay eggs that prolong life indefinitely — showing that, from the egg's viewpoint, a chicken is primarily a lonely egg's way of getting another egg.

From the egg's viewpoint, a chicken is primarily a lonely egg's way of getting another egg.

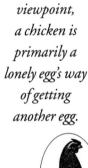

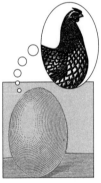

This line of thinking perforce leads us to our long-awaited answer to the ancient dilemma of "Which came first, the chicken or the egg?" The egg wins hands down — literally by half a billion years! It is well known to evolutionists that eggs are more than ten times as ancient as chickens, because eggs antedate chickens by well over 400 million years. In fact, fish have been laying eggs almost since Cambrian times 500 million years ago. And then came the first bugs, followed by amphibians and reptiles, all of whom lay eggs, as well as many birds older than the relatively recent barnyard fowl who evolved in what's known as the order of Galliformes a mere 40 million years ago.

Of course, some pedants will argue that the egg in the original question has to be a chicken egg, not just any old egg. But I'd say that, if you want to be pedantic, as well as logical, you really should define your terms — in which case you can create any outcome you choose (or no outcome) depending on your definitions. Should you, for example, insist on a chicken egg and define it as "an egg capable of hatching a chicken," the egg still wins. But if you define a chicken egg as "an egg laid by a chicken," the chicken beats the egg, because the first chicken could not have hatched from a chicken egg since there were no previous chickens around to have laid it. If your definition requires that all chickens be hatched from chicken eggs, which in turn could only have been laid by chickens, then the sequence of egg-chicken-egg-chicken-egg must go back endlessly into history without any beginning — something no evolutionist (nor any reasonable mortal living in a finite world) would accept.

1911

American newspaper publisher Joseph Pulitzer dies. His will endows the journalism school at Columbia University in New York City and establishes a fund for annual prizes to be awarded for excellence in journalism.

> ■ *When it comes to investigating a theoretical creature, a cryptozoologist must never be discouraged by the lack of physical evidence.*

In Search of Animals That Don't Exist

BY MARK SUNLIN

TODAY, WHEN ENVIRONMENTALists are dedicating themselves to protecting animals threatened with extinction and paleontologists are delving into reasons for prehistoric extinctions, another group is seeking out animals that might never have existed in the first place. Welcome to *cryptozoology*.

Cryptozoologists define their discipline as "the science of hidden animals." Foremost on their "wanted" list are not only the familiar bigfoot, yeti, and Loch Ness monster, but also such lesser-known creatures as the *ri* (which some cryptozoologists insist is a mermaid and most regular zoologists say is a sea cow) and the *mokele-mbembe* (allegedly a dinosaur lurking in the swamplands of the Congo). Shakespeare must have been thinking of cryptozoology when he wrote, "There are more things in heaven and earth than are dreamed of."

In defense of the theoretical existence of these creatures, cryptozoologists often note that native legends of hairy, manlike monsters haunting the African jungles were likewise treated by Europeans with scorn until the discovery of gorillas in 1847. Ergo, they say, the likes of bigfoot and the mokele-mbembe may also exist.

Ergo *nothing,* said zoologist Tim Berra of Ohio State University, an avowed skeptic who, like most mainstream zoologists, is not inclined to see a logical connection between the unexplored African jungles of 200 years ago and, say, the outskirts of modern-day Seattle as a viable habitat for exotic giants. Deftly, Berra lunged for the cryptozoologists' weak point: their lack of "a single shred

1911

The Indianapolis Motor Speedway is the site of the International Sweepstakes, a 500-mile race that will become an annual event known as the Indianapolis (or Indy) 500.

of physical evidence of such creatures" despite numerous expeditions and sightings.

One of the most frustrating (or comic, depending on your sympathies) aspects of cryptozoology is the embarrassing hex it seems to cast over cameras. In 1983 anthropologist Roy Wagner and Richard Greenwell, editor of the journal *Cryptozoology*, were searching the seas 300 miles from New Guinea in an effort to locate a "shred of physical evidence" for the existence of the mermaidlike ri, described by natives of the area as having a fishlike body and a human head. The duo claim they actually spotted one and got within 50 feet of their quarry, whereupon Wagner quickly grabbed his camera. But alas (and this could happen to anyone), at that point the ri submerged, and Wagner wound up with some fuzzy snapshots of a tail-like apparatus and another tale of the big one that got away.

That same year, the camera hex struck once again when biologist Agnagna Marcellin was in the Congo searching for the mokele-mbembe. There, in the tropical waters of Lake Tele, an oval lake about three miles in diameter, he spotted his quarry. Like Wagner, he had his camera in hand, but this time the camera's settings had not been adjusted, and an exasperated Agnagna ended up with no photos at all! (I mean, couldn't you just *spit?*)

But at the same time these photo attempts were being made, A. B. Wooldridge was hiking along an exposed snow slope in the Himalayas at 13,000 feet when he happened upon — what else? — a yeti, otherwise known as the abominable snowman. "The head was large and squarish, and the whole body appeared to be covered with dark hair," he reported. Wooldridge had his camera ready and set properly, and he began firing away at the creature, who obligingly remained as motionless as a bump on a proverbial log. Perhaps a little *too* much like a bump, for in all the photos taken by Wooldridge, the entity never changes position, suggesting to some that it may have been nothing more exotic than a yeti-shaped rock. Science writer William Corliss, who is generally sympathetic to cryptozoologists, laments, "If only it had moved significantly during the picture taking. Instead of a smoking gun, all we have is the smoke — enticing, but still unconvincing, data."

Far from being discouraged by such setbacks, cryptozoologists are all the more stimulated and are continuing to search for more than 100 animals unknown to science, including the likes of a black-and-white-spotted dolphin with two dorsal fins (one on the head like a horn), a sea serpent in Canada's Lake Ogopogo, and various other phantoms.

1912

Juliette Low of Savannah, Georgia, organizes the Girl Scouts in the United States.

Keeping an Eye on the Sky

I HAVE A CONFESSION TO MAKE: Although I have always loved astronomy, I lasted only one lecture in my only college astronomy course. Attempting to understand the simplest mathematical concept — angular momentum, I think it's called — sent me out the door with my head spinning.

And so it comes as no surprise that, upon reading Guy Murchie's article "The Music of the Spheres," all I could say was, "What the *hell* is this man talking about?"

I had to go for a walk to recover my senses. As I did, it occurred to me that "The Music of the Spheres" could use some lyrics that the rest of us can understand.

The Sun Always Shines at Noon

(Tune: "I Only Have Eyes for You")

Sextants out, take a sight.
I don't care if it's cloudy or
    bright.
'Cause the Sun always shines
    at noon.

1912

The Olympics introduces its first women's events, all three in swimming and diving.

This fact rarely fails.
(Now and then when it snows
    or it hails.)
Oh, the Sun always shines at
    noon.

The reason why is that it's
    closer
Than at dawn or the evening,
    so — sir —

Its rays penetrate.
Makes it easier to navigate,
And for me to make up this
    tune:
'Cause the Sun always shines
    at noon.

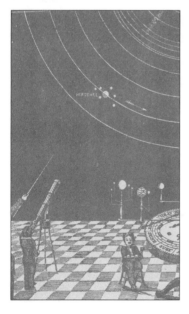

All Planets Spin

(Tune: "Turn! Turn! Turn!")

All planets spin
Turn, turn, turn,
At different rates
Turn, turn, turn,
Why they do,
I can't tell you.
It's a mystery.

The Earth turns around
In 24 hours;
If we lived on the Sun,
We'd take lots of showers.
A day in the park
Lasts eight months on
    Venus —
Oh, don't let rotation
Come between us.

Big Bang

*(Tune: "Bang Bang [My Baby Shot
Me Down]")*

Big Bang!
Began the show.
Big Bang!
We found the glow.
Big Bang!
So now we know.
Big Bang!
Einstein said, told you so.

1912

Tiny toy surprises first appear
in boxes of Cracker Jack.

Balaklava!

(Tune: "Oklahoma!")

Baaaaaaaa-laklava!
Where the steamboat *Prince*
    sank in a gale!
Where the Russians slayed
The Light Brigade,
Who were nursed by Florence
    Nightingale!

Baaaaaaaa-laklava!
Urbain Jean Joseph Leverrier
Was the smart French guy
Who said, let's try
To predict the weather every
    day!

And so we owe our forecasts
To those miserable Crimean
    blasts!

So hip hurray — hey!
For old Leverrier — hey!
And for the storm that blew
    into old Balaklava,
Balaklava! B-A-L-A-K-L-A-
    V-A! Balaklava!

Quarter Moon

(Tune: "Only a Paper Moon")

Oh, it's just the first quarter
    Moon,
And it always comes up at
    noon,
Though it looks like a half,
    you loon,
It's just a quarter Moon.

Lunar ignorance is a crime,
But there's more of it all the
    time,
It annoys me, so that's why
    I'm
Composing this short rhyme.

New Moon at dawn;
And first quarter at midday.
Full Moon at dusk;
And third quarter ascends,
    when the day truly ends.

I'd explain how the tides
    work, or
Maybe even Metonic lore;
But you'd think me an awful
    bore —
If I said any more.

1913

Journalist Arthur Wynne creates the first U.S.
crossword puzzle, which is published in the
December 21 edition of the *New York World*.

Nothing Can Enthrall Us Like Aurora Borealis

(Tune: "Carolina in the Morning")

Nothing can enthrall us
Like Aurora Borealis
Where it's polar.

Molecules of oxygen
And nitrogen blow in a wind
That's solar.

All that agitation
Causes them to glow;
This illumination
Is visible down below.

Arcs and rays of light appear
And ripple in the atmosphere
Like curtains.

Making noise, say Eskimos,
Like whistling, but no one
    knows
For certain.

So uncommon a phenomenon
Deserves our applause.
Let's hope it doesn't hurt
    Santa Claus!

Nothing can enthrall us
Like Aurora Borealis
Where it's polar!

I Saw the Quake in San Francisco

(Tune: "I Left My Heart in San Francisco")

I saw the quake in San
    Francisco
From Auriga in '94.
And though I know it's hardly
    news,
Were I on Betelgeuse,
I'd have to wait 500 years —
    maybe more.

To keep an eye on San
    Francisco,
And its lovely Golden
    Gate —
I'll have to move to Alpha
    Centauri
So I can stay more up-to-date!

1913

The Internal Revenue Service is officially
established as a result of the
16th Amendment to the U.S. Constitution,
which authorizes an income tax.

I Taught Bode's Law, but I'm All Done

(Tune: "I Fought the Law")

I teach mathematics in a high
school:
I taught Bode's law, but I'm
all done,
I taught Bode's law, but I'm
all done.

Not a lot of geniuses in my
school:
I taught Bode's law, but I'm
all done,
I taught Bode's law, but I'm
all done.

I told them there's a gap between Jupiter and Mars —
I guess I shouldn't have done.
'Cause they just laughed and
went right back to fixin'
their cars.
I taught Bode's law, but I'm
all done,
I taught Bode's law, but I'm
all done.

Tim Clark

1914

The first regularly scheduled
air passenger flight begins
between Tampa and
St. Petersburg, Florida.

■ *For the past 2,500 years, man has searched unsuccessfully for a simple harmonic or mathematical law to explain the relationship of the planets. And yet the possibility of a universal harmony, encompassing everything from atomic particles to celestial bodies, seems more real now than ever.*

The Music of the Spheres

BY GUY MURCHIE

IS THERE ORDER AMONG THE PLANets? Or, as Pythagoras once put it, is there "Music in the Spheres"?

Pythagoras is believed to have been the first person ever to demonstrate a connection between music and geometry. In the sixth century B.C., he discovered that using a finger to divide a harp string precisely in half produces a tone exactly an octave higher. This in turn led him to theorize that, because of this obvious geometry in the humming of the strings, there must conversely be music in the spacings of the spheres.

Two millennia later, Kepler, the great 17th-century German astronomer, went a step further in speculating that the planetary "spheres," or orbits, might fit together like the regular solids of Plato (tetrahedron, cube, octahedron, dodecahedron, icosahedron), each inside the next. Needless to say, this medieval surmise didn't pan out, but partly through it and other failures, Kepler eventually

proved that orbits are not circles, as the ancients presumed, but rather ellipses. And from that base, he eventually worked out the fundamental laws of planetary motion. Had he lived beyond the age of 59, he might even have discovered the law of gravitation, which required no less a genius than Isaac Newton a few decades later.

One of Kepler's least well-known observations, closely related to our subject, was that he found a mysterious gap in the order of the spheres. In fact, he declared that a planet was unaccountably missing between Mars and Jupiter, the fourth and fifth planets out from the Sun, and he urged astronomers to look for it — which they did. But before they could find anything in this empty region, one Johann Titius devised a mathematical progression to express the intervals of all the six known planets plus the "missing" one, a progression that the German astronomer Johann Elert Bode later developed into what has since become widely known as

1915

Robert Frost writes his poem
"The Road Not Taken."

Bode's law. It was done by writing down a series of 4s, one for each planet, then adding the numbers 0 for Mercury, 3 for Venus, 6 for Earth, 12 for Mars, 24 for the missing planet, 48 for Jupiter, and 96 for Saturn, doubling the number for each additional member. The resultant progression (with its decimal points moved one place) represented the approximate planetary distances from the Sun in terms of the Earth's distance as the unit length (1).

Even when Uranus, the seventh planet, was

Pythagoras ... discovered that using a finger to divide a harp string precisely in half produces a tone exactly an octave higher. This in turn led him to theorize that ... there must conversely be music in the spacings of the spheres.

discovered in 1781, and when Ceres, the first asteroid, on the first night of the 19th century (January 1, 1801) was hopefully hailed as "the missing planet" (though later found to be a mere 480 miles in diameter), Bode's law stood up as remarkably true to reality. For it was not until 1846, when the eighth planet, Neptune, was discovered, that a serious flaw appeared in Bode's law. This happened because Neptune turned out to be more than 8 billion miles too close to the Sun to fit the law, even approxi-

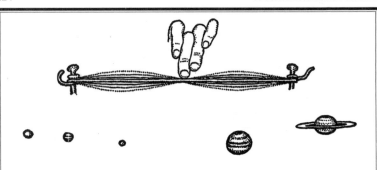

mately. And despite the fact that Pluto, the little ninth planet, partially redeemed Bode when it was discovered in 1930, circling the Sun at roughly the right distance for the next planet beyond Uranus, Neptune has stubbornly remained the unexplainable fly in Bode's ointment.

As a result, astronomers ceased taking Bode's law seriously after 1846, regarding it as a mere mathematical curiosity, and they still reject attempts to reestablish order in this apparently limping music of our spheres. Most notable of such attempts in this century, so far as I know, is that of William Arnold, an American mathematician who has worked Neptune into what he terms a "two-way sequence model"

There developed a natural geometric order in the endless collisions that formed these planets and kept reducing the number of separate particles, for the particles that least often intersected the orbits of others survived in the greatest numbers.

in the "ideally arc'd" proportions of 0, 1, 2, 3, 4, 8, 15, 30, 60, 90, 120, which includes the Sun in the beginning and Ceres in the middle.

Although it seems to me that rather too much rationalization is required to make either Bode's or Arnold's mathematical sequences come usefully close to fitting the actual firmament, there is nevertheless a genuine harmony among the spheres, especially in the spacings of the inner planets. This has been explained most plausibly, I believe, by Carl von Weizsacker in his theory of the birth of the solar system, first published in 1943. He postulated the proto-Sun as a rotating star clot surrounded by revolving rings of gas and dust that during hundreds of millions of years

1916

A Piggly Wiggly opens in Memphis, Tennessee. It is the first modern supermarket.

coagulated into planets. And there developed a natural geometric order in the endless collisions that formed these planets and kept reducing the number of separate particles, for the particles that least often intersected the orbits of others survived in the greatest numbers in a pattern of bean-shaped eddies that girdled the central mass like a series of necklaces. Moreover, because of the way their shapes fitted together, each necklace inevitably contained about five bean eddies, or beads, and the next necklace outside it tended to be about 1.7 times larger, the whole concentric array forming a simple geometric progression from the Sun core outward. This logically would lead to a fairly regular sequence of spacings of the planets as they grew, but, as the cells of turbulence had room to be larger and consequently more complex and irregular in the outer reaches, the progression there was more apt to have aberrations — which could account for Neptune's anomalous position in the Sun's system.

Notwithstanding these irregularities, the "music" in celestial formations appears far from really haphazard or random and may well have been the very thing that has most impressed every great pioneer of science from Pythagoras to Kepler to Einstein with the sublime order of the universe. Nor should we forget, in saying this, that the per-

vasive harmony goes inward as well as outward and without doubt rules the microcosm as much as the macrocosm, indeed likely with an even firmer hand inside the atom, to judge by the rigor of the quantum theory.

Have you heard tell of the unfortunate position philosopher Auguste Comte got himself into in the 1800s when he rashly announced that man must reconcile himself to "eternal ignorance" of the compo-

If fowl roll in the sand, rain is at hand.

sition of the stars? Comte had barely spoken before the invention of the spectroscope eloquently refuted him in what has been called the language of the atom. It is a language in refracted rainbow colors with dark lines that sort out starlight to tell not only what the

1917

Edwin W. Cox, a door-to-door kitchenware salesman in San Francisco, makes the first S.O.S pads.

stars are made of but also how hot they are and whether they are coming or going. The lines are created by the absence of light at the frequency bands representing the chemicals that absorbed that particular light on its way to the spectroscope.

LETTERS TO THE ASTRONOMER

Do all planets spin? Why?

ALL PLANETS SPIN, though at different rates. One day on Jupiter lasts a mere 10 hours, while Venus turns so slowly that a day stretches for more than 8 of our months. Even the Sun spins on its axis — once every 25 days. Why everything rotates is quite a mystery. Something must have started them off that way when they were formed billions of years ago. Since there is no friction in space, the rotation will continue forever.

An example of this is the "ladder" worked out by a Swiss mathematician named Johann Jakob Balmer in 1885, consisting of a climbing sequence of the frequencies of all the known hydrogen lines, each frequency being a definite fraction of the ladder's limiting frequency of 3,287,870,000 megacycles per second. And these fractions form a beautiful harmonic series — each denominator a cardinal square in natural succession, each numerator four less than its denominator: $5/9$, $12/16$, $21/25$, $32/36$, $45/49$, $60/64$, $77/81$, and so on. It seemed to be a kind of Bode's law for hydrogen, smallest of the inner spheres, even to including Bode's familiar series of 4s, one for each fraction or frequency. Although no one else, to my knowledge, has ever attempted to equate these series of 4s in the macroworld and microworld or has so much as noticed the suggestive similarity between Bode's law and Balmer's ladder, intuitively I feel a mystic resonance here, a consonance of things unseen, a sense that no matter how many imperfections ultimately show up, none can help but be, like thorns on a rose, just parts of a greater perfection — that the total music expresses a truly universal harmony that somehow must include not only hydrogen and the solar system but all the elements of all the worlds everywhere and forever.

1917

U.S. Rubber introduces Keds, the first popularly marketed sneakers.

■ *The ancient Egyptians set their calendars by the brightest star in the night sky. Keep your eye on this glowing giant, and you can do the same.*

A Case for the Dog Star

BY MICHAEL McNIERNEY

ONE WINTER NIGHT NOT LONG ago, I glanced out my window at about two in the morning. The snow glowed in the platinum light of the Moon, and in the barren branches of cottonwoods to the south, a single white light shone so brightly that it startled me.

It was Sirius, the Dog Star, lead star of the winter constellation Canis Major, the Greater Dog. Sirius

is far and away the brightest star in the night sky. In fact, at magnitude -1.46, it is nearly ten times as bright as the average first-magnitude star. It can actually be seen in broad daylight with a small telescope, if you know where to look.

From prehistory until urban civilization began to blast the night

sky with artificial illumination, people looked to this magnificent celestial light as a beacon telling the change in seasons and predicting the future. The origin of the name *Sirius* is unknown, but ancient writers explained it as relating to a word for blazing, burning, or parching. This association is at least as old as Homer, whose *Iliad* mentions "Orion's Dog" as a star in the summer dawn and also as a star in the evening sky at harvesttime. In both cases, it "brings down killing fevers on wretched men."

In ancient Egypt, the appearance of Sirius above the eastern horizon just before dawn occurred around the time of the summer solstice. This event, called the heliacal rising of the star, was an occasion of great joy. The return each year of Sirius to its place near the morning Sun meant that the Nile was about to flood, bringing water and rich soil to the desert along its banks. The Egyp-

1917

President Woodrow Wilson pastures a small flock of sheep on the White House lawn to free up groundskeepers to serve in World War I.

tians began their year with the heliacal rising of Sirius and calibrated their calendar according to it.

To inhabitants of the Mediterranean shore farther north, however, the same summer rising of Sirius portended disease and death. Both the Greeks and the Romans noted that the star's appearance seemed to bring on the worst heat of summer, a time when people felt lethargic and feverish, and crops withered. Since Sirius was the dominant star in the constellation of the Dog, it was called the Dog Star, and the time after its solstice rising was known as the Dog Days, a term we still use for the 40 or so days in the hottest part of the summer.

Ancient medicine sought to explain disease and health as various combinations of heat and cold, dryness and moisture. If the Dog Star was thought to cause fevers in people, then naturally it must affect dogs, too. Under its influence, dogs could become so hot and dry that they developed rabies — *lyssa* in Greek, meaning "wolfishness."

The Greeks made the connection between madness, rabies, and wolves and associated Sirius with the "excessive dryness" that caused men to act like or even change into wolves.

About midnight on New Year's Eve, [Sirius] is as high in the southern sky as it ever climbs.

To describe the insane, uncontrollable rage of men in battle (*berserk* in Old Norse), the Greeks used the word for rabies. When Achilles mangled the corpse of his fallen enemy for days after the battle, Homer says he was seized by *lyssa*.

For us today, all the mythical mysteries and dire associations of Sirius are gone. It is simply a star a little less than twice the size of our Sun. Though 23 times as bright as the Sun, it is a fairly ordinary star by astronomical standards. Its prominence in our sky and our history is due to the accident of distance: It is only 8.7 light-years away, the fifth-closest star known.

To regain a little of the fear and awe once felt at the sight of Sirius, try this: During fall and winter, keep an eye on the star. Gaze at that burning arc light in the sky a few times a month and notice how its position changes in relation to the hour and the horizon. As it rises earlier each night, the Dog Star leads us into the season of our own special days of celebration. On Thanksgiving, it rises shortly before 9:30 P.M., EST. By Christmas Eve, it appears in the east around 7:30 P.M. About midnight on New Year's Eve, it is as high in the southern sky as it ever climbs, a symbol of the inexorable revolution of the years.

1918

The first Raggedy Ann dolls are sold by John Gruelle. Gruelle based the doll on one his invalid daughter had. Marshall Field will begin marketing the dolls in 1920.

FARMER'S CALENDAR

Discovery of Worlds

NIGHTS IN LATE FALL, when the frost is hard and the air clear and sharp, are best for looking at the sky. There is wood smoke in the air. Overhead, the sky bends over the Earth like the top of a great circus tent, crowded with the familiar beasts: the bull, the ram, the winged horse. About halfway up the eastern sky is a very bright star, and just above it to the right is a fuzzy, vague patch in the sky. That patch, if you have a pair of binoculars, can give you a hint of the excitement of discovery.

The big star below the bright patch is Aldebaran; the patch itself is the Pleiades. The Pleiades is not a star but a so-called open cluster of stars. There are altogether something like 1,400 stars in the Pleiades, but only 9 are bright enough to have been named. Simple binoculars resolve the cluster into a startling array of hundreds of stars, 6 of which form a brilliant hook, with the lesser stars scattered among them. The  Pleiades fairly leap down at you from the haze of their great distance, and where you saw only a fog, you find detail, complexity, and an intimation of the strangeness of the heavens.

Galileo in 1609 pointed his new telescope at the Pleiades one night and found 40 formerly invisible stars in one of the early steps in what was perhaps the richest period of discovery in history. In a way, it's a breakthrough that can still be made. Only in the sky can you come close to repeating the discovery of worlds. You can't return to New York Harbor in 1524 and find it as Verrazano did, and similarly for the source of the Nile and the Newfoundland Capes. The Pleiades endure. They have been found but not changed. The consolations of astronomy.

1919

Charles Strite of Stillwater, Minnesota, patents the first pop-up toaster.

■ *Ever wondered what Einstein's 95-year-old "theory of relativity" really means to you and me? Like, is it even possible for us to understand it? Well, here's a pretty good attempt at a simple explanation.*

$E = mc^2$
So What?

BY MICHAEL McNIERNEY

THE PROBLEM WITH THE THEORY of relativity is not so much that it is difficult to understand but that it is almost impossible to believe. What it says about reality so contradicts common sense and everyday experience that it seems absurd.

Most normal people (that is, people who aren't physicists) live in a Newtonian universe, whether they call it that or not. In the 17th century, Isaac Newton, using the calculus he invented for the purpose, was able to describe how the physical universe works through the force of gravitation. His mathematical laws explain everything from the fall of an apple to the elliptical orbits of the planets around the Sun. His system was so complete and satisfying that it came as a revelation to people of his time. It seemed that there was little left to discover. Alexander Pope wrote:

Nature and Nature's laws lay
*   hid in night:*
God said, Let Newton be! *and*
*   all was light.*

Fundamental to the Newtonian worldview is that space and time are absolutes. They are the unchanging stage on which all the events of the universe are acted out.

But Newton was wrong. On the human scale, even on the scale of the solar system, Newton's laws work almost perfectly. *Almost* perfectly. With extremely sophisticated instruments, scientists can now detect slight discrepancies here. But on the scale of massive stars and galaxies and clusters of galaxies, the discrepancies are enormous.

Scientists of Newton's time, of course, didn't have these instruments, and they didn't know of the existence of galaxies, let alone clusters of galaxies. Even so, a clue to the fact that not all was right with the Newtonian system was present for those who could see. And Newton himself was the one to see it. The haunting question he could not answer was, How do light and gravitational force travel through the emptiness of space?

1920

Johnston McCulley creates a swashbuckling hero from Spanish California in his novel *The Mark of Zorro.*

The attempt to answer this question led to the theory of relativity.

Light moves so fast that for centuries attempts to measure its speed seemed to indicate that it propagated instantaneously. Across a park, you see a batter hit a ball. A moment later, you hear the crack of the bat. Sound obviously has a speed, but light seems instantaneous. For a long time, technology was simply too crude to measure light's speed, which was finally determined to be about 186,282 miles per second. (Sound moves at about 12.5 miles per second.)

Light behaves like a wave. (It also behaves like particles, but that story would get us into quantum physics.) Scientists reasoned that sound waves are carried in the air. Water waves are carried in water. Therefore, although space is empty, light waves must be carried in something.

But Newton was wrong. On the human scale, even on the scale of the solar system, Newton's laws work almost perfectly. Almost perfectly.

This conclusion led to the theory of the luminiferous ether — a light-carrying "substance" in space.

Determining if your boat is moving through the water is easy: You can look for the bow wave or put your hand in the water and feel motion. On this analogy, 19th-century scientists tried to detect an ether wind or drift as the Earth moved through space. Many attempts were made, and finally, in July 1887, the definitive experiment was performed by Albert Michelson and Edward Morley. The results shocked the scientific world. They could find no ether wind.

Scientists scrambled to find an explanation for the failure of the experiment. Almost no one wanted to consider the most obvious explanation: There is no ether. Physics had reached a frustrating dilemma. If the ether existed, why couldn't it be

1921

Band-Aids are created by Earle Dickson, an employee of Johnson & Johnson in New Jersey. They are the first small, adhesive, sterile bandages.

detected experimentally? If it didn't exist, why didn't it exist? In 1905 the answer was provided by a theory that not only solved the problem of the ether but also made far-ranging predictions in other areas.

The theory belonged to an obscure man of 26 working as a "technical expert third class" in the Swiss patent office in Bern.

Albert Einstein had been a dreamy child, not even speaking until he was three years old. He failed his first college entrance exam but finally graduated in 1900 with mediocre grades (he preferred playing the violin and hanging out in cafés to studying). He ended up working in the patent office after trying, and failing, to get a job as a scientist or high school teacher.

1921

The first Miss America beauty pageant is held in Atlantic City, New Jersey, in an attempt to extend the tourist season. Margaret Gorman wins the title.

Einstein had been fascinated with physics since he was a child and never stopped thinking about the subject. He applied himself to the problem of light and the ether wind and wrote a short paper on it titled "On the Electro-Dynamics of Moving Bodies." After Max Planck, a renowned physicist and editor of a German journal of physics, read the paper submitted by this unknown young man, he knew immediately that the standard view of the world had changed forever. Einstein's paper set forth what would later be known as the special theory of relativity.

In his paper, Einstein offered and proved two postulates:

1. The ether, if it exists, cannot be detected.

2. The speed of light is always constant relative to an observer.

Neither of these will seem all that dramatic to a nonphysicist, but the deductions and conclusions that follow from them are earthshaking. Relativity can't be completely explained or comprehended without mathematics, but we can at least sketch out an idea of what the Einsteinian, relativistic universe is like. Incidentally, don't be misled by the word *theory*. Relativity was only a theory when Einstein published it, but it is a fact now. Its truth has been repeatedly verified by experiment.

Einstein discovered two extraordinary facts about light (and about all other electromagnetic radiation). The first is that its speed never changes, even if an observer is moving directly toward the light source or directly away from it. This means that the light leaving a star travels at 186,282 miles per second relative to you even if you are approaching or separating from the star at a speed of 186,281 miles per second!

This kind of behavior is not true of anything else, including other types of waves. If two cars approach each other head-on, each traveling at 60 miles per hour, the speed of the other car relative to each observer is 120 miles per hour. Or if they are traveling parallel to each other, the relative speed of each is 0 miles per hour. This principle also applies to sound waves. Yet with light, the relative speed remains constant.

The second fact that Einstein discovered about light is that the

> *Einstein discovered two extraordinary facts about light (and about all other electromagnetic radiation). The first is that its speed never changes, even if an observer is moving directly toward the light source or directly away from it.*

1922

Moviegoers, wearing special glasses with one red and one green lens, enjoy the first 3-D movie.

speed of light — 186,282 miles per second — is the speed limit of the universe. Nothing can travel faster than that.

This brings us to the heart of the special theory of relativity and the most famous formula in the history of science: $E = mc^2$. In simple terms, what this equation says is that energy and mass are equivalent; they are the same thing in different forms. Mass is frozen energy. $E = mc^2$ means that equivalent energy (E) is equal to mass (m) times the speed of light (c) squared.

You are familiar with the implications of this equation, even if you don't realize it. If you will recall a little of your high school algebra, you can figure it out for yourself. You know that the speed of light is a very large number. Multiply it by itself, and you get an astronomically large number. If you substitute even a small number for the mass in the equation, just a few pounds, say, and multiply it by the squared speed of light, the result is another enormous number. And this is E, the pure energy that is equivalent to those few ounces of mass.

The second fact that Einstein discovered about light is that the speed of light — 186,282 miles per second — is the speed limit of the universe. Nothing can travel faster than that.

Take 110 pounds of uranium. If you drop it on a house, it will crash through the roof, but that's about all the damage it will do. Put it into a special device (military-speak for "bomb") that converts it into pure energy, however, and you level the city of Hiroshima. All forms of nuclear power are implied in that simple equation.

The reason nothing can exceed the speed of light is that the faster an object goes, the more its mass increases. As it approaches light speed, its mass approaches the infinite, and since energy is required to move a mass, the energy needed also approaches the infinite. It would take an infinite amount of energy to move something, anything, faster than light, and that is more energy than is available in the entire universe. Faster-than-light travel is therefore impossible.

In 1916, 11 years after Einstein published his special theory, he introduced the general theory of relativity to the scientific world. Building on his earlier work, he finished off the Newtonian worldview for good.

1924

Celluwipes, the world's first disposable handkerchiefs, are introduced. They will later be called Kleenex.

The implications of general relativity are still being worked out in the realm of quasars, pulsars, and black holes. But what the combined general and special theories say is that on the largest scale of the universe, there is no such thing as gravitation or independent, absolute space or time. Everything exists in space-time, which is the three dimensions of space plus the fourth dimension of time. Space-time is curved in the vicinity of mass — the greater the mass, the greater the curve. What Newton thought of as the mysterious force of gravitation is not a force at all. It is the sliding and falling of a body along the curves made by a more massive body in space-time.

The Earth, for example, is sliding along the walls of space-time curved around the mass of the Sun. Great mass can even bend light. Black holes, formed in the collapse of huge stars, contain the mass of their parent stars in incredibly dense spheres of matter only a few miles in diameter. Space-time is so curved in their vicinity that not even light can escape; it is curved back on itself.

If your mind is beginning to feel a little scrambled, don't worry. General relativity is not comprehensible without the mathematics. It's a little like trying to hear music from a verbal description. We just have to trust the physicists when they say it is true.

Some people have rejected the whole idea of relativity because they think that it makes everything relative, even values, or even that God does not exist because there is no such thing as good and evil. This is an unfortunate misunderstanding. The theory of relativity has nothing whatsoever to say about spiritual values; it describes only the physical universe.

But what a universe! It's a place of infinite mystery and awe. Albert Einstein, himself a deeply religious man, drew unlimited inspiration

The sharper the blast, the sooner it's past.

from the universe he had discovered. "I want to know," he said, "how God created this world. I am not interested in this or that phenomenon. . . . I want to know His thoughts, the rest are details."

1924

Harold Gray creates the comic strip character "Little Orphan Annie" for the *Chicago Tribune.*

■ *If someone on the star Canopus had a powerful enough telescope, he would be able to view the entire San Francisco earthquake and fire of 1906 in April 2004.*

How Old Is the Starlight You'll See Tonight?

BY FREDERICK F. BIRD

T HE SPEED OF LIGHT IS SO GREAT that there are literally no experiences on Earth to make us aware of the fact that it really does take time for light to travel a certain distance. The idea becomes real only when we move beyond the Earth and into space.

The distance between the Earth and the Moon is about 250,000 miles. Light travels at about 186,000 miles per second, so sunlight reflecting off the Moon's surface takes 1.3 seconds to reach the Earth. When men walked on the Moon and reported the events, the

1926

Winnie-the-Pooh, written by A. A. Milne and illustrated by Ernest H. Shepard, is published.

messages took 1.3 seconds to reach the Earth because radio waves travel at the speed of light. Still, 1.3 seconds is a barely noticeable delay.

The Sun is about 93 million miles away. This means that light from, say, a solar prominence (a surface flare) does not reach the Earth for eight minutes. Another way of visualizing the time it takes for light to travel from the Sun to the Earth is to realize that the image we see of the solar disk is actually where the Sun was eight minutes ago.

The greater the distance, the longer the delay. The American spacecraft that photographed Saturn took 1 hour and 16 minutes to transmit its signals back to Earth at the speed of light. And if an astronomer looks at the outermost planet in our solar system, Pluto, the image he sees is how Pluto looked five and a half hours earlier.

Outside our solar system, the distances are magnified immensely. The nearest star to the Earth is Centauri A (or Alpha Centauri), about 25 million million miles away. Using miles as a measure of distance becomes too awkward now, so astronomers use the distance that light travels in one year — a light-year — to measure the distance between stars. One light-year is about 6 trillion miles. Centauri A is 4.3 light-years away. Light seen [in 2000] from Centauri A was generated on that star in [1996].

The situation can also be reversed. Light from the great San Francisco fire of 1906 has reached out [94] light-years into space. An observer on a planet near the star

LETTERS TO THE ASTRONOMER

Why do some stars appear to be different colors than others?

BECAUSE THEY *are* different colors. Every star has its unique color, and some are very different from the Sun. If these stars have planets (and they might), beings living on them would have a "sun" whose color could be quite extraordinary: deep red for some, blue-white for others, and so on.

Canopus will be able to view the entire San Francisco disaster in April 2004 if he has a telescope large enough.

(*Note:* Information in the original article has been updated, in brackets, to be current in the year 2000.)

1926

The Book-of-the-Month Club is the first mail-order book club.

■ *If a halo signifies goodness and purity, then perhaps our world isn't all that wicked after all. It has a halo — two of them, in fact, which, if viewed from far outer space, appear to wobble like glowing hula hoops. Science is just now beginning to comprehend their mysteries.*

Understanding Northern (and Southern) Lights

BY BLANTON C. WIGGIN

Some say that the Northern Lights are the glare of the Arctic ice and snow;
And some that it's electricity, and nobody seems to know.

— Robert Service, "The Ballad of the Northern Lights"

IMAGINE THAT YOU ARE SITTING UP on the Pole Star, or maybe in the Big Dipper, looking down on our solar system with a very powerful telescope. You see a bright star, the Sun, with some smaller bodies revolving about it.

Counting outward, the third of these satellites occupies our interest. It appears to be a double planet — two planets in the same orbit. They weave in and out past each other, like alternate strands in a wicker basket. The smaller of the two is cratered and bare, lacking atmosphere. The larger one is mostly blue and wreathed with white clouds. Between the clouds one can see the outlines of irregularly shaped bright areas of yellow,

brown, and green, and two white polar caps.

As you focus on the darker side of this interesting planet, the side facing away from the Sun, you may see two broad rings of light, one around each pole. These luminescent halos are usually in view and wobble like glowing hula hoops as the planet rotates. Sometimes you can see the halos as complete rings, but usually the portion of the rings that lies over the lighted side of the planet is washed out by the Sun's bright glare. The halos disappear at times but become brighter and much larger at other times.

If you look very closely, you will see that there are two concentric off-center bands at each pole. The inner one is sharp and irregular, while the outer one is duller, broader, and more diffuse. They undulate in a kaleidoscope of colors — green, yellow, red, and gray.

The planet, of course, is our Earth, and the bright halos are au-

1927

Wonder Bread appears on grocery store shelves.

roras, named after the Greek goddess of the dawn. If any other planet has such halos, they haven't yet been seen.

So much for the overview; let's head back to Earth. The view is dramatic from space but even more startling from the planet's surface.

As we go, let's take a closer look at the Sun. This bright torch seems to be burning smoothly and evenly, as it must if life on Earth is to continue. It has been assumed that the long-term radiation of the Sun is very constant, but now, with more sensitive instruments and standards, this assumption — the "solar constant" — is getting closer scrutiny.

We find, for instance, that every eleven years or so, there is an in-

1927

Belgian astronomer Georges Lemaitre proposes his big bang theory — that the universe began with a single event, such as a great explosion, between 10 billion and 20 billion years ago.

crease in the Sun's activity, which we detect by the increased presence of sunspots and solar flares, fiery streamers lifting off the star's surface as far as a quarter million miles. These solar flares not only spray visible tongues of fire, but, as they cool, they continue rushing outward as streams of subatomic particles, mostly protons and electrons. The particles travel more slowly than light, taking a couple of days to traverse the 93 million miles to Earth, whereas light pops across in eight minutes. The particles sweep across the solar system like water from a rotating lawn sprinkler.

Even when there are no flares and the Sun is "quiet," there is a constant flow of particles moving outward from the Sun in all directions at 500 miles per second or more. There is no ducking this "solar wind" in space. It varies widely, and during flares it can get quite gusty. Sometimes the gusts plow right through the slower-moving wind, causing shock edges, eddies, and locally unpredictable effects, such as the brightening or dimming of comet tails. The wind carries its own magnetic fields, like any electrical flow, and the wind variations cause changes in those fields.

There are between 100 and 10,000 particles per cubic inch in the ordinary solar wind — virtually nothing when you consider that there are 440 quintillion particles per cubic inch in air. And yet the influence of the solar wind is very significant in our affairs. It can drag down satellites by its friction, and someday it may propel huge sails across space, like old-time clipper ships.

We are most interested in its effect on the Earth. Remember, our planet is a huge magnet surrounded by three-dimensional fields of influence, like the skin of a fat apple. The fields curve down at the ends and meet the Earth in the polar regions.

Now imagine that around the middle of that fat apple, about 1,000 miles above the equator, is a large doughnut-shaped region, and around that, still larger, an inner tube perhaps ten times the size of the Earth itself. Technically, these doughnuts of inner

These solar flares not only spray visible tongues of fire, but, as they cool, they continue rushing outward as streams of subatomic particles, mostly protons and electrons. . . . The particles sweep across the solar system like water from a rotating lawn sprinkler.

1928

The *Oxford English Dictionary* is completed 71 years after it was started.

tubes are the Van Allen belts, which trap the solar wind particles and shield us from the worst of the solar storms.

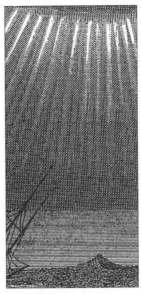

Around this entire still life of Earth apple, doughnut, and inner tube is a loose envelope of almost ephemeral space, shaped rather like an airport wind sock in reverse. The narrow, closed end points toward the Sun, into the solar wind. The Earth and the Van Allen belts are in the closed end. The open end trails off downwind from the Sun. This enveloping shroud is the magnetosphere. It ebbs and flows with the solar wind, its eddies, the passages of the Moon, magnetic anomalies on Earth, and the seasonal tilt of the Earth's axis.

The magnetosphere is also distorted by the impact of solar flares, which may contain up to 10 billion charged particles per cubic inch. Most of those particles are trapped in the Van Allen belts, but many protons and electrons escape and are guided down the curving magnetic surfaces (remember the fat apple?) to the polar regions. On their way, they give us a fireworks display.

Below the Van Allen belts, about 1,000 miles up, the protons and electrons fall into the "exosphere," where, as they descend below 600 miles, they encounter enough atmosphere that they may interact with it, agitating the gases so that they glow red, just as a neon light glows when electricity is passed through it.

Falling still farther, the particles enter the ionosphere, so named because of the ions, or charged particles, it contains. The ionosphere extends downward to a point about 40 miles above the surface and is composed of at least four layers, which bend or absorb longer-wave radio signals. These layers are strongly affected by solar storms and will play all sorts of tricks on radio transmission at those times.

Throughout the region from 40 to 200 miles up, the particles from the Sun are hitting oxygen and nitrogen, causing them to give off green, yellow, red, and blue glows that we associate with auroras. The chemistry of this interaction is well understood, but there are still gaps in our understanding of how solar particles reach the magnetosphere, bounce around inside it, and finally drop down into the lower atmospheric levels.

1928

Mickey Mouse, a cartoon character created by Walt Disney, makes his debut in the short film *Plane Crazy*.

Severe magnetic storms that upset ships' compasses have long been associated with auroras, disrupted radio signals, and sunspots. Now we understand that magnetic storms are actually the result of solar storms pushing and pulling the magnetosphere out of shape.

One hears mostly about the northern lights, or aurora borealis, Boreas being the Greek god of the north wind and a son of Aurora. One seldom hears about "southern lights," probably because the southern halo lies entirely over water or ice most of the time and nearby lands are sparsely inhabited. Still, Captain Cook recorded some "aurora australis" events during his epic voyages, and data developed during the International Geophysical Year of 1957–1958 support the idea that southern lights occur at the same time as their northern counterparts, and with equal intensity.

When the solar outbursts are major, the lights are seen in temperate zone skies, and occasionally in the tropics. Every few decades, after a gigantic solar tempest, they may be seen on the equator — in Singapore, for example. Man has occasionally created his own auroras by firing H-bombs into the ionosphere.

The auroras come in all sorts of shapes and colors. There are arcs across the heavens; general glows; and plain, rayed, and folded curtains. There are flashes, sudden brightenings, and rapid lateral motions.

It has been speculated that the curtain forms are really the bottom of sheet currents that surround the poles in an east–west around-the-pole direction. It's not hard to imagine instabilities in sheets sometimes only a few hundred feet thick by many hundreds or thousands of miles long. Folds should easily appear and do. Arcs also have been measured extending very long distances.

There seem to be two auroras possible at a particular location. One ranges from 450 to 650 miles up; the other 40 to 200. Generally, the lower edge of an aurora is 40 to 70 miles high, depending on the type, with some ranging up to 200 miles. They have been measured by triangulation from two or more observatories simultaneously. They may extend upward 10 to 80

Do auroras make noise? One usually thinks of silence in the deep snowy woods at night, and most displays are indeed silent. . . . But Eskimos, explorers, and old Arctic hands have all reported swishing, rustling, and faint whistling.

1929

The first Academy Awards are given at a quiet event attended by 200 members of the film community.

miles above the bottom. Do the northern lights come any lower? Definitely. During major displays, astronomers and professional observers have seen the aurora against nearby hills and icebergs, and actually down into valleys. This is a frequently disputed point, but the data are there.

If one trusts professionals, such as scientists expressly measuring the auroras, another controversial point is resolved: Do auroras make noise? One usually thinks of silence in the deep snowy woods at night, and most displays are indeed silent. Many question, reasonably, how any air glow at great elevation can be noisy. But Eskimos, explorers, and old Arctic hands have all reported swishing, rustling, and faint whistling. Some Eskimos blow gently through the lips to imitate the sound they know. In Scandinavia, the renowned aurorologist F. C. M. Stormer heard these sounds caused by, or associated with, the northern lights.

Other accompanying phenomena are an 8-kilohertz radio hiss, gyrating or even reversed compass needles, and radio interference.

If you wish to learn more about this fascinating subject, there are many interesting books to be found in most libraries today. Good, older encyclopedias may have extensive observational material, much of which has been omitted from newer editions and as a result is unknown

There'll be one snow in the coming winter for every fog in August.

and discounted. Modern general and technical encyclopedias illustrate the advances in understanding the mechanism of the northern lights.

Nothing can substitute for the real thing, though: the magic of a crystal-clear night over a northern lake or valley, and the "merry dancers" silently playing across the sky. You may be so fascinated, as the hours slip away, that you suddenly find dawn breaking while you are still under the spell, thrall, and grandeur of the northern lights.

All night long the northern streamers
shot across the trembling sky;
Fearful lights that never beckon;
Save when kings or heroes die.

— W. E. Aytoun, "Edinburgh After Flodden"

1929

The comic strip hero Popeye, created by Elzie Crisler Segar, first appears in the strip *Thimble Theatre.*

■ *In 1992 the Almanac celebrated its bicentennial and featured this article of astronomical highlights: the most spectacular, memorable, and even scary sky phenomena visible to the naked eye since the Almanac's first year of publication, 1792.*

Greatest Sky Sights of the Past 200 Years

BY FRED SCHAAF

Solar Eclipse of July 29, 1878

FOR ANY SPOT ON EARTH, A TOTAL solar eclipse occurs an average of only once every 300 to 400 years. Only 16 such eclipses have passed over parts of the 48 contiguous states in the past 200 years. The 1878 eclipse ran down the Rockies over Boulder, Denver, and Colorado Springs, then across Texas and Louisiana. Observing the eclipse from Pikes Peak, astronomer Samuel Langley (later director of the Smithsonian Institution) drew a naked-eye sketch that showed coronal streamers extending an amazing 12 times the Sun's diameter (more than 10 million miles). His drawing made the cover of *Harper's Weekly*. But Langley was upstaged by young Thomas Edison, who observed the eclipse from a chicken yard in Rawlins, Wyoming, where his preposterous new invention, the "tasimeter," accurately measured heat from the corona.

Lunar Eclipse of July 6, 1982

JUST 8 LUNAR ECLIPSES IN WHICH the Moon has virtually vanished have occurred in the past 200 years. The 1982 total eclipse, which many readers may remember, was the Western Hemisphere's longest total lunar eclipse since 1736. There was an extra bonus to the 1 hour and 46 minutes of totality. The acid haze from Mexico's El Chichon volcano had spread far enough to darken part of the Earth's shadow. The result was a Moon black at the top and middle but deep red at the bottom.

The Great Comet of 1882

THIS MAGNIFICENT LONG-PERIOD comet could be seen easily even in broad daylight, a shining knife beside the blazing Sun. When visible right at the Sun's edge, it shone 100 times brighter than the Moon. As it pulled away to become visible in twilight, the first ten degrees of the comet's tail was brighter than the brightest star.

1930s

Ruth Wakefield, owner of the Toll House Inn in Whitman, Massachusetts, creates the Toll House cookie. Nestlé will popularize the cookie by printing the recipe on its packages of chocolate morsels.

Comet hunter E. E. Barnard of Tennessee dreamed he saw the sky filled with comets; he went outside and found that the Great Comet had spawned many smaller comets.

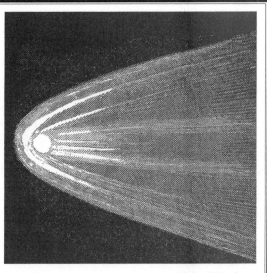

Return of Halley's Comet, 1910

HALLEY'S HAS paid the Earth three visits since 1800. The 1910 show was the best. In May of that year, Halley got as bright as the brightest star, and Earth passed right through an outer edge of its tail. Many people feared (unnecessarily) being poisoned by the gases. At its closest approach, the comet's glowing tail extended two-thirds of the way across the sky.

Leonid Meteor Showers of November 17, 1966

THE GREATEST METEOR "STORMS" have been those supplied, usually about every 33 years, by the annual Leonid showers. On November 13, 1833, came the night "the stars fell on Alabama" — and all over America; the brightest of the 14,000 meteors an hour woke people from their beds in Boston. But the night of November 17, 1966, was even more dazzling. This time, the western states got the best show. Folks out that night, especially on Kitt Peak in Arizona, said it was like a waterfall of shooting stars pouring down from the sky — as many as 500,000 meteors an hour!

The Great Meteoric Procession of February 9, 1913

THOUSANDS OF PEOPLE FROM Saskatchewan to Bermuda sighted the procession of several hundred meteors streaming across the sky, taking about three minutes to complete the arc. When last spotted from a ship in the South Atlantic, they were going strong. The best guess is that they were fragments of a temporary small "second moon" of Earth as it entered the atmosphere for one last fiery orbit.

1930

Boeing Air Transport (later United Airlines) hires the first female flight attendants.

The Northern Lights of March 13, 1989

WHEN CHARGED PARTICLES from the Sun are sped by Earth's magnetic field toward the poles, they collide with atoms and molecules of upper atmosphere gases. Thus is born the sky's greatest display of moving lights: the aurora borealis, or northern lights. The best show documented is the March 13, 1989, outbreak, in which red northern lights were seen as far south as Central America and the associated magnetic storm knocked out electric power for about 6 million people in Quebec.

Expect rain when dogs' tails straighten.

The Meteorological Optics Effects (Beautiful Sky Colors) of 1883 and 1950

THE 1883 ERUPTION OF THE IN-donesian volcano Krakatoa threw huge amounts of volcanic ash into the air and caused numerous meteorological phenomena worldwide. Most prominent were the vast crimson and purple twilights that glowed for as long as one and a half hours after sunset.

A different-size particle — ash from vast forest fires in Alberta, Canada — caused green, blue, and brass-colored sunshine and odd "dark days" over much of the northeastern United States in 1950. But the full Moon on September 25, by strangest luck, was the most memorable of all. The Moon, already blue from the smoke, was totally eclipsed that night. The reddening of the eclipse across the Moon created the rarest lunar sign of all — a purple Moon!

1930

Clyde W. Tombaugh discovers the ninth planet, Pluto.

■ *The Moon seems to be larger when low in the sky near the horizon. Yet, strangely, quite the opposite is true!*

How Big Is the Moon?

BY LEWIS J. BOSS

THE FACT THAT THE MOON looks remarkably larger when it is near the horizon than when it is high in the sky has been noted by almost everyone. Philosophers and astronomers alike — such as Aristotle, Ptolemy, Kepler, Gauss, and von Helmholtz — have offered explanations of this for more than 2,000 years. Aristotle, for example, thought that light passing through the Earth's atmosphere in a horizontal direction caused the phenomenon.

Ptolemy referred to the apparent variations in the Moon's size as it moved from horizon to zenith in his descriptions of various natural events, but no accurate observations were made until the 16th century. Then Johannes Kepler noted that the Moon exhibited varying diameters at different altitudes in the sky, but he did not pursue the matter further. Carl Friedrich Gauss, early-19th-century philosopher, astronomer, and eminent mathematician, made the first significant progress in solving the puzzle by proposing a physiological solution. He considered that the answer lay in the difference between the image perceived when the rising Moon was viewed over a horizon, which provided a scale for the eyes, and the image perceived when the eyes

1931

New York City's Empire State Building, the world's tallest building, is completed.

were raised to view the same object high overhead. In developing this theory, he came surprisingly close to the truth.

It seems probable that the German physicist Hermann von Helmholtz, whose early years were contemporary with Gauss's later ones, was quite familiar with this theory. Helmholtz is known for his research in physiological optics and appears to have found an acceptable explanation for the Moon's variation in size with its altitude in the sky. His theory asserts that the reason the Moon appears larger when it is seen near the horizon is that it is viewed in apparent proximity to terrestrial objects and, as Gauss surmised nearly 50 years before, the brain unconsciously assigns to it a dimension comparable to these objects.

Actually, the phenomenon is probably a combination of physiological and optical effects, as can be demonstrated by the following simple experiment. Roll up a sheet of paper into a tube about ½ inch in diameter and 11 to 12 inches long. Look through the tube with one eye at the seemingly enlarged full Moon near the horizon: At once the Moon's disk will contract to its normal proportions. Now close this eye and open the other one: Immediately the Moon will resume its enlarged appearance. Repeat this action as often as desired, and you will find that the eye looking through the tube is never deceived

— the reason being that there is only a very thin ring of sky around the Moon when it is viewed through the tube and none of the neighboring trees or buildings on the landscape at the horizon are visible.

As a matter of fact, the Moon should appear very slightly larger to our eyes when it is in the zenith, since it is closer to us. This is shown in the accompanying diagram. Let the small circle M represent the Moon and the large circle the Earth. When M is on the horizon of a

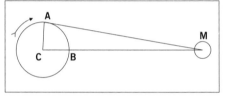

place A on the Earth's surface and later on is observed from this place after it has moved into position B, the Earth having turned on its axis by about 90 degrees, it is obvious that the Moon is nearer to B than it is to A by almost the length of the Earth's radius, C-B. The average distance of the Moon from the Earth, C-M, is about 240,000 miles, and C-B is around 4,000 miles. Consequently, the zenith Moon should appear to be slightly larger than the horizon Moon by about one-sixtieth part. Our visual mechanism appears to be so programmed by continual viewing of terrestrial objects, however, that this is not the case.

LETTERS TO THE ASTRONOMER

Most astronomy books state that the period of one lunation is 29 days, 12 hours, and 44 minutes. However, in *The Old Farmer's Almanac* for 1980, the time between the new Moon in June and the new Moon in July was 29 days, 13 hours, and 43 minutes — a difference of about 59 minutes. What is the reason for this?

THE DISCREPANCY between the value given in the Almanac and the value in textbooks occurs because the textbook value is an *average*. If you look at the phases of the Moon over many months, you will find that they do not come at precisely regular intervals. This is because the orbit of the Moon is elliptical, not circular. It is only if you calculate the lengths of the months over many years and average them that you will get the standard textbook figure of 29 days, 12 hours, and 44 minutes for one lunation.

Does only the Moon have phases?

NO. ALL THE PLANETS have phases, but they occur in varying degrees. Only two planets — Mercury and Venus — go through the complete cycle of phases from new to full. The outer planets, Mars through Pluto, are almost always full. These phases are most striking for Venus and can be seen with even a small telescope. They progress very slowly, however. The Moon takes a month to go through its cycle of phases, but Venus takes more than a year.

Venus's phases are only partially responsible for its changing brightness over the seasons. For example, when Venus is in the new phase, it cannot be seen, just like the Moon. When it is full, it also cannot be seen (*unlike* the Moon), for it lies directly behind the Sun. Venus in not brightest when it is full. It is brightest when it is in a partial phase, is not obscured by the Sun, and is not too far from Earth.

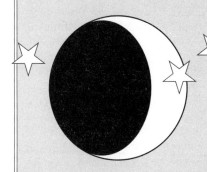

1933

Charles B. Darrow
creates the game Monopoly,
which Parker Brothers will
produce in 1935.

■ *Although men have walked on the Moon, most of us here on Earth know very little about our only natural satellite. For instance, do you know why a "quarter Moon" is actually a "half Moon"?*

When One-Quarter Equals One-Half

BY ROBERT X. PERRY

IN CASE YOU DIDN'T KNOW IT, THAT half Moon you saw in the sky last night was the first quarter. Both of the Moon phases known as "quarters" are observed in the sky as half Moons. This apparent contradiction, that a quarter is a half, is easily explained, but over the years many calendars, newspapers, authors, and artists have exhibited incorrect sketches of these phases. Some err when they show the first and last quarters as one-quarter of a full Moon. The correct profile is that of a half Moon. In this case, the word *quarter* refers to time: one-fourth of a lunar month. It does not indicate the shape of the visible Moon.

On the "Space Coast" of Florida, the Apollo series of Moon shots was completed with the liftoff of *Apollo 17* on December 7, 1972. In this area, there are a great many sophisticated people devoted to our space program. Yet the two daily newspapers arriving at this writer's doorstep in Cocoa Beach committed common Moon errors. One

showed the quarters incorrectly as one-fourth of a full Moon. The other showed them correctly as half Moons, but the sketches were reversed. The first quarter should be arched to the right, because here the Moon is waxing. This particular paper had it arched to the left, which is correct only for the waning third or last quarter. All of this in an area that boasts of more Moon savvy than anyplace else on this planet. If two of the primary newspapers in this region can be that careless, how do you suppose it goes elsewhere? In Figure 1, the four principal phases are shown in their proper form reading chronologically from left to right.

Football Analogy

Many romantic songs extol the beauty and influence of the Moon, but most of us fail to comprehend just why the first quarter is a half Moon. Although we have made tremendous scientific strides in lunar exploration and knowledge, the

1934

Shirley Temple, at age six, is the youngest person to receive an Oscar.

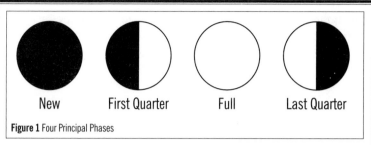

Figure 1 Four Principal Phases

person on the street is still pretty confused about simple everyday information about our lunar satellite in the heavens. Perhaps a good way to begin to correct this is to compare a lunar month with a football game.

The four quarters of a lunar month (29 days plus) are somewhat akin to the four quarters of a football game. During the first two quarters the Moon is waxing, and at the half it puts on a brilliant show and appears as a full Moon. During the last two quarters it is waning, and on the 19th day time has expired and a new game begins immediately. The first quarter is a period of 7 days plus, and when this period closes, we see a half Moon arched to the right. The same thing happens at the end of the third period, only the Moon is arched to the left.

The terms "first quarter" and "third quarter" have been with us for a long time, and I am not recommending that they be changed. However, the first person to choose the names of the four principal phases was not too consistent. The

term "full Moon" refers to the shape, while "first quarter" relates to time. Had he stuck to shape all the way, it would go like this: new — first half; full — second half. Understanding that the two phases known as quarters are visible in the sky as half Moons is step 1 in Moon lore.

Perpetual Time of Moonrise

Folks who enjoy the out-of-doors and the wonders of nature may wish to commit to mind the following gem of Moon knowledge, which is a rule of thumb for the time of rising for the man in the Moon.

*The new Moon always rises at
   sunrise
And the first quarter at noon.
The full Moon always rises at
   sunset
And the last quarter at midnight.*

At the risk of becoming too verbose, I developed the above into a verse, which runs like this:

1935

The first parking meters, invented by Carl C. Magee, are installed in Oklahoma City.

The new Moon will rise —
  In the eastern skies
At dawn it climbs with the Sun —
  A new lunar month begun.

The first quarter will rise —
  In the bright eastern skies
On the horizon at noon —
  Waxing as a pale half Moon.

The full Moon will rise —
  In the eastern skies
Starting the show at twilight —
  To reign as the queen of night.

The last quarter will rise —
  In the dark eastern skies
At midnight it will appear —
  As the waning days are here.

The time of moonrise (and, incidentally, the time of high tide) occurs about 50 minutes later each day. To determine the time of moonrise for all the days of the month, one can add this amount for each day after a phase or subtract it for each day prior. The new Moon is invisible because the Sun blots it out. One or two days after the date of the new Moon, we can see it in the western sky as a thin crescent setting just after sunset. In using the above rule, care must be taken about the terms "noon" and "midnight." These are affected by Daylight Saving Time and, to a lesser degree, by one's longitude in the time zone. Sunrise and sunset are definite times regardless of man's tampering with the clock. Since the Moon has no light of its own and reflects sunlight, we see a full Moon rise in the east when the Sun is setting in the west. The time of moonrise is probably step 2 in getting closer to understanding our Moon, about which so much has been written.

● ◐ ○ ◑ ●

The Moon's Effect on Earthlings

Step 3 might be the effect the Moon has on earthly things such as ocean tides, land, air, and living animals both human and otherwise. It is well known that the Moon governs our tides with an assist from the Sun. There are many who claim that it also has an effect on human behavior — when to plant crops and when to go fishing, for example. Police crime records are said to be more numerous during the days of the full or new Moon. Hospital records of patients bleeding are likewise said to increase

Police crime records are said to be more numerous during the days of the full or new Moon. Hospital records of patients bleeding are likewise said to increase during these days.

1935

Englishman A. E. Stevens develops an electronic hearing aid that weighs 2½ pounds!

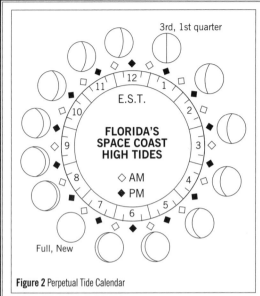

Figure 2 Perpetual Tide Calendar

Moon, and it forecasts the time of high water for London Bridge. The perpetual tide chart exhibited in Figure 2 is also based on the age of the Moon. It is unusual because it introduces an interesting phenomenon about the effect of the Moon on earthly things. In this Space Coast tide chart, there are 14 Moon circles around a conventional face of a clock. Each circle represents 2 Moon shapes, or phases. This totals 28 Moons, which is about 1 less than a lunar month. One Moon was dropped to have each of the 4 quarters equal in time (7 days). This chart indicates that the full or new Moon produces the same time of high tide. The first and third quarters are likewise the same, as are all the intermediate phases shown around the clock. In other words, a waxing and a waning Moon with complementary shapes causes the exact same time of high tide. This phenomenon can be extended to include the same action on other earthly bodies. That is to say, the effect of the new Moon is the same as that of the full Moon. Figure 3 shows this point in greater detail.

during these days. There is also some evidence of great historic storms hitting our coasts during certain lunar periods. Some almanacs and books on weather have quoted an old saw about the weather changing when the Moon changes and a new lunar month begins:

The Moon and the weather
May change together
But a change of the Moon
Does not change the weather.

● ◐ ○ ◑ ●

Perpetual Tide Calendar

One of the world's first tide calendars was developed by a 14th-century astronomer. It is now on exhibit in a marine museum in Greenwich, England. Its predictions are based on the age of the

1935

Dr. George H. Gallup conducts his first public opinion poll.

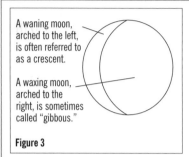

A waning moon, arched to the left, is often referred to as a crescent.

A waxing moon, arched to the right, is sometimes called "gibbous."

Figure 3

An additional point about the effect of the Moon on Earth concerns the quantity of this effect. Everyone knows that the time of tide is different each day in most of the world's harbors and beaches. What they don't know is that the height of tide or the quantity of water also differs from tide to tide in the same harbor. A simple explanation might be that old story about cooperation or working together. When the Sun, Moon, and Earth are in a straight line (such as at full or new), their combined gravitational pull will produce a spring, or big, tide. At the time of the quarters, the Sun and Moon are 90 degrees apart, and we experience a neap, or small, tide. The combined efforts of these heavenly bodies cause other effects on

When the Sun, Moon, and Earth are in a straight line (such as at full or new), their combined gravitational pull will produce a spring, or big, tide. At the time of the quarters, the Sun and Moon are 90 degrees apart, and we experience a neap, or small, tide.

Earth. Scientists have proved that there are land tides as well as atmospheric tides. A tide of several inches is experienced on the Great Lakes in the United States and Canada. There is a "tide" in other smaller bodies that may not be sufficient to be detected, yet the influence is there.

The Metonic Cycle

In the first century B.C., a Greek astronomer by the name of Meton discovered what became known as the Metonic, or lunar, cycle. Meton found that the Moon repeats itself approximately every 19 solar years. Each year in the cycle has been assigned a golden number from I to XIX. In the current cycle, 1995 was Golden Year I. The year 2000 will be Golden Year VI, and a new Metonic cycle will begin in the year 2014. The dates of Moon phases, eclipses, and the like very nearly repeat themselves in years with the same golden number. They may vary by 1 or 2 days because the cycle is not exactly 19 years. Leap year also throws a curve when we compare

1936

A New York law forbidding men to wear topless bathing suits is revised to allow swimming trunks.

2 years with the same golden number and one is a leap year and the other is not. I have constructed my own Metonic cycle that gives the approximate dates of Moon phases to use in checking historic storms or great battles of yesteryear. How do you suppose the moonlight was on the night Paul Revere muffled his oars and rowed to Charlestown? My Metonic cycle will answer that question quickly, but it is doubtful whether anyone has an almanac handy for April 1775.

The Dark Side of the Moon

It is well documented that we can see only about one face of the Moon. As the Earth turns on its axis, the Moon does likewise, always exposing the same face. Through the ages, the face we see has been well studied through powerful telescopes. Until our astronauts exposed the so-called dark side of the Moon, there were many amusing stories told about this unknown side. A short play was written some years ago about what was on that side. The point of the play was that there was a nude woman there, and that's why God had caused the Moon to revolve in harmony with the Earth and keep that side hidden from earthly Peeping Toms and their telescopes. Our astronauts have ended many such yarns about the dark side of the Moon.

The Heartbeat of Earth

SEE THE MAN in the Moon —
   He's a restless tycoon,
Waxing and waning —
   Shrinking and gaining.

The tide in the ocean —
   Performs a set motion,
In tune with the gaze —
   Of his lunar phase.

As today's tide reaches —
   The shores of these beaches,
The Moon in the sky —
   Tells the hour of high.

The daily ebb and flood —
   Flows as the earthly blood,
Refreshing each bay —
   Two times every day.

Like the breathing of man —
   In God's eternal plan,
The tide has a berth —
   The heartbeat of Earth!

1937

Amelia Earhart's plane disappears in the South Pacific during her attempt to fly around the world.

■ *Now is as good a time as any to become fully acquainted, at long last, with the personal relationship we all have with the Moon each month.*

The Moon and You

BY MARTHA WHITE

ON JULY 20, 1969, NEIL ARM-strong took his historic steps on the Moon. President Richard M. Nixon, in a moment of national pride, proclaimed it the greatest event since Creation.

Some say that the Sun gives life, while the Moon regulates it. The tides, rains, reproduction and fertility, plant life, and even the life cycles of animals and humans all seem affected by the Moon's pull. Without that steady gravitational pull, the Earth's axis would undergo chaotic variations; in keeping the spinning Earth stabilized, the Moon helps regulate the seasons and climate.

To many sky watchers, the Moon is home to the gods. Plutarch, a first-century Greek essayist, considered it a way station for the coming and going of souls. Lunar eclipses, some believed, were instances of the Moon being eaten up. Various rituals were enacted to

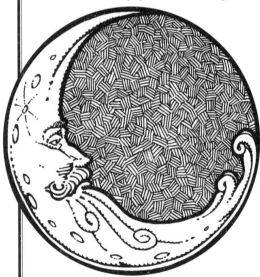

bring the Moon back, whether from eclipse or its monthly new Moon phase disappearance. "Shooting the Moon" — now an expression of great ambition — was an attempt to rekindle the light of the Moon with fiery arrows.

Man in the Moon?

In our culture, we speak of seeing the "Man in the Moon," an image of a face imposed on the illuminated lunar surface. In Polynesia, it is the

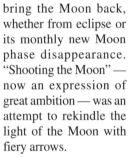

1938

Walt Disney completes the first feature-length animated film, *Snow White and the Seven Dwarfs.*

"Woman in the Moon," and she has her child with her. The Selish Indians of the American Northwest see a toad that escaped to the Moon when a wolf courted her. Other cultures see a man with a bundle of sticks on his back, the finger marks of mischievous boys, Judas, the severed head of an outcast, a giant who controls the tides, or a hunchback. To Japanese viewers, it's a rabbit in profile, while Scandinavians see a boy and a girl holding a water bucket.

The Selish Indians of the American Northwest see a toad that escaped to the Moon when a wolf courted her. To Japanese viewers, it's a rabbit in profile, while Scandinavians see a boy and a girl holding a water bucket.

Man ON the Moon!

Two dozen American astronauts have traveled to the Moon, and half of those have walked on its surface. Through all this intensive scientific research, the Moon nevertheless has retained its aura of mystery and romanticism. Colonel James Irwin, pilot of the *Apollo 15* lunar module, spoke of "the grand spiritual change of seeing the Earth as God must see it," viewed from the surface of the Moon.

Neil Armstrong is known for his words, "That's one small step for [a] man, one giant leap for mankind." (In his excitement, he forgot to say "a," he later confessed.) Charles "Pete" Conrad Jr., in the next Apollo landing (November 1969), was allowed a little more candor. "Whoopee!" he cried. "Man, that may have been a small step for Neil, but that's a long one for me."

Courting, Tomcatting, and Birthing

Folklore has it that if a young woman sees a dove and glimpses the new Moon at the same instant, she should repeat, "Bright Moon, clear Moon, Bright and fair, Lift up your right foot, There'll be a hair." When she removes her shoe, she'll find a hair the color of her future husband's. Marriages consummated during the full Moon are most prosperous and happy, according to the ancient Greeks, while a waning Moon bodes ill for wedded bliss. The full Moon is an ideal time to accept a proposal of marriage as well.

Certain plants believed to be ruled by the Moon carry romantic associations. The poppy, particularly, has been considered an inducement for dreams predicting love. Both poppies and cucumbers are folk reme-

1938

The nylon-bristle toothbrush, replacing hog hair – bristle brushes, revolutionizes the dental industry.

dies to enhance fertility. Succulents are thought to attract romance, while eating lettuce has been prescribed for those with an overabundance of lust. (Are your salads giving you mixed messages?)

Dreams and Superstitions

To DREAM of a clear Moon portends success, say some, while a red or "bloody" Moon warns of catastrophe or war. A new Moon in your dreams promises increased wealth or a happy marriage. If a young woman dreams of the Moon growing dimmer, she should mind her sharp tongue, lest happiness elude her. Dreams of an eclipsed Moon are said to predict a contagious disease close at hand.

It's lucky to:

■ See the first sliver of a new Moon "clear of the brush," or unencumbered by foliage.

■ Own a rabbit's foot, especially if the rabbit was killed in a cemetery by a cross-eyed person at the dark of the Moon.

■ Hold a moonstone in your mouth at the full Moon. It will reveal the future.

■ Have a full Moon on the "Moon's day" (Monday).

■ Expose your newborn to the waxing Moon. It will give the baby strength.

■ Move your residence during the new Moon. Prosperity will increase as the Moon waxes.

It's unlucky to:

■ See the first sliver of a new Moon through a window. You'll break a dish.

■ Point at the new Moon or view any Moon over your shoulder.

■ Sleep in the moonlight, or worse, be born in the moonlight. If a woman must sleep in the moonlight, she should rub spit on her belly, or she risks becoming pregnant.

■ See "the old Moon in the arms of the new," or the faint image of the full disk while the new crescent Moon is illuminated, especially if you're a sailor. Storms are predicted.

■ Have a full Moon on Sunday. (Some say Saturday.)

1938

Orson Welles produces a radio dramatization of H. G. Wells's *War of the Worlds* (1898), about an invasion by martians. The broadcast causes widespread panic.

"Tomcatting," whether practiced by felines or humans, is reputed to be most successful at the bright Moon. Carousers will be refreshed rather than exhausted by their exertions and are less apt to suffer physical maladies as a result. Men's virility is enhanced and fertility is at a peak, believe some.

The Navajos, among others, believe that the full Moon's pull on a woman's amniotic fluid increases the chances of birthing at this time. Some nurses and midwives also claim that the new Moon is an active time for births.

The Moon and Weather Predictions

Farmers, sailors, and other sky watchers have long used the Moon to predict the weather. The waxing Moon is sometimes called the right-hand Moon, its curve following that of the right-hand index finger and thumb. The waning Moon is the left-hand Moon. "In the wane of the Moon, a cloudy morning bodes a fair afternoon," reads one old saw. If the crescent Moon holds its points upward, able to contain water, it predicts a dry spell. If the new Moon stands on its points, expect precipitation to spill out.

In general, the new Moon is considered a time of weather changes, and, indeed, weather records confirm that the days following both the new and full Moons are most likely to be rainy or stormy.

A winter full Moon is a time for long cold snaps. In April, it brings frost. Western Kansans claim freedom from storms if the full Moon is near, and sailors agree that the full Moon "eats clouds." Two full Moons in a month increase the chances of flood, a pale full Moon indicates rain, a red one brings wind, and a Christmas full Moon predicts a poor harvest.

Halos (also called rings or "Moon dogs") are another sign. Henry Wadsworth Longfellow wrote in "The Wreck of the Hesperus":

For I fear a hurricane;
Last night the Moon had a
golden ring,
And tonight no Moon we see.

The halo, marking an abundance of moisture in the atmosphere, predicts wet or stormy weather. One should count the number of stars visible within the halo to know the number of days before rain. The stars also may signify the number of days of rain. Science confirms that the fewer visible stars, the more moisture there is in the atmosphere.

1939

In Williamsport, Pennsylvania, Little League Baseball starts with 30 boys on 3 teams.

The Right Times to Plant, Wean, Build Fences, Castrate, and Harvest

The age-old practice of performing farm chores by the Moon stems from the simple belief that the Moon governs moisture. Pliny the Elder, the first-century Roman naturalist, states in his *Natural History* that the Moon "replenishes the Earth; when she approaches it, she fills all bodies, while, when she recedes, she empties them."

Moonrise occurring in the evening brings fair weather, says one proverb, harking back to the belief that the waning Moon (full and last quarter, which rise in the evening) is dry. New Moon and first quarter, or waxing phases, are considered fertile and wet.

The new and first quarter phases, known as the light of the Moon, are considered good for planting aboveground crops, putting down sod, grafting trees, and transplanting. From full Moon through the last quarter, or the dark of the Moon, is the best time for killing weeds, thinning, pruning, mowing, cutting timber, and planting belowground crops. The time just before the full Moon is considered particularly wet, best for planting during drought conditions. Seed germination, some farmers insist, is much better then.

According to folklore, rail fences cut during the dry, waning Moon will stay straighter. Many say wooden shingles and shakes will lie flatter if cut during the dark of the Moon, but others swear by the waxing Moon. Logs cut in the dark of the Moon are thought to sink into the ground quickly; for a pig fence, this is desirable. Similarly, fence posts should be set in the dark of the Moon to resist rotting. Ozark lore adds that a fence post should always be set as the tree grew. To set the root end upward makes a short-lived fence.

Don't commence your weaning when the Moon is waning, nor (ideally) should you be birthing then. Turn your feather beds to make them smooth; a waxing Moon attracts the feathers too strongly. Castrate

> *The dark of the Moon is the best time for killing weeds, thinning, pruning, mowing, cutting timber, and planting belowground crops.*

1939

Robert May of Chicago writes the poem "Rudolph the Red-Nosed Reindeer." Johnny Marks will put it to music in 1949.

and dehorn animals on the Moon's wane for less bleeding, but slaughter on the wax for juicier meat. Crabbing, shrimping, and clamming are thought to be best when the Moon is full, but wait for the days between the new and full Moons for fishing. Mushrooms gathered by the full Moon may be poisonous, even if ordinarily palatable, but dig your horseradish in the full Moon for the best flavor. And always set eggs to hatch on the Moon's increase, but not if a south wind blows.

Lunacy

Paracelsus, the 16th-century physician, said the Moon has "the power to tear reason out of man's head by depriving him of humors and cerebral virtues." There are those who will not sleep in moonlight for fear of courting insanity. In England, a distinction was made between lunatics and the insane: Lunatics were affected only by the full Moon, while insanity was more permanent. Epilepsy, once called *lunaticus,* or "moonstruck," was believed by the early Greeks and Romans to be caused by moonlight. Lycanthropy, the belief that the full Moon can cause a person to become a werewolf, remains a well-known form of Moon madness and, whether fact or delusion, has its sufferers even today.

Scientific studies over the years have tried to link the full Moon with times of increased violence, sui-

Moon Facts and Figures

Age: Approximately 4.6 billion years

Circumference: 6,790 miles

Density: 3.34 times that of water

Diameter: 2,160 miles, about one-quarter of the Earth's diameter

Direction of orbit: Counterclockwise

Distance (mean) from the Earth: 238,857 miles, with variations of more than 30,000 miles

Sidereal period (Moon's mean rotation around the Earth): 27 days, 7 hours, 43.2 minutes

Surface area: 23,712,500 miles, or less than one-thirteenth that of Earth

Surface gravity: About one-sixth that of Earth

Synodical or lunar month (from one new Moon to the next): 29 days, 12 hours, 44.05 minutes

Temperature: 243° F at the lunar equator, with the Sun directly above; at sunset 58° F; after dark -261° F

Weight: 81 quintillion tons, or just over one-tenth the Earth's weight

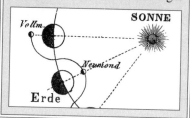

1939

Actor John Wayne gets his big break in acting with a role in the motion picture *Stagecoach.*

cide, mental disorders, fits and seizures, increased fertility or virility, and times of menstruation and birthing. Some small-scale studies have shown correlations between the full Moon and increased police activity, hot-line calls, and hospital emergencies.

Healing Powers

Not all of the Moon's effects on health are considered negative. The flow of blood, especially, has been suspected of responding to the gravitational tug of the Moon in folklore, astrology, and more recently, even in medicine.

LETTERS TO THE ASTRONOMER

Which has the stronger gravitational pull, the North Pole or the South Pole?

THEY ARE the same. The equator, however, is different, because the Earth is rotating. Things are lighter there.

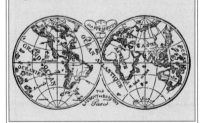

Believers in the influence of the Moon may consider dental care and elective surgery unwise around the times of the full Moon because of the risk of increased bleeding. (Similarly, Civil War doctors noted the tides, suspecting greater blood flow during a flood tide.) A Florida physician, Dr. Edson Andrews, ran an informal study between 1956 and 1958 that pointed to excessive bleeding in operations done between the new Moon and full (waxing) phases, with a peak at the full Moon days.

Lunar folk remedies lean heavily toward myth and superstition. Wart cures, particularly, have relied on lunar magic. For instance, to remove warts, you might blow on them nine times during a full Moon or "wash" your hands in the Moon's rays captured in a shiny metal basin. Be careful not to offend the Moon, however. A surefire route to becoming a witch is to fire a silver bullet at the Moon while spouting obscenities. An even quicker path is to fire seven bullets at the Moon and recite the Lord's Prayer backward.

Do you get the blues on Mondays? Maybe you're engaging in the wrong activities. Literally "the Moon's day," Monday in legend and lore is auspicious for peace and happiness, raising spirits of the dead, water activities and travel, home and family, dreams, medicine, cooking (but watch those salads), love spells and reconciliation, learning the truth, clairvoyance, and becoming invisible. So if it's Monday, shoot for the Moon.

1940

Maurice and Richard McDonald open a hamburger stand, which they will turn into a self-service restaurant in 1948. Entrepreneur Ray Kroc will convince them to sell franchises beginning in 1952, then buy them out in 1961.

■ *That midday ray of sunshine might have seemed like a random occurrence, but there is a reason, easily explained with simple geometry, we always see the Sun at noon, even on cloudy days.*

The Sun Always Shines at Noon

BY ROBERT X. PERRY

HAVE YOU EVER NOTICED THAT on an overcast day, the Sun will often break through the clouds close to midday? Sometimes it may not actually break through, but it tries hard and the atmosphere brightens. On such days, if you observe the cloud cover above, you will get a brief glimpse of the Sun's upper limb and then the lower limb as the Sun crosses the meridian. Sunshine may not actually reach Earth, but through smoked glasses you can detect a piece of the Sun through the cloud cover.

During World War II, I served as navigation officer aboard a U.S. Army hospital ship. The skipper taught me something I'd never learned in school: The Sun always shines at noon.

It took our ship nine days to cross the Atlantic, and on this particular voyage, it was overcast for the entire trip. Every day at noon, the captain would prop himself up on a wing of the bridge, put his hat on backward, and scan the horizon with the telescope of his sextant, searching and waiting for a piece of the Sun to break through. Every day he succeeded, and if he didn't see the Sun exactly as it crossed the meridian, he got it a little before

1941

noon or just after it crossed, for what is known as an ex-meridian altitude.

Before this cloudy voyage was over, he had us all shooting the somewhat invisible Sun just the way we'd do on a clear day. The doctors, nurses, and others who were strolling on deck were amazed to see the deck officers all lined up with their sextants peering into a leaden sky, where there was apparently nothing but thick clouds.

Ever since learning this lesson on the hospital ship, I've paid attention at noon on overcast days wherever I have lived. Seldom has the Sun disappointed me. (All of my observations have been made in the temperate zone, and these comments may not apply to an observer in the extreme northern or southern latitudes, where the Sun follows a different pattern.)

At noon the Sun penetrates less cloud cover and contends with less atmospheric pollutants because it is directly above and not at an oblique angle.

There are some simple reasons for this phenomenon. At noon, the Sun is 4,000 miles closer to an Earth observer than at dawn. (Since the Sun is 93 million miles from Earth, this might be considered a small point.) More important is the fact that at noon the Sun penetrates less cloud cover and contends with less atmospheric pollutants because it is directly above and not at an oblique angle.

As I write these lines, the weather is bad. It's raining, and it's been overcast for 3 days, but a ray of sunshine just broke through for a moment, and I note that it's 10 minutes to 12:00 (standard time). It's been a long time since the captain taught me this little weather wrinkle, and I thought that some of you out there might like to put on your sunglasses and say hello to ol' Sol and brighten a dreary overcast day before you go to lunch.

Dog Days bright and clear Indicate a happy year.

1942

Jack Norworth, the author of the 1908 song "Take Me Out to the Ball Game," attends his first baseball game.

ANECDOTES & PLEASANTRIES

It's OK, Florida — We Love You Anyway

IS FLORIDA *really* the "Sunshine State"? The answer, alas, is no — not by a long shot.

A quick check of 30-year averages compiled by the National Oceanic and Atmospheric Administration (NOAA) reveals that Boston and New York City both have more clear days annually than does Miami: 94 and 107 to Miami's 76. Even snowy Concord, New Hampshire, has more—92. A sample of other eastern cities that outstrip Miami in the number of clear days per year includes New Haven, Connecticut (100); Wilmington, Delaware (94); Washington, D.C. (101); Atlanta (108); Portland, Maine (107); Baltimore (106); Atlantic City (96); Charlotte, North Carolina (111); Philadelphia (92); Providence (103); Charleston, South Carolina (101); and Richmond (103).

One state that deserves to use the motto is New Mexico: Albuquerque, for instance, has 172 days of clear skies a year. In general, the West and major portions of the Midwest are sunnier than the East. Topping them all is Las Vegas, Nevada, with 216 annual days of sunshine. Other cities include Phoenix (214); Denver (115); Colorado Springs (124); Des Moines (103); Wichita, Kansas (127); New Orleans (109); Minneapolis (100); Kansas City, Missouri (132); St. Louis (105); Omaha (113); Reno, Nevada (165); Tulsa (101); Rapid City, South Dakota (110); Dallas (139); El Paso, Texas (194); Salt Lake City (129); and Cheyenne, Wyoming (106).

So when you're thinking about installing a fancy new solar panel on your house, check out the amount of sunshine in your area first.

Courtesy of Heinz D. Woehlk,
based on statistics in Climatological
Data, *put out by the NOAA*

1942

The Grand Coulee Dam, across the Columbia River in Washington State, is completed. It is the largest concrete dam in the world.

■ *To some it's frightening, while others find it exhilarating, and although it seems like an occasional event, lightning is constantly striking the Earth. And it's a good thing, too, for without lightning, we could not live!*

What Is Lightning?
(Besides Scary)

BY GARTH LONGENE

THE STAGE IS SET. DARK CLOUDS form the backdrop, wildly highlighted by brilliant flashes, followed by the crashing crescendo of thunder — and another thunderstorm is being staged. Nature is, again, presenting an exciting, unparalleled, and sometimes frightening spectacular!

It's not a once-a-year or once-a-month show. It's estimated that some 1,800 thunderstorms are in progress over the Earth's surface at any given moment and that lightning strikes the Earth 100 times each second.

What is lightning? It is a gigantic electric spark; a surge of electrical charges rushing to meet their opposites. This interchange may be from cloud to cloud or from cloud to Earth. When storm clouds gather, there is a wild turbulence inside them. Humid air condenses to raindrops, water turns to ice crystals inside air currents, and there is a resulting separation of electrical charges.

Usually negative charges accumulate in the lower part of a cloud, while positive charges build up in the Earth and in the upper part of the cloud. When the attraction between these opposite charges becomes strong enough, they leap across the gap of nonconducting air between them. This is lightning.

It's something that has always been a marvel to man. In past civilizations, man has given lightning supernatural powers, often making it the ultimate weapon of primitive gods. It has been taken as an omen of punishment and warning, or even as good fortune. Places touched by lightning were considered sacred. Whether for religious or practical reasons, man has always given lightning a high degree of respect.

As simple as the basic identification of lightning is today, it was a complete mystery before 1752. It was Benjamin Franklin who, eager to learn if the little spark of electricity he could make with a cell in his workshop was the same as the lightning he observed in the sky, decided to experiment. Franklin's kite

1944

With an interest in contributing to the war effort, 18-year-old Princess Elizabeth of England joins the Auxiliary Territorial Service. She enrolls in a mechanics course to learn how to service and drive military vehicles.

and key are nearly as famous as the man himself.

Today our study of lightning is more scientific than mystical; our techniques of investigation are more experimental than intuitive. Still, we are awed and sometimes frightened when lightning strikes nearby and we feel the charged air, see the flash, and hear the crack of thunder.

When lightning strikes, the air through which the charge travels becomes heated so quickly that it virtually explodes, causing violent waves in the surrounding air. These shock waves travel in all directions. Sometimes the clouds cause echoes to occur, and these echoes make the sound that is known as thunder.

When lightning is close by, the thunder is a sharp explosive sound. More distant strokes produce the familiar growl and rumble of thunder, a result of sound being refracted and modified by the turbulent movement or environment of a thunderstorm. Because the speed of light is about a million times that of sound, the distance (in miles) to a lightning stroke can be estimated by counting the number of seconds between lightning and thunder, then dividing by five. Be-

Without lightning, plant life could not exist.

fore the sound reaches you, the lightning has already struck somewhere.

If the lightning occurs between two clouds, it does no damage, whereas lightning between a cloud and the Earth may cause considerable damage. Yet in this evil, there is good. Without lightning, plant life could not exist. And without plant life, humanity would cease to exist. So who can say that lightning is all bad?

Eighty percent of our atmosphere is nitrogen — an essential food for plant life. About 22 million tons of this nutrient float over each square mile of the Earth. But in this aerial form, the nitrogen is insoluble and, consequently, unusable. Before plants can use the nitrogen, it must undergo a series of chemical reactions. And this is where lightning assumes its role of goodness.

Air particles are rendered white-hot by lightning. Under this intense heat, the nitrogen combines with the oxygen in the air to form nitrogen oxides, which are soluble in water. The rain dissolves the oxides and carries them down to Earth as dilute nitric acid. It is this acid that causes that pungent tinny odor that hangs in the rainy air of a thunderstorm.

1945

Earl Tupper, a Du Pont chemist, produces his first molded polyethylene item, starting his Tupperware empire. He will go on to develop a unique marketing scheme: in-home sales parties.

Reaching the Earth, the nitric acid reacts with minerals and becomes the nitrates on which plants can feed. In simple language, lightning actually transforms the upper air into fertilizer for Earth-bound plants.

Lightning is mystifying, fascinating, and horrifying, but it has its good points. You may be able to move away from ice and snow, but you'll find lightning wherever you go — at least within the United States. All 50 states have electrical storms. Although some areas have them more often and have more severe storms than others, the average number for any given area is about 40 yearly. All of which shows that when nature goes about something, it's done in a big, spectacular way.

ANECDOTES & PLEASANTRIES

The Ol' Goose Bone Method

BACK AROUND the turn of the 19th century, there was the so-called goose bone method for weather forecasting, famous in the days prior to the establishment of the U.S. Weather Bureau. Here's how it worked.

Around Thanksgiving, Grandma would cook a freshly killed goose. She would roast it, carve it, and serve it, always being careful not to cut the breastbone from the carcass.

After the goose had been eaten, she would carefully remove the breastbone and cut away all the meat and fat left clinging to it. Grandpa would take the bone and put it on a shelf to dry, keeping an eye out for the coloration that would follow.

If the bone turned blue, black, or purple, a cold winter would be assumed. White would indicate a mild winter. Purple tips to the bone were a sure indication of a cold spring.

A blue color branching out in lines toward the edge of the bone meant open weather until New Year's Day.

If the bone was a dark color, or blue all over, look out for a really bad winter.

That's it. And there was even an explanation. The reason for a dark color prevalent in a goose bone was because the bird had absorbed more oil than usual, which acted as a natural protection against the cold. So the darker the blue coloring spreading over the breastbone, indicating oil intake and storage, the tougher the winter ahead would probably be. Logical?

Courtesy of Warren Evans

1946

Frenchman Jacques Heim designs the *Atome,* the "world's smallest bathing suit," which is quickly copied and called the bikini. The name was inspired by the U.S. atomic bomb testing on Bikini atoll this year.

■ *Let's face it, the idea that every snowflake is unique is hard to accept. Yet it turns out that there is a simple (but mind-boggling) mathematical explanation that solves this puzzle once and for all — sort of.*

How Come No Two Snowflakes Are Alike?

BY CHET RAYMO

IS THERE ANY TRUTH TO THE OLD saw "No two snowflakes are alike"?

Of course, the question could be laid to rest if someone succeeded in observing two identical flakes. The person who had the best opportunity for doing this was Wilson A. Bentley of Jericho, Vermont. Bentley was a farmer and amateur meteorologist. For 50 years, he dedicated himself to observing flakes of snow.

Bentley was born in 1865 near Jericho. He had almost no formal schooling, but his mother had been a teacher, and he acquired from her a lively curiosity and a love for nature's minutiae. Drops of water, bits of stone, or the feather of a bird could equally excite his interest. But it was snow that became his lifelong passion.

On his 15th birthday, Bentley's mother gave him the use of an old microscope. It was snowing that day, and the boy succeeded in get-

ting a glimpse of a six-sided snowflake with the instrument. By the age of 20, the unschooled farm boy had perfected a technique for photographing the beauty of snow. When death ended the adventure half a century later, Bentley had accumulated nearly 5,000 microphotographs of snow crystals. He also had won worldwide fame as an expert on the meteorology of snow. In his own neighborhood, he was known simply as the "Snowflake Man." An editorial in the *Burling-*

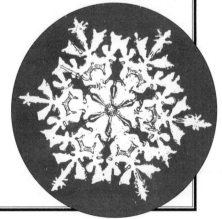

1946

Dr. Benjamin Spock publishes
*The Common Sense Book of
Baby and Child Care.*

ton Free Press after his death said, "He saw something in the snowflakes which other men failed to see, not because they could not see, but because they had not the patience and the understanding to look."

We have Bentley's word for it that no two snowflakes in his collection were alike. That fact was a source of satisfaction for him. In the simple snowflake, he stood face-to-face with one of nature's deepest mysteries, what the Greeks called "the problem of the One and the Many": How does any form endure in the face of almost limitless possibilities? The snowflake exemplified for Bentley the kaleidoscopic balance of order and disorder that is the basis of beauty in nature and in art.

In the simple snowflake, he stood face-to-face with one of nature's deepest mysteries, what the Greeks called "the problem of the One and the Many": How does any form endure in the face of almost limitless possibilities?

cup of snow, there are more than 10 million flakes. I estimate that something like 10^{22} snowflakes fall on New England in a typical snowstorm (that's 1 followed by 22 zeros). During the 4-billion-year history of the Earth, perhaps as many as 10^{34} snowflakes have fallen on the face of the planet (add 12 more zeros). Could it really be possible that among that unimaginably large number of flakes, no two were alike?

Twentieth-century physics has made substantial progress toward understanding the genesis of the snowflake's form. The hexagonal symmetry of snowflakes has its origin in the shape of the water molecule. A water molecule consists of an atom of oxygen and two atoms of hydrogen. The hydrogens are connected to the oxygen in such a way that the two hydrogen "arms" make an angle about like the arms on the side of this *x*. The angle of the "arms" ensures that when water molecules link together to form a crystal, the resultant symmetry will be hexagonal, just as the

But 5,000 snowflakes is a small number. If we had the patience and understanding to inspect 5 million snowflakes, or 5 billion, might we find at least one pair of twins? The answer is almost certainly no.

A single crystal of snow weighs about a millionth of a gram. In a

---

1947

R. R. Reynolds (nephew of tobacco king R. S. Reynolds) begins manufacturing with aluminum in Louisville, Kentucky.

placement of the holes in the knobs of a Tinkertoy set determines the symmetry of the structures that can be built with the set.

Now we turn to the probabilities of combination. A deck of 52 cards can be shuffled into 10^{68} different combinations. A small Tinkertoy set may have something like a hundred pieces; consider, if you will, the huge number of different structures that could be built with such a set. A single snow crystal consists of something like 10^{18} (1 quintillion) molecules of water. The number of ways that many molecules can be arranged into six-sided crystals is astronomical, vastly larger than the number of snowflakes that have ever fallen on the face of the Earth. The odds are very great indeed that no two flakes have ever been exactly identical!

Science has revealed another surprising aspect of the snowflake's form. The apparent stability of a crystal of ice, it turns out, is an illusion. On the atomic scale, the snowflake is a hubbub of activity. Electrons leap and dance. Molecules furiously wave their hydrogen "arms." Crystal imperfections jump from place to place. If you could shrink to subatomic size and enter a crystal of ice, you would think yourself caught in a hurricane of chaos. And yet somehow, in the midst of all that chaos, nature constructs and maintains a crystalline architecture of delicate beauty.

In one sense, no two snowflakes are alike. In another sense, all snowflakes are alike. The staggering diversity of snowflakes is a measure of nature's potential for novelty and change. The constancy of the snowflake's six-sided form reassures us that nature is ruled by law.

Wilson Bentley once wrote, "The farm folks up in this north country dread the winter, but I was always supremely happy, from the day of the first snowfall — which usually came in November — until the last one, which sometimes came as late as May." For the "Snowflake Man," snow was a continuing lesson in the way nature's beauty arises from a delicate balance of law and chaos, fixity and change.

1947

Jackie Robinson becomes the first African-American major league baseball player in the modern era when he joins the Brooklyn Dodgers. In 1949 he will be voted Most Valuable Player, and in 1962 he will become the first black member of the Baseball Hall of Fame.

No Two Snowflakes Are Alike, Right?

WRONG. (Is there nothing sacred anymore?)

Both Nancy Knight and her husband, Charles, were cloud physicists with the National Center for Atmospheric Research in Boulder, Colorado, in 1990. And both were fully aware that no two snowflakes had *ever* been alike in the 4.5 billion years of the Earth's history. (Charles estimated that about 10^{35} snowflakes had fallen during that period of time.)

Then, in the winter of 1989, Nancy was on a routine flight over Wausau, Wisconsin, conducting scientific research. While flying through snow clouds, she was collecting snowflakes on an oil-coated piece of glass suspended beneath the plane. (We're not quite sure why — but no matter.) During the course of that particular flight, she collected two specific snowflakes — among many others, of course — which, she says, "if not identical, are certainly very much alike." Her photographs of them attest to that. Each is exactly .009 inch long, and each has thick columns with hollow, pyramidal cores that look just alike. Today she has these two snowflakes preserved for posterity in a freezer in her laboratory back in Boulder.

"When my wife showed me the slide, I said, 'Impossible,'" said George, adding, "and I still think it's impossible." He points out there are a million different combinations of temperature and saturation a snow crystal might pass through on its way to the ground. This translates into $10^{5,000,000}$ different sequences, any one of which could make a single snowflake different from all the others that have ever fallen in all of history.

So it's impossible to find identical snowflakes — except, perhaps, over Wausau, Wisconsin.

1948

Inspired by annoyingly clingy cockleburs, Swiss mountaineer George de Mestral develops Velcro.

FARMER'S CALENDAR

Snowstorm Etiquette

AS A DEMOCRATIC PEOPLE, Americans are supposed to be mostly indifferent to manners and likewise to all other considerations of what used to be called "good breeding." If that's true, they miss a lot of fun, not because manners are really important, but because to ignore them is to lack a whole system for describing the world and making distinctions between things — not only in matters of etiquette but even in the field of weather.

Consider snowstorms. Clearly, our vocabulary for describing them is pretty poor. There are northeasters and Canadians, dusters and ten-inchers. If we introduce the idea of *snowstorm etiquette,* we immediately acquire far richer, more informative categories.

As with the etiquette of behavior — that is, real manners — so good breeding in winter storms is almost less a matter of what is said and done than of timing, setting, inflection, and style. A well-bred storm occurs at night — a weeknight, please, not a Friday or a Saturday night. A well-bred snowstorm knows what it is: a *snow*storm. Therefore it eschews ice, sleet, and rain. A well-mannered storm does not knock out the electric power, any more than a gentleman gets drunk and hurls the hors d'oeuvres against the drawing-room wall. A well-mannered storm knows what is enough; it does not make the loutish error of supposing that if 6 inches of snow is good, 18 is three times better. Above all, a well-bred storm, like a well-bred gentleman or lady, knows when to take its leave. It does not linger awkwardly an instant over the time it is wanted. It slips fastidiously away in plenty of time for shoveling, plowing, and road clearing to take place. In weather as in human relations, manners are a way of making life easy, sensible, and, especially, predictable. Boreas, take heed.

1948

The first broadcast of Milton Berle's *Texaco Star Theater* launches the era of television.

■ *Things might have gone differently at the Battle of Balaklava had they known what kind of weather was on the way.*

The Birth of Daily Weather Reporting

BY W. EMORY WARDWELL

WHEN ANCIENT MAN FIRST began to till the land, centuries before the dawn of history, he was constantly surveying the heavens and talking with the older people in an endeavor to learn what the weather would be. His knowledge was limited to the small area in which he lived. The ancient proverbs and sayings of the oldsters were passed down by word of mouth. Perhaps one of the better

known of these ancient proverbs is the one found in the Gospel of St. Matthew, chapter 16, verses 2 and 3: "When it is evening, ye say, it will be fair weather for the sky is red, and in the morning it will be foul weather today, for the sky is red and lowering."

Here and there, prior to 1850, spasmodic attempts were made by individuals to work out some system of weather reporting. But such efforts were abortive. Space will not permit a detailed history. Notable, however, were the meteorological stations established by Frederick II, grand duke of Tuscany, in 1653 and the availability of the thermometer and barometer at that time.

Among the danger spots in the world in 1854 was the Crimea, or as it was called in ancient times, Crim Tartary. Here the allies, composed of the French, English, and Turks, were engaged in forcing the Russians, who had attempted to overrun Turkey, back within their own boundaries.

The war between the allies and Russia developed into a series of

1949

Captain James Gallagher and a crew of 13 take off in *Lucky Lady II* for the first nonstop airplane flight around the world. They make it in 4 days, having refueled 4 times in flight.

battles around the Black Sea, finally ending in the tragic Battle of Balaklava. This resulted in the Russians being forced into a state of siege. But for the intervention of fate, the Battle of Balaklava would have been merely another battle. The tragic aftermath of this battle, however, leading to the establishment of daily weather forecasting, made it immortal.

Early in the evening of November 13, 1854, after a series of days comparable to our Indian summer, a rain started. Soon it developed (on the 14th) into a tempest with gale-force winds. Tents were torn down, and wooden tent flooring was blown away together with the men's spare clothing and accoutrements. The cold wind caused the greatest misery. Shipping in the harbor was destroyed, including France's largest battleship, the *Henri IV.* The huge steamboat owned by the British navy, the *Prince,* containing winter clothing and supplies, was sunk.

When the news reached England and France, the public clamor was high, but as in so many cases, it was soon hushed by their parliaments. There was one man in France who could not be silenced. This was Marshal Jean Baptiste

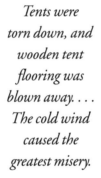

> *Tents were torn down, and wooden tent flooring was blown away. . . . The cold wind caused the greatest misery.*

Philibert Vaillant. He felt very keenly his responsibility to his emperor, Napoleon, for the loss of the *Henri IV* and was determined that, if possible, some way would be found to warn the armed forces of these sudden and often tragic storms.

He secured the permission of the emperor to employ the services of the most brilliant scientist in all of Europe, Urbain Jean Joseph Leverrier. Leverrier was undoubtedly the best selection that could have been made. He was in charge of the meteorological work at the Imperial Observatory in Paris. He had succeeded, by purely mathematical deductions, in discovering a new planet. On receiving his assignment from the emperor, he immediately communicated with all the European observatories, asking that they send their data relative to weather observations for November 11 to 16, 1854. When he received these, with his assistants, he correlated the information. On January 31, 1855, he reported to the Royal Academy that a storm warning could have been issued to the military forces in the Crimea a day in advance of the debacle. Later he submitted to the emperor a memo-

1949

"If anything can go wrong, it will." This facetious comment by Edward Murphy of California earns him the honor of being the namesake of "Murphy's Law."

randum outlining a project for weather advisories, which Napoleon approved at once. The emperor ordered that necessary steps be taken to put these plans to work immediately. He authorized the director general of telegraphic lines to cooperate with the plans.

Thus was born the daily weather reporting system — as was, incidentally, the eternal flame of Florence Nightingale, a volunteer nurse at the scene of the Balaklava disaster, and the Light Brigade, which made its famous disastrous charge at Balaklava in September.

ANECDOTES & PLEASANTRIES

Forecasting the Weather by Observing a Leech in a Jar

YOU'VE HEARD, surely, that when a frog is pale yellow, the weather will be fine. The same frog will, of course, turn brown or green before a storm. Everyone knows those things. Hear a crow before dawn and expect rain. Well, along the same lines, here's how to predict the weather with leeches (or, as some call them, bloodsuckers), available in most freshwater ponds.

First of all, put the leech in a large glass jar about two-thirds full of water. Change the water once a week during the summer and once a fortnight during the winter. Now, according to the early Victorian encyclopedia *Enquire Within*, "If the weather is to be fine, the leech lies motionless in the bottom of the glass;

if rain may be expected, it will creep up to the top of its lodgings and remain there till the weather is settled; if we are to have wind, it will move through its habitation with amazing swiftness and seldom goes to rest till it begins to blow hard."

If heavy storms are to be expected, "it will lodge for some days before, almost continually out of the water, and discover great uneasiness in violent throes and convulsive motions; in frost as in clear summer weather, it lies constantly at the bottom; and in snow as in rainy weather, it pitches its dwelling at the very mouth of the phial. The top [of the jar] should be covered with a piece of muslin."

Courtesy of Bridget Boland and her book Gardener's Magic and Other Old Wives' Lore

---

1950

United Feature buys and syndicates a comic strip by Charles Schulz called "Li'l Folks," featuring a character named Charlie Brown. The strip is renamed "Peanuts," referring to the "peanut gallery" (juvenile studio audience) on The Howdy Doody Show.

■ *If there's one thing that humbles man, it's the weather. Despite our attempts to make plans based on weather forecasts, we still get caught in unexpected rain, snow, and other inconveniences. Here are seven occasions when weather changed the course of American history.*

If It Hadn't Rained ...

BY NORM D. BLOOM

If it hadn't been so cold in 1604 ...

New Englanders might speak French. French explorers under the Sieur de Monts were the first to establish a colony on the North Atlantic coast, on an island in the St. Croix River in 1604. But the winter was so "cold and dreadful" that the little group decided to move to a more sheltered spot in Nova Scotia. The first English settlement, near the mouth of the Kennebec River in Maine, was also abandoned after the fierce winter of 1607–08.

If it hadn't been so warm in 1620 ...

The Pilgrims might not have survived their first winter in Massachusetts. That winter of 1620–21 was described as "a calm winter such as never seen here since," with mild temperatures and only one substantial snowstorm. Even so, only 50 of the 102 settlers lived until spring.

1951

Bette Nesmith Graham of Texas concocts a correction fluid for painting out errors on paper. This fluid will be marketed as Liquid Paper.

If it hadn't been so foggy on August 29, 1776 . . .

George Washington and most of the Continental Army might have been annihilated at the Battle of Long Island. After British troops won a smashing victory on August 27, 1776, the Americans were trapped at the western end of Long Island. Washington managed to save his army by crossing the East River to Manhattan Island under cover of a thick fog on August 29–30. Although he had suffered a defeat, Washington preserved his army as a fighting force.

In the middle of the crossing, a violent thunderstorm dispersed the flatboats, pushing some of them five miles downriver, where they were captured by the French. The crossing had to be abandoned.

If it hadn't been so stormy on October 16, 1781 . . .

British commander Lord Cornwallis might have escaped from Yorktown to prolong the Revolutionary War. On the night of October 16–17, 1781, Cornwallis proposed to evacuate his trapped army across the York River estuary on flatboats, then fight his way north to join British forces in New York. But in the middle of the crossing, a violent thunderstorm dispersed the flatboats, pushing some of them five miles downriver, where they were captured by the French. The crossing had to be abandoned, and "thus expired the last hope of the British army," according to one of its officers. Cornwallis surrendered on October 19, ensuring American independence.

If it hadn't rained on July 4, 1863 . . .

General Robert E. Lee's Confederate army might have suffered worse losses, or even been destroyed, in the aftermath

1952

Austrian candy maker Eduard Haas brings his Pez mints to the United States in a dispenser topped with Mickey Mouse's head. The first mints were made in 1927, the first dispensers (resembling a cigarette lighter) in 1948.

of Gettysburg. The great battle took place on July 1–3, 1863, and on the last day, Pickett's Charge, the Confederates' final assault on the Union lines, was repulsed with enormous losses. Lee expected Union general George Meade to counterattack, but Meade hesitated. Rain began to fall on the night of the third and continued throughout July 4. Under cover of the rain and darkness that night, Lee began his retreat to Virginia. Despite President Lincoln's frantic urgings, Meade was slow to pursue the battered rebels, and the Confederate Army of Northern Virginia escaped intact to fight on for another 21 months.

If it had snowed harder on November 7, 1916 . . .

President Woodrow Wilson might have lost his reelection bid. In one of the closest elections in history, Democratic incumbent Wilson defeated Republican Charles Evans Hughes and went on to take the United States into World War I in 1917. Wilson won the state of California by fewer than 2,000 votes on a day when heavy snow kept Democratic turnout low in mountain counties. Had the storm been worse, the turnout would have been even lower, and Hughes would have won the state — and the national election. America probably would have entered the war anyway; Wilson had been regarded as the peace candidate. But as histo-

rian Paul F. Boller Jr. said, Wilson "made world pacification . . . the primary objective of American foreign policy," a position that has shaped our history — and the world's — ever since.

If there hadn't been a freeze on January 28, 1986 . . .

The *Challenger* disaster might have been avoided. The space shuttle exploded shortly after takeoff from Cape Canaveral, Florida, killing seven astronauts, including Concord, New Hampshire, schoolteacher Christa McAuliffe. An investigation showed that a sudden temperature drop the night before the launch had caused O-rings sealing the joints between segments of the solid-fuel booster rockets to become brittle and fail. The disaster forced a temporary halt in the U.S. space program, which has since been dogged by technical troubles and doubts about its costs and benefits.

Wet June, dry September.

1953

Edmund Hillary of New Zealand and Tenzing Norgay of Nepal reach the summit of Mount Everest. They are the first people ever to climb to the top of the highest peak on Earth.

FARMER'S CALENDAR

Information Overload

I T'S POSSIBLE we have gotten to know too much about the weather. Broadcast weather bulletins inundate us with information and half-understood principles. The forecasters tell us much more than we want or need to know, to the point that, with the weather as with politics, art, and the conduct of life, we are overcome with information and lose our way.

Consider a typical weather report on the radio. A *meteorologist* (note that he or she is not a weatherman or an announcer, but a scientist) clears his throat and carries on something like this: "A preponderant Arctic system originating east of Great Slave Lake is rapidly autorelocating southwesterly across the Laurentian Highlands, encountering a subsidiary low-pressure configuration emanating from the region of the Bay of Campeche, rendering it probable that should these two meteorological entities converge at high altitude over Churubusco, the likelihood of solid  or semisolid precipitation will be in the range of 22.1 to 37.4 percent, *whereas* should the Arctic superbarometric eventuality and the Oaxacan sub-barometric abstraction fail to effect conjunction before reaching the latitude of the Fishkill Salient, the probability of such precipitation achieves the inverse of the range hypothecated immediately above. We'll keep you posted. Now back to you, Edgar."

OK, it's not really that bad. But you get the point: a blizzard of data driven by a hurricane of lingo, most of it only remotely relevant. What we need is this: "It's going to snow tonight, probably. Probably start about dark. Might snow a foot or so. If you have to go to town, go now. Back to you, Edgar."

1953

The Swanson company offers the first heat-and-eat frozen meals, dubbed TV dinners.

■ *If you should find yourself outside wondering what the temperature is — with no thermometer in sight — get in tune with the insects around you. They'll let you know, with surprising accuracy, just how hot or cold it is.*

Use Insects as Thermometers — They're Free!

BY ERICA L. GLASENER

D ID YOU KNOW THAT YOU CAN tell how hot it is by listening to insects? Insects are very sensitive to temperature changes, and the reaction of some species to heat and cold is a good indication of temperature, wrote J. Henryette Hallenbeck in a 1931 edition of *Boys' Life.*

The grasshopper is loudest at 95° F and is unable to chirp when the temperature falls below 62° F. He cannot fly at a temperature below 45° F, and at 36° or 37° F he is unable to jump. Whenever you hear a grasshopper, you know the temperature is at least 62° F.

Crickets are still more accurate. Two species of crickets — the common house cricket and the white tree cricket — are excellent thermometers. To calculate the temperature from the house cricket's tune, count the number of chirps he makes in 14 seconds, add 40, and you will have the temperature — that is, the temperature at the location of the cricket.

The number of chirps in the song of the white tree cricket and its relation to the temperature have been reduced to a similar mathematical formula, which Hallenbeck attributed to a Professor Dolbear of Massachusetts (although a Dr. Robert Ede found this formula 1 degree too high). The white tree cricket chirps four times per minute for every degree of temperature above 40° F.

The white tree cricket is a more useful thermometer than the house cricket because although each proclaims the temperature of the air around him, the former is out in the open, while the latter usually is in some warm nook in the house,

1954

NBC's *Tonight Show,* hosted by Steve Allen, airs for the first time.

where the temperature may be quite different from that outdoors.

The katydid's night call is most emphatic above 80° F — "Katee did it!" His cadence drops by approximately 4-degree intervals to "Katy didn't!" to "Katy did!" to "She didn't," "She did," and "Katy." Below 60° F, the cry is a feeble "Kate." The first call ("Katee did it!") rarely is heard, for in the katy-

did season (late summer), the temperature usually is below 80° F by sunset. The last two ("Katy" and "Kate") are also seldom heard, for most people are in bed asleep before the little fellow gets down to his last notes.

Honeybees cluster outside their hive when the temperature reaches 102° F and cluster compactly inside their hive when the temperature falls to 57° F. At 48° F, the clustered bees begin buzzing to generate heat. The best working temperature for bees is 85° F; at this temperature, they are also very gentle. But at temperatures below 70° F, they are very irritable and will attack people without provocation.

Ants do not emerge from their subterranean dens until the temperature has risen to 55° F, and they return home when it reaches 105° F. It is said that there are species of ants in Arizona, however, that remain active at temperatures above 105° F.

At 40° F all insects are silent, and at 33° or 34° F our insect thermometer ceases to register because all insects are helpless.

1955

Disneyland opens in Anaheim, California. In 1971 a new park, Disney World, will open outside of Orlando, Florida, on a parcel of land twice the size of Manhattan.

Measuring Time and Space

I HAD A FRIEND in college with a peculiar talent for what might as well be called "Yogi Berra-isms." He would scramble two familiar aphorisms — for example, "Seize the day" and "Strike while the iron is hot" — into a new and beguiling, if somewhat illogical, amalgam: "Seize the iron while it's hot."

There was also the mysterious "It's no skin off my back," which I believe was the offspring of "It's no skin off my nose" and "He'd give you the shirt off his back."

But every now and then, he'd come out with a piece of unadulterated wisdom. My favorite was his response to my question, one foggy (mental, not meteorological) morning: "What day is it?"

"Any day you ask 'What day is it?' is a Wednesday," he intoned.

More often than not, I've found that to be true. Wednesday takes up more room than it ought to, somehow. It sprawls across the middle of the week like a golden retriever on a sofa. Tuesday, by contrast, is a slender day, the

1955

Cincinnati inventor Joseph McVicker develops a modeling clay that he calls Play-Doh.

skinniest day of the week. You could fit three of them into the average Wednesday.

Arbitrary nonsense, you say. Well, sure. But as the following chapter should make clear, a lot of our notions about time and measurement are essentially arbitrary, if not outright capricious.

According to Winifred H. Scheib, the unit of measurement we call a "foot" came from the length of some ancient chief's foot, and an "inch" from the breadth of the king's thumb. But while 12 inches make a foot, a size 12 shoe on that foot is not 12 inches

long — it is 12 barleycorns long. And the mile is 5,280 feet long, because that is eight times the length of a furlong, which was based on the length of a furrow. Don't ask.

Andrew Rothovius tells us that Ember Days have nothing to do with embers, and Boxing Day (December 26) has nothing to do with fighting, unless it's your kids fighting over who got more Christmas presents, in which case you can follow an ancient custom and whip them soundly on Holy Innocents Day (December 28) — although the logic of beating children to commemorate Herod's slaughter of the innocents escapes me.

That's because logic has little to do with it. U.S. Supreme Court justice Oliver Wendell Holmes once remarked that the life of the law is not logic but experience. Just so, we measure time and space based on our experience with particular environments. Plough Monday, which falls on the first Monday after January 6, is so called because farmers could get out into the fields for the

1956

"In God We Trust" becomes the national motto of the United States. (It had been used on U.S. currency since 1864.)

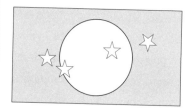

first time that day in the milder climate of Old England. In New England, we'd have to call it Snowplow Monday.

Likewise, the names of the full Moons used by American Indian tribes depended on the particulars of their culture and environment. A full Moon in April, for example, was the Full Pink Moon in some areas, the Sprouting Grass Moon or Egg Moon in others, and the Fish Moon along the coast. If we were doing it today, we might call it the Form 1040 Moon or the Moon of Lamentation.

Woe betide the crusader who tries to reform the way we measure space (how's your metric conversion plan coming along?) or time! John White's article "The Year Ten Days Disappeared from October" recounts how Pope Gregory XIII rejiggered the Julian calendar, which failed to take into account the eccentricities of the

Earth's orbit. The Pope ordered 10 days removed from the calendar in 1582 to get it back in line with the actual spring equinox. But it took 170 years for the English to go along with the idea (the English, as we might say today, had issues with the pope), and when they finally got around to it, workers rioted in the streets, demanding to be paid for the missing days.

Considering how long it took the pope to reform the calendar, Charles

1957

The Soviet Union launches the first artificial Earth satellite, *Sputnik 1*. Later this year, *Sputnik 2* will be launched, carrying the first living being (a female dog named Laika) into space.

Dowd should have been relieved that it took only 13 years to persuade American railroad executives to adopt his standard time zones. Until 1883 every town and city in America had its own local, or "Sun" time, noon being determined by observation of the Sun at its zenith. So a traveler going by train from Portland, Maine, to California, would have to adjust his watch 20 times. How ironic that this reformer, who saved untold thousands of lives that might have been lost in railroad accidents caused by inconsistent time zones, should have been killed by a train at a Saratoga, New York, railroad crossing.

So the calendar, too, is ruled more by eccentricity than logic. Roosters don't always crow at dawn. Perhaps our universe dances to a music we don't even understand. I was amazed to read John Burnham's article about cycles — the weird coincidence of stock prices, cheese consumption, and field mouse abundance all following 4-year cycles, for example. What do bank deposits have to do with the number of cows milked? Why do UFO sightings increase every 61 months? And does the increased ability of bean

1957

Inspired by pie tin–tossing Yale students, an executive at Wham-O develops a plastic toy called the Frisbee, named for the Frisbie Pie Company of Bridgeport, Connecticut, but spelled differently.

seeds to take up water every 7.4 days have anything to do with the lunar cycle? Could that be why our ancestors relied on planting by the Moon's phases?

Perhaps someday we will understand those mysterious cycles that rule our lives. Perhaps someday we will eliminate all eccentricity, natural and human, from our measurements of time and space. I can't imagine how we'd do it, and I'm not sure I'd like living in such a world. But as my college friend would say, we'll burn that bridge when we come to it.

Tim Clark

1957

Theodor Seuss Geisel, using
the pen name Dr. Seuss, writes
The Cat in the Hat.

■ *True, the turn of the third millennium is a great milestone in history, but only if you follow the Christian era, also called the Common Era. Those who adhere to the calendar of the Byzantine era, for instance, will be looking forward to the dawning of the ninth millennium, a mere 491 years from now.*

New Eras: When They Began and When They Didn't

BY ANDREW ROTHOVIUS

EACH YEAR, *THE OLD FARMER'S Almanac* carries a listing of chronological eras — that is, calendars calculated from a starting point in time different from the one that assumes the year beginning January 1 to be the 2000th from the birth of Jesus Christ. That figure is almost certainly in error, being from 2 to 4 years too low, depending on the correct date of the death of King Herod, who was reigning at the time. The point is still unresolved with exactness 14 centuries after an Italian monk calculated it from the best data available to him, his probably erroneous result having in the intervening span become sanctified by usage.

Much greater uncertainty attaches to many of the other eras in the Almanac's annual listing. Two — the Byzantine era and the Jewish era (AM, or *anno mundi,* Latin for "in the year of the world"), still in use for the religious calendars of the Orthodox (Greek) Christian and Hebrew faiths — start their count from the creation of the world as narrated in the Book of Genesis, but differ by 1,748 years (5509 B.C. and 3761 B.C., respectively) in their calculation of the date. (Neither agrees with the 4004 B.C. figure arrived at by the 17th-century Protestant archbishop Ussher and generally accepted by American fundamentalist sects.)

The Japanese era uses a more localized starting point — the legendary creation of the Japanese islands by the Sun goddess in 660 B.C.

Against these chronologies, which have to be accepted on faith rather than on any hard evidence, the remaining seven in the listing can be related with reasonable accuracy to known historical events. The Islamic era of the Hegira ("flight"), which starts from Muhammad's exile in our A.D. 622 to Medina, where he received his revelation, is unquestionably correct in its year count. But, unfortu-

1959

Mattel produces the first Barbie doll.

nately, it is computed in lunar years, which are shorter than our Western solar years, and thus it is difficult to correlate with our own calendar. If the Muslims used solar years as we do, 2000 would be their year 1338 instead of 1421.

In India, the traditional calendar is based on the era of the Sakas, a central Asian tribe that overran northern India in the first century A.D. The Sakas are said to have started ruling India in our A.D. 78, and the era starts from that date. But so far historians have been unable to determine whether it is exact or only approximate.

For something like a thousand years, until the Christian era started to be used in the sixth century A.D. (and well beyond that in some areas), the Western world counted its years from the traditional founding of Rome in 753 B.C. (AUC — *ab urbe condita,* Latin for "from the founding of the city"). No historical record of that event has survived, and the date

For something like a thousand years, ... the Western world counted its years from the traditional founding of Rome in 753 B.C.

may be only a wild guess, but the Roman era that was based on it did duty long and well, and out of respect to it, almanacs (including *The Old Farmer's Almanac*) still tell us what year it would be if it were still in use (2000 = 2753).

None of these eras — except, obviously, the Christian one, and even that is now starting to be called by the neutral appellation "Common Era" — has the name of an individual person. But three that are still to be described do have that distinction. The oldest of the three is the era of Nabonassar, which by recent recomputation is now counted to start in 749 B.C. instead of 747 B.C., as stated in older almanacs. Oddly, Nabonassar himself — one of the most insignificant rulers of the ancient world — had nothing whatever to do with initiating the era.

He had been dead for around nine centuries when the great classical astronomer Claudius Ptolemy decided about A.D. 150 to compile dated lists of the Babylonian, Persian, Greek, and Roman kings and rulers. He went as far back as he could lo-

1960

Etch-A-Sketch is mass-marketed based on Arthur Granjean's original design (late 1950s), which he called L'Ecran Magique.

cate any references to them, for the purpose of providing cross-checks on the ancient astronomical observation of which he was making a study. The resulting "Canon of the Kings," as it is called, has been an invaluable resource for historians ever since. The oldest dates in it are those in the Babylonian king list, which commences with Nabonassar in a year that Ptolemy calculated was six years later than the founding of Rome (that is, 747 B.C.) but that is now believed to have been 749 B.C.

Nabonassar was a mere puppet king of Babylonia under the Assyrian conqueror Tiglath-Pileser IV. The king list commences with him simply because there is a gap of several generations before, during which Babylonia fell into general decline and records were either lost or not even kept. Later, Babylonia revived and became great again, until it fell to the Persians two centuries down the line. For all that stretch, the list of kings was maintained from Nabonassar on, providing a continuous link from them to the Persians, and from the latter to the Greeks and Romans. That is why the era of Nabonassar, with its proven corre-

The list of kings was maintained from Nabonassar on, providing a continuous link from them to the Persians, and from the latter to the Greeks and Romans.

lations, continues to serve astronomers and historians.

The second era named for an individual is the Seleucid (or Grecian), which can be fixed to an exact year — 312 B.C. — although there is some question whether it commenced in September or October. It takes its name from Seleucus Nicator (Seleucus the Victorious), one of the generals of Alexander the Great. After that great conqueror's death in 323 B.C., his army chiefs contended over who should inherit and rule the Middle Eastern lands he had wrested from the Persian Empire. Seleucus, the most energetic and enterprising of them, and a bold and daring adventurer, seized Babylonia with a small band of followers in the late summer of 312 B.C. and established there the kingdom that by his death 30 years later had become the great Seleucid Empire, stretching from Turkey to India. The exploit that laid its foundation caught the imagination of the peoples of the Middle East so wholly and swiftly that in a few months they started using it as year 1 of a new era, which is still used in some Greek communities in the Levant.

1960

The United States launches the first weather satellite, *Tiros 1.*

The era of Diocletian is named for the Roman emperor who, somewhat on the model of Seleucus, emerged from obscurity as an army commander to proclaim himself supreme ruler of the Roman Empire in A.D. 284 and proceeded to dispose quickly of all competitors and to institute a series of thoroughgoing reforms to prop up the empire's disintegrating fabric. He also initiated the last great persecution of Christians. For this and for his renovation of the empire, his reign came to be regarded as a break with the past and the starting point of a new computation of time. (The count was actually started, for reasons not very clear, from 283, the year before he seized power.) Except in the Middle East, use of the era of Diocletian was never very widespread, and it survives now only as a historical curiosity.

Finally, there is the Chinese era. Its beginning, 2637 B.C., is based on a legendary date—the founding of the Chinese Empire by the equally legendary emperor Fo-Hi. However, archaeological evidence indicates that the empire was founded by the Shang Dynasty in approximately 1700 B.C. As with the Byzantine and Hebrew eras, the story is apocryphal—the Chinese version of the creation of the world.

Eras

IN THE GENERAL SCHEME of things, our Christian era is a relatively young one. The chart below delineates the various eras, the age each will be in our year 2000, and how long before its new millennium will turn.

Era	Age in 2000	Number of Years Before Next Millennium	Next Millennium
Byzantine	7,509	491	8,000 (9th millennium)
Jewish (AM)	5,761	239	6,000 (7th millennium)
Chinese (Lunar)	4,698	302	5,000 (6th millennium)
Roman (AUC)	2,753	247	3,000 (4th millennium)
Nabonassar	2,749	251	3,000 (4th millennium)
Japanese	2,660	340	3,000 (4th millennium)
Grecian (Seleucid)	2,312	688	3,000 (4th millennium)
Christian (Common)	**2,000**	**0**	**2,000 (3rd millennium)**
Indian (Saka)	1,922	78	2,000 (3rd millennium)
Diocletian	1,717	283	2,000 (3rd millennium)
Islamic (Hegira)	1,421	580	2,000 (3rd millennium)

1960

A new television cartoon series called *The Flintstones* debuts.

■ *In the United States, why should total bank deposits, the number of milking cows, and the number of new church members follow the same six-year rhythm?*

Cycles: Nature's Incredible Time Clocks That Rule Our Lives

BY JOHN BURNHAM

NEARLY EVERYONE HAS SOMEthing to say, good or bad, about prophets and the science of prediction. And although it is generally accepted that the seer is without honor in his own country, a shrewd prophet is not without tools to make certain very accurate predictions. For instance, I can say with some assurance that in the middle of 2003, there will be a peak in the number of new members joining the Congregational, Episcopal, Methodist, and Presbyterian Churches in the United States. After that, the number of new members will decline.

How can I say this? Simply by studying the cycles of new members in all these churches over the past 100 years. Our lives are ruled by cycles — night and day, the seasons, a biological rhythm within our own bodies, and many other rhythms, some of which we are not even aware of — and yet many people remain skeptical of the study of cycles.

Skepticism is not a commodity in trade at the Foundation for the Study of Cycles in Wayne, Pennsylvania. Here the foundation publishes six issues a year of the scholarly magazine *Cycles,* which discusses current research in rhythmic phenomena. Let's look at a sample of cycles of varying lengths that are documented in nature, economics, astronomy, and other fields.

Gardeners would be interested to note that there is a 7.4-day cycle in the ability of bean seeds to take up water. Interestingly, this cycle corresponds closely with the phases of the Moon: Peaks in water uptake occur at the new Moon, full Moon, and intervening quarters. This lends credence to the practice of planting by the Moon.

Over 122 years, U.S. stock prices show a 4-year cycle, as do cheese consumption and field mouse abundance.

Abnormally large numbers of UFO (unidentified flying object) sightings occur every 61 months and in a regular pattern — usually 1,500 to 2,000 miles apart.

1961

Folksinger Bob Dylan is discovered in Greenwich Village by Columbia Records and releases his first album.

The index of international war battles shows a 6-year cycle recurring over a period of 2,557 years. Also on a 6-year rhythm are steel production and wholesale sugar prices, as well as diphtheria outbreaks in the United States until 1938.

Precipitation in Philadelphia shows a very pronounced 8-year cycle over 145 years of data, as does rainfall in all of the United States. Oddly, cigarette production falls into the same cycle period.

Over a span of 133 years, bank deposits in all the banks in the country vary on a clear 9-year cycle, as do the number of cows kept for milk on U.S. farms and the number of new members joining the

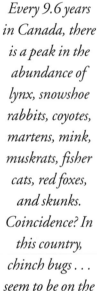

Every 9.6 years in Canada, there is a peak in the abundance of lynx, snowshoe rabbits, coyotes, martens, mink, muskrats, fisher cats, red foxes, and skunks. Coincidence? In this country, chinch bugs . . . seem to be on the same cycle.

Congregational, Episcopal, Methodist, and Presbyterian Churches.

One hundred years' worth of records show that grasshopper abundance rises and falls rhythmically every 9.2 years.

Every 9.6 years in Canada, there is a peak in the abundance of lynx, snowshoe rabbits, coyotes, martens, mink, muskrats, fisher cats, red foxes, and skunks. Coincidence? In this country, chinch bugs and tent caterpillars (at least in New Jersey) seem to be on the same cycle, as is human heart disease in New England.

Sunspots are on a 12-year cycle, coinciding with the amount of rainfall in London.

In Arizona, studies of rings in trees more than 1,000 years old reveal a growth cycle that reappears each $16\frac{2}{3}$ years.

1962

Rachel Carson's controversial book *Silent Spring* launches a worldwide environmental movement.

Records kept for more than 1,300 years reveal that the Nile River floods highest on a regular 17⅓-year cycle.

Real estate activity apparently follows an 18.2-year cycle, as does immigration to the United States.

Without exception, every president of the United States elected or reelected to office at 20-year intervals since 1840 has died in office. Some believe (but we don't) that this death cycle is the result of a curse placed on William Henry Harrison by a Shawnee Indian prophet after Harrison defeated the Shawnees at the Battle of Tippecanoe in 1811.

All drug company sales show a

Copper prices, coal production, and interest rates . . . not only have the same period, but they all crest at the same time, too. Can this be chance?

nice 22-year cycle, the same as post office revenues.

Sunspots, in addition to their 12-year cycle, also exhibit a 54-year rhythm. Coinciding with this is a remarkable number of economic cycles: shipbuilding, worldwide iron production, U.S. cotton acreage, copper prices, coal production, and interest rates, among others. These cycles not only have the same period, but they all crest at the same time, too. Can this be chance?

What does all this prove? The philosopher in each of us would like to discover some "grand scheme" quietly surfacing here and there among all these cycles, but such is not the case. Interviewed in the early 1960s, when his research was only beginning, former Foundation for the Study of Cycles president Edward Dewey said that he hoped his work would lead to an understanding of what it is "out there" that directs events in our daily lives and in the history of the world. His personal philosophy mellowed, and by the mid-1970s he felt strongly that the study of cyclical phenomena will be able to help mankind predict certain impending natural disasters. Dewey said that although "we cannot be masters of our fate, we can at least know when to run and hide."

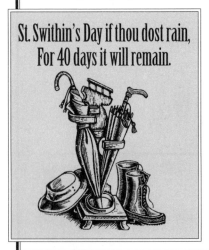

St. Swithin's Day if thou dost rain, For 40 days it will remain.

The Beatles sign a record deal with EMI, and "Love Me Do" is released.

■ *Ever wonder why the first Monday after January 6 is Plough Monday, why Groundhog Day is always February 2, or why Boxing Day has nothing to do with pugilism?*

How Certain Holidays and Just Plain "Days" Came to Be

BY ANDREW ROTHOVIUS

MOST OF THE HOLIDAYS AND other name-remarkable days in our calendar originated from two main sources: ancient pre-Christian seasonal observances and the tradition that arose in the third century A.D. of memorializing the days on which noted martyrs for the Christian faith gave up their lives.

Some festival days, of course, derive from other beginnings, such as the Jewish ones based on Old Testament usages and rituals. A few come from the ancient Roman calendar. A handful are of more or less modern date, mainly commemorating historical events such as the end of World War I (Veterans Day).

The Romans were of two minds as to when the year should begin: on January 1, when the days were noticeably longer, or at the spring equinox, then on March 25. This confusion lasted in Catholic countries until the calendar was put in its present form by Pope Gregory XIII in 1582 (see page 306) and much longer in Protestant countries (un-

til 1752 in Britain and America). Overlapping the January 1 year-start date were the 12 days of the winter solstice celebration, the first of which, December 25, came in the mid-fourth century A.D. to be identified with the birthday of Christ. The last day was January 6, hence Twelfth Night in English folk custom as the end of the Christmas merrymaking. In the church calendar, this date came to be called Epiphany — the manifestation of the infant Christ to the three Wise Men who came to see him.

No work used to be done on those 12 joyous days. Not until the first Monday after January 6, Plough Monday, were the teams hitched up to start plowing for the spring sowing. In the usually mild winter climate of western Europe, it was feasible to do this in January. The law courts and the schools did not resume their terms until January 13, St. Hilary's Day, hence "Hilary Term," often referred to in old chronicles.

As the year progressed, a succession of festive days — some

fixed on the same date each year, some varying annually in relation to the great festival of Easter, regulated by the equinox full Moon — marked the advance of the seasons. The steadily lengthening daylight was hailed by the Candle Mass (Candlemas) on February 2, commemorating the Virgin Mary's presentation of the baby Jesus in the temple; earlier it had been the Celtic Iamolc, the feast of light and purification. It was the day on which weather sages tried to foresee the end of winter, a custom we perpetuate in Groundhog Day. It was also the occasion for springtime marriages. By the 15th century, however, this latter function had been transferred — perhaps because it was thought to be inappropriate for a day associated with the Virgin — to the February 14 feast of an obscure saint named Valentine.

In the church calendar, [January 6] came to be called Epiphany.

The penitential season of Lent followed, preceded by a period of boisterous fun and games culminating on Shrove Tuesday, the 48th day before Easter. On that day, after a final round of revelry (still surviving in New Orleans's Mardi Gras, or "Fat Tuesday"), one confessed one's sins and was shriven (cleared) of them by a priest. Thus properly shriven, the penitent had his forehead marked the following morning (Ash Wednesday) with ashes to signify his contriteness for the beginning of the Lenten season of abstinence from the pleasures of the flesh.

To remind people of the approach of Lent and Easter, the three Sundays immediately preceding Shrove Tuesday were observed as Septuagesima, Sexagesima, and Quinquagesima — Latin for 70th, 60th, and 50th, indicating roughly the number of days until Easter. There were six Sundays in Lent, the last being Palm Sunday. The fourth Sunday was traditionally a break from the austere rigors of the season. Boys living away from home, such as apprentices or students, were allowed to go and visit their mothers on this day. It was customary for them to bring a simnel (a highly spiced

1963

Soviet cosmonaut Valentina Tereshkova becomes the first woman in space.

fruitcake) as a suitable present on "Mothering Sunday."

Usually halfway through Lent was a day of ill omen — the Ides of March in the old Roman calendar (the 15th in ours), on which Julius Caesar was assassinated in 46 B.C. It remained traditionally a bad-luck day, one to be wary of. A little earlier, in the first full week of Lent, occurred the three Ember Days — from the Old English *ymbren* (remembering), having nothing to do with embers — on which special fasting and prayer were observed in expiation of past misdeeds. Later it became customary to ordain priests on these and the other three groups of Ember Days occurring in May, September, and December.

The precession of the equinoxes has moved the astronomical beginning of spring forward four days to March 21 in our time, but its previous date of the 25th became identified with the Virgin Mary, who was told by the angel Gabriel on that day that she would become the mother of Christ nine months later. Annuncia-

The steadily lengthening daylight was hailed by the Candle Mass (Candlemas) . . . the day on which weather sages tried to foresee the end of winter, a custom we perpetuate in Groundhog Day.

tion, or Lady Day as it was more commonly called, was one of the great quarterly dividing points of the year (the others being Midsummer Day, Michaelmas, and Christmas). As such, it was traditionally the day for paying rents, signing or vacating leases, and hiring farm laborers for the year. This date was also the alternate year-beginning day.

A "feast of fools," on which all sorts of ridiculous tricks were played, has been known since Roman times. In the Middle Ages, it was usually held a little before Lent. When the pope fixed January 1 as the official beginning of the year in 1582, this day of foolery shifted to April 1, which thus was no longer the start of the government or civil year as it had been, but so only in joke. From that our All Fools Day tradition developed.

Following Easter, the next great seasonal holiday was May 1, or May Day, the Celtic Beltane, when the cattle were led into the upland pastures for the summer. It lent itself to all sorts of fertility rituals, of which

1963

New Hampshire runs the first state-sponsored lottery.

the maypole is a survivor. The opposite of May Day was November 1, Samhain, or All Saints Day, as Pope Gregory IV named it in A.D. 835 to clear it of its pagan associations. On that day, the cattle were brought back into their winter pens.

The Christian church commemorated Christ's ascension into heaven on a Thursday, the 40th day after Easter. The preceding Sunday was Rogation Day (from the Latin *rogare,* "to ask"), on which prayers were offered for bountiful crops from the sowings just completed. Ten days after Ascension Day is Pentecost (Greek "fiftieth," the 50th day after Easter), commemorating the descent of the Holy Spirit on the apostles (Acts 2). Having long been favored for baptisms, this day was usually called White Sunday or Whitsunday, because of the white robes worn by the newly baptized.

Formerly, the Sun reached its northernmost point on June 24 (now, by the precession of the equinoxes, on June 21). Hence it was called Midsummer Day, in terms of sunlight rather than weather. To the church, it was the birthday of St. John the Baptist, the herald of Christ. The wildflower that blooms at this time, St. John's-wort, reputedly has peculiarly effective properties against witches and all other evil. In many lands, Midsummer Day is still marked by bonfires and all-night revelry.

Lammas (Loaf Mass) Day, August 1, the Celtic Lugnasaid, hailed the beginning of the wheat harvest. Loaves made from the first new wheat were handed out at Mass. It is usually a time of great heat, attributed to the Dog Star, Sirius, which rises concurrently with the Sun from July 26 through August 11. We call these the Dog Days.

The completion of the harvest was marked by "Harvest Home" celebrations that varied in date by locality and weather, although the Feast of the Ingathering attained some stature on the fixed date of

Annunciation, or Lady Day as it was more commonly called, was one of the great quarterly dividing points of the year.

The tab-top soda (and beer) can eliminates the need for a can opener.

September 24. It was overshadowed, however, by Michaelmas, the festival of St. Michael the Archangel and overcomer of the Devil, on September 29. In addition to being the terminal date of the growing season, it was one of the four great quarterly dividing points of the year, and, like Lady Day in March, was a day for settling rents, making or breaking leases, paying off laborers, and hiring new ones. The custom of electing municipal officials at Michaelmas also grew, presumably so that they might be under Michael's protection.

Soon it was time to bring the cattle in from the pastures on November 1, a day whose associations with darkness were turned by the church into a festival honoring all saints in general. The souls of all others who had left this mortal life were remembered by special Masses the next day, November 2, All Souls Day. The twin days were referred to together as All Hallows, and the preceding day, October 31, thus became All Hallows Eve, now Halloween, when the powers of evil were allowed their fling before the sanctified days that followed.

*October 31
. . . became
All Hallows Eve,
now Halloween,
when the powers
of evil were
allowed their fling
before the
sanctified days
that followed.*

Some of the fattened cattle now had to be slaughtered and the meat salted for the winter. This task became associated with Martinmas, November 11, the day honoring the apostle of Celtic Gaul (now France) in the fourth century A.D. The winter solstice and Christmas approached, and gifts had to be prepared to give to family and friends. The distribution to the poor was on December 21, the feast day of St. Thomas the Doubter, so that recipients would have something to celebrate with. The other gifts, done up in beribboned boxes, were not exchanged until the day after Christmas, hence the Old English name of Boxing Day for December 26.

Perhaps one of the oddest of festivals was Holy Innocents Day, December 28, honoring the children of Bethlehem slain by King Herod in his mad attempt to kill the infant Christ. It used to be the custom to whip one's own children soundly on this day to remind them of those poor slaughtered unfortunates and to impress on them how fortunate they were to have had their own bountiful Yuletide holiday.

1963

The U.S. Post Office introduces the zip (zone improvement plan) code to aid in the routing of mail.

■ *You have guests coming for dinner, and you don't know what to serve. Well, just consult your calendar.*

Dining by the Calendar: Traditional Foods for Feasts and Fasts

BY E. BRADY

JANUARY

Feast of the Circumcision: Black-eyed peas and pork (United States); oat-husk gruel or oatmeal porridge (Scotland).

Epiphany: Cake with a lucky bean baked in it; the one who finds the bean is the king or queen of the feast, in memory of the three Wise Men (France).

Robert Burns Day: Haggis — sheep's stomach stuffed with suet, chopped organ meat (heart, lungs, liver), onions, oatmeal, and seasonings (Scotland). Haggis is a traditional Scottish delicacy served on all holidays of national importance.

FEBRUARY

Candlemas Day: Pancakes eaten today will prevent hemorrhoids for a full year (French-American).

St. Agatha: Round loaves of bread blessed by a priest (southern Europe).

Shrove Tuesday: Pancakes (England); oatcakes (Scotland); rabbit (Ireland). Rich foods are eaten to usher in the Lenten fast; pancakes use up the last of the eggs and butter.

Lent: Simnel, a large fruitcake baked so hard it has sometimes been mistaken by recipients for a hassock or footstool (Great Britain).

MARCH

St. David: Leeks, to be worn (Wales) or eaten raw (England). Recalls a Welsh victory over the Saxons in A.D. 640; the Welsh wore leeks in their hats to distinguish them from the enemy.

St. Benedict: Nettle soup (ancient monastic practice). Picking nettles, which irritate the skin, was a penance in keeping with the spirit of the monastic rule of St. Benedict.

Purim: Strong drink and three-cornered cookies flavored with poppy seeds (Jewish). These cookies, called hamantaschen, are said to represent the three-cornered hat of Haman, the enemy of the Jewish people, whose downfall is celebrated on this holiday.

Maundy Thursday: Green foods or foods colored green (southern Europe). The medieval liturgical observance called for green vestments; in some parts of Europe, it is still called Green Thursday.

Good Friday: Hot cross buns. If made properly on this day, they will never get moldy (England).

1964

Hassenfeld Bros. (later Hasbro) introduces G.I. Joe, an action-figure toy. It is an instant success despite the traditional view that boys will not play with dolls.

APRIL

Easter: Lamb, as a symbol of sacrifice; ham.

Beltane, May Day Eve: Strong ale (England); oatcakes with nine knobs to be broken off one by one and offered to each of nine supernatural protectors of domestic animals (Scotland).

MAY

Ascension Day: Fowl, or pastries molded in the shape of birds, to commemorate the taking of Jesus into the skies (medieval Europe).

Whitsunday (Pentecost): Dove or pigeon, in honor of the Holy Spirit (southern Europe); strong ale (England).

St. Dunstan: Beer. Cider pressed today will go bad (England).

Corpus Christi: Orange peel dipped in chocolate; chicken stuffed with sauerkraut (Basque provinces).

JUNE

St. Anthony of Padua: Liver, possibly based on the pre-Christian custom of eating liver on the summer solstice.

St. John the Baptist: First fruits of spring harvest eaten.

JULY

St. Swithin: Eggs, because the saint miraculously restored intact a basket of eggs that had been broken by a poor woman taking them to market; he also looks after apples (medieval England).

St. James: Oysters, because James was a fisherman (England).

AUGUST

Lammas Day: Oatcakes (Scotland); loaves made from new grain of the season (England); toffee; seaweed pudding. Blueberries in baskets as an offering to a sweetheart are the last vestige of this holiday as a pagan fertility festival (Ireland).

St. Lawrence of Rome: Because the saint was roasted to death on a gridiron, it is courteous to serve only cold meat today (southern Europe).

Feast of the Assumption: Onions, possibly because they have always been considered wholesome and potent against evil (Polish-American).

SEPTEMBER

St. Giles: Tea loaf with raisins (Scotland).

Nativity of Mary: Blackberries, possibly because the color is reminiscent of the depiction of the Virgin's blue cloak (Brittany).

Michaelmas Day: New wine (Europe); goose, originally a sacrifice to the saint (Great Britain); cake of oats, barley, and rye (Scotland); carrots (Ireland).

1964

The world's first discotheque, the Whisky-a-Go-Go, opens in Los Angeles.

OCTOBER

Rosh Hashanah: Sweet foods; honey; foods colored orange or yellow to represent a bright, joyous, and sweet new year (Jewish).

Yom Kippur: Fast day; the day before, eat kreplach (filled noodles), considered by generations of mothers to be good and filling (Jewish).

St. Luke: Oatcakes flavored with anise and cinnamon (Scotland).

Sts. Simon and Jude: Dirge cakes, simple fried buns made for distribution to the poor. Also apples or potatoes, for divination (Scotland and England). Divination with apples is accomplished by peeling the fruit in one long strip and tossing the peel over one's shoulder. The letter formed by the peel is then interpreted.

All Hallows Eve: Apples and nuts, for divination (England); buttered oat-husk gruel (Scotland); bosty, a mixture of potatoes, cabbage, and onions (Ireland).

NOVEMBER

All Saints Day: Chestnuts (Italy); gingerbread and oatcakes (Scotland); milk (central Europe); doughnuts, whose round shape indicates eternity (Tyrol).

All Souls Day: Skull-shaped candy (Mexico); beans, peas, and lentils, considered foods of the poor, as penance for souls in purgatory (southern Europe).

St. Martin: Last religious feast day before the beginning of the Advent fast. Goose, last of fresh-killed meat before winter; blood pudding (Great Britain).

St. Andrew: Haggis — stuffed sheep's stomach (Scotland).

DECEMBER

St. Nicholas: Fruit, nuts, candy for children (Germany). Commemorates, in part, the miracle by which the saint restored to life three young boys who had been murdered by a greedy innkeeper.

St. Lucy: Headcheese; cakes flavored with saffron or cardamom, raisins, and almonds (Sweden). The saffron imparts a yellow color to the cakes, representing sunlight, whose return is celebrated at the solstice.

Christmas: Boar's head or goose, plum pudding, nuts, oranges (England); turkey (United States); spiced beef (Ireland).

St. John the Evangelist: Small loaves of bread made with blessed wine (medieval Europe). This is a feast on which wine is ritually blessed in memory of the saint, who drank poisoned wine and miraculously survived.

Chanukah: Latkes — potato pancakes (Jewish).

Holy Innocents Day: Baby food, pablum, Cream of Wheat, in honor of the children killed by King Herod of Judea (monastic observance).

St. Sylvester: Strong drink (United States); haggis, oatcakes and cheese, oat-husk gruel or porridge (Scotland).

1964

The most intense earthquake ever recorded in North America strikes southern Alaska.

■ *Native Americans had a calendar: the Moon. Each of the 12 full Moons had a name describing the season of the year. It was that occasional 13th Moon that kept everyone guessing.*

Full Moon Names: How Each Came to Be

BY ANDREW ROTHOVIUS

THE NATIVE INDIANS OF WHAT is now the northern and eastern United States kept track of the seasons by assigning distinctive names to each recurring full Moon. These names were applied to the entire month in which the Moon occurred. There was some variation in the Moon names, but in general the same ones were used among all the Algonquin tribes from New England to Lake Superior.

Since the lunar month is only 29 days long on the average, the full Moon dates shift from year to year, and the Indian names for them fit the seasons best in those years when each full Moon occurs at about the middle of our calendar months.

January: Full Wolf Moon

Amid the cold and deep snow of midwinter, the wolf packs howled hungrily outside the Indian villages. This was also known as the Old Moon. In some tribes, it was the Full Snow Moon, although most applied that name to the next Moon.

February: Full Snow Moon

Usually the heaviest snows fall in this month. Hunting becomes very difficult, and so some tribes called this the Full Hunger Moon.

March: Full Worm Moon

In this month, the ground softens and the earthworm casts reappear, inviting the return of the robins. The more northern tribes knew this as the Full Crow Moon, when the cawing of crows signals the end of winter, or the Full Crust Moon, because the snow cover becomes crusted from thawing by day and freezing at night. The Full Sap Moon, marking the time of tapping maple trees, is another variation.

April: Full Pink Moon

The grass pink, or wild ground phlox, is one of the earliest widespread flow-

---

1964

Jerrie Mock is the first woman to complete an around-the-world solo flight. Mock made the 22,858.8-mile flight in 29½ days (with 21 stops) in a single-engine Cessna.

ers of the spring. Other names are the Full Sprouting Grass Moon, the Egg Moon, and, among coastal tribes, the Full Fish Moon, when the shad come upstream to spawn.

May: Full Flower Moon

Flowers are abundant everywhere. It is also known as the Full Corn Planting Moon or the Milk Moon.

June: Full Strawberry Moon

Europeans called it the Rose Moon.

July: Full Buck Moon

This name comes from the time when the new antlers of buck deer push out from their foreheads in coatings of velvety fur. It is also called the Full Thunder Moon, as thunderstorms are most frequent now.

August: Full Sturgeon Moon

This large fish of the Great Lakes and other major bodies of water, such as Lake Champlain, is most readily caught now. A few tribes knew this as the Full Red Moon, because the Moon rises looking reddish through a sultry haze, or the Green Corn Moon.

September: Full Harvest Moon

Corn, pumpkins, squash, beans, and wild rice — the chief Indian staples — are now ready for gathering.

October: Full Hunter's Moon

With the leaves falling and the deer fattened, it is time to hunt.

November: Full Beaver Moon

It's time to set beaver traps before the swamps freeze to ensure a supply of warm winter furs.

December: Full Cold Moon

Among some tribes, this was the Full Long Nights Moon. In this month, the winter cold fastens its grip, and the nights are at their longest and darkest.

AND SO WE COME around to January and the Full Wolf Moon again, as another year has made its cycle. Because there are always a few days left over in the lunar year, about every six years or so there has to be a 13th Moon to keep the seasons straight. This brings up a Moon name that has no American Indian background — "blue Moon," which has come to denote the second full Moon within the same month. The expression "blue Moon" derives from the extremely rare, actually blue-tinged Moon caused by atmospheric layers of forest fire smoke or volcanic dust at just the right height and visual angle. "Once in a blue Moon," people say when referring to something that in all likelihood will never happen at all or is far off in the future. In this century, the only literal "blue Moon" visible in New England was that of September 26, 1950, caused by forest fire smoke from western Canada.

1965

Social activist and consumer advocate Ralph Nader publishes his first book, *Unsafe at Any Speed,* exposing the irresponsibility, corruption, and deceit of the auto industry.

FARMER'S CALENDAR

Litter Calendar

H OW DID THE EARLY SETTLERS in the wilderness keep track of time? They used a litter calendar. Simplicity itself!

Settlers would naturally have some animals, domestic or captured wildlife. OK. They segregated the males from the females until a predetermined day in the spring — April 1 if they could find out when it was, or the full Moon, say — when they mated them and sent them all off to a flying start. Now they were set! The opossums would pop on the 11th day thereafter, the white mice the 22nd, the rabbits the 30th, the ferrets the 40th, the dogs the 63rd, the hogs the 120th, the sheep the 150th, the horses the 346th, and the walruses the 365th, and there they were! And Ma and the cows at 280, and the elephants at 600 gave them additional checks. It was really a cinch.

Suppose they wanted to give a neighbor a note. They merely said, "1 Rabbit from date I promise to pay —." But, you may ask, how many opossums ago did they plant the spinach? Elementary: They went to the opossum pen and counted the animals, divided by 18, and there was the answer. They could invite their friends for a Walrus Eve Party. Once they could find out when January 1 came, they could start fresh and be in step with a regular calendar.

1965

The movies *Dr. Zhivago* and *The Sound of Music* are box-office hits.

■ *At one time, our calendar was so out of step with the Earth's precisely timed journey around the Sun that it showed January was coming in the fall!*

The Year Ten Days Disappeared from October

BY JOHN I. WHITE

UNTIL RECENTLY, WE AMERIcans celebrated the birthday of our greatest national hero, George Washington, on February 22. Then a new law shifted the observance of Washington's birthday and several other national holidays to Mondays, to give workers in factories and offices more three-day weekends.

Some of our patriotic citizens feel that changing this time-honored holiday so that more people can go skiing or take longer trips in their cars is a shabby way to treat the memory of the soldier and statesman whom we call the "Father of His Country." History tells us, however, that this was not the first time Washington's birthday was shifted. The great man once changed it himself, for a very good reason.

As a youth in Virginia, Washington observed his birthday not on February 22, but on February 11. He did this until he was 20 years of age. Changing to February 22 was related, believe it or not, to the movement of our Earth around the Sun.

The huge sphere on which we live travels slowly around the Sun in a circular path, or orbit. One complete trip around, which we call a solar or Sun year, requires just a bit less than 365½ days. The exact time is 365 days, 5 hours, 48 minutes, and 45.7 seconds.

For thousands of years, people have tried to divide up the solar year and keep track of time with calendars. It was important to the citizens of ancient Rome and Greece to know when their festivals would take place, just as it is important to us to know when the next school term ends. Imagine your own home without a calendar hanging on the wall.

The calendars of the ancients contained serious errors, largely because no one knew how long it took the Earth to make its huge circle around the Sun. Even when they found out, it was difficult to settle on a good way of dividing up approximately 365 days and showing it on a calendar.

The early Romans had a 12-month calendar somewhat like ours

1966

The U.S. Department of the Interior publishes its first rare and endangered species list, including 78 species. Passage of the Endangered Species Act of 1973 will protect endangered animals and plants from extinction.

today. But 2,000 years ago, it had gotten so out of step with the Earth's annual journey around the Sun that it showed January coming in the fall instead of in the winter. Julius Caesar attempted to correct this. In the belief that the year was exactly 365¼ days long, he gave 31 days to six of the months. Except for February, which was given 29, the other months were given 30 days. As this adds up to exactly 365 days, there was still that troublesome one-quarter of a day to worry about. To make the calendar come out right, or so he thought, Caesar announced that every fourth February would have 30 days instead of 29.

But there was still a tiny error in all this. When some 1,600 years had gone by, it began to be serious. In the year 1580, with the arrival of the spring equinox, one of two days in the year when day and night are of equal length, Caesar's calendar said the

As a youth in Virginia, Washington observed his birthday not on February 22, but on February 11. He did this until he was 20 years of age.

date was March 11, when it actually should have been March 21, the first day of spring. The so-called Julian calendar, named for Julius Caesar, was gaining a day every 128 years and was out of step with the solar year by 10 whole days. Something had to be done.

The problem was tackled and, fortunately, solved by Pope Gregory XIII. The key to his success in calendar reform

1966

A new science fiction television series called *Star Trek* debuts.

was the way he handled what we call leap year. Three years in a row, February was given 28 days; every fourth year (leap year) it got 29. But Pope Gregory and his calendar experts realized that if things were not to get out of kilter again, it was necessary to skip this extra leap year day, February 29, once in a great while. Pope Gregory's rule, which seems to make things come out just right, is that leap year (giving February that extra day every four years) is ignored in the first year of a century whose date cannot be evenly divided by 400. The year 1600 was a leap year, and February had 29 days. But the years 1700, 1800, and 1900, all of which would have been leap years, are not evenly divisible by 400, and therefore their Februarys were given only 28 days.

Pope Gregory, who was 80 when he accomplished his great task of calendar reform, got the world off to a fresh start calendar-wise in 1582 by dropping ten days from

Mother England, strangely enough, was a bit behind the times. She was still using Caesar's old calendar even though most countries had adopted Pope Gregory's new one many years before.

October of that year. The day after October 4 became October 15. Then the new calendar went into effect in many countries. The Gregorian system is the one we use today.

Now, to get back to George Washington.

When Washington was born in Virginia in 1732, the American colonies still belonged to England. And Mother England, strangely enough, was a bit behind the times. She was still using Caesar's old calendar even though most countries had adopted Pope Gregory's new one many years before. Washington was born on February 11, as reckoned by Caesar's old calendar. When the British finally changed over to the new one, he was 20 years old. As the two calendars were out of whack by 11 days, the young surveyor knew that he would not be a full year older until February 22 came up on the new Gregorian calendar. So George Washington chose that date for the observance of his birthday for the remainder of his long and illustrious life.

1966

The Soviet *Luna 9* is the first spacecraft to land intact on the Moon. *Luna 9* transmits only a few pictures before its batteries die.

The Pros and Cons of Leap Year

L OOKING BACK, it appears that leap years have brought both good and bad luck. For instance, during various leap years Rome was burned to the ground, Custer fought the Battle of the Little Bighorn, and the *Titanic* sank. The massacre at Deerfield, Massachusetts, in 1704 occurred on February 29. By contrast, during other leap years the Pilgrims landed in Plymouth, Franklin proved that lightning is electricity, and gold was discovered in California.

For sure, during the years when there's an extra day, more money is spent, made, and lost. For instance, these days the government takes in close to $2 billion* in extra receipts when there is a February 29. But then again, members of the armed forces and others who are paid on a monthly basis will have to work that day for free.

Finally, there's the romantic side. The tradition of women being able to propose to men during a leap year supposedly began about 1288 when the Scots passed a law providing that "for il yeare knowne as lepe year, ilk mayden ladye of bothe highe and lowe estait shall Law liberte to bespeke ye man she likes." But isn't that pretty much like every year these days?

Research courtesy of Mark Muro and the Boston Globe

*This figure is based on 1991 data.

1967

Amana introduces the first microwave oven for household use. It is based on the invention of Raytheon employee Percy Le Baron Spencer in 1947.

ANECDOTES & PLEASANTRIES

Wanna Fool Around with the Calendar — Again?

IF YOU ARE one of the many people who have trouble remembering what comes after "Thirty days hath September," you might be interested in calendar reform. There was a movement in the 1930s to simplify the calendar by making a year consist of 13 months, each month exactly 28 days long. The extra month would be called Sol (after our Sun) and fall between June and July, thus giving those of us in the Northern Hemisphere an extra month of summer.

Among the advantages of this system, called the International Fixed Calendar, is the fact that nobody would need new calendars every year. Every month would begin on a Sunday and end on a Saturday, and every date would fall on the same day of the week every year. (For those of you who have been doing some quick calculating, you are right — the International Fixed Calendar has only 364 days in the year. Don't worry, though — the extra day would be stuck in between December 28 and January 1 and designated a World Holiday, identified with no month or day of the week. On leap years, there would be a second World Holiday wedged between June 28 and Sol 1.)

One of the disadvantages of the International Fixed Calendar is that 13 months can't be easily divided into quarters for business purposes. This has led to a counterproposal — the World Calendar, made up of four 91-day quarters, each consisting of a 31-day month followed by two 30-day months. Once again, it adds up to 364 days, and so one day would be set aside for general hoopla.

But perhaps you are a traditionalist. "Why fool around with the calendar?" you ask. It was good enough for Moses, and it's good enough for me. In fact, people have been fooling around with the calendar for as long as calendars have existed. But that's another story (see page 306).

Courtesy of Tim Clark

1967

The world's first heart transplant is performed in Cape Town, South Africa, by Christiaan Barnard. The surgery is successful, but the patient lives only 18 days.

■ *No more logic supports seven days than, say, eight or five, yet the seven-day week has resisted any and all attempts at change.*

The Real Reason the Week Has Seven Days

IT HAS BEEN PRAISED AS "THE most ancient monument of astronomical knowledge" and damned as "illogical arrangement," but the seven-day week appears to be here to stay.

Unlike the year and the month, which correspond to the movements of the Earth around the Sun and the Moon around the Earth, the week has no astronomical analogue. It is roughly the same as the length of a phase of the Moon — seven days, nine hours — but any system of timekeeping based on the Moon's phases quickly falls apart due to those extra hours piling up. The seven-day week is artificial, the first truly man-made unit of time.

Officially adopted by the emperor Constantine in A.D. 321, the seven-day week goes back thousands of years before that to the first civilizations of the Middle East. Mesopotamian astrologers designated one day for each of the seven most prominent objects in the sky — the Sun, the Moon, and the five major planets visible to the naked eye. The Jews also adopted a seven-day cycle, based on the time it took the Lord to create the universe as reported in Genesis. A new wrinkle in their week was the Sabbath, a day set aside for rest. According to sociologist Eviatar Zerubavel, author of *The Seven Day Cycle: The History and Meaning of the Week,* no other culture had yet invented a holiday that occurred on a regular basis, unrelated to natural phenomena. "This was one of the great breakthroughs of human civilization," Zerubavel wrote.

But other cultures adopted different weeks, probably for business rea-

R. Buckminster Fuller's geodesic dome is a big attraction at Expo '67 in Montreal, Canada. Fuller's design embodies his philosophy of gaining the maximum benefit by using the minimum resources.

sons. The Romans thought of a week as the 8 days between market days. West African societies preferred a 4-day market cycle. In Assyria, 6 days was the rule; in Egypt 10, in China 15.

The ancient Germans used a five-day cycle named for their primary gods, which is how our week ended up honoring Norse deities such as Tiw (Tuesday), Odin (Wednesday), Thor (Thursday), and Frigga (Friday). They borrowed Saturn from the Romans to make Saturday. In fact, our word *week* probably comes from the Old Norse word *vikja,* which means "to turn." Sunday and Monday, of course, honor the Sun and the Moon.

Our word week *probably comes from the Old Norse word* vikja, *which means "to turn."*

Atheistic revolutionaries tried unsuccessfully to get rid of the seven-day week. In 1793 the leaders of the French Revolution produced a new calendar with each month divided into 3 ten-day "decades." It never caught on, and Napoleon abandoned it in 1805. In 1929 the Soviet Union tried a five-day week, with one day of rest. Instead of the traditional day names, the days were given colors: yellow, orange, red, purple, and green. To keep mass production going, each Soviet citizen was assigned a different day of rest, so that a husband might have a yellow day off, while his wife took her leisure on a green. This produced mass confusion. In 1932 the plan was revised to a six-day week, with numbers replacing the colors. That didn't work either, and by 1940 the Russians were back on the familiar seven-day cycle.

Somebody is always trying to come up with something better. In 1936 the League of Nations solicited proposals for world calendar reform and considered almost 200 different schemes, many of which rejiggered the week. Edward Skille of Drummond, Wisconsin, suggested a year consisting of 73 five-day weeks called metos. The days of the week would be called Ano, Beno, Ceno, Deno, and Eno.

There is no doubt that the seven-day week is illogical. It doesn't divide evenly into 365- or 366-day years, so holidays fall on different days of the week from year to year, creating problems determining the dates of important ones. Easter, for example, can be celebrated on any one of 35 different days. But human beings are not logical creatures. Who can imagine saying, "Thank God, it's Eno!" or "What are you doing next purple?" And as a member of the British Parliament remarked in a 1944 debate on calendar reform, "It is bad enough to be born on April 1, but to have one's birthday always on a Monday would be perfectly intolerable."

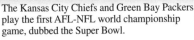

1967

The Kansas City Chiefs and Green Bay Packers play the first AFL-NFL world championship game, dubbed the Super Bowl.

■ *Even the most rational among us pauses when Friday the 13th rolls around, and the cautious folks might even reschedule their day's activities. What's behind all the superstitions, and do we have anything to worry about?*

Have a Happy Friday the 13th

BY RICK HOROWITZ

FEELING A LITTLE BIT EDGY ONE particular day a month? Do the little hairs on your arms start darting around with minds of their own? Do you find you're looking behind you everywhere you go? Are you sure there's something out there, but you can't quite name it?

Wrap your tongue around this one: triskaidekaphobia.

Triskaidekaphobia is the fear of the number 13. If you have it, you're not alone. And you're probably at your worst on a 13th that's also a Friday.

The town fathers of French Lick Springs, Indiana, once decreed that all black cats in town should wear bells on Friday the 13th.

"If you want to break the spell of a broken mirror on Friday the 13th," suggested a man in Denton, Texas, "go to the top of the highest mountain or building and burn all your socks with holes in them."

In years past, ocean liners scheduled to leave port on the 13th (Friday or not) would often contrive to delay their departures until after midnight, and there are other people who simply won't travel on that day.

But why all the fuss? What's made 13 such a worrisome number, Friday such a troublesome time? The people who claim to know such things offer two contending possibilities. There were 13 people at the Last Supper, they point out, and the crucifixion of Christ occurred on a Friday. That's one.

Here's two, from Norse mythology: Twelve Norse gods were enjoying a dinner feast in Valhalla when a 13th — the cruel, mischievous god Loki — intruded and caused the death of Baldur the Beautiful, the embodiment of joy and gladness. Nobody knows what day of the week that was.

1967

The first cordless, battery-powered telephone is developed.

In any event, that's where the experts think it came from, but where has it gone? *Are* 13ths particularly unlucky?

Well, as with so many things, where you stand depends on where you sit. For example:

■ On Friday the 13th in July 1900, Theodore Roosevelt laid the cornerstone for a new county courthouse in New York and spoke of the need for honesty in government. "During the exercises," a newspaper reported the next day,

What's made 13 such a worrisome number, Friday such a troublesome time? . . . There were 13 people at the Last Supper . . . and the crucifixion of Christ occurred on a Friday. That's one [possibility].

"Nathaniel Ketcham, who was on the platform, had his pockets picked of $140, another man lost $103, and several watches were stolen." It was a good day for Roosevelt, who in a year's time would succeed to the presidency. It was a pretty good day for folks who like courthouses and for pickpockets. But it was not so good a day for Nathaniel Ketcham.

■ Some 750,000 pounds of paper fluttered down around Charles Lindbergh dur-

The television variety show *Laugh-In* first appears on NBC.

ing a ticker-tape parade in New York City on June 13, 1927. That was lucky for "Lucky Lindy," less lucky for the garbagemen.

▉ On September 13, 1857, Milton S. Hershey, candy maker, was born. Hershey also died on a 13th, in October 1945.

All in all, the 13th has a mixed record, historically speaking. Still, some people just don't take very kindly to it. The Turks, it's said, almost expunged the number from their vocabulary. In many of the streets and squares of Florence, Italy, 12½ substitutes for 13. French socialites known as *quatorziens* (fourteeners) once made themselves available as emergency fill-ins when a dinner party unexpectedly contained exactly 13 people.

In Madagascar, however, 13 means nothing. People there consider 6 the most unlucky number. In Japan it's 3. But in China the number 3 — and also 9, which is 3 times 3 — is considered very lucky indeed.

Then there are those who consider the number 13 quite lucky, like some theatrical people of old, who tried to sign all their contracts on that day. In Great Britain, eating Christmas pudding in 13 different houses before January 1 was supposed to bring joy and prosperity in the next year.

President Dwight D. Eisenhower was made honorary president of

Missouri's Lucky 13 Club, consisting of that state's 13 presidential electors, because they liked the fact that "Ike Eisenhower" has 13 letters. In fact, the United States is so full of lucky 13ths that even normally superstitious political types should put their minds at ease. George Washington laid the cornerstone for the White House on a 13th (October 1792). The cornerstone for the Supreme Court was laid on the same date in 1932. There were 13 original colonies, of course, and the Great Seal of the United States contains 13 stars, 13 bars, and an eagle with 13 tail feathers, holding 13 arrows and 13 olive branches in its feet. "E pluribus unum" even has 13 letters.

You'd think all that would calm at least the American triskaidekaphobes, but no such luck.

To dream of a calendar is a sign of good fortune.

1968

The Motion Picture Association of America establishes a movie rating system: G (general audience), PG (parental guidance), R (restricted to adults or children accompanied by adults), and X (restricted to adults).

■ *Literature and legend tell us that the rooster crows at dawn, but don't set your watch by it.*

Cocks, Cockcrows, and Weathercocks

SINCE ANCIENT TIMES, THE COCK has been the bird of light. This concept was inherited by the ancient Christians from pagan times, and since early Christendom the cock has been placed atop church towers. The cock weather vane on Notre Dame in Paris, for example, contains sacred religious relics, as do many other old cock weather vanes.

As the bird of light, the cock is the symbol of Christ and the Resurrection. It also stands for the pastor who leads and watches over his parish and for the position of the church in the community.

In the symbolism of the cock vanes, we also must recognize Peter's denial that he knew Christ. Christ foretold his denial and said Peter would deny him before cockcrow. Cockcrow is commonly thought of as early dawn. However, cocks have been known to have crowing watches all through the night. As these happen at or about dark, midnight, three in the morning, and dawn, the night is thus divided into "night watches." It is supposed that evil spirits walk in the night and that the final cockcrow just before the dawn disperses them to their devilish habitats.

The unseasonable crowing of cocks has always been reckoned ominous, particularly as it relates to wars. The cock was sacred to Mars, the Roman god of war, and presaged the victory of the Athenian general Themistocles, as well as that of the Boeotians over the Lacedaemonians (Spartans).

In still dark weather, which often happens at the time of the fall solstice, cocks will often crow all day and all night. Cocks also will crow in almost any crepuscular (twilight) light, such as during an eclipse of the Sun or in the semidarkness of a thundercloud.

■ *Granted, the Sun was always a reliable timekeeper, but there were some very good reasons for making the shift to clock time.*

Sun Time Versus Clock Time

BY BLANTON C. WIGGIN

B EFORE THE DAYS OF RAPID communication, man lived by Sun time, which varies everywhere. In the temperate zones, Sun time may vary several minutes within only 30 miles. Therefore, in today's closely linked world, we

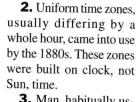

have a global network of *averaged* time to which we set our clocks. There are three main differences between Sun and clock time.

1. The Earth varies its orbit speed around the Sun, while rotating at a nearly constant speed. Thus Sun day lengths vary seasonally by

30 minutes or so. Man created an average day length for clocks and navigation a few centuries ago. This is "mean" time, sometimes called "civil" time. Greenwich (England) mean time was and still is the starting point for the averaged Sun time.

2. Uniform time zones, usually differing by a whole hour, came into use by the 1880s. These zones were built on clock, not Sun, time.

3. Man, habitually using the clock more than the Sun, discovered that he could trick himself by setting his clock ahead. He got up sooner in the early-summer sunlight and had more daylight left after work for recreation (or saving electricity). Starting in the 1910s, Daylight Saving Time spread and now covers almost entire time zones. In the United States, the period of Daylight Saving Time has been extended to half the year, and there is pressure in some areas to observe it all year, or at least all but the three winter months.

1968

First Philadelphia Bank installs the first cash-dispensing machine, or automated teller machine (ATM).

> ■ *We should all aspire to be as punctual as the fiddler crab.*

Time, Tide, and the Fiddler Crab

BY W. L. DOUGHERTY

DOWN BY THE SHORES OF THE sea around us lives a small crustacean who scuttles obliquely about the tide-packed sand. He carries a violin. His day is a perennial scavenger hunt for algae. He is *Uca minax*, boy fiddler crab, and immediately familiar to any parent who has ever unpacked a child's suitcase after a seaside vacation.

He has always been considered unique because of the one giant claw that gives him his common name. In an emergency, he can shuck off this instrument to travel light. Yehudi Menuhin, in this position, would have to give up music, but not *Uca minax*. Offhandedly, his other normal claw begins to grow into a new Stradivarius. And the right hand, knowing what the left is doing, sprouts a new small pincer to tie the score.

But recently, marine biologists have discovered that there is more to this beady-eyed chap than a simple talent for ambidexterity. By shrewd observation and a little prying, they have learned that he also has a built-in Swiss movement — a biological clock — which automatically varies his wardrobe.

At dawn, for example, when this saltwater musician is attired in business gray, his internal clockwork tells him it is time for a change. As the day brightens, his carapace darkens until it has become a sporty, and protective, tweedy brown. This littoral translation accomplished, our friend is less apparent to airborne predators. He is dressed for his excursions on the dark, wet beach — his supermarket.

At this point, almost anyone but a biologist would have exclaimed, "Isn't nature wonderful!" and gone right back to his science fiction. But science, being an inquisitive party, wanted to know why. This was no blush like the chameleon's giddy fluctuation. Was metabolism responsible? Was it a response to the Earth's rotation? To light and dark?

Almost anyone but a biologist would have exclaimed, "Isn't nature wonderful!" and gone right back to his science fiction.

1968

The first emergency 911 telephone system is installed in New York.

To find out, crabs were kidnapped and held in dark rooms where conditions of light and temperature were constant. Notebooks were produced, and the men who care about these things sat down for a little clock-watching.

Now, removed from their natural habitat, did these crabs wear gray for a monotonous 24 hours? Or brown? Did they become confused and fumble in the closet for brown jacket and gray slacks? No, indeed. They varied their dress around the clock, as always, with the regularity of a conductor's watch. Whatever happened, it appeared to the trained eye, went on inside the crab.

The scientists nodded to each other and tried another experiment. They began parcel-posting crabs to surprised fellow scientists in

Did these crabs wear gray for a monotonous 24 hours? . . . Did they become confused and fumble in the closet for brown jacket and gray slacks?

different parts of the country. They pressed packages of crabs upon acquaintances who were traveling, with instructions for compiling statistics. When enough of these had accumulated, a fact that had only been suspected was proved: The crab's clothing changes were also responsive to the 12½-hour tidal, or lunar, cycle. His shell was darkest when the tide was low — when

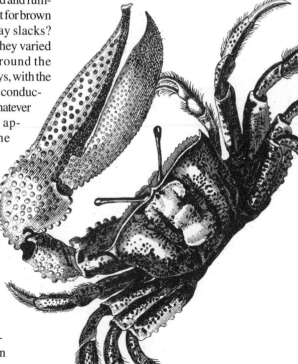

1969

Neil Armstrong and Edwin "Buzz" Aldrin are the first Americans to land on the Moon.

he had to range farthest down the wet sand from his burrow above high water. By the time of high tide, when he was feeding in shallow water, he wore the pearliest gray.

And no matter how far he was mailed from the beach where he was born or with how many crabs from different shores he was associated, he was always true, with old-school-tie fidelity, to the tides on the beach of his origin. This phenomenon was superimposed on his response to the solar cy-cle. He had a clock within a clock.

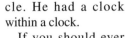

Back in their laboratory, the biologists tried one more experiment. They had noticed that, on his travels across the country, the fiddler crab would "run slow" by an hour for each man-made time belt through which he passed.

If you should ever feel like dabbling in science on your own, you might try airmailing a clutch of Boston Harbor crabs to some indifferent pen pal in the Midwest. Your old college roommate, from whom you have not had an intelligent word in 15 years, would do nicely. Tell him what to look out for. See if he won't drop whatever he is doing to join you in your pursuit of nature's mysteries. However, you may get a package by return mail that the postman will hand you and run because it ticks. He could be right. It might not be shellfish.

Back in their laboratory, the biologists tried one more experiment. They had noticed that, on his travels across the country, the fiddler crab would "run slow" by an hour for each man-made time belt through which he passed. To see what would happen, they refrigerated their good-natured subject to a point slightly above freezing.

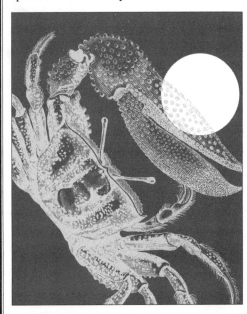

His clock stopped. They warmed him up. He began to tick again like an electric clock after a power failure, running "behind" to the exact extent of his frigid siesta in the icebox. The theory of an internal stimulus was strengthened. For the present, this dramatic detective story rests at this firm conclusion. But it hints of possible exciting things to come.

For the crab's intricate adaptability is by no means singular in nature, nor does he attempt to give that impression. Many animals, insects, and even vegetables demonstrate a rhythmic response to natural forces. Man, too, has his ups and downs, independent of the martini, frequently blamed on the phases of the Moon. It is in relation to these that the findings about the fiddler crab could be important. The unraveling of the mysterious effect of rhythms and cycles on man's behavior may have progressed one step further.

Perhaps the day is now closer when man will discover that he is the proprietor of latent natural powers that were necessary to him for survival in an earlier era and that, if they could be revived, could be manipulated to his advantage. Perhaps he already possesses what any commuter thirsting after a second cup of coffee would envy the fiddler crab: a biological sense of time. Even if the only result were to relegate Baby Ben to the Smithsonian, it could be interpreted as progress.

ANECDOTES & PLEASANTRIES

Count to a Trillion?

BET YOU CAN'T, but won't take your money because here is why you can't. You can count to about 170 in a minute—even 200. An hour will therefore produce 12,000; a day 288,000; and a year, or 365 days (you may rest a day every 4 years), 105,120,000. Even if Adam had started counting the day he was born, he would not yet be up to a trillion. For it would take 9,512 years, 34 days, 5 hours, and 20 minutes to count to a trillion at the above rate.

1969

Preschoolers enjoy the first airing of *Sesame Street.*

■ *Until 1883 a traveler going from Maine to California had to adjust his watch 20 times to match variations in timekeeping. Then along came Charles Ferdinand Dowd and his invention: standard time.*

The Man Who Unraveled a Tangle in Time

BY H. I. MILLER

THE CHAMPIONS OF INDIVIDUAL liberty who voice their yearly objections to Daylight Saving Time should have lived about a century ago. They would not only have found plenty to complain about, but they also would probably have thrown brickbats at a certain mild-mannered Yale graduate and principal of a female seminary in Saratoga, New York — namely Charles Ferdinand Dowd. Born in Madison, Connecticut, on April 25, 1825, Dowd is credited in the archives of the National Library in Washington with being the inventor of the system of standard time that ended a welter of confusion across the land and forever enshrined his name in the nation's history.

Such a uniform time system had long been the goal of the nation's railroads. Fact is, the railroads, in desperation, put the entire country on standard time in 1883. It was high time.

Up to November 18 of that year, a state of confusion had existed among the railroads. Prior to adoption of standard time by the nation's railroad systems, many communities based their time on the position of the Sun over their city halls. This resulted in no end of chaos.

Moreover, railroad timetables, lacking a nationally synchronized master time system, gave arrival and departure times in terms of the time of each particular city. A traveler going from Maine to California had to adjust his watch 20 times to match local variations in timekeeping. In Kansas City, jewelers vied with one another by setting up their own "standard times," which varied as much as 20 minutes from one jewelry store to another. In Pittsburgh, 6 different time standards governed train movements. But it was in Buffalo, a crossroads city, that the confusion that irked Professor Dowd reached its zenith. There, a traveler coming in from Portland, Maine, would find four variations in time. With the New York Central clock indicating

1969

Sony (formerly Tokyo Telecommunications Co.) invents the videotape cassette.

noon, the Lake Shore clock might point to 11:25 A.M., the Buffalo city clock to 11:40 A.M., and his own watch to 12:15 P.M.

Then came standard time, and the confusion ended. The man who merits a national monument for this great advance was an 1853 graduate of Yale University. Charles Dowd, a man of meticulous methodology, found

In Kansas City, jewelers vied with one another by setting up their own "standard times," which varied as much as 20 minutes from one jewelry store to another.

timetables a mass of confusion. It took him less than a year to work out a basic formula that would unravel the snarled skeins of time, but it took him 13 years to convince apathetic public officials and railroad executives to give his plan a try.

At each annual convention of railroad trunk lines, he aired his idea of hourly divisions. It called for the establishment of

1970

American brothers David and John Kunst begin their walk around the world. John will die en route; David will complete the 14,500-mile journey in 1974.

four geographical zones, each 14 degrees of longitude wide. While each zone would observe a uniform time, the time would vary exactly one hour from zone to zone. The zones were Eastern, Central, Mountain, and Pacific. This meant that if it were four o'clock in the Eastern zone, it would be three o'clock in the Central zone, two o'clock in the Mountain zone, and one o'clock in the Pacific zone.

In 1869 one of his plans was finally given the nod when railroad convention delegates expressed a desire to see it worked out in detail. After much time, effort, and money, Dowd published a pamphlet titled *A System of National Time for Railroads*. A copy of this is now in the National Library in Washington and attests to the priority of Dowd's work. The book includes a map dividing the country into sections exactly like those adopted 13 years later, when standard time was adopted.

If Dowd thought that the railroads would eagerly embrace his advanced method of ending time confusion, he was doomed to disappointment. Embroiled as they were in rate difficulties, fast-train competition, and other rivalries, the railroads showed

> *Embroiled as they were in rate difficulties, fast-train competition, and other rivalries, the railroads showed no disposition to improve their aggravating time schedules.*

no disposition to improve their aggravating time schedules. However, leading scientific organizations also were agitating for a solution to the time dilemma. They joined forces with Dowd, and William Allen, secretary of the American Railroad Association, finally gave his hearty endorsement to the four-zone time system.

Delegates to the association's 1883 meeting in Chicago pledged their officers to run all trains "by the standards agreed upon (Dowd's plan) . . . and to adopt same . . . at 12 o'clock noon, Sunday, November 18." From *Harper's Weekly,* leading periodical of the day, comes this description of the historic event:

> *On the last day under the old system, when the Sun reached the 75th meridian, the clocks began their jangle for the hour of noon and kept it up in a drift across the country for four hours, like incoherent cowbells in a wildwood.*
>
> *But on Monday, the 19th, no clock struck for this hour until the Sun reached the 75th meridian. Then all the clocks on the continent struck together, those in the Eastern Belt striking 12, the Central Belt 11, in the Mountain Belt 10 and in the Pacific Belt 9.*

1970

American boxer Cassius Clay changes his name to Muhammad Ali.

Time tables everywhere became intelligent.

Although the railroads benefited from the improvement to a degree too prodigious to determine, they gave scant recognition to Charles F. Dowd — never even naming a Pullman car after him. And fate decreed that it was a railroad train that killed the inventor of standard time at a Saratoga railroad crossing 21 years after the historic occasion. All that remains to mark his achievement, according to a member of Dowd's family, is a small plaque on a monument in the yard of Skidmore College, placed there by students.

ANECDOTES & PLEASANTRIES

People Who Wait Five Months for the Traffic Light to Change

(Almost everyone does, eventually.)

SEVERAL YEARS BACK, the *New York Times* reported a study made by an outfit called Priority Management Pittsburgh. It said that, over the course of a lifetime, the average American spends a year looking for misplaced objects, such as dry cleaner slips, glasses, and checkbooks. It said we spend eight months opening junk mail. And two whole years are lost trying to return the phone calls of people who never seem to be in.

Furthermore, four years in our lives are spent doing things such as washing dishes, mopping the bathroom floor, vacuuming the rug, and taking out the garbage. Eating takes up six years of our lives, said the study, and waiting for the traffic light to change takes up five months.

Well, except for the eating, all that sounds pretty awful. But these statistics could definitely have a brighter side. For instance, on the same basis, one might say we spend one whole year in our lives watching gorgeous sunsets. We probably laugh for something like seven and a half years and are entertained for eight. Maybe we spend nine years, four months, two weeks, and a day — making love (just a guess).

Come to think of it, life ain't so bad.

Expressing their concern for the environment, an estimated 20 million people across the country participate in the first Earth Day.

■ *You might be surprised to discover that certain measurements that we consider arbitrary — such as the length of a furrow — are in fact quite precise, and that some measurements that seem precise to us now — such as inches and feet — actually originated as rather random measures.*

How Long Is a Furrow?

BY WINIFRED H. SCHEIB

HOW LONG IS A FURROW? ASK this question of an experienced Yankee farmer, and he'll probably drawl, "Well, that depends." Yet in the English system of measurements that we Americans inherited, the length of a furrow was established at 220 yards by decree of the Tudor kings, and a furrow-long became a furlong, or one-eighth of a mile.

Today we accept many common units of measurement without realizing that they exist because some early ruler pronounced that they would be so. Take the foot, for example; this basic measurement is based on the length of the human foot. There are a lot of corns and bunions around as testimony to the fact that human feet vary considerably in size, so it was usually the

1970

The Postal Reorganization Act creates the U.S. Postal Service, an independent agency of the federal government. Previously, the Post Office Department was run by the postmaster general, a member of the president's cabinet.

chieftain's foot that determined the standard. Thus it was also with the inch, originally a thumb's breadth, depending upon who was under whose thumb.

"Make yourself an ark," God instructed Noah, "three hundred cubits long, fifty cubits wide, and thirty cubits high."

Noah, as we are all aware, was quite willing to get busy on an ark, but how long was a cubit? It turned out to be the distance from the elbow to the tip of the middle finger, and as long as Noah was boss of the construction project, he undoubtedly used his own body measurements, the result being that a cubit came to be about 18 inches.

Measurements went along in this haphazard fashion for centuries, and many tribal wars possibly were caused because one leader's foot was longer than that of some equally powerful rival. The Romans, however, were great or-

As conquerors do, the Romans introduced this 5,000-foot mile into Britain. . . .

By statute of [Queen Elizabeth I], the mile was increased to 5,280 feet so that 8 furlongs would fit into it neatly.

ganizers, and they needed some standardized system to keep the empire in line. They insisted that the mile be defined as 1,000 paces, a pace being 5 Roman feet, an easy double step for a lusty Roman legionary.

As conquerors do, the Romans introduced this 5,000-foot mile into Britain. That probably would be the distance of our mile today if it were not for Queen Elizabeth I. In her reign, it was decided that this Roman mile was most inconvenient in England, as it failed to accommodate our old friend the furlong. By statute of the queen, the mile was increased to 5,280 feet so that 8 furlongs would fit into it neatly.

English royalty was a domineering lot when it came to measurements. Tradition says that it was Henry I who decreed that the yard should be the distance from the tip of his nose

1970

IBM (International Business Machines) invents the floppy disk.

to the end of his thumb, a measurement still beloved by Yankee housewives at yardage counters. The Saxon kings had previously been content to consider a yard as being the length of the girdle around the waist. Perhaps Henry I was slimmer through the middle than his predecessors and used his prerogative to change the yard for some kingly gain.

At any rate, this was the case with Charles I of England when he decided to increase his revenues with a tax on milk, honey, and wine as measured by the "jack" or "jackpot." Not only did he impose the tax, but he also reduced the size of the jack, which was half a gill or four fluid ounces. Some scholars maintain that the old nursery rhyme about Jack and Jill is a 17th-century protest song against this royal skulduggery, for if the jack fell in value, would not the gill come tumbling after?

If most of our early colonists had been French instead of English, our own schoolchildren would not be droning through arbitrary tables about how many inches go into a yard, how many ounces into a gallon, and how many pounds into a ton.

In matters involving taxation, this flexibility of measurement almost always worked out to the ruler's advantage. The acre, for example, was, in British tradition, the amount of land a man could plow in a day with a team of oxen. Obviously, much maneuvering was possible here, as an acre would vary according to the type of terrain as well as the ambition of the farmer and his animals. With such imprecise standards, it's no wonder the poor farmer found it hard to buy shoes for his children.

When it came to shoes, the nobility naturally had the best chance of being well shod, yet it may have been a farmer who decided that footwear should be measured by the length of a barleycorn. If you wore a size 12, your shoes were 12 barleycorns long, and each full size was 1 barleycorn longer than the preceding one. Though much barleycorn has long

1971

The 26th Amendment to the
U.S. Constitution lowers the voting
age from 21 to 18 in all elections.

since been diverted to the manufacture of whiskey and malt liquors, we are still measuring shoes by barleycorns. If you don't believe this, ask your shoe salesperson whether your size 12 isn't one-third inch longer than a size 11. That's a barleycorn, John.

The measurement whims of English royalty were transplanted to New England with the British colonists. Today most American units roughly parallel the British ones. That is, they *did*. In recent years, Britain elected to join most of the rest of the world in using metric measurements, and, as the other Commonwealth countries follow suit, the United States will be alone in conforming to a system largely evolved by the dictates of long-dead royalty.

If most of our early colonists had been French instead of English, our own schoolchildren would not be droning through arbitrary tables about how many inches go into a yard, how many ounces into a gallon, and how many pounds into a ton. The practical French adopted the metric system back in 1791, thereby guaranteeing their offspring freedom from all but decimal fractions thenceforth. The logical terminology of the metric system applies whether the units are of length, weight, volume, or electrical output; a "kilo" always means a thousand, whether it is meters, grams, liters, or watts.

Many people are now wondering whether measurements that were good enough for the "in-group" in ancient times are not archaic in the era of computers, space exploration,

When the new Moon falls on a Saturday, the following 20 days will be wet and windy.

and international trade. Conversion to the metric system would be expensive for American manufacturers and require a drastic change of habit by all of us Yankees.

If you could ask the opinion of one of the Tudor kings, he might reply, "In these times, our English measures can't survive fur long."

1971

The Greenpeace Foundation, an international organization to protect the Earth's environment, is founded in Vancouver, Canada.

FARMER'S CALENDAR

Mowing to Maryland

HAVING MADE the necessary measurements and finished a series of computations, I have discovered that by summer's end, I will have walked, in the course of cutting the grass in my backyard, a distance of a little over 7 miles. I worked that out by mapping the yard, finding its area, measuring the swath cut by my mower, figuring out how many passes the mower took to cut the whole area of the yard, dividing, and multiplying. The result, 7.3 miles, seemed insufficiently remarkable, however, so I extrapolated it over a lifetime of mowing and arrived at a prospective total of miles walked by me in pushing a lawn mower around my yard: 292, or the distance from this house to Havre de Grace, Maryland. *That's more like it,* I thought.

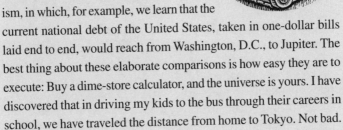

I decided to go through the process just recounted for the sake of applying to my own humble life the kind of grandiose statistical translation so common in journalism, in which, for example, we learn that the current national debt of the United States, taken in one-dollar bills laid end to end, would reach from Washington, D.C., to Jupiter. The best thing about these elaborate comparisons is how easy they are to execute: Buy a dime-store calculator, and the universe is yours. I have discovered that in driving my kids to the bus through their careers in school, we have traveled the distance from home to Tokyo. Not bad.

In the end, though, I found, arrived a certain ennui. Havre de Grace is a long way to push a mower, Jupiter longer still. These majestic comparisons are offered by clever writers who wish to make abstract mathematical facts accessible to peasants, but in the end they don't tell us anything that helps. They only make us tired.

1971

The television sitcom *All in the Family,* featuring outspoken bigot Archie Bunker, premieres.

How to Become a Prophet

HERE'S A PREDICTION: At the start of the new millennium, people will be nervous about the future. And that means big opportunities for prophets.

In the old days, it took *years* to establish yourself as a big-time prophet. You had to journey to far-off lands, wear poorly cured animal skins, and run the risk of martyrdom in order to make a splash. Now we have the Internet. Set up a Web site with a snazzy URL, post your most attention-grabbing prophecies, and bingo — in less than 24 hours, you're being denounced by Responsible Prophets for reckless disregard of (their) revealed truth.

H. L. Mencken once said, "The prophesying business is like writing fugues; it is fatal to everyone save the man of absolute genius." Mencken was too pessimistic; you don't have to be a genius (or a man) to be a prophet. Just follow a few simple rules.

1. Predict the past. Samuel Goldwyn, the legendary Hollywood

1971

Texas Instruments introduces the first electronic calculator.

producer and malapropist, once advised, "Never make predictions. Especially about the future."

There is more wisdom in that comment than you might think. Just about anything that might happen has happened before, and it's a safe bet it will happen again — someday. Wars and rumors of war? Guaranteed. Signs and portents in the heavens? A lead-pipe cinch. Earthquakes, volcanoes, floods, famines, plagues, riots, the fall of kingdoms, and the rise of false prophets? Check your daily newspaper.

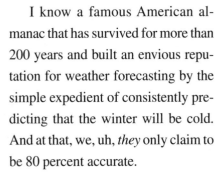

I know a famous American almanac that has survived for more than 200 years and built an envious reputation for weather forecasting by the simple expedient of consistently predicting that the winter will be cold. And at that, we, uh, *they* only claim to be 80 percent accurate.

The trick is not to let yourself be pinned down on when these things are going to happen. Which leads to our next rule . . .

2. Avoid specifics. Geronimo Cardano, a 16th-century astrologer, foretold that King Edward VI of England would fall desperately ill at the age of 55 years, 3 months, and 17 days. Unfortunately, the king ruined everything by dying at the age of 16. Cardano tried to recover his reputation by predicting his own death at the age of 75, and went so far as to kill himself to make it so.

Most successful prophets employ vague but colorful language to get around this problem. "In the fullness of time" is a convenient

1972

The video game Pong, created by Norman Bushnell, is released by Atari.

phrase, if a bit archaic. "Lo, it shall come to pass" has a nice ring to it. Modern prophets like to invent new words, or new uses for old words, to attract attention and elude exactitude. Faith Popcorn is one of the best at this. She not only came up with "cocooning" and "clicking," but she also came up with "Faith Popcorn."

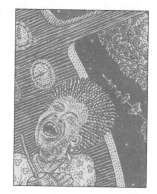

Another way to escape is to make sure your prophesied events take place far enough in the future that nobody currently living will be around long enough to see you proved wrong. Guy Murchie's "What Will the Future Bring?" makes casual use of phrases such as "within a millennium or two" and "by the fourth millennium." Anything might happen in the long run. As the economist John Maynard Keyes pointed out, "In the long run, we are all dead."

3. Predict the obvious. You have to stay in touch with current events. For example, a smart would-be prophet would have looked at the newspapers in the late fall of 1998 and issued a prophecy that sounded something like this: "Lo, there will be signs and portents in the heavens [the Leonid meteor shower comes every November]. And there will be a great wailing and gnashing of teeth [midterm elections], and a mighty man of the South [Bill Clinton or Newt Gingrich — they couldn't *both* win] will fall, yea, even unto the dust. And the false prophets [the media] will be confounded."

A corollary of this might be, "Predict what's *possible*." For example, saying the Moon will turn the color of blood is not only

1972

Sally Stanford becomes the first (known) former bordello madam to be elected mayor of a U.S. city — Sausalito, California.

poetic and exciting; it's something that happens every now and then under certain atmospheric conditions. But you don't want to predict that the Moon will turn lime green.

4. Leave home. As it says in the Bible, "A prophet is not without honor, save in his own country." A guy on a city street raving about the end of the world hardly merits a passing glance. Old Frank the hermit, who lives in an unfinished foundation just outside of town and claims to be Woodrow Wilson, has trouble recruiting members of his League of Nations. And your Uncle Ike, who has been intercepting E-mail from the Trilateral Commission

through his fillings ever since that unfortunate incident with the sump pump, almost never sees his letters to the editor published. You, a prophet? Get a grip. We've known you all your life.

Ah, but bill yourself as the Master Sukkimam, just in from the foothills of Bangladesh, and people will sit up and take notice. List a few advanced degrees from foreign educational institutions (the University of Illyria, Freedonia Technical-Mystical Institute, the Center for Intergalactic Pulchritude), and you'll be invited to the best parties.

5. Leave yourself an out. When I was a freshman in college, my professor in introductory psychology told us about something called cognitive dissonance. If I remember correctly, the term refers to situations in which the facts conflict with what we wish to believe. Very often, in such situations, we find a way to ignore, deny, or distort the facts so as to defend a cherished belief or activity.

1972

Richard Leakey discovers a
2.5-million-year-old human skull
in Kenya.

For example, the professor said, a cigarette smoker, confronted with studies showing links between smoking and cancer, heart disease, and other illnesses, experiences cognitive dissonance. He may resolve it by quitting smoking, but more likely he will choose to believe that the studies are wrong. Or, even if he accepts the validity of the studies, he may say, "Nobody lives forever," and light up.

Another example the professor used was flying saucer cults. Every now and then (especially approaching a new millennium), some prophet or other (such as Montanus or William Miller — see "Doomsday: It's Always Just Ahead") warns that the Earth is about to be destroyed but that the faithful will be saved. Often the faithful are ordered to gather in high places, where they will be picked up in the nick of time by angels — or a flying saucer. So the faithful pack their bags, close their bank accounts, quit their jobs, and show up on the mountaintop at the appointed time. No flying saucer. No end of the Earth. They all go home disillusioned and resolve never to be suckered again, right?

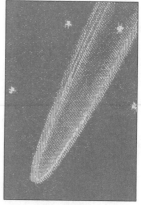

Wrong. *They believe in the prophet more strongly than ever.* Why? Cognitive dissonance. The clever prophet left himself an out. Maybe it was the wrong mountaintop. Maybe his calculations of the time of the Earth's destruction were off. Or, more likely, the prophet appears to his people and says, "Your faith has saved the whole world! God was so impressed that you quit your jobs and came up here that he's called off the Apocalypse!"

1974

American baseball great Hank Aaron hits his 715th home run, breaking Babe Ruth's career record 714 home runs.

Well, it's not every day one gets to save the Earth. Those folks go home a little cold and stiff but feeling pretty darn good about themselves — and their prophet.

Next time you read or hear about predictions of the end of the world, notice how they start with statements like this: "If humankind doesn't get its act together, the following humongous and grossly terrifying calamity is going to happen." See? A convenient out.

6. Predict interesting stuff. I once represented *The Old Farmer's Almanac* on Geraldo Rivera's TV show (the old one, before he got respectable). It was taped for a New Year's Day broadcast, and the theme was "What to Expect in the Coming Year."

The guests included a Hollywood astrologer, a specialist in fashion trends, a political pundit, an expert in economic forecasting, and me, the hick from New Hampshire. Guess who got the most questions from the studio audience?

I gave it my best shot. Before the cameras rolled, the director told us he'd begin the show by focusing briefly on each of us for a

quick prediction. "Make it short and exciting," he advised us. As I was on the extreme end of the line, I went first.

"What's happening in the weather?" the announcer boomed.

"Hurricanes early and often," I said.

"Great!" the director cried.

"What's the latest in fashion?"

"Legs and cleavage!" shouted the fashion maven.

1974

Nineteen-year-old Bill Gates founds Microsoft with Paul Allen, 22. Microsoft will become one of the world's largest producers of microcomputer software.

"Perfect!"

"What do the stars tell us about the stars?"

"Michael Jackson hears wedding bells!" the astrologer twinkled. The director was in ecstasy.

And so on down the line, until he reached the economic forecaster.

"What's going on in the economy?"

"Big business will look more like small business, as executives try to respond more quickly to market trends, while medium-size business —"

"Cut!" the director cried.

"I wasn't finished," the economic forecaster said.

"Shorter. More exciting," said the director. "Let's try it again, shall we?"

"What's going on in the economy?" the announcer intoned.

"Big business will look to small business for models of economic behavior, while —"

"Cut!"

You get the picture, even if the economic forecaster never did. The folks wanted to know whom Michael Jackson was going to marry. The astrologer was the star of the show. None of the rest of us got a single question.

By the way, the astrologer predicted that Michael would marry Whitney Houston. He actually married Lisa Marie Presley. And that poor clueless economic forecaster was dead right: Big companies did start imitating smaller ones. But who cares? The successful prophet is often wrong but never boring.

Tim Clark

1975

Garry Trudeau's "Doonesbury" becomes the first comic strip to win the Pulitzer Prize for editorial cartoons.

■ *A supernova will explode near the Earth, or we'll all drown in the floods from melting polar ice caps. Maybe we'll collide with a large asteroid. Then there are, of course, good old famine, disease, and war. Whatever. Mankind invariably seems to have the urge to bring on a day of reckoning.*

Doomsday: It's Always Just Ahead

BY TIM CLARK

IN 1755 A SEVERE EARTHQUAKE shook New England. One witness described the people's reaction to it this way: "Upon the first Shock of the Earthquake, many Persons jump'd out of their Beds, and ran immediately into the Streets, while others sprung to the Windows, trembling, and seeing their Neighbours, as it were naked, *shrieked with Apprehension of its being the Day of Judgment,* and some tho't they heard the LAST TRUMP sounding, and cry'd out for Mercy."

Doomsday was deferred. But the belief in an impending Day of Judgment lived on, as it has throughout human history. People look forward to it joyfully as a Second Coming, or fearfully as Armageddon, or with scientific interest as the inevitable evolution of our planet. And as long as there are those who believe that The End Is Near, there will be others who will try to predict the exact moment of its arrival.

So far, the accuracy of Doomsday predictions has been disappointing. A few examples:

■ During the second century A.D., a prophet called Montanus announced that the New Jerusalem would come to Earth on a plain in Phrygia, which we now call Turkey. Many thousands of his adherents left their homes and settled in the area to await the great event. Montanus predicted the imminent end for seven years in succession before he died. In spite of that, the cult of Montanism flourished.

■ Various arcane mathematical formulas have been used to predict Doomsday, most of them based on the Book of Revelation by St. John the Divine, which is an extraordinary vision of the struggle between the forces of good and evil. Revelation predicts that Christ will reign for a thousand years, and so A.D. 1000 was thought by many to mark the end of the millennium. After its passing, some recalculated that the millennium would end in 1030 (a thousand years after Christ's death). A great deal of excitement centered on the year 1260, because that number appears in the Book of

1975

The first personal computer, the Altair 8800, goes on the market.

Revelation, and dates ending in 33 continued to figure prominently in prophecies of Doom: The End was predicted in 1533, 1733, and 1933 by various experts and scholars. Another school of thought seized on 1998, that being the number of weeks Christ lived on Earth, according to their calculations. Others have looked to the year 2000, which is a nice round number with an apocalyptic ring to it.

■ Another approach to Doomsday predictions might be termed astrological/historical. In 1524 the planets Saturn, Mars, and Jupiter appeared in the constellation of Pisces, leading to predictions of a Second Flood. The attack of the Spanish Armada on England in 1588 and the Great Fire of London in 1666 also convinced many that the world was about to end, as did the earthquakes in New England in 1727 and 1755.

Some famous people were interested in predicting Doomsday. Cotton Mather, the great Puritan thinker of Massa-

During the second century A.D., a prophet called Montanus announced that the New Jerusalem would come to Earth on a plain in Phrygia. . . . Montanus predicted the imminent end for seven years in succession before he died.

chusetts, published a sermon called "Things to Be Look'd For" in 1691, hinting that the Day of Judgment might be imminent. The following year, in another

1976

The United States celebrates its Bicentennial, marking the 200th anniversary of its independence.

sermon, he predicted that it might arrive as soon as 1697. When that year passed without event, he was not discouraged and returned to his calculations. The next date he chose was 1736, but he later changed that to 1716.

One of Mather's contemporaries, Samuel Sewall, was more interested in where the New Jerusalem would be located. His research eventually fixed the spot as Mexico, a conclusion supported by the astronomer Timothy Clark, who observed that "a line drawn to the comet [which had been recently discovered] strikes just upon Mexico." A number of Massachusetts Puritan families discussed moving south to the Carolinas to be nearer to the Holy City.

Perhaps the single most famous and widely believed prophet of Doom was William Miller, founder of the Adventists, who began in 1831 to preach that the world would end in or about the year 1843. Miller estimated that as many as 100,000 persons believed in his prophecy, and as the fatal year approached, there were reports of many Millerites preparing to meet their Maker. It is hard to determine the accuracy of such reports, which tended to come from the popular press. One story said that a New Hampshire adherent of Miller's views put on white robes, climbed a tree, and tried to fly up to heaven, thus meeting his Maker as a result of a broken neck.

The passing of the year 1843 became known as the First Disappointment among the Millerites. In spite of that, a new date was set by some of Miller's followers, although they refused to be specific. The new date was October 22, 1844. It later came to be called the Great Disappointment. The Millerite movement collapsed in 1845, although in time it produced as an offshoot the Seventh-Day Adventists, who still believe in the imminent Second Coming.

There are still people trying to decipher the Book of Revelation, with its seven seals, seven vials, seven trumpets, beasts, Whore of Babylon, and other colorful ingredients. But

1976

U.S. Viking probes
land on Mars.

there is now a growing community of Doomsday prophets working the scientific side of the street. They foresee the end of the world not in terms of rivers of blood or plagues of hailstones, but in catastrophes ecological and astronomical.

In the early 1980s, Dr. George C. Reid of the Aeronomy Laboratory of the National Oceanic and Atmospheric Administration suggested two possible scenarios for the destruction of our planet. The most frightful one described the explosion of some nearby star — a supernova — that could vaporize our entire solar system if it occurred near enough. Such a stupendous explosion, even one occurring 60 light-years away (1 light-year is about 6 trillion miles) could erase life on Earth with deadly radiation. Dr. Reid said that such an explosion should not occur in our vicinity but once in a hundred million years. But before you heave a sigh of relief, be advised that geological evidence indicates that there has been no nearby supernova in the past 500 million years. Statistically speaking, we may be living on borrowed time.

Closer to home, our own Sun could be a menace. Although astronomers expect our local star to expand and engulf the Earth eventually, they say that time is still comfortably distant — 3 billion to 4 billion years away. But Dr. Reid and his colleagues raised the possibility that a deterioration of the Earth's protective magnetic field could expose life on this planet to deadly ultraviolet radiation. The magnetic field, scientists say, has a tendency to deteriorate and strengthen periodically. It is now in a period of declining strength.

Either of these catastrophes — the nearby supernova or the weakened magnetic field — might explain the relatively sudden extermination of the dinosaurs that once ruled the planet, which is still a mystery.

If radiation seems an unlikely end, consider the possible effects of a cosmic traffic accident — the collision of this planet with a large asteroid or a comet. Some authori-

> *The most frightful [scenario] described the explosion of some nearby star — a supernova — that could vaporize our entire solar system if it occurred near enough. Such a stupendous explosion, even one occurring 60 light-years away ... could erase life on Earth with deadly radiation.*

1977

The "King of Rock and Roll," Elvis Presley, dies.

ties estimate that the Earth has been struck by large extraterrestrial objects a mile or more in diameter 50,000 times in the past 500 million years. The evidence is found in huge impact craters, many of them in Canada, where the glaciers scraped away obscuring layers of sediment. One of those craters, in Quebec, is more than 40 miles in diameter.

A different but equally ghastly possibility in the minds of some scientists is widespread ecological disruption caused by the greenhouse effect. The burning of fossil fuels such as coal, oil, and wood release carbon dioxide into the atmosphere in much greater amounts than ever before. As it accumulates in the atmosphere, the carbon dioxide, or CO_2, acts like a one-way mirror, permitting solar radiation to pass through it but keeping it from being reflected back out into space. Thus, just as a greenhouse creates and maintains a warm atmosphere for indoor plants, the greenhouse effect would warm up the Earth's surface to the point where, eventually, ecological disaster would erupt. Deserts could increase in some areas, and the polar ice caps could melt and flood coastal areas, which contain most of the world's population.

Back in the early 1980s, Dr. Dewey McLean, a geologist at the Virginia Polytechnic Institute, said that at the rate carbon dioxide is increasing in the atmosphere, global average temperatures could rise by six degrees in the next hundred years — more than enough to trigger some profound changes in the planetary ecological balance.

In addition to these complicated problems, there remain some of

There remain some of the oldest threats to mankind: famine, disease, and war. Even though the Earth's population growth has begun to level off, most of the world's inhabitants live dangerously near the subsistence level in terms of food.

Xavier Roberts begins making dolls he calls Little People. In 1983 the dolls will be mass-produced and sold as Cabbage Patch Kids.

the oldest threats to mankind: famine, disease, and war. Even though the Earth's population growth has begun to level off, most of the world's inhabitants live dangerously near the subsistence level in terms of food. And although great progress has been made in eradicating the ancient plagues of mankind such as smallpox, medical experts admit that there might arise new strains of disease fatal to man, or to the plants and animals on which he depends for survival, especially when one considers the current research into the creation of new life forms by manipulation of DNA. As for war, it has always acted as a final solution to disputes over insufficient resources or living space.

With so many forms of annihilation seemingly upon us, why bother to get up every morn-

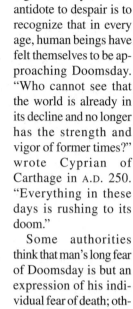

In every age, human beings have felt themselves to be approaching Doomsday. "Who cannot see that the world is already in its decline and no longer has the strength and vigor of former times?" wrote Cyprian of Carthage in A.D. 250.

ing? Probably the best antidote to despair is to recognize that in every age, human beings have felt themselves to be approaching Doomsday. "Who cannot see that the world is already in its decline and no longer has the strength and vigor of former times?" wrote Cyprian of Carthage in A.D. 250. "Everything in these days is rushing to its doom."

Some authorities think that man's long fear of Doomsday is but an expression of his individual fear of death; others consider it part of our collective unconscious, a shared dream as old as man himself. But in much of the rhetoric of Doomsday throughout history, there has been a paradoxical emphasis on the future. It is as if the prophets of Doom have held The End over our heads like a stick, using it as a threat to achieve spiritual reforms.

1977

Star Wars wows moviegoers with its special effects and interstellar adventure.

If You Can Understand Catastrophe Options, You're a Genius (or a Fool)

EMANATING FROM unlikely origins on the volatile trading floor of the Chicago Board of Trade comes a glimmer of hope for softening the economic blow of high winds, flooding, earthquakes, volcanoes, tidal waves, even asteroid collisions — and even for predicting their occurrence. It's a financial device called catastrophe options contracts. "Cat options," as they are called, are emerging as a way for individuals, insurers, and entire nations to weather the tremendous costs of events such as 1992's Hurricane Andrew (estimated $20 billion in losses) by spreading the costs around.

And because so much money is at risk, "cat option investors" are scouring the universe for every available scientific indicator of an upcoming disaster. If you're concerned about the potential for disaster in your area, consider tossing out the Ouija board and reading the financial columns instead.

Catastrophe futures work in the way familiar crop futures work: Hedgers (those who are attached to the status quo, such as insurance companies) shift their risk to speculators (who are willing to bet on a change in the status quo in pursuit of profit). Those who want to dabble in this relatively new way to make (or lose) a pile of money buy cat options through Property Claims Services (PCS), a recognized property-

There is no doubt that religions have found the fear of Doomsday an effective recruiting device, a means of keeping the faithful pure in spirit. And many of the current prophets of ecological doom are equally intent on scaring us into changing our habits of life. The greenhouse effect becomes an argument on behalf of alternative forms of energy; the threat of world famine, an argument for birth control programs. The other side of the Doomsday coin has always been the New Jerusalem, the paradise promised to the righteous.

Historian Barbara Tuchman studied the terrible effects of the Black Death, which killed a third of mankind in the 14th century, and

1978

Louise Brown, the first test-tube baby, is born in England. She is the first baby to be conceived outside the body of a woman through a process called in vitro fertilization.

casualty insurance authority for calculating property damage estimates through nine indices for trading at the Chicago Board of Trade. There are five regional indices for the United States; three indices specific to the states of Florida, Texas, and California, and a national index. Each index is based on estimated upcoming quarterly "loss periods" calculated by the insurance industry. If losses for the quarter are less than the price of the index at the time of sale, the speculator earns a profit.

Russ Ray, professor of finance at the University of Louisville's College of Business and Public Administration, described the potential of catastrophe futures in *The Futurist:* "Once they become more common, catastrophe futures may become an invaluable tool for predicting natural catastrophes. . . . This is because futures are nothing more than predicted prices, and people become very good predictors when their own money is on the line."

However, here's one caveat for anyone anxious to jump on the bandwagon: Do not try this at home! Call your broker! And don't be too surprised if he or she has never heard of cat options.

Where else can you make money by betting on how bad the weather's going to be?

Courtesy of David Lord

came up with a message of hope for our own times:

As our century enters its final quarter, I am not persuaded, despite the signs, that the end is necessarily doom. The doomsayers work by extrapolation; they take a trend and extend it, forgetting that the doom factor sooner or later generates a coping mechanism. I have a rule for this situation that is absolute: You cannot extrapolate any series in which the human element intrudes; history — that is, the human narrative — never follows, and will always fool, the scientific curve. I cannot tell you what twists it will take, but I expect that, like our ancestors, we too will muddle through.

1979

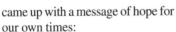

A nuclear-related accident at Three Mile Island, near Middletown, Pennsylvania, causes the evacuation of more than 100,000 people.

■ *Whatever happens to our world in the future, Guy Murchie assures us, won't be an untimely death of the planet, but more akin to a plant's bloom stage. Here is an excerpt from a much longer essay published in 1978.*

The Flowering of the Planet

BY GUY MURCHIE

WHAT IS WRONG WITH THE world these days? All of a sudden, we find ourselves hit by a shortage of fuel and food and a plague of poisons at a time when myriad inscrutable computers are making more and more of the world's vital decisions, people are expressing bewilderment, and astronomers are tuning in for help from the Milky Way.

Actually, if one will just stand back a little and look at things with a long view, such as the perspective of a mature historian or scientist, the world soon reveals itself to be neither dying nor even critically ill. Rather it is germinating!

Indeed, in the eyes of astronomy and evolution, every viable planet or celestial body sooner or later must grow, ripen, ferment, germinate, and, in a cosmic way, come into flower. In the case of a star, this normally means a stupendous explosion called a nova or supernova that suddenly blasts forth heavy atoms, sowing them like seeds over hundreds of light-years of sky.

In a planet it comes more gently, more subtly, yet is no less important as a climactic event that happens once per world.

Understandably, it is disturbing. So is being born. But it is fundamental and vital and, by a seemingly extraordinary coincidence after 5 billion years of evolution, it is taking place on Earth right now in our own age — in the very age the prophets of old, for lack of a better term, referred to as "the latter days" or the "time of the end."

1979

Compact discs (CDs) and CD players become available for the first time.

HOW TO PREDICT THE 𝓕UTURE ACCURATELY EVERY TIME

Astrology Has the Answers — if You Believe

WE LIVE IN an oscillating universe, where cycles repeat and interact with each other," said David Solte of San Diego. For about 20 years, Solte has been analyzing historic and current events in relation to planetary cycles.

Solte began wondering about political astrology in the 1970s and was puzzled that the "birth sign" of the United States would be Cancer (a relatively shy and nurturing sign), based on the July 4, 1776, "birthday" of the country. It was not until he recast the country's chart using the date of the approval of the Articles of Confederation on November 15, 1777, that he felt he had found the real national horoscope. Using the Scorpio perspective, Solte said he found evidence for the nation's superpower ambitions, military might, and love of guns; for our history of Yankee ingenuity and tradition of volunteerism; for status as the world's superconsumer; and for our tendency to continually reinvent ourselves.

Solte believes that the planetary cycle most important in shaping American history is the 14-year Jupiter-Uranus cycle. Every seven years, the two planets are at either opposition or conjunction. Both aspects coincide with major "discovery events," from Columbus's discovery of the New World to Neil Armstrong's landing on the Moon. "No other culture in history is as obsessed with discovery

as we are," Solte said.

What does Solte see for the future? Quoting Thomas Jefferson, he said, "We may consider each generation a distinct nation." To Solte this means a transition from the Age of Gemini, which began in 1964 (according to the astrologically "progressed" chart) and was characterized by experimentation, polarization, and division, to the Age of Cancer, which began in 1995 and will usher in a 30-year "era of nurturing and inner healing."

Courtesy of Peg Boyles

1980

Ted Turner founds CNN (Cable News Network), the world's first live, around-the-clock, all-news TV network.

■ *Feeling chilly? Solar scientists who study farming records in medieval England and geological residue on the shores of Hudson Bay think we may be in for a spell of cold, wet weather. Here's how they use the past to mirror the future.*

Predicting the Weather for the 21st Century

BY CLIFFORD NIELSEN

REMEMBER 20 YEARS AGO, when the weather buzzword was "global cooling"? The Brazilian coffee crop and the grain yield in the Soviet Union had both just been devastated by unusual cold. Glaciers showed an alarming advance throughout the Northern Hemisphere, and for the first time in 80 years, sea ice had become a problem for shipping in both the North Atlantic and the Arctic Ocean. Scientists warned that Earth was headed into a devastating ice age, with particulate matter in the atmosphere (from industrial burning and even the contrails of jet aircraft) acting to screen out sunlight, thus causing the cooling.

But by 1978, the weather was warming up. Since then, the weather buzzword has been "greenhouse warming." Scientists who in the 1970s had predicted massive world crop failures due to frost began to warn of similar crop failures from drought and parching caused by man-made greenhouse gases, primarily carbon dioxide. Given this dramatic seesaw in popular scientific opinion, one might well ask, Is there any means of gauging climate in the near future, the next century, or even the next half century?

The answer is that there may well be. The evidence comes from geological residue on the east coast of Hudson Bay that portrays the dynamic nature of our climate since the Ice Age.

That huge burden of ice, which originated more than 100,000 years ago and grew to more than a mile thick, compressed Earth's crust in a wide area surrounding what is now Hudson Bay. About 12,000 years ago, when the glaciers had completely melted, the land began rising at a predictable rate in what is known as *isostatic rebound*. The continued rising has made it possible to read the record of sea-level fluctuations on the east shore of the bay for the past 10,000 years. That record, in turn, may give us a dis-

---

1980

Mount St. Helens, a volcanic peak in Washington State, erupts. The shock wave and rushing gases flatten surrounding forests.

tant mirror that can reflect future climate.

What is most striking about the Hudson Bay record is a repeated pattern of sea-level rise for 350 to 360 years, followed by a period of falling levels for an identical time span. The best scientific explanation is that sea levels fall when increased cold locks water in glaciers and ice caps; sea levels rise when warming releases the water. The entire cycle from a cold trough, known as a *climatic pessimum,* to a warm peak, called a *climatic optimum,* and back to cold requires 700 to 720 years. If the record of sea-level change during a complete cycle is as accurate as it seems to be, it is possible to look back from our own time to what may well have been a similar period of climate 700 years ago in the late 13th century.

The decade of the 1280s seems to have been a prosperous and optimistic period in Europe. In southern England, small vineyards had flourished for much of the century. The quality of wine produced was high enough to

What is most striking about the Hudson Bay record is a repeated pattern of sea-level rise for 350 to 360 years, followed by a period of falling levels for an identical time span.

worry French vintners, who attempted to have English vineyards closed down as part of a treaty settlement.

The fact that the English vineyards prospered indicates that temperatures were something like 1.1° to 1.6° F warmer than during our own warmest period of the 20th century, a period that has been defined as a climatic optimum.

The relatively good growing conditions during the 13th century were not limited to vineyards. Tillage and general agriculture were practiced at much higher altitudes and latitudes than is possible today. In the British Isles, records exist of farm-

1981

Sandra Day O'Connor becomes the first woman appointed to the U. S. Supreme Court.

ing at altitudes 500 to 600 feet higher than is now practicable. In Scandinavia, grain was cultivated and boreal forests grew 200 miles farther north than has been possible since.

The prosperity of the 1280s did not last long, unfortunately. The best evidence indicates that the vineyards had completely quit producing by 1300 or a bit later. Oncoming colder conditions also made farming impossible in the northern reaches of Scandinavia and the highlands of the British Isles. Continued cooling in the next decade led to one of the greatest weather disasters in Europe. The cold in itself was not as intense as it became in the late 1600s and early 1700s (a period now seen as the depth of what is known as the Little Ice Age), but the cooling caused a phenomenon equally as devastating: torrential rainfall.

Throughout the decade beginning in 1310, crops failed in many parts of Europe because the fields were

The prosperity of the 1280s did not last long, unfortunately. The best evidence indicates that the vineyards had completely quit producing by 1300 or a bit later.

too swampy to support growth. The most disastrous year was 1315, when virtually the entire grain harvest failed in Europe. Great numbers of sheep and cattle also died in *murrains,* or epidemics of disease, that swept the sodden landscapes. So dire was the famine that instances of cannibalism were recorded. It was a disaster thought by many historians to have been the cause of the century of chaos that is best remembered for the Hundred Years' War between England and France.

In Asia, significant flooding of China's central river valleys was common from about 1300 on. The greatest flood, in 1332, led to the deaths of more than 7 million people. Almost every year after 1327 saw famine caused by flooding and poor harvests in much of China. And in 1344, the dikes on the Yellow River were breached, flooding vast areas and causing the dislocation of a previously isolated rodent,

1981

Some firsts in personal computing: IBM introduces its PC, the laptop computer debuts, and the first mouse is available.

which carried fleas that, in turn, were host to the bubonic plague. Within a quarter century, the Black Death was decimating Europe, deepening the misery.

One explanation for that historical quick shift in climate is that the period was marked by a decline in solar activity. Unfortunately, no one in Europe was counting sunspots that early. But during the warm period from 1050 to 1250, the Chinese had recorded what could be called a riot of sunspots. After 1300 accounts of sunspots are rare in Chinese chronicles.

Solar scientists now believe that solar activity became unusually quiet during the early 1300s. They have named that period the Wolf Sunspot Minimum. It was the first of three periods of quiet solar activity, followed by the Spörer Sunspot Minimum (latter part of the 1400s) and Maunder Sun-

One explanation for that historical quick shift in climate is that the period was marked by a decline in solar activity. Unfortunately, no one in Europe was counting sunspots that early.

spot Minimum (late 1600s), all of which are now associated with the colder periods of the Little Ice Age.

Much of this analysis is conjectural. The greatest argument against a solar influence on climate is that the change between an active Sun (the period when sunspots appear) and a quiet Sun is minuscule, only one to three watts per square meter at the top of the atmosphere. Opponents argue that no physical mechanism has been discovered to explain such a solar-climate relationship.

The historical record, however, remains. Sea-level fluctuations along Hudson Bay averaging 710 years have been recorded 14 times, accounting for a span of nearly 10,000 years. By the mid-1600s, sunspots (the few that happened) were finally being counted in Europe. Looking back to that period, a correlation exists between low solar activity

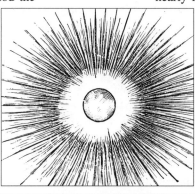

1981

The space shuttle *Columbia,* the first reusable spacecraft, completes a successful test flight.

and falling sea levels caused by cooling. The record since has allowed us to witness exactly half of a Little Ice Age Cycle, a 360-year period during which climate has, with ups and downs, grown progressively warmer while the Sun has become intermittently more active, peaking in intensity in the

Neither fear to die nor refuse to live.

1950s. Sea levels in Hudson Bay have risen proportionally.

Assuming that the Sun and climate follow the anticipated cooling pattern predicted by the Hudson Bay record, the obvious question is, What are the implications for mankind in the 21st century? One viewpoint is that we can adapt to it, as did the 17th-century colonials in North America, who flourished during the coldest period of the Little Ice Age. Because too much rain is deadly to grain crops, development of other crops may well be an answer. During the Little Ice Age in Europe, for example, people made potatoes a staple crop when heavy rains made the grain crop vulnerable.

By contrast, a climate change such as that experienced in 1310 could spell global disaster rivaling the scenarios predicted about global warming. Should the atmosphere cool by as little as 1° F, an onslaught of precipitation similar to that of the 1300s might well be expected. Such continued heavy precipitation is easy to understand in meteorological terms. After a period of great warmth, the oceans, which are highly efficient heat sinks, remain warm, while the atmosphere cools. The combination of cold air and warm water is the perfect recipe for deluge after deluge.

Given the record, it might almost be hoped that greenhouse warming would occur to help mitigate any coming cool period. A repeat of the 50 or so years of the Wolf Sunspot Minimum may bring about a recurrence, in the coming century, of some of the coldest weather of the past millennium, when ice fairs were held on the frozen Thames, livestock froze in the fields, and hens' eggs were worth their weight in silver.

1981

AIDS (acquired immunodeficiency syndrome) is conclusively identified in the United States and reaches the level of an epidemic worldwide.

■ *Someday a huge wall of ice will scrape Seattle, Chicago, New York, and Boston from the face of the Earth. But not to worry. Surely we'll have something worked out by the time it arrives.*

The Ice Age Is Coming!
The Ice Age Is Coming!

BY CHET RAYMO

ONCE I STOOD WITH A FRIEND ON a high bluff in New Hampshire's White Mountains. "Do you realize," I said, "that 15,000 years ago all of these valleys about us were filled with ice? Only the peaks of the highest mountains stood above the glacier, like islands in a frozen sea. If we had stood here then, the ice would have reached in every direction as far as the eye can see."

"I don't believe it," said my friend.

"But it's true," I insisted.

"Oh, I know it's true," he replied, "but I don't believe it."

I can easily forgive my friend his incredulity. When the Swiss-American geologist Louis Agassiz suggested early in the 19th century that large parts of the northern continents were once covered by glaciers, the idea met with general skepticism. But once people knew what to look for, the evidence for an ice age became persuasive. Today no geologist doubts the former existence of those continent-spanning glaciers.

Ten times during the past million years, ice has advanced from polar regions to cover one-third of the land area of the Earth. When the glaciers achieved their maximum

1982

Dr. Barney Clark becomes the first recipient of an artificial heart. Dr. Robert Jarvik designed the heart and is a member of the surgical team.

extent, North America was mantled by ice as far south as Cape Cod, Massachusetts; Long Island, New York; and the valleys of the Ohio and Missouri Rivers.

If the cycle of glaciation continues, sometime within the next few thousand years the planet will begin to slip into another era of ice. How would we recognize the initiation of an ice age? The answer: We wouldn't, at least not within a lifetime or even many lifetimes. There are too many short-term climate controls that would likely mask the initiation of a true ice age.

Major volcanic eruptions can significantly affect the climate. The eruption of the volcano Tambora in the East Indies in 1815 caused the famous "Year Without a Summer," when snow and freezes ruined crops in New England in June and August. The explosion of Krakatoa in 1883 spread dust into the stratosphere that cooled the Earth for several years.

The so-called Little Ice Age, which chilled the Earth from 1400 to 1850, is believed by some scientists to have been caused by a slight change in the energy output of the Sun. The coldest of those years coincided with a period of minimum sunspot activity,

Sooner or later, most climatologists agree, the glacial cycle will prevail, and an ice age will return.

called the Maunder Sunspot Minimum. Several other historical sunspot minima have been tentatively identified and correlated with a cooling climate (see page 351). There is some evidence that even now the energy output of the Sun is slightly waning.

Our own interventions in climate might also mask the return of the ice. By burning fossil fuels, we are dumping vast quantities of carbon dioxide into the atmosphere. By cutting down the tropical forests, we are diminishing the Earth's capacity to remove carbon dioxide from the atmosphere. Carbon dioxide acts like glass in a greenhouse: It traps the Sun's heat. The trapped heat may tend to keep the Earth warm. Carbon dioxide also can stimulate plant growth, which in turn gives off oxygen. Oxygen has a *cooling* effect — so perhaps the whole thing becomes a standoff.

But sooner or later, most climatologists agree, the glacial cycle will prevail, and an ice age will return. What then? There will be a downward trend of temperature prevailing over many millennia. The average drop in global temperature during the most recent ice age was about 10° F. By contrast, the temperature drop during the Little Ice Age or the

A network for the use of cellular phones is established in the United States.

Year Without a Summer was less than 2° F. If the pattern of the last Ice Age is repeated, 80,000 years will be required for the full 10-degree drop.

Meanwhile, glaciers will begin an inexorable glide down mountain valleys. On the tundra of central Canada, ice sheets will begin to grow and move radically outward under the influence of their own weight. They will push down across the continent like mile-thick bulldozers, scooping, grinding, and breaking. They will plane off the tops of hills and excavate valleys. They will scrape Seattle, Chicago, New York, and Boston from the face of the Earth.

The average progress of the ice toward its southern terminus will be measured in tens of feet per year. On the human time scale, the growth of the ice sheets will be almost imperceptible. Eighteen thousand years ago, when the Earth was last in the deep freeze, it was our Cro-Magnon ancestors who hunted mammoths on the frozen tundra. One hundred thousand years ago, when the climate was last as warm as it is today, Neanderthal humans enjoyed the balmy weather.

If humans are around to experience the beginning of the next cycle of glaciation, they will have plenty of time to respond to impending disaster. As the ice caps build, the level of the sea will drop. New York will have ceased to be a port tens of thousands of years before a wall of ice appears in the Bronx. One by one, northern cities will be abandoned and new cities built farther south on land now covered by the sea.

It was the month of June when I challenged my friend to imagine New Hampshire buried in ice. We were standing at the rim of Tuckerman Ravine on the shoulder of Mount Washington. In the bowl-shaped valley below us, a few dedicated skiers exploited the last remaining fields of winter snow in all of New England.

The snow in Tuckerman is sometimes skiable into July; not many weeks later, the first of the next

Unlooked-for often comes.

winter's snow arrives. Only a modest drop of average temperature would allow snow to go unmelted from one winter to the next. Year by year, the snow cover would thicken and turn to ice.

"Keep your eye on this place," I said to my friend. "One of the first signs of a returning ice age will be an alpine glacier growing once more in Tuckerman Ravine."

1983

Sally Ride becomes the first American woman to travel in space.

HOW TO PREDICT THE *F*UTURE ACCURATELY EVERY TIME

Volcanoes: Perhaps Mountains Sing Before They Erupt

FIGURING OUT when a known volcano will erupt next is a science in its infancy. Volcanologists study the eruptive history of an area and monitor it with sensitive equipment but still have trouble predicting (accurately) the timing, size, and nature of any eruption. Time and again, veteran scientists have been caught by surprise, sometimes with fatal results, while studying a volcano thought to be quiet.

As it turns out, volcanic mountains aren't quiet at all. Scientists put sensitive recording devices on the slopes of Mount Semeru, an active volcano and the highest mountain on the Indonesian island of Java. The researchers hoped that underground movement of gases and magma would send distinct vibrations toward the surface, and they expected to find irregular sounds much like the rumbling of a hungry stomach. To their surprise, they recorded a single, deep, constant sound, like one note from a pipe organ. The tone, or song, of the mountain was measured at below 8 hertz, inaudible to human ears (our low threshold is 20 hertz). What the scientists do not yet know is the meaning of this lonely note sounding from the heart of a volcano.

1984

A wristwatch-size television set
is available to consumers.

■ *A California geologist predicts earthquakes — not by fancy seismic monitoring, but by counting the number of lost pets in the classified ads! In 1991 we featured this story on James Berkland's successful earthquake predictions — a success that continues to this day.*

The Earthshaking Theories of James Berkland

BY RIC BUCHER

JAMES BERKLAND, A COUNTY geologist with the U.S. Geological Survey (USGS) in the San Francisco area, has anticipated more earthquakes and how big they'll be than anyone inside or outside the scientific community, and he's not about to stop. He stands on his record: 270 predictions over the past 15 years, and in no one year did he miss more than 1 out of 4.

How does he do it? To the dismay of the established scientific community, which is still struggling with the "seismic gap" theory developed by a Japanese scientist early in this century, Berkland does it by counting the number of missing pets in the classified ads and measuring ocean tides. He also classifies such uncharacteristic animal behavior as elephants refusing to have their nails manicured, homing pigeons losing their way during races, worms wriggling up out of the soil, snakes deserting their dens, and confused swarms of bees flying

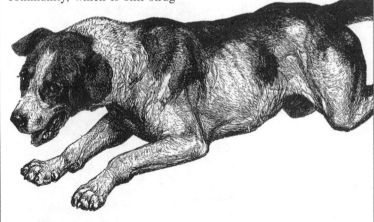

1984

Jaron Lanier takes the concept of 3-D graphics to a new level with his virtual reality. Lanier develops the special goggles, gloves, and software needed for this new interactive experience.

into churches as harbingers of earthquakes.

When the Loma Prieta fault near San Francisco yawned on October 17, 1989, it measured 7.1 on the Richter scale and killed 67 people. Berkland was ready. In September, while most people within driving distance of Candlestick Park, site of the World Series, had been scrambling for tickets, he had been scanning the classified ads. "Someone asked me, 'What numbers of animals advertised as lost would scare you?'" he related. "I told them, 'Oh, about 25 or 26 cats and 60 dogs.'" On September 22, cats listed as missing peaked at 27; dogs reported lost numbered 57.

Berkland warned the people in his office to be ready for a 5-plus magnitude quake before the end of

Short-Term Signals of Earthquakes

ALTHOUGH MANY scientists are concentrating on the ability to make accurate long-term predictions of earthquakes, the following phenomena have been observed to signal imminent quakes.

■ The release of radon, a mildly radioactive gas, from wells.

■ An increase in creep, the slow movement along a fault or gentle tilting of land near a fault.

■ Flashes of bright lights in the sky, possibly related to gas release and dust.

■ A rise or drop in the level of well water.

■ Earthquakes may be more likely when the Moon "rides high" or "runs low" during each lunar cycle or when the Moon is on the equator.

■ An increased intensity of low-frequency electromagnetic waves.

■ Cattle may bellow and plant their feet widely apart for support.

■ Certain weather is thought to presage and accompany earthquakes: fog, mists, darkness, and lurid vapors.

1985

The British Antarctic Survey discovers a hole in the ozone layer over Antarctica.

the month. The end of September came and went; the ground remained quiet. Berkland said that at that point he realized he had been fooled, that what he had taken as foreshadowing an impending medium-size tremor was actually the early signs of a larger jolt. In situations where a record earthquake had struck, the first indication had

come about one month in advance.

He checked the tide tables and found that on October 14, the highest tidal forces in three years would batter the northern California coast. He felt he was on the right track. After noting a second rise in missing cats developing in mid-October, Berkland was convinced. When the number of AWOL cats hit 21, along with 58 missing

When the number of AWOL cats hit 21, along with 58 missing canines, on Friday the 13th of October, [Berkland] convinced the Gilroy Dispatch *to print his prediction.*

canines, on Friday the 13th of October, he convinced the *Gilroy Dispatch* to print his prediction of an earthquake of a magnitude between 6.5 and 7.0 to strike between October 14 and 21.

Most people did not pay heed, but some did. A USGS colleague who lives in a San Jose suburb known as Los Gatos (The Cats) strapped down his water heater the night of October 16. When it, unlike those of his neighbors, survived the October 17 earth-

1985

A severe earthquake rocks Mexico, killing an estimated 5,000 to 20,000 people and leaving more than 100,000 homeless.

quake, he sent Berkland a note of thanks. Another family thanked him for his advice, which had led them to safeguard $6,000 worth of china and crystal.

Berkland's belief that unusual animal behavior can serve as alerts to upcoming seismographic disturbances is illustrated by this example: A woman who owns a well-behaved dog reported to Berkland that her dog had disappeared a few days before the October 17 earthquake. The dog returned a few hours after the quake, caked with mud and choking on a willow stick. Willow bark, Berkland explained, contains an ingredient that Indians used to cure headaches. He deduced that the dog had developed a whopping headache from the impending quake and attempted to use the same remedy.

Even as recovery drives were being launched to restore order after the October earthquake, Berkland warned publicly that a second serious vibration would assault the Bay Area in November. The *Oakland Tribune* contributed to the panic by stating that Berkland expected the November quake to register 8-plus on the Richter scale. Although the paper later ran a correction stating that Berkland's prediction was for a tremor between 3.5 and 5.5 (which actually occurred), Berkland was in trouble with his superiors at the USGS; he was suspended from his job for more than two months for causing undue panic. He was reinstated with the understanding that he would not make predictions while on the job.

In any event, catastrophic or otherwise, Berkland will continue to read the classifieds and the tide tables, collect data and documented episodes of bizarre animal behavior, and use that information to predict the time, place, and severity of future earthquakes.

You must shift your sail with the wind.

1986

The U.S. Congress establishes a national holiday in honor of Martin Luther King Jr., to be observed on the third Monday in January.

HOW TO PREDICT THE *F*UTURE ACCURATELY EVERY TIME

Earthquakes: When in Doubt, Apply the Chaos Theory

A NEW THEORY about earthquake mechanics emerged late in 1995 when two researchers, a geophysicist from the United States and a seismologist from Chile, proposed that explosive quakes along known fault lines can be predicted according to the position of the two colliding tectonic plates. When the plates are pushing against each other from opposite directions, increased friction makes large earthquakes more likely. When one plate dives beneath another and both are moving in the same direction, there is less friction and less likelihood of a cataclysmic quake. Although this theory may not be a predictor of whether a given location will have an earthquake tomorrow, it may be useful in identifying high-risk areas. According to this model, one such area considered likely to produce a powerful earthquake is the northern California–Oregon–Washington basin known to seismologists as Cascadia.

However, many leading seismologists have concluded that earthquakes are inherently unpredictable, a classic example of a chaotic sys-

tem. Those who support the chaos theory point out that the Earth's crust is always shifting, especially along fault lines, and small earthquakes occur all the time. For example, in California more than 25,000 small earthquakes a year are detected. For reasons not well understood, occasionally a small earthquake will set off a slightly larger one, and the effect will mushroom into a large quake. Dr. Thomas Heaton, a seismologist at the U.S. Geological Survey in Pasadena, California, hypothesized that a large earthquake may simply be "a small one that ran away." He said that we may never be able to predict which of the small quakes will explode into a large one.

1986

A major accident at the Chernobyl, Ukraine, nuclear power plant results in the release of radiation into the atmosphere that spreads over much of Europe.

FARMER'S CALENDAR

Old Weather Predictors

I F YOU WANT TO KNOW what the future has in store in any field, you ask those especially concerned. Is your interest sports? Ask a player. Is it loan rates? Ask a banker. Is it elections? Ask someone who has to run for office. Skip the experts and find a witness whose own life will be affected by the course of events you're inquiring about. Find someone on the ground, so to speak.

This principle, no more than common sense, is part of the reason people stubbornly hang on to folk weather lore in a scientific age in which that lore ought to be obsolete. Most of us, no doubt, get our weather forecasts from TV and radio — that is, from broadcasters who pass on the conclusions of meteorologists. We have confidence in these scientific forecasts for the best possible reason: We have found them to be generally accurate. Nevertheless, the prescientific indicators of weather — the acorns, groundhogs, woolly bear caterpillars, and so on — are not forgotten. Although they survive mainly as humor, they do survive.

Why don't we let the old weather signs go at last and put all our faith in meteorology? Because meteorology isn't on the ground. Those likable, attractive people on TV, even the scientists whose findings they report, aren't concerned with the weather the way a deer mouse, say, is. If the former get it wrong, they may have to find a job in Sioux Falls. But for them, that's the worst thing that happens. The deer mouse has a different stake. If he underestimates the winter to come and fails to provide in his nest, he starves.

1987

In Yugoslavia, a boy said to be the 5 billionth living human inhabitant of Earth is born.

■ *As we head into the 21st century, perhaps we should rethink how we refer to our planet and Moon. After all, the other planets and their various moons have nice names. Why not ours?*

Is It Time Now for the Earth and the Moon to Have Their Own Names?

BY DENNIS L. MAMMANA

WE KNOW OUR WORLD AS THE Earth. But is that its name? The other planets of our solar system are all named for mythological beings. Venus is the Roman goddess of love and beauty; Mars, the Roman god of war; Jupiter, the king of the Roman gods. But the Earth — what is *it* named for? Dirt?

And what about the Moon? It, too, has fallen between the proverbial cracks. Other planets' satellites have been endowed with beautiful names from mythology: Miranda, Titan, Ganymede, Charon. But our Moon is just, well, "the Moon." The explanation for this dates back many centuries.

"During antiquity, people knew of five planets," explained E. N. Genovese, professor of classics and humanities at San Diego State University. "In the fourth century B.C., they called Jupiter 'Zeus-Star,' Saturn 'Chronos-Star,'

Venus 'Aphrodite-Star,' Mercury 'Hermes-Star,' and Mars 'Aries-Star.' The Moon was given the name 'Selene' in Greek. It's just a generic name for something that shines, as is the Latin 'Luna' — neither word has anything to do with divinities, but they were later applied to divinities of those bodies. This happens frequently in mythology; it's called personification. Then, as mythology develops, be-

The stock market crashes in October when the Dow Jones Industrial Average plummets a record 508 points (22.6 percent).

cause there are two names, people make a separation and lose touch with the original application of the name.

"The same goes for 'Earth.' The word is Germanic — the German word for Earth is *Erde*. It's just a word for the ground or dirt, and it got extended to something larger. Of course, when the word was first derived, people had no sense of the Earth being one of the planets. Once that was established, the name got transferred rather quickly."

This worked just fine for many centuries. Then, in March 1781, astronomer William Herschel found something peculiar among the stars of the constellation Gemini. It was a planet — the first to be discovered since ancient days. Herschel wanted to name it Georgium Sidus after King George III of England, who was then eager to fund his work. Others in Europe thought this was ridiculous and fought it vigorously. The body was finally christened Uranus, following the convention of using mythological names.

Strictly speaking, Uranus was the only Greek name among the Roman names of the planets. But since Uranus was the god of the

The German word for Earth is Erde. It's just a word for the ground or dirt, and it got extended to something larger.

heavens, it seemed appropriate for the first planet found in modern times. With the discovery of Neptune (god of the sea) in 1846 and Pluto (god of the underworld) in 1930, scientists resumed the practice of using the names of Roman gods.

Today, as astronomical discoveries are being made at a record pace, astronomers spend great amounts of time coming up with names. Charged with this task is the Working Group for Planetary System Nomenclature (WG-PSN) of the International Astronomical Union (IAU).

"We try to follow a consistent theme," said Merton Davies of the Rand Corporation, a member of that group back in the early 1990s. "For instance, the names of all except one of the original satellites of Uranus were taken from Shakespeare. So when new satellites were discovered at Uranus, we selected names from Shakespeare. At Neptune, we use a theme of water gods."

Has the IAU ever considered creating and approving a proper name for *our* planet — something to replace the generic terms Earth and Moon? "I suspect not," Davies said. "The main reason is that the names

1987

Archaeologists in Israel unearth a Neanderthal skeleton dating back 60,000 years. Studies indicate that Neanderthal man was anatomically able to talk.

work. They're within the literature, and they're useful in communication. It would be a terrible chore to try to change them."

Granted, there are more pressing problems facing us today. But suppose we did want to name the Earth and the Moon — what might we come up with?

Our first thought might be to call our planet Terra, from which words such as *terrestrial* have sprung. After all, it seems most natural. But it wouldn't fit the scheme — Terra is not the name of a god. More appropriate might be Tellus, the Roman goddess of the earth, protector and developer of the sown seed. (We, then, would be named Tellurians.)

The Moon has been known by many names over the ages: Artemis, Diana, Phoebe, Cynthia, and Selene. Perhaps most fitting is Luna, Roman goddess of the Moon and the months. Future inhabitants of that world might then be known as Lunarians.

At present, of course, it's all academic. The Earth is the Earth, and the Moon is the Moon. And that suits most people just fine. "To me, the most beautiful words are the simplest and the oldest," said Charles Elster, author of the book *There Is No Cow in Moscow.* "They're the most flexible and the most useful. The fixed names of the planets that came from classical mythology are quite lovely. But

you'll never change Earth and Moon."

Beautiful words, yes. Proper names, no. And though it's true that having no official name for our planet and its natural satellite may not seem important now, it may become necessary someday. Imagine the confusion in trying to draw up treaties, diplomatic arrangements, and trade agreements with future human colonists of other worlds without having an official name for ours. And just wait until our first encounter with an extraterrestrial being — one who has visited worlds throughout our galaxy. I'd love to see the smirk on his little green face when we tell him our planet doesn't have a name!

Proverbs contradict each other. That is the wisdom of mankind.

1988

A drought, the worst in more than 50 years, affects one-half of the agricultural counties in the United States.

Predicting Weather by the Moon
(Or is it the elves?)

IS THERE such a thing as "Moon weather"? Country wisdom says that the full Moon brings frosts in spring and fall and periods of extreme cold in winter (see page 259). But researchers are finding that there is a striking correlation between the full Moon and cloudiness, rainfall, and thunderstorms. Astronomer Bob Berman, reporting in *Discover* magazine, wrote that the full Moon raises temperatures in the lower four miles of the Earth's atmosphere by a few hundredths of a degree — a subtle change, to be sure, but not negligible. Some scientists think that the full Moon's gravity is strong enough to distort the Earth's magnetic field, which in turn could trigger thunderstorms.

Which brings us to the subject of elves. These are not Santa's merry workers. To geophysicists, elves are extremely bright flashes of lightning at the very edge of space, high above garden-variety lightning storms. Researchers theorize that elves and their kin, called jets and sprites, introduce large amounts of nitrogen oxides into the stratosphere and just might affect global weather, ozone depletion, and storm formation. Elves materialize in the ionosphere right after large bolts of lightning hit the ground and can appear as fiery disks. (UFOs, anyone?)

Finally, there is, of course, *The Old Farmer's Almanac* method

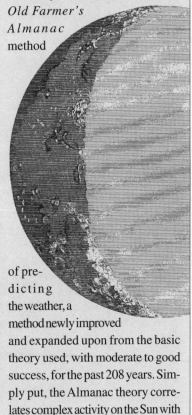

of predicting the weather, a method newly improved and expanded upon from the basic theory used, with moderate to good success, for the past 208 years. Simply put, the Almanac theory correlates complex activity on the Sun with fluctuating weather here on Earth.

1989

Alaska's Prince William Sound is the site of a devastating oil spill (the largest in U.S. history) when the *Exxon Valdez* strikes Bligh Reef.

■ *The ideas expressed in this essay emanated from the mind of Guy Murchie while he was writing and illustrating his book* The Seven Mysteries of Life *(Houghton Mifflin, 1978).*

What Will the Future Bring?

BY GUY MURCHIE

I HAVE NO PARTICULAR CREDENtials as a prophet, but somehow I sense the inadequacy of trying to predict the unknown future by extrapolating from the known past. This sense helps me to visualize a future that is, in many respects, unrelated to the past.

Most obvious is the approaching period of severe famine and deprivation that cannot but increase. Starvation will inevitably become widespread on Earth during droughts in undeveloped and overpopulated tropical regions. But by sometime in the 21st century, if my surmise is right, man will, for the first time, make the sacrifices and decisions resulting in the disarming of all nations. And the ensuing relaxation of tensions will doubtless enhance harmony among all people. At the same time, a world monetary system will stabilize commerce. And a standardized world language,

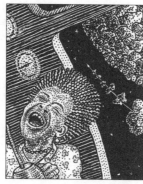

taught in schools on every continent, will increase understanding.

Although economic and political synthesis must exert a conservative influence on man's progress next century, his technological ingenuity need not be so restrained. In fact, that is where Earth's most dramatic changes can be expected.

■ Within a millennium or two, there may even be tunnels straight through the molten heart of the Earth, using natural gravitational power to convey cargoes and passengers anywhere on the surface in 42.2 minutes (that being half the 84.4-minute period of a Schuler pendulum or a satellite orbiting the planet), the 42 minutes made up of falling downward in frictionless acceleration for 21 minutes, then coasting upward again in frictionless deceleration for another 21 minutes according to the natural harmonics of Earth.

■ For airliners, surface tension levitation (as used by

1990

The largest science satellite to date, the Hubble Space Telescope, is launched aboard the space shuttle *Discovery*.

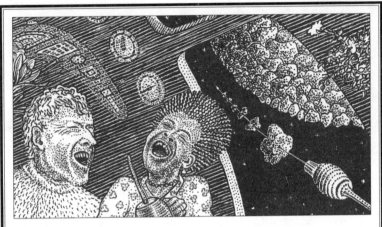

"unwettable" water bugs) is a possibility by the fourth millennium, and there may be cars at ground level rolling on superconductive circular electric current instead of wheels, permitting each vehicle to travel as a solid moving whole without solid moving parts.

■ Next century, fusion power will be used, among other things, for desalting ocean water in massive quantities, and saline agriculture (using seawater) will also grow phenomenally in some areas.

■ Personal two-way television already is developing from an electronic challenge into one in economics, which, when solved, will make it possible to shop, confer, and conduct almost any kind of business at home — something that, in turn, should ease commuting around cities, eventually doing away with rush-hour traffic problems.

■ Medical research is actively studying artificial vision, hearing, smelling, and so on for the sensorially deprived by way of brain waves electronically shaped by sensory instruments and channeled into the visual, auditory, and olfactory centers of the brain. And it has made dramatic progress in the repair, replacement, and improvement of body parts, which means grafting on either artificial organs or natural tissue from another spot if not another body, or possibly inducing the same body to regenerate itself as does a worm.

■ Physicist Gerard K. O'Neill of Princeton proposed harnessing cheap, plentiful solar power in space by building huge, parabolic mirrors there to collect heat and generate electric power to be beamed to Earth. The construction crews and permanent operators with their families will also live in space in great cylindrical "pieces of Earth" a mile in circumference and perhaps half a mile long, containing towns of up to

1991

Disney's *Beauty and the Beast* makes Academy Awards history when it becomes the first animated film to be nominated for "Best Picture."

10,000 people nestling amid wooded farmland with ponds, fish, birds, flowers, atmosphere — indeed everything that might promote a fulfilling life, including Earth-strength "gravity" by rotating the cylinders. Power for the space towns would be generated in pollution-free solar panels between the movable mirrors that would direct sunlight inward for any agreed number of hours per "day," regulating "weather" and "seasons" to common need.

■ More ambitious, in the sense of looking ahead not just thousands but actually millions of years, is the elaborate proposal of another Princeton physicist, Freeman Dyson, of the famous Institute for Advanced Study and former chairman of the Federation of American Scientists. Dyson proposed that an advanced planetary race like man must, in time, redesign and rearrange his entire solar system, not only commandeering its moons and asteroids and reorbiting or towing them about with powerful "space tugs," but even dismantling the giant planets like Jupiter and Saturn and steering asteroid-size chunks of

Dyson proposed that an advanced planetary race like man must, in time, redesign and rearrange his entire solar system . . . commandeering its moons and asteroids and reorbiting or towing them about with powerful "space tugs."

them into orbits nearer the Sun, where they will soon warm up and be made to fall together into moonish spheres that can be tailored into hospitable annexes for expanding man. These spheres will eventually form a kind of doughnut ring of thousands of small, inhabited "planets," using appropriate asteroids as mines for needed minerals, fertilizing some as nurseries or laboratories, rigging others for solar energy.

■ I think the Earth's cities will continue to grow (at a slowing rate), at least into the 21st century. By this time, megalopolises will have spread in crystalline patterns for thousands of miles across America, Europe, Japan, China, India, and even through parts of Africa, South America, and Australia.

■ But the counter-movement (away from concrete and asphalt) will be developing too (at a faster rate), increasing wooded park areas in ratio to city populations, humanizing housing, creating giant automated cities like Babelnoah (designed by Paolo Soleri for 6 million people) and the huge, mobile, floating ones (promoted by Buckminster

1991

A cyclone with winds up to 145 miles per hour strikes coastal areas and offshore islands of Bangladesh, killing 150,000 people. The cyclone causes 20-foot waves.

Fuller) that may begin to populate the oceans any decade now; also smaller idealized cities like Auroville, in southern India, dedicated to Sri Aurobindo and world unity, and shaped like a spiral galaxy, for about 50,000 people on 15 square miles of land; and a wide spectrum of planned villages where everybody can go fishing, to shops or church, and children can walk to school without crossing any streets.

In Conclusion

Of course, it is impossible for any mere human to know the distant future with any certitude, but I cannot help feeling that the familiar think-tank approach to prediction has stressed future technology overmuch in its extrapolation of the obvious accelerations of the recent past, while almost no one mentions the less obvious coming of spiritual maturity that (to me) seems overdue. Many reject out of hand the concept of God as an intelligent humanlike being, but I am convinced that any deep-thinking person will ultimately admit there must be tremendous forces dominating this universe that are hidden and unknowable to us, therefore essentially mysterious and in effect playing the part of a Supreme Being. In consequence, as science and religion intermittently continue to merge toward a rational synthesis, the ancient hypothesis of divinity must sooner or later also regain acceptance as science reaches beyond the tangibility of matter that physicists now explain as waves of energy, and into the measurable cousinhood of all creatures from worms to stars — to the eventual realization that our mortal life on Earth in essence constitutes a school for evolving souls, indeed a school in which the rapidly evolving human spirit is in perpetual transcendence from terrestrial finitude (using the tools of space, time, and self) to the greater life of infinitude (beyond all tools) outside the shell of death.

> **Don't ride the high horse; the fall, when it comes, is hard.**

1991

A 5,000-year-old mummified body is found in the Austrian Alps.

ANECDOTES & PLEASANTRIES

An Old Prediction That Is Soon to Come True

*I*T WAS MADE *by several prominent chiropodists at the turn of the century and announced in a 1903 edition of the* Chicago Record-Herald, *from which the following is excerpted verbatim.*

Now it is asserted that the small toe of the human foot will be crowded out of existence by the end of the present century. Such is the view of chiropodists generally and of physicians who have given the matter more than passing consideration.

Just as, according to Darwin, the tail was crowded out of the human bony skeleton many ages back because it had absolutely no useful function to perform; just as the vermiform appendix, the only apparent function of which is to necessitate dangerous and expensive operations, will eventually find no place in human anatomy, so, according to present indications, the little toe must ultimately disappear altogether.

The conditions prevailing at the present day are such, indeed, that but a short period of evolution will be necessary to bring about this radical change in the human system. The little toe is at its best in childhood, but even then it is seldom much more than an apology for a toe, while it is a fact well known to physicians that after a certain age has been reached, in ninety cases out of a hundred the two end joints of the toe become ankylosed — that is to say, so united as to make separate movement impossible.

The disappearance will, of course, be gradual. As the use of the foot is more and more confined to the big toe, the little toe will slowly but surely diminish in size with each successive generation.

It is estimated that by the beginning of the twenty-first century, unless some very radical change is made in footwear and in locomotion, the eight-toed man and woman will be the rule, the ten-toed ones the exception.

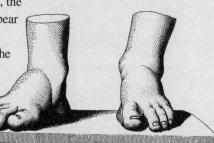

1993

The Great Flood of 1993 inundates 8 million acres in 9 midwestern states, leaving 50 people dead.

■ *All you need to do to travel into the future is to be able to move somewhere close to the speed of light. Theoretically, that's possible. Traveling into the past is a bit more complicated, but very intriguing.*

Is Travel to the Past Possible?

BY MICHAEL McNIERNEY

THE 1993 MOVIE *TIME COP* CONcerns travel backward in time. People traveling to the past cause so many problems that a special police force must be set up to deal with them. Travel to the future is dismissed out of hand by one character with the remark that it is impossible because the future hasn't happened yet.

So much for Hollywood's knowledge of physics. The situation is in fact the opposite. Travel forward in time is theoretically possible, according to the predictions of Albert Einstein's special theory of relativity (1905), which has been proved experimentally many times (see page 230). All you need to travel into the future is to be able to move at a reasonable fraction of the speed of light (about 186,282 miles per second). Neither the laws of classical physics nor the dictates of logic and common sense forbid it.

Traveling backward in time, however, seems impossible because of what is known formally as the inconsistency paradox and informally as the grandfather paradox. This

paradox could just as accurately be called the grandmother paradox or the ancestor paradox. It is simply explained. If you travel back in time, meet any of these ancestors, and kill them — or kill them all, if your taste runs to mass murder — you will never come into existence and be available to go back in time and do the dirty deed. Yet you just did it! Hence a paradox, and our logic and common sense (and classical physics, too) yell "Stop!" at this point.

Special relativity does allow for backward time travel. If you could move faster than light, you would go back in time. This outrageous idea was given popular expression by Arthur Buller's famous limerick that appeared in 1923 in the British magazine *Punch:*

There was a young lady named Bright,
Whose speed was far faster than light;
She set out one day
In a relative way
And returned home the previous night.

1993

Toy maker H. Ty Warner introduces Beanie Babies, understuffed plush toys that appeal to children and collectors alike.

Of course, special relativity also maintains that nothing can travel faster than light, because to accelerate any mass to light speed would require an infinite amount of energy, and there just isn't that much available in the universe.

Too bad. But Einstein again comes to the rescue of would-be time travelers with his general theory of relativity (1915). Like the special theory, it has been experimentally

If you travel back in time, meet any of these ancestors, and kill them . . . you will never come into existence and be available to go back in time and do the dirty deed. Yet you just did it! Hence a paradox.

proved to be true many times. Ramifications of it allow travel to the past because of something called warped space-time.

In the universe of general relativity, time does not exist as an isolated phenomenon. It is part of space-time. Space, as we ordinarily think of it, is three-dimensional and consists of points — one point here, one there. Space-time is four dimensional: the three dimensions of space plus the fourth dimension of time. It consists of *spatiotemporal points*, or

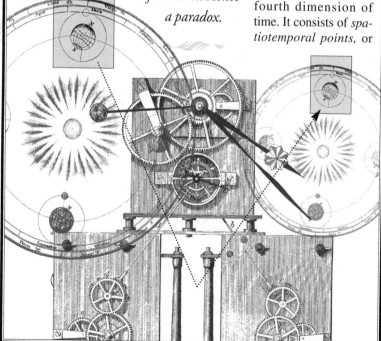

1994

The Internet comes under private management after 25 years of government control.

events. Each event is at a specific place at a specific time.

Everything that exists — including you (and me) — forms a sort of worm through space-time. The tail of the worm is your birth, and the head of the worm is your death. The line that your worm makes is called your world-line. Some world-lines are relatively short, like yours and mine, and some are very long, like that of a piece of granite billions of years old. Our world-lines are squiggles as we move here and there in space. Time, as we measure it with clocks, also has a world-line that goes in one direction — forward — and is straight.

However odd this talk of world-lines may seem, it is just a way of describing our ordinary reality in different terms.

The general theory of relativity predicts that massive bodies such as stars and black holes warp space-time and bend world-lines. This is, in fact, what is happening when we notice the effects of gravity. The reason the Earth is bound in an orbit around the Sun is not that there is a mysterious force emanating from the Sun, but that the mass of the Sun bends the Earth's world-line around it. Space-time is warped near the Sun.

Time, as we measure it with clocks, also has a world-line that goes in one direction — forward — and is straight.

What if an object, say a black hole or neutron star, is so massive that it dramatically warps space-time so that world-lines actually bend back on themselves, forming a loop? This phenomenon is possible and is called a closed timelike curve (CTC). If you were present at any point along the loop, time would seem to "flow" normally. *But* the closed loop would be a pathway into the past.

If you traveled all the way around the loop, you would run into your own world-line in the past — that is, you would run into yourself! And if the loop were large enough, you could go around and come back before your world-line started, meet your ancestors, and, if you wanted to, *kill them.*

The paradox! Classical physics is totally deterministic: It doesn't actually say you can't travel around the CTC and meet your grandfather, but it does say that however much you may want to kill your grandfather, you can't. Something will stop you. What could this something be? Nobody has a clue. This paradox is why most physicists don't like even to think about time travel.

But help is on the way. It lies in one particular theory that has evolved to explain the weirdness

1994

Explorers near Vallon-Pont-d'Arc in southern France discover a cave containing some 300 Stone Age animal paintings that experts estimate to be about 20,000 years old.

of the quantum world of subatomic particles. Things are very different down there. They do not obey the laws of the macroworld we live in. They boggle the mind, in fact.

A few examples are enough to give you a taste. A photon can be in two places at the same time. The famous "quantum leap" is when an electron moves from one "orbit" around a nucleus to another *without ever occupying the space in between.* Light is at the same time both particles and a wave. The quantum world simply doesn't exist in a definite state until we observe it.

The best-known explanation of quantum weirdness is the Copenhagen interpretation of Werner Heisenberg and Niels Bohr that says, among other things, that objective reality is a fiction and that the quantum world is not as real as our macroscopic world.

Another interpretation was first proposed by Hugh Everett III in 1957 and provides a way around the grandfather paradox. It is the "many worlds" or "multiverse" interpretation. It is a minority view but has a respectable and increasing following of physicists.

According to this theory, if something can happen, it will — if not in this universe, then in another. For example, if we look for light to behave like particles, it will. If we look for it to behave like a wave, it will. But there is no contradiction. The moment we choose, the uni-

verse splits. In one universe at that moment, the light we observe is a collection of particles; in another, it is a wave. This splitting happens every time we observe or make a decision or act. Reality is constantly splitting into an infinite number of universes.

The way out of the grandfather paradox is now clear. You travel back in time and murder your grandfather. The universe splits at that moment. In the future of one universe, you never exist. In the future of another, you do.

If the multiverse interpretation of reality is correct, we could some-

It is not clever to be always wise.

day travel into the past once we learned how to harness the power of warped space-time, of CTCs. This raises many questions, of course, but ask yourself this one: Has someone from the future come back and interfered with your life? You will never know. Or will you?

1994

A 31-mile tunnel under the English Channel is completed. Public train service begins between Britain and France.

■ *Living forever is much simpler than you might think. Undying fame — or disgrace — can be had by a person whose name becomes an eponym, a part of the language.*

How to Become Immortal

BY TIM CLARK

Alzheimer's Disease

Alois Alzheimer (1864–1915) was a German neurologist who, in 1906, first described what he called "presenile dementia" — the loss of memory and other mental functions in persons under age 65. But no one followed up on Alzheimer's work for half a century.

Bloomers

Amelia Bloomer (1818–1894) was editor of *The Lily*, the first women's magazine in America. Her enthusiastic promotion of Gerrit Smith's fashion bombshell made her name synonymous with the loose, baggy pantaloons for women that one critic claimed would land wearers "in the lunatic asylum or perchance the state prison."

Condoms

Someone in the court of the rakish King Charles II of England — some sources say a Dr. Conton, others a Colonel Condum — devised the prophylactic from lamb's intestines around 1665. Giovanni Casanova (1725–1798), an eponym himself, is said to have been a customer.

Derrick

Godfrey Derrick was a soldier in the service of the Earl of Essex in the Spanish campaign of 1596. Convicted of rape, Derrick was pardoned by Essex, who made him a hangman. Derrick became so well known that the gallows, and later any kind of hoisting machine, came to be known as a derrick. In 1601 Essex himself was executed — by Godfrey Derrick (perhaps the origin of the exclamation "By Godfrey!").

Eiffel Tower

Gustave Eiffel (1832–1923) was a French engineer who designed and built what was then the world's tallest structure for the Paris Exposition of 1889. He was also responsible for the interior

1995

Major U.S. newspapers create an on-line newspaper network.

gineer came up with a wheel, 250 feet in diameter, that could lift passengers 140 feet in the air in 36 cars capable of holding 40 persons each. Because the great wheel was built on the Midway Plaisance in Chicago, the central avenue of any fair is now called the midway.

[Amelia Bloomer's] enthusiastic promotion of Gerrit Smith's fashion bombshell made her name synonymous with the loose, baggy pantaloons for women that one critic claimed would land wearers "in the lunatic asylum or perchance the state prison."

framework of the Statue of Liberty.

Ferris Wheel

George Washington Gale Ferris (1859–1896) was chosen by organizers of the 1893 Chicago Exposition to build an attraction that would rival Eiffel's tower. The Galesburg, Illinois, en-

Guillotine

Joseph Guillotin (1738–1814) did not invent the decapitation machine that bears his name, nor did he lose his head to it, as legend claims. Guillotin, a physician and legislator during the French Revolution, merely endorsed the use of the machine invented by one of his colleagues, Dr. Antoine Louis, as a more humane method of execution than hanging. It was Louis who got chopped by what was then called a "Louisette." Guillotin was sentenced to death by Robespierre but was spared when Robespierre himself was guillotined first. Later on, Guillotin's family petitioned the French government to

1996

NASA announces scientific evidence pointing to the possible existence of life beyond Earth.

change the name of the device. The government suggested that the family change *its* name instead.

Heisman Trophy

John Heisman (1869–1936) coached college football for 36 years and invented the center snap, the division of the game into 4 periods, the athletic dormitory, and forerunners of the T and I formations. A perfectionist and relentless competitor, Heisman once told his Georgia Tech team, which led Cumberland College 126–0 at the half, "Men, we're in front, but you never know what those Cumberland players have up their sleeves. Don't let up." Tech won 222–0, earning their coach the nickname "Shut the Gates of Mercy" Heisman.

Immelmann

This aerial combat maneuver, in which a pilot pulls his plane up sharply in a loop that brings him down on his pursuer's tail, was invented by German fighter ace Max Immelmann (1890–1916) during World War I. It didn't prevent him from being shot down and killed in a dogfight.

This aerial combat maneuver, in which a pilot pulls his plane up sharply in a loop that brings him down on his pursuer's tail, . . . didn't prevent [Immelmann] from being shot down and killed in a dogfight.

Josh

Josh Billings, the pen name of Henry Wheeler Shaw (1818–1885), was a New England humorist, and some authorities believe that "joshing" can be traced to his popular jokes and stories. Others disagree, bringing to mind one of Billings's favorite sayings: "It is better to know nothing than to know what ain't so."

Kinsey Report

Alfred Charles Kinsey (1894–1956) was the world's leading authority on the gall wasp when he turned his attention to a new subject — human sexuality. His two reports — *Sexual Behavior in the Human Male* (1948) and *Sexual Behavior in the Human Female* (1953) sold hundreds of thousands of copies and inspired much debate. Ironically, the gall wasp reproduces by parthenogenesis — the male does not fertilize the female.

Leotard

Jules Leotard (1838–1870) was a French acrobat who not only invented the one-piece gymnastic costume but was also the first man to

1996

Scottish embryologist Ian Wilmut stuns the world when a sheep named Dolly is born. She is the first mammal to be successfully cloned from an adult cell.

perform a somersault on the flying trapeze.

Martinet

This word for a strict disciplinarian comes from Colonel Jean Martinet, an officer in the army of the French king Louis XIV. Martinet was killed in 1672 by a shot from his own men. Everyone agreed it must have been an accident.

Nobel Prize

Alfred Nobel's (1833–1896) invention of dynamite and other explosives, as well as detonators used to set them off, made him a fortune that he left in trust to establish prizes for peace, physics, chemistry, medicine, and literature. He saw no contradiction in this. "The day when two army corps will be able to destroy each other in one second," he wrote, "all civilized nations will recoil from war in horror and disband their armies."

Oscar

In 1931 Margaret Herrick, an employee of the Academy of Motion Picture Arts and Sciences, took a look at the nameless statuette presented since 1929 to the best actors, directors, and technicians in the industry and said, "It reminds me of my Uncle Oscar." Oscar Pierce was actually her second cousin, a Texas wheat farmer who retired and moved to California.

Pullman Cars

If it hadn't been for the assassination of President Abraham Lincoln, George Pullman's (1831–1897) name would never have been associated with railroad sleeping cars. In 1863 Pullman, an Illinois cabinetmaker, spent every penny he owned making a luxurious sleeping car he called the Pullman Pioneer. Trouble was, it was too tall to fit under bridges and too wide to slide past station platforms. But in 1865,

1997

Septuplets — Alexis, Brandon, Joel, Kelsey, Kenny, Natalie, and Nathan — are born to Bobbi and Kenny McCaughey of Carlisle, Iowa.

Illinois officials ordered state bridges and platforms rebuilt so that Lincoln's body could be brought home to Springfield in the finest style. General Ulysses S. Grant, who accompanied the body, liked the Pullman enough to ask for it again when he became president. Eventually, Pullman went into business with Andrew Carnegie and became a millionaire.

Quisling

Vidkun Quisling (1887–1945), a Norwegian fascist and admirer of Adolf Hitler, was appointed führer of Norway in World War II. Arrested by Resistance fighters in 1945, Quisling was so hated that Norwegians made an exception to their long-standing policy against capital punishment and executed him. His name has become a synonym for *traitor.*

Richter Scale

Charles Francis Richter (1900–1985) established in 1935 the commonly used method for determining the intensity of earthquakes. Born in Ohio, he lived and taught in California for most of his life. "I don't know why people worry so much about earthquakes," he once said. "They are such a small hazard compared to things like traffic."

Remembered chiefly for his long side-whiskers, . . . [Burnside] fared better than his successor as commander of the Army of the Potomac, the equally undistinguished "Fighting Joe" Hooker.

Sideburns

Ambrose Burnside (1824–1881) went bankrupt making rifles in 1857, ordered the Union Army of the Potomac into an appalling slaughter at Fredericksburg in 1862, illegally jailed opponents of the war in Ohio, and finally left military life in disgrace after another debacle in 1864. Nevertheless, Rhode Islanders elected him to three terms as governor and then to the U.S. Senate, where he died in office. He is remembered chiefly for his long side-whiskers, called "burnsides" in his day, but later transmuted to "sideburns." At that, he fared better than his successor as commander of the Army of the Potomac, the equally undistinguished "Fighting Joe" Hooker, whose name survives as a synonym for the prostitutes he ruled off-limits to his troops.

Typhoid Mary

Mary Mallon was a cook who, despite being in good health, was a carrier of the deadly disease typhoid fever. Ordered by health authorities

Jeanne Calment of France, the world's oldest person according to verifiable records, dies at the age of 122.

to stop cooking (the disease is easily spread through contaminated food) in 1898, she avoided the authorities and continued under an assumed name until she was caught again in 1906. She was confined until her death in 1929.

Uncle Sam

Samuel Wilson (1766–1854) was a patriotic meat packer who supplied provisions to the American army during the War of 1812. Goods for the soldiers were always stamped "U.S." The story goes that when visitors asked what the initials stood for, plant workers joked that they meant "Uncle Sam" Wilson. The name stuck because Wilson had a reputation for hard work and integrity.

Volleyball

The story goes that a French warden named Jacques de Vollet invented an exquisite form of torture in which male prisoners chained to a wall were forced to watch naked chambermaids batting a loaf of bread over a line hung with their underclothes. When the loaf was finally smashed, the prisoners were fed the crumbs. It's almost certainly apocryphal but too good to pass up.

Wedgwood

Josiah Wedgwood (1730–1795) was an English potter whose inge-nuity and business skills made him a leader of the Industrial Revolution. He passed his talents down to his descendants. His son Thomas was a pioneer of photography, and his grandson was Charles Darwin.

Xantippe

The wife of Socrates and some say the reason he drank the hemlock. Her name is occasionally used, as in Henry Fielding's *Tom Jones,* to mean "an errant Vixen of a Wife."

Yale Lock

Linus Yale (1821–1868) invented the compact cylinder pin-tumbler lock that is the model for most ordinary door locks today. No relation

to Elihu Yale, whose gift of books and other valuables to a struggling new college in Connecticut was acknowledged by naming it after him.

Zamboni

Frank J. Zamboni made the first ice-resurfacing machine out of an old Jeep at his skating rink in Paramount, California, in 1949. Zamboni wanted to call his company Paramount Engineering, but somebody else was already using the name. "Zamboni" was the second choice.

1997

NASA sends its *Mars Pathfinder* spacecraft along with the roving vehicle *Sojourner* to Mars. *Sojourner* explores the climate and terrain of Mars and analyzes the various rocks and minerals on the planet.

FARMER'S CALENDAR

Seeds of Chance

WE LOOK OUT AT OUR WORLD just at sunset. There is a roll of thunder. The leaves of the maples jump as the first swollen drops begin to fall. A fitful squall lashes and then dies.

Our fields are plowed, harrowed, seeded. And there is nothing now that we can do for these fields of ours. We need rain, surely, but as light dims, we see the first churning clouds above, and behind, the sullen, solid bar of the true storm, a gray wall with bullets of rain.

No robins sing, but the swallows squeak and jibber and soar and swoop and flitter like bats in the face of the weather. Mindless morons of the air while we wait and worry.

Before the gray wall of cloud, the lightning flicks the mountain. We must think as simply and as philosophically as our brother tiller of the soil from an age on the verge of man's being: that we may plant this good earth, but there is no surety of its reaping.

Only the swallows give welcome gladly, for the storm is *their* brother — though our barn is their haven. No haven for my seeds and my furrows, but just the prayer of the sower.

This we must know, and take such comfort in it as we may, that though our seeding, growing, harvesting are planned things, there are always the seeds of chance that are sowed along with our seeds — and always will be. Yet the odds are for us.

1999

Swiss psychiatrist Bertrand Piccard and British balloon instructor Brian Jones complete the first round-the-world balloon flight. The trip took 20 days.

Sources and Credits

TEXT

This collection consists, in large part, of previously published material from *The Old Farmer's Almanac*. Below is a list of each piece and the date, in parentheses, of its original appearance in the Almanac. Material from other sources is marked accordingly.

THE HUMAN CONNECTION

pp. 18–22: "How Big is the Family Tree?" by Guy Murchie (1980). Reprinted with permission of the author's estate. *p. 23:* "How Long is a Thousand Years?" by Jon Vara (1996). Reprinted with permission of the author. *p. 24:* "Ancestors" by Benjamin Rice, originally appeared as the Farmer's Calendar for March (1960). *p. 25:* "A Handy Chart for Identifying Five Generations of Blood Relatives" by Frederick Rohles (1992). Reprinted with permission of the author. *pp. 26–30:* "200 Years of Counting Noses" by Tim Clark (1990). *p. 31:* "Happy (?) Birthday" by A. J. Frost, originally titled "Still Another Difference Between Men and Women," (1995). *pp. 32–38:* "Solving the Mysteries of Love (and Sex)" by Christine Schultz (1994). *pp. 39–45:* "Beauty Was in the Eyes (and Nose) of the Beholder" by Elenor L. Shoen (1975). *p. 46:* "Nostalgia" by Benjamin Rice, originally appeared as the Farmer's Calendar for January (1958). *pp. 47–53:* "The Sinister Truth About Handedness" by Jon Vara (1995). Reprinted with permission of the author. *pp. 52–53:* "Does Anyone Care to Know the Origin of 'Hello'?" (1993). *pp. 54–58:* "For Crying Out Loud (or Otherwise)" by Jamie Kageleiry (1998). *p. 59:* "The Golden Rule" by Elizabeth Pool (1992). *pp. 60–64:* "Alas, Brave, Foolish Sam Patch" by Tim Clark (1980). *pp. 65–66:* "Why My Great-Uncle Gave Up the Ministry" by Marcia Barnard Chandler (1984). *p. 66:* "Old English Prayer" by Mrs. C. B. Terrell (1957).

GOOD HEALTH, GOOD FOOD

pp. 72–76: "The Breath We Share" by Guy Murchie (1984). Reprinted with permission of the author's estate. *pp. 77–78:* "The Great Lowell Measles Epidemic" by Barbara Craig (1977). *pp. 79–85:* "Cures for the Common Cold" by Tim Clark (1982). *p. 86:* "Folk Remedies" by Castle Freeman, originally appeared as the Farmer's Calendar for October (1993). Reprinted with permission of the author. *pp. 87–90:* "The Bloodstoppers" by Margo Holden (1982). *p. 90:* "Fingernails" from *The Old Farmer's Almanac 1997 Advice Calendar*. *pp. 91–96:* "The Top Ten Feel-Good Herbs" by Martha White (1999). Reprinted with permission of the author. *pp. 97–100:* "Surefire Home Remedies for the Hiccups" by Tim Clark (1985). *p. 101:* "Do You Really Know Yourself?" (1987). *pp. 102–107:* "The Healthiest Vegetable of All" by Georgia Orcutt (1995). Reprinted with permission of the author. *p. 108:* "The Birthplaces of Our Vegetables" (1953). *pp. 109–114:* "From the Highest Table in the Land" from the *The Old Farmer's Almanac 1994 Hearth & Home Companion*. *pp. 115–119:* "Meat Loaf Can Be Quite Personal" by Al Sicherman (1990). *pp. 120–122:* "In the Event You Have a Cow…" (1974). *pp. 123–126:* "Anyone Can Make a Perfect Cup of Coffee" by Leslie Land (1985). *p. 126:* "Let's Have Another Cup of Coffee" by H. L. Miller (1978).

THE ART OF SELF-RELIANCE

pp. 132–133: "The Forgotten Art of Building a Long-Lasting Fire" by Raymond W. Dyer (1975). *p. 134:* "Wood Sniffing" by Castle Freeman, originally appeared as the Farmer's Calendar for November (1994). Reprinted with permission of the author. *p. 135–137:* "Some Good Ways to Find North Without a Compass" by Dougald MacDonald (1984). *p. 138:* "Snow to Water" by Castle Freeman, originally appeared as the Farmer's Calendar for December (1995). Reprinted with permission of the author. *p. 139:* "How to Estimate Distances Easily" by Jon Vara (1999). Reprinted with permission of the author. *pp. 140–144:* "The Four Fundamentals of Successful Fishing" by Harold F. Blaisdell (1981). *p. 145:* "Shovel with Style" by Castle Freeman, originally appeared as the Farmer's Calendar for January (1982). *pp. 146–147:* "How to Tell Time by the Stars" and "How to Check Your Watch by the Stars" Edward Barnatowics (1978). *pp. 148–153:* "Growing Vegetables in Small Spaces" by Helen Tower Brunet (1980). *p. 153:* "A Tricky Method for Fixing Shoes That Pinch" (1983). *p. 154:* "Blackflies" by Castle Freeman, originally appeared as the Farmer's Calendar for June (1990). Reprinted with permission of the author. *pp. 155–157:* "How to Predict a Frost Accurately" by Calvin Simonds (1984). Reprinted from *The Weather-Wise Gardener* © 1983 by the children of Calvin Simonds. Permission granted by Rodale Press, Inc., Emmaus, PA 18049. *pp. 158–159:* "A Case for Weeding in the Dark" by Jon Vara (1993). Reprinted with permission of the author. *p. 160:* "The Ultimate Example of Yankee Ingenuity" (1991).

FELLOW CREATURES

pp. 166–171: "Solving the Evolution Riddle Once and for All" by Guy Murchie (1982). Reprinted with permission of the author's estate. *p. 171:* "How Happy *Is* a Clam" by Tim Clark (1980). *pp. 172–176:* "The Only Potentially Immortal Creature on Earth" by Peg Boyles (1981). *p. 177:* "Analyzing Ants" by Castle Freeman, originally appeared as the Farmer's Calendar for July (1999). Reprinted with permission of the author. *pp. 178–181:* "The Case for a Pet Cricket" by Kathleen Kilgore (1982). *pp. 182–187:* "Unforgettable Gifts from Pandora's Box" by Art Sordillo (1988). *p. 188:* "Animal Hero: Horace the Frog" by Yolanda Jarvis excerpted from "Amazing Animal Heroes" (1985). *p. 189:* "Cold-Blood Envy" by Castle Freeman, originally appeared as the Farmer's Calendar for May (1994). Reprinted with permission of the author. *pp. 190–194:* "Nature's Amazing Laws of Speed and Locomotion" by Guy Murchie (1990). Reprinted with permission of the author's estate. *p. 195:* "Allies and Adversaries" by Castle Freeman, originally appeared as the Farmer's Calendar for August (1998). Reprinted with permission of the author. *pp. 196–202:* "Three Incredible Pets Who Will Never Be Forgotten" by Henry N. Ferguson and Kenneth W. Mirvis (1984). "The Cat Who Came to Dinner" is reprinted with permission of Kenneth W. Mirvis. *pp. 203–207:* "Who's Smarter: Cats or Dogs or Human Beings?" by Sy Montgomery (1996). Reprinted with permission of the author. *p. 208:* "Animal Hero: Rags, the Farm Dog" by Donna Steen excerpted from "Even More Amazing Animal Heroes" (1986). *pp. 209–211:* "Why (and How) Do Cat's Purr?" by Jean Burden (1981). *p. 211:* "Animal Hero: Dumb-Dumb the Cat" by Yolanda Jarvis excerpted from "Amazing Animal Heroes" (1985). *p. 212:* "Uncouth Jays" by Castle Freeman, originally appeared as the Farmer's Calendar for February (1985). Reprinted with permission of the author. *pp. 213–214:* "Which *Really* Came First — the Chicken or the Egg?" by Guy Murchie (1979). *pp. 215–216:* "In Search of Animals That Don't Exist" by Mark Sunlin (1992). Reprinted with permission of the author.

KEEPING AN EYE ON THE SKY

pp. 222–226: "The Music of the Spheres" by Guy Murchie (1981). Reprinted with permission of the author's estate. *p. 226:* "Do All Planets Spin?" from "Letters to the Astronomer," Dr. George Greenstein, Astronomer, (1984).

pp. 227–228: "A Case for the Dog Star" by Michael McNierney (1998). Reprinted with permission of the author. *p. 229:* "Discovery of Worlds" by Castle Freeman, originally appeared as the Farmer's Calendar for November (1992). Reprinted with permission of the author. *pp. 230–235:* "E=mc² So What?" by Michael McNierney (1995). Reprinted with permission of the author. *pp. 236–237:* "How Old Is the Starlight You'll See Tonight?" by Frederick F. Bird (1983). *p. 237:* "Why Do Some Stars Appear to be Different Colors?" from "Letters to the Astronomer," Dr. George Greenstein, Astronomer, (1984). *pp. 238–243:* "Understanding Northern (and Southern) Lights" by Blanton C. Wiggin (1980). *pp. 244–246:* "Greatest Sky Sights of the Past 200 Years" by Fred Schaaf (1992). *pp. 247–248:* "How Big Is the Moon?" by Lewis J. Boss (1977). *p. 249:* "How Long is a Lunation?" and "Does Only the Moon Have Phases?" from "Letters to the Astronomer," Dr. George Greenstein, Astronomer, (1981). *pp. 250–255:* "When One-Quarter Equals One-Half" by Robert X. Perry (1974). *pp. 256–262:* "The Moon and You" by Martha White (1994). Reprinted with permission of the author. *p. 262:* Which [Pole] Has the Stronger Gravitational Pull? from "Letters to the Astronomer," Dr. George Greenstein, Astronomer, (1984). *pp. 263–264:* "The Sun Always Shines at Noon" by Robert X. Perry (1984). Reprinted with permission of the author. *p. 265:* "It's OK, Florida — We Love You Anyway" by Heinz D. Woehlk (1980). Reprinted with permission of the author. *pp. 266–268:* "What Is Lightning? (Besides Scary)" by Garth Longene (1977). *p. 268:* "The Ol' Goose Bone Method" by Warren Evans (1980). *pp. 269–271:* "How Come No Two Snowflakes Are Alike" by Chet Raymo (1986). *p. 272:* "No Two Snowflakes Are Alike, Right?" (1990). *p. 273:* "Snowstorm Etiquette" by Castle Freeman, originally appeared as the Farmer's Calendar for December (1989). *pp. 274–276:* "The Birth of Daily Weather Reporting" by W. Emory Wardwell (1956). *p. 276:* "Forecasting the Weather by Observing a Leech in a Jar" by Bridget Boland (1994). *pp. 277–279:* "If It Hadn't Rained . . ." by Norm D. Bloom (1992). *p. 280:* "Information Overload" by Castle Freeman, originally appeared as the Farmer's Calendar for December (1992). Reprinted with permission of the author. *pp. 281–282:* "Use Insects as Thermometers — They're Free" by Erica L. Glasener (1997). Reprinted with permission of the author. *p. 282:* "The Formula for Converting Cricket Chirps to Celsius" by Douglas Havens (1992).

MEASURING TIME AND SPACE

pp. 288–291: "New Eras: When They Began and When They Didn't" by Andrew Rothovius (1987). *pp. 292–294:* "Cycles: Nature's Incredible Time Clocks That Rule Our Lives" by John Burnham (1976). *pp. 295–299:* "How Certain Holidays and Just Plain 'Days' Came to Be" by Andrew Rothovius (1983). *pp. 300–302:* "Dining by the Calendar: Traditional Foods for Feasts and Fasts" by E[rika] Brady (1986). Reprinted with permission of the author. *p. 303–304:* "Full Moon Names: How Each Came to Be" by Andrew Rothovius (1984). *p. 305:* "Litter Calendar" by E. F. Hinkle, originally appeared as the Farmer's Calendar for August (1952). *pp. 306–308:* "The Year Ten Days Disappeared from October" by John I. White (1974). *p. 309:* "The Pros and Cons of Leap Year" by Mark Muro (1992). *p. 310:* "Wanna Fool Around with the Calendar — Again?" by Tim Clark (1982). *pp. 311–312:* "The Real Reason the Week Has Seven Days" (1988). *pp. 313–315:* "Have a Happy Friday the 13th" by Rick Horowitz (1987). Reprinted with permission of the author. *p. 316:* "Cocks, Cockcrows, and Weathercocks" (1972). *p. 317:* "Sun Time Versus Clock Time" by Blanton C. Wiggin (1973). *pp. 318–321:* "Time, Tide, and the Fiddler Crab" by W. L. Dougherty (1958). *p. 321:* "Count to a Trillion?" originally appeared as "Count to a Billion?" (1950). *pp. 322–325:* "The Man Who Unraveled a Tangle in Time" by H. I. Miller (1973). *p. 325:* "People Who Wait Five Months for the Traffic Light to Change" (1990). *pp. 326–329:* "How Long Is a Furrow?" by Winifred H. Scheib (1972). *p. 330:* "Mowing to Maryland" by Castle Freeman, originally appeared as the Farmer's Calendar for June (1996). Reprinted with permission of the author.

HOW TO BECOME A PROPHET

pp. 338–345: "Doomsday: It's Always Just Ahead" by Tim Clark (1981). *pp. 344–345:* "If You Can Understand Catastrophe Options, You're a Genius (or a Fool)" by David Lord, excerpted from "How to Predict the Future Accurately Every Time" (1997). Reprinted with permission of the author. *p. 346:* "The Flowering of the Planet" (excerpt) by Guy Murchie (1978). *p. 347:* "Astrology Has the Answers — if You Believe" by Peg Boyles, excerpted from "How to Predict the Future Accurately Every Time" (1997). Reprinted with permission of the author. *pp. 348–352:* "Predicting the Weather for the 21st Century" by Clifford Nielsen (1998). Reprinted with permission of the author. *pp. 353–355:* "The Ice Age is Coming! The Ice Age is Coming!" by Chet Raymo (1987). *p. 356:* "Volcanoes: Perhaps Mountains Sing Before they Erupt" excerpted from "How to Predict the Future Accurately Every Time" (1997). *pp. 357–360:* "The Earthshaking Theories of James Berkland" by Ric Bucher (1991). *p. 361:* "Earthquakes: When in Doubt, Apply the Chaos Theory" excerpted from "How to Predict the Future Accurately Every Time" (1997). *p. 362:* "Old Weather Predictors" by Castle Freeman, originally appeared as the Farmer's Calendar for December (1999). Reprinted with permission of the author. *pp. 363–365:* "Is It Time Now for the Earth and the Moon to Have Their Own Names?" by Dennis L. Mammana (1992). Reprinted with permission of the author. *p. 366:* "Predicting Weather by the Moon" excerpted from "How to Predict the Future Accurately Every Time" (1997). *pp. 367–370:* "What Will the Future Bring?" by Guy Murchie (1979). *p. 371:* "An Old Prediction That Is Soon to Come True" (1992). *pp. 372–375:* "Is Travel to the Past Possible?" by Michael McNierney (1996). Reprinted with permission of the author. *pp. 376–381:* "How to Become Immortal" by Tim Clark (1992). *p. 382:* "Seeds of Chance" by Benjamin Rice, originally appeared as the Farmer's Calendar for March (1958).

ART CREDITS